1987

IDEAS IN CONTEXT

THE LANGUAGES OF
POLITICAL THEORY IN
EARLY-MODERN EUROPE

IDEAS IN CONTEXT

Edited by Richard Rorty, J. B. Schneewind, Quentin Skinner
and Wolf Lepenies

The books in this series will discuss the emergence of intellectual traditions
and of related new disciplines. The procedures, aims and vocabularies that
were generated will be set in the context of the alternatives available within
the contemporary frameworks of ideas and institutions. Through detailed
studies of the evolution of such traditions, and their modification by
different audiences, it is hoped that a new picture will form of the development of ideas in their concrete contexts. By this means, artificial distinctions between the history of philosophy, of the various sciences, of society
and politics, and of literature, may be seen to dissolve.

Titles published in the series:

This series is published with the support of the Exxon Education Foundation.

THE LANGUAGES OF POLITICAL THEORY IN EARLY-MODERN EUROPE

EDITED BY

ANTHONY PAGDEN

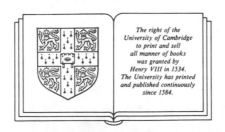

The right of the
University of Cambridge
to print and sell
all manner of books
was granted by
Henry VIII in 1534.
The University has printed
and published continuously
since 1584.

CAMBRIDGE UNIVERSITY PRESS

CAMBRIDGE

LONDON   NEW YORK   NEW ROCHELLE

MELBOURNE   SYDNEY

Published by the Press Syndicate of the University of Cambridge
The Pitt Building, Trumpington Street, Cambridge CB2 1RP
32 East 57th Street, New York, NY 10022, USA
10 Stamford Road, Oakleigh, Melbourne 3166, Australia

Cambridge University Press 1987

First published 1987

Printed in Great Britain at the University Press, Cambridge

British Library cataloguing in publication data
Pagden, A. R.
The Languages of political theory in early-modern Europe.
(Ideas in context)
1. Sociolinguistics   2.   Europe – politics and government
I.   Title   II.   Series
320'.094   JN5

Library of Congress cataloguing in publication data
The Languages of political theory in early-modern Europe.
(Ideas in context)
'Earlier versions of seven of these essays . . . were originally
delivered at a conference on political languages held at the
European University Institute in Florence in September 1983'
– Acknowledgments.
Includes index.
1.   Political science – Europe – History.
I.   Pagden, Anthony.   II.   Series.
JA84.E9L36 1986   320',094   86–14714

ISBN 0 521 32087 9

For Geoffrey Hawthorn

CONTENTS

PART III

PART IV

CONTRIBUTORS

ANTHONY PAGDEN is a Lecturer in History at the University of Cambridge and a Fellow of King's College. He is the author of *Hernán Cortés: Letters from Mexico* (2nd edn, 1986) and *The Fall of Natural Man* (2nd edn, 1986), and co-editor (with Nicholas Canny) of *An Identity in the Atlantic Colonial World* (forthcoming 1987). He is currently working on a history of the human sciences in the early-modern world.

J. G. A. POCOCK is Harry C. Black Professor of History at the Johns Hopkins University. He has published *The Ancient Constitution and the Feudal Law* (1957; reissued 1986), *Politics, Language and Time* (1971), *The Machiavellian Moment* (Cambridge, 1975), *The Political Works of James Harrington* (1977) and *Virtue, Commerce and History* (1985). He is currently at work on studies of Burke and Gibbon.

NICOLAI RUBINSTEIN is Emeritus Professor of History at the University of London. His works include *The Government of Florence under the Medici, 1434–1494* (1966) and numerous articles on the history of political thought, a collected volume of which is forthcoming from the Cambridge University Press. He is also general editor of the Letters of Lorenzo de Medici.

DONALD KELLEY is Wilson Professor of History at the University of Rochester. He is the editor of *The Journal of the History of Ideas* and the author of *The Foundations of Modern Historical Scholarship* (1970), *François Hotman: A Revolutionary's Ordeal* (1973), *The Beginning of Ideology* (1981), *Historians and the Law in Postrevolutionary France* (1984) and *History, Law and the Human Sciences* (1984).

RICHARD TUCK is a University Lecturer in History at the University of Cambridge and Fellow and Director of Studies in History at Jesus College. He is the author of *Natural Rights Theories* (1979).

QUENTIN SKINNER is Professor of Political Science at the University of Cambridge and a Fellow of Christ's College. His publications include *The Foundations of Modern Political Thought* (1978) and *Machiavelli* (1981).

MAURIZIO VIROLI is a Jean Monnet Fellow at the European University Institute and a Research Fellow of Clare Hall, Cambridge. He is the author of numerous articles on the history of political thought in nineteenth- and twentieth-century Italy, and a book on Rousseau's theory of justice is forthcoming from the Cambridge University Press.

ECO HAITSMA MULIER is a Senior Lecturer in the Department of History of the University of Amsterdam. His publications include *The Myth of Venice and Dutch Republican Thought in the Seventeenth Century* (1980) and numerous articles on the historiography of early-modern Europe. A *Dictionary of Dutch Historians (1500–1800)*, written in collaboration with G. A. C. van der Lem, is forthcoming with the Nederlands Historisch Genootschap.

MARK GOLDIE is a Fellow and Lecturer in History at Churchill College, Cambridge. He has published several articles on the political and intellectual history of later Stuart England, and has a book, *Tory Ideology: Politics, Religion and Ideas in Restoration England* forthcoming from the Cambridge University Press.

M. M. GOLDSMITH is Professor of Political Thought at the University of Exeter. He is the author of *Hobbes's Science of Politics* (1966), *Private Vices and Public Benefits: Bernard Mandeville's Social and Political Thought* (1985) and a number of articles on contemporary political philosophy as well as on seventeenth- and eighteenth-century political thought.

ISTVAN HONT is a former Senior Research Fellow of King's College, Cambridge and a Professor of Politics at Columbia University. He is the editor (with Michael Ignatieff) of *Wealth and Virtue: The Shaping of Political Economy in the Scottish Enlightenment* (1983) and the author of several articles on the history of Political Economy and of Marxism.

RICHARD BELLAMY, a former student of the European University Institute, is a Fellow of Jesus College and Lector of Trinity College, Cambridge. His publications include *Modern Italian Social Theory* (1986) and articles on the history of political thought from the eighteenth century to the present. He is currently engaged on a study of Liberalism.

GIGLIOLA ROSSINI is *attachée de recherche* in Political Philosophy at the European University Institute and the author of a forthcoming study on Hobbes's philosophy of science.

JUDITH N. SHKLAR is John Cowles Professor of Government at Harvard University and a 1984 McArthur Fellow. Her publications include *After Utopia* (1957), *Legalism* (1964), *Men and Citizens: A Study of Rousseau's Social Theory* (1969), *Freedom and Independence: A Study of the Political Ideas of Hegel's Phenomenology of Mind* (1976) and *Ordinary Vices* (1984).

ROBERT WOKLER is Senior Lecturer in Government at the University of Manchester. His publications include monographs on eighteenth-century political and anthropological thought and *Rousseau on Society, Politics, Music and Language* (1986).

ACKNOWLEDGEMENTS

Earlier versions of seven of these essays, those by Pocock, Rubinstein, Tuck, Haitsma Mulier, Rossini and Bellamy, were originally delivered at a conference on political languages held at the European University Institute in Florence in September 1983. I owe those seven an apology for having made them wait so long to see their work in print. The other essays were written specifically for the volume. I would like to thank the President and the Department of History of the European University Institute for having appointed me to a chair in cultural history during 1982–3 which enabled me to organise a meeting in what must surely be one of the most spectacular settings in Europe, and my former secretary, Beatrijs de Hartogh, whose organisational abilities made the whole affair practicable. The final shape of the book also owes much to discussions with Judith Shklar and Geoffrey Hawthorn.

My greatest debt, however, is to Professor Quentin Skinner who is, in every sense, the co-editor of this volume. He is largely responsible for its present form; and he has guided the preparation of the manuscript at every stage of its slow and sometimes tortuous development. Without his generosity and, as an editor of this series, his forbearance, the book would certainly never have been completed.

Introduction

ANTHONY PAGDEN

I

In the past few decades historians have become increasingly concerned with the role played by language in our understanding of social and political life. The theoretical sources for this concern are several and not infrequently contradictory. But if the works of Wittgenstein, Heidegger, Austin, Ryle, Foucault, Derrida and Rorty (to take only a random sample) often have little else in common, they have all, in different ways and with different ends in view, insisted upon the interdependence of the propositional content of an argument and the language, the discourse, in which it is made. At the most fundamental level such languages will be composed of precise vocabularies, metaphors and topoi, even recognised authorities, all readily identifiable and easily transmitted from one author to another. But there are also other levels, less easy to identify, at which it makes sense to say that a particular author is speaking in the language of, say 'humanism' or 'scholasticism' or 'political economy'. Such languages are, as J. G. A. Pocock says here, 'distinguishable language-games of which each may have its own vocabulary, rules, preconditions and implications, tone and style' which the historian has to learn to 'read'. They are, to borrow a term from Hobbes, 'registers' in which specific kinds of propositions may intelligibly be cast.

The authors represented in this volume are committed to the view, which this series is intended to advance, that ideas can only be studied in what the series editors call 'their concrete contexts', their 'procedures, aims and vocabularies'. This is an explicit, and now familiar, rejection of those older modes of intellectual history which studied texts in terms of sources and influences, or some variation of Lovejoy's famous 'unit ideas', and which frequently imputed inten-

1

tions and meanings to past authors which they could not possibly
have held. It is equally, however, and far more urgently, a rejection
of the deconstructionists' anti-humanist claim that no text is, in any
meaningful sense, the work of a conscious agent. The discursive
practices discussed here were, certainly, the product of long processes of linguistic change. But we believe that those changes were
brought about by agents who clearly intended to say some things and
not others, and who *employed* the discourses which they had, in part at
least, inherited. This is not, of course, to deny that the 'prison house
of language' is a real one. For there clearly is a part of every author's
text which can be shown to be derived, in some sense of which the
author may seem unaware, from an assembly of past utterances. But
any analysis which concentrates upon that *alone* must ultimately be
only circuitous. It, like Paul De Man's assault on Locke's use of
metaphor, 'is bound to continue this perpetual motion that never
moves beyond tautology'.[1] The essays in this volume are concerned,
not with the architecture of the linguistic prisons of the past, but
with the necessarily limited, but nevertheless intelligible, freedom
of those who inhabited them.

   Nor do we believe that languages, discourses, are self-limiting. An
author may employ the idiom or the vocabularies of one language
while speaking predominantly in another. He or she may also combine different languages within the same text. Nor, of course, do
languages remain unchanging over time. They may, as Richard Tuck
shows, become wholly transformed, almost to the extent of
constituting new languages by their exposure to other discursive
practices and changes in the external circumstances they seek to
describe. The vocabularies of which they are constituted may also, as
Nicolai Rubinstein demonstrates in his essay on the history of the
term *politicus*, undergo radical change. The context in which
Aristotle used the term *politikos* and the language in which Michel de
l'Hôpital situated the term *politique* are so very different that it might
even seem reasonable to speak of two distinct terms sharing the
same semantic origin. But, as Rubinstein has also been able to show,
the word never lost its central constitutionalist application, and with
it the understanding of what area of experience 'the political' was
intended to describe. Such continuities of sense serve, as Judith
Shklar says, to demonstrate 'the extraordinary capacity of intellectual and moral dispositions to survive intact under the assaults of
social change'. But those changes which do occur – the shift in the

---

[1] 'The epistemology of metaphor', in Michael Shapiro (ed.), *Language and Politics*
  (Oxford, 1984), p.199.

value given to 'citizen' or 'luxury', the transformation of *otium* into 'idleness' or *negotium* into 'business' – are also crucial to any account of how those intellectual and moral dispositions are able to survive, since they help to monitor the ways in which the languages of politics adapted to changing historical circumstances. They are also one of the unifying themes of this volume.

II

No single collection of essays on so vast a subject as this one could hope to be comprehensive in its range. But the contributions to this volume cover four of the most important, most easily identifiable languages of political theory in use in early-modern Europe. They are: the language of the law of nature and what has come to be called 'political Aristotelianism'; the language of classical republicanism; the language of political economy; and the language of the science of politics.

The first of these to achieve widespread recognition *as* a political language was political Aristotelianism. This was largely the creation of St Thomas Aquinas and his immediate followers, Tolomeo of Lucca and Giles of Rome. It was, as Rubinstein says, William of Moerbeke's translation of the *Politics*, which effectively 'introduced *politicus* and its Latin equivalent *civilis* into Western political language', and with the term came the Greek concept of the 'politic', the idea that man was *zoon politikon*, one, that is, who was literally made for the political life in the sense that his true end, his *telos*, as a man, could be achieved in no other context.

For Aquinas, and for the large and varied number of those who can be described as Thomists, the political regime was more than merely a practical arrangement. Political societies were, as Donald Kelley says, *personae fictae*, worlds constructed on the basis of a rational understanding of man's moral potentialities. Political science was, therefore, like moral philosophy (and for Aquinas, as for Aristotle, the two were inseparable) a form of knowledge, an *episteme*. And because it was a science, it was concerned not with the understanding of the human (or positive) law, but rather with the interpretation of the law of nature, the *ius naturae*, that body of rationally perceived first principles which God has inscribed in the hearts of all men. For the Thomists, the law of nature was the efficient cause of man's relationship with the natural world. It was, as Kelley describes it, 'metahistorical, and metalinguistic as well as metatextual'. And since the theory of natural law relied upon the vocabulary of

Aristotelian logic and Aristotelian anthropology, the language of
political Aristotelianism became inseparable from the language of
what, in the seventeenth century, became known as 'iusnaturalism'.
From Aquinas himself to the 'modern' natural-law theorists discussed by Richard Tuck, the project was to create a political
philosophy which could be fully accountable in terms of a set of
rationally conceived, and thus universally acceptable, first
principles.

The application of these principles was, however, consensual.
Knowledge was, in Francisco de Vitoria's blunt phrase, 'that thing
on which all men are in agreement',[2] and it could, as Grotius and
Pufendorf were to argue, be made identical with men's interests on
the same understanding: that this is, self-evidently, what God must
have intended for man. Human societies were, therefore, sources of
knowledge. But they must, it was argued, have come into existence
through an agreement or contract among the first men. By this
'social contract' men willed away their original liberty in exchange
for the protection and the possibility of moral understanding which
civil society alone could provide. They chose rulers to create for
them a world in which they might live essentially private lives, and be
able to defend their common interests. But although in order to
leave the state of nature they had given up natural liberty, they still
retained against their rulers certain natural rights. Rights, therefore,
became central to the language of the natural-law theorists.

In the traditional histories of the development of the theory of
natural law, Grotius and Pufendorf, since they used a recognisably
scholastic idiom, have often been regarded as the successors of the
Spanish Thomists. For the post-Kantian historians of philosophy,
this continuity of vocabularies between the 'old' natural-law
theorists and the 'moderns' made the radical break between Grotius
and Suárez almost imperceptible. It also obscured the principal
objective of the seventeenth-century theorists, which was to rework
the older language of natural rights into what was to become 'a
modern science of natural law'. For, as Tuck argues, whereas the
scholastics had attempted to build up a Christianised version of the
Aristotelian moral virtues into a fully autonomous ethical system
which could then be used to support the traditional moral order, the
Grotian project was to refute the sceptics' claim that, given the
enormous diversity of human customs, there could exist no certain
moral knowledge, that society was held together only by the rule
of laws which were neither natural nor divine but human, positive,

[2]   *De justitia*, ed. V. Beltrán de Heredia (Madrid, 1934), I, p.10.

customary. This belief could, of course, offer no reason at all 'why the fanatic was wrong in holding his moral belief and acting on it', and in a world where, as Tuck puts it, 'large areas of life needed defending from fanatics', that is precisely what the moral theorist had to be able to provide. It was precisely in the knowledge that the iusnaturalist's project was to create a 'minimalist ethics' capable of meeting the 'challenge of Carneades' that Pufendorf could hail Grotius as the heir to Suárez the metaphysician rather than Suárez the jurist.

The use of the language of natural law to contest a moral scepticism which the traditional exponents of that language had never held to be even 'an intellectual possibility' finally came, in Pocock's phrase, 'to highlight the presuppositions of the old language' – in this case, presuppositions about the centrality of the Aristotelian moral virtues. This had subsequently created 'tension in the old conventions', and it was the awareness of this tension which, as Istvan Hont shows, led ultimately to the creation of an entirely new language.

Grotius and Pufendorf's concern to answer the sceptical challenge was also the consequence of another feature which marked them off from their predecessors: their humanism, or at least their humanist training. This was evident not only in their willingness to recognise that scepticism *was* a challenge, but also in their attempts to reduce the innumerable stages of the natural law assumed by the scholastics to a minimalist core, concerned, as Pufendorf insisted, only with the preservation of society on the grounds that what was right (*honestum*) was so only because it was useful (*utile*). The natural law was thus made to approximate as far as possible to the condition of the positive law, which increased its dependence upon the other major component of the language of the natural law, Roman jurisprudence. The 'civil science', as Kelley calls it, constituted not only a discourse (and, of course, a methodology) of its own, but also served to underpin many of the natural-law theorists' more pragmatic claims. Roman lawyers had, of course, always provided the naturalists with much of their conceptual vocabulary – not least of all the terms *lex* and *ius* themselves – what Kelley calls, 'an extended family of socialising and communalising concepts and terms'. The Roman jurists, in particular Bartolus and Baldus, had figured prominently in scholastic discourse as *auctoritates* while the 'language and ideas of the ius naturale' had always been deeply embedded in the civil science. But the ground on which the two idioms met most frequently was the law of nations, the *ius gentium*. For the modern natural-law

theorists, as for Suárez, the law of nations, although a human positive law, was that area where the teaching of the law of nature could
be translated into a body of enforceable precepts. Of the three parts
of Gaius's triad – persons, actions and things – persons and actions
were 'subjected finally not to civil law but, as Baldus had said, to the
law of nations' and increasingly during the Renaissance Roman
jurists had come to work 'within the confines not of the *ius civile* . . .
but rather of the "law of nations" '. Both the civil lawyers and the
natural-law theorists were, as Kelley insists, committed to what
Leibniz was to call the 'ars hermeneutica' and both believed that
interpretation, whether of the text of the civil law or the 'text' which
God had inscribed in men's hearts, would lead to a full understanding of 'the nature and behaviour of collectivities as well as
individuals'.

But while the jurists came increasingly to speak in terms of the
natural law, they were never, as Kelley says, 'fully "naturalised" '.
The difference between their two projects lay in the ancient
distinction between a science (or *episteme*) and practical understanding (or *phronesis*). Jurisprudence was always bound, in ways that
iusnaturalism was not, by its anthropocentric orientation; and
although it, too, had always claimed to be a *scientia*, in the sense that
it sought to describe human affairs in terms of cause and effect, 'the
idea of *causa* was permeated with questions of value and motive'.

III

This distinction between *episteme* and *phronesis* was also central to the
second of the languages discussed in this volume: the language of
'civic humanism' and, more generally, of classical republicanism. As
early as the fourteenth century the term *politicus* had been, in
Rubinstein's words, 'squarely pre-empted in Italy for the republican
regime', and by insisting that Aristotle's definition of the *politeia*
could only apply to republics, William of Moerbeke 'provided
republican and later constitutionalist theory with a fundamental
argument', namely that it was only possible to live a fully civil life
under a republican government. The humanists were the
immediate, and lasting, beneficiaries of this sleight of hand and it
was the humanists and their Enlightenment heirs who gave the
language of civic humanism its most powerful expression. That
language still drew heavily on Greek, and in particular Aristotelian,
sources but its principal inspiration came from the Roman moralists
and historians, from Livy, Seneca, Sallust and above all Cicero. The
humanists' prime concern was with the *practice* of politics, and the

major objective of their enterprise was to provide an account of 'the best state of the commonwealth'. This became, as Quentin Skinner says, 'a standard subject of debate throughout the Renaissance' and, in one idiom or another, was to remain the goal of republican political theory during the whole of the early-modern period.

In his discussion of *Utopia*, Skinner explores More's use of two terms which constitute two of the major classificatory principles of early-modern political thought: the terms *otium* and *negotium*. On the one hand, there is the life in which the citizen is free to pursue his own private happiness ' "living and living well" in the manner most befitting to the nature and dignity of man'; on the other, the life of active participation in the affairs of the state in which 'all the praise of *virtus* derives from action'. This dichotomy was associated, to the point of interdependence, with the classical distinction between monarchies and republics. For the life of *otium*, the declared aim of most Greek political philosophy, was believed to be possible only within a society in which affairs of state had been entrusted to a single, strong and just ruler, a *pater patriae* whose role it was to take upon himself the burdens of the *vita activa*, leaving everyone else free to pursue their higher purposes and so attain their happiness. The life of *negotium*, on the other hand, was clearly only possible when the entire citizen body was able to engage in the active political life, and when each individual regarded his happiness as constituted by that engagement. It was also clear that, in practice, the life of *otium* could only be realised under a monarchy, that of *negotium* only under a republic. The language of republicanism therefore stood in broad opposition also to the language of political Aristotelianism and the natural law. While the latter may not be explicitly a language of *otium*, it was a language in which, as we have seen, the citizen was required to surrender his natural freedom to a sovereign whose task it is to rule in his interests, but with neither his assistance nor his immediate and active consent. The definition of 'republic' and 'monarchy' was, of course, remarkably flexible. It is clear that for More the best state of the commonwealth can only be a *respublica*, a community, that is, of 'active citizens within a self-governing commonwealth'. It was certainly easier for a true *respublica* to be achieved under a republican form of government where what Boccalini called 'that mutual love which prolongs the liberty of all commonwealths'[3] had a far greater chance of success than under a monarchy; but it is equally clear that a true 'republic' can also exist under a formal monarchy provided that, as in Sir John Fortescue's

---

[3] Trajano Boccalini, *De' ragguagli di Parnaso*, I, V.

dominium politicum et regale, the people 'constituted itself as a "body
politic" ', a situation which even observers less partial than Fortescue
and More believed to have existed in England, where, as Montesquieu
said, a 'republic hides itself under a monarchy'.[4]

It was this stability, the fact that an electoral system and the
succession of governments made republics seemingly immortal,
which led the theorists of the early Dutch Republic discussed by
Haitsma Mulier to take Venice as their model. If Venice was clearly
not the optimal state, it was at least the best that could possibly be
achieved in practice. The so-called 'myth of Venice' became,
therefore, the most powerful contemporary embodiment of the
discourse of civic humanism. Because it *was* a virtuous republic,
Venice had, or at least so it seemed, been stable for longer than any
other European state. It was superior even to Sparta and Rome for it
had never shown any bellicose or expansionist ambitions; and its
citizens lived in liberty and prosperity, free from the faction
struggles and the tyranny of over-powerful ministers, weak or infant
kings, which were characteristic of monarchies.

For the Dutch, who knew the limits of monarchical tyranny, and
who required a language with which to legitimate their rebellion
against Spain, only a republican form of government was acceptable.
Any single ruler possessed of legislative power could threaten the
integrity of the state: only in a republic was it possible to achieve the
'political balance' the De la Courts were working for.

In institutional terms, however, this meant that the government
of the state must be, as Aristotle had prescribed, a mixed constitution. It should, that is, be composed of the 'one, the few and the
many', a progressive diffusion of power which would permit the
interests of 'the people' to be translated into political action. For
most civic humanists, however, 'the people' meant not the classical
demos (few republicans, not even Rousseau, were very enthusiastic
about the idea of a *democratic* republic), but the citizen body. To
qualify for citizenship one had to be free, and this excluded not only
slaves, women and children, but also all those who were in any way
dependent. One had in fact to be, literally, 'of independent means'
because dependence was believed to make a man liable to persuasion and corruption.

The De la Court brothers, who in the 1660s attempted to provide a
programme for the new Dutch Republic, went to great lengths to
insist on the exclusion of all 'dependents'. To practise the life of

---

[4] *De l'esprit des lois*, XI, 6.

negotium one had to have a stake in the community. For the humanists, however, the independence which came from inherited wealth was not, as it had been for both Aristotle and Aquinas, a sign of that *nobilitas* which every citizen must possess and which both raised him above the morally corrupting pursuit of 'trade' and permitted him to be 'liberal' with his fellow citizens. For the humanists, nobility could only be the consequence of inherent virtue. *Virtus vera nobilitas est* thus became 'almost a slogan of humanist political thought'. By stressing this they were, in effect, making the claim that only through the life of *negotium* would a man be able to acquire true virtue, which is why in Utopia 'the quality of virtue has been made the ruling principle'. In the language of civic humanism the term *otium* becomes one of mere abuse. It is no longer the life of (active) contemplation but merely Erasmus's *iners otium*, 'sluggish idleness'. The nobility of the courts of Europe, claims Hythloday, are driven by what he calls 'civil greed' to damage the larger political community to which they belong and for whose welfare they are supposedly responsible. And this withdrawal from the active life into one of otiose luxuriousness to the detriment of one's fellow citizens is what the humanists understood by 'corruption'. Luxury and corruption – and the supposition that one must flow from the other – thus became powerful terms in the vocabulary of civic humanism. They also, as Maurice Goldsmith demonstrates, provided civic humanism's eighteenth-century critics with a means for overturning the whole republican ethic.

The contrast between the life of *otium* and that of *negotium* also depended upon another pair of antimonies which became prominent in the vocabulary of later classical republicans, and of Rousseau in particular. For the life of *otium* was clearly a 'private' life, a life that is in which the individual pursues his own private interests – as well as enjoying his *private* property – behind closed doors *as* an individual. The life of *negotium*, on the other hand, is the life of the public individual whose affairs are conducted in full view of his fellow citizens *as* a citizen. *Utopia*, the epitome of such a life, is a society in which literally nothing is private. The Utopians eat together in communal dining halls, wear identical clothes and live in houses which, by some unexplained architectural means, always give 'admission to anyone who wishes to enter'. Private property, and the money economy which supports it, which for the natural-law theorists – and for their eighteenth-century heirs – was ultimately the basis of all true civil societies, was for the civic humanists only 'the root of all evil'. Few humanists were, of course, prepared to go as far as Hythloday, and the majority of his utopian successors, in abolishing private property. Most, as Skinner points out, still insisted that, even in the optimal republic, considerations of 'degree, priority and place' were indispensable as the 'preconditions of any well-ordered society'. But if Hythloday's conclusions are extreme they are also inescapable. The humanist ethic required the eradication of any purely private existence and the ultimate abolition of property if the *optimus status reipublicae* was ever to be realised.

Classical republicanism is also, of course, a language of liberty. For only the republic can guarantee men their true liberty since this does not consist merely in an absence of constraint but in active service to the community. And if the republic was to achieve this end it had, in Cicero's famous phrase, to be *bene et recte ordinata*: it had to be a community in which, as in Utopia, 'there is no disorder'. It was, of course, Rousseau who most insisted that all discussions of politics were discussions about liberty and it was Rousseau who, as Maurizio Viroli argues, made the concept of order, as represented by a body of law, central to any definition of liberty. For most classical republicans, liberty could only be achieved by each man's willingness to renounce his purely private concerns for the greater good of the community. Rousseau claimed, however, than any society in which legitimate private interests – the interests of artisans or Genevan traders – are excluded is merely another form of tyranny. The well-ordered republic is, he claimed, one in which the laws truly reflect the general will, in which *all* individual interests are reconciled.

One of the devices by which the difficult task of reconciliation may be achieved – and to which Rousseau dedicated an entire chapter of the *Contrat social* – is a 'civil religion', a religion which, irrespective of its truth-value, could be used to persuade the most recalcitrant citizens that their private interests formed a part of the common good. It had, of course, for long been an important component of humanist political discourse. Machiavelli's famous description of Christianity as a creed which had made 'the world weak' and thus a prey to the ambitions of 'vicious men'[5] was not, of course, a rejection of the truth of divine revelation. It was a rejection of the civic value of the ethical code which that revelation seemed to demand. Christianity, or at least Christianity in its unreformed state, was a threat to any political community not only because it taught subservience, but because it was the instrument itself of a powerful and politically independent Church. What was needed was a religion

[5] *Discorsi*, I, II, III.

whose interests were wholly identified with those of the civil community. The Utopians, who have not had the benefit of revelation and who are thus invincibly ignorant, have been able to devise for themselves a form of worship which (in that the priesthood is, for instance, elective) is as near as a good Catholic could come to describing the kind of civil religion which would support a classical republic.

For Machiavelli, the form the religion might take had been largely a matter of indifference, as long as it was not the Church of Rome. For Harrington and Rousseau, however, there now existed in the reformed religion an ideology, the doctrine of 'priesthood of all believers', which could transform the civic humanists' essentially pagan, optimal commonwealth into a Christian state. As Mark Goldie describes it, 'For Harrington, and for Hobbes, as much as for Hegel, the mission of the state, of the Godly Prince, was to realise in the commonwealth the religion which, in its corrupt medieval form, had held all commonwealths under its tutelage.' The sacred and secular, what Rousseau called 'the two heads of the eagle', could now be reconciled in a community where the patriot and the Christian were one, where it was possible for religious beliefs to be realised *in* the commonwealth. For Harrington then, as Goldie describes him, Machiavelli's condemnation of the Church could be met with the claim 'that the [ancient] Roman and Christian religions, when properly understood, were identical'. Once the civil religion had successfully been translated into the terms of an essentially Calvinist providentialism it became possible to re-describe the classical republican distinction between virtue and corruption as a distinction between a true and a false religion. Government is then, in Harrington's words, only reason 'brought forth and made into virtue', and what he called the 'soul of government' became nothing less than the 'true and perfect image of the soul of man'. By Christianizing the language of civic humanism, Harrington had succeeded in reconciling the needs of a *rational* moral and political order with the only ideology force which could make that order compelling, and by so doing he had explained why, as Goldie puts it, 'the Greek ideal of human fulfilment in the *civitas* simply *was* the freedom promised by the Gospel'.

IV

The fourth language discussed in this volume, the language of political economy and the commercial society, challenged and finally transformed the discourse of both civic humanism and natural jurisprudence. Natural jurisprudence, as Istvan Hont and Michael Ignatieff have shown elsewhere, provided Adam Smith 'with the language in which his theory of the functions of government in a market society took place'.[6] It also provided, if only in the form of a reluctant recognition, the elements of the principal theoretical strategy of political economy – the concept of unintended consequences, the belief that the pursuit of private interests, which the humanists had seen as the source of all public discord, might bring inadvertent public goods. Smith and Millar's attempts to 'historize the origins of private property' on the basis of Pufendorf's theory of sociability also led, as Hont argues here, to the conceptualisation of the commercial society as a 'fourth stage' in the theoretical natural history of human society. The seventeenth-century natural-law theorists, Pufendorf and Grotius in particular, had already recognised the existence of such a stage, although they were distinctly unhappy with its possible implications. For Smith, however, this stage, regulated by a market economy, was the highest to which civil man could attain, because, since the market was responsible for distributing wealth throughout the entire community, it had precisely the power required to translate the short-term pursuit of private interests into long-term public benefits.

These unintended consequences could, then, in Mandeville's notorious phrase, convert 'private vices into public virtues'. If the language of political economy was a perhaps unforeseen (if not exactly unintended) product of iusnaturalism, it was also, as Maurice Goldsmith points out, quite specifically directed *against* most of the assumptions of civic humanism. In the commercial society the man whose activities most benefit the community is not the virtuous man of *negotium*, but the luxurious man of *otium*, since in the civilisation of the 'fourth stage', urban and mercantile, where 'sociability' and 'commerce' have become interdependent, it is the private consumer who generates the wealth the market will distribute. And it could be argued that, since the market was a natural mechanism, any but the minimal necessary participation by the citizen body in public life – since this would inevitably lead to active interference with the economy – would constitute a threat to the proper functioning of the society. The citizen, as the political economists never tired of saying, now had a *duty* to pursue his private interests. The language of political economy had thus made the old distinction between *otium* and *negotium* redundant by collapsing one into the other.

[6] 'Needs and justice in the *Wealth of Nations*: an introductory essay', in I. Hont and M. Ignatieff (eds.), *Wealth and virtue: The Shaping of Political Economy in the Scottish Enlightenment* (Cambridge, 1983), p.43.

For the political economist, the role of government was only to ensure that the natural mechanism was allowed to function as far as possible without interference. The form of government therefore became largely a matter of indifference. So long as those in power knew that their task was effective administration, it might be either republican or monarchical. What it clearly could not be was either the humanists' virtuous republic or the traditional absolute monarchy whose principle, in Montesquieu's formulation, was honour. For both honour and virtue had in their turn become purely private goods. Politics, as Goldsmith says, had 'become a matter of keeping the machine going rather than a theatre for displaying virtue and honour'. With Saint-Simon, as Wokler shows, this claim became an argument for a new system of administration which would effectively replace the pursuit of political power altogether by a society where 'men of the highest intellectual and scientific capacity would assume responsibility for public administration'.

Smith and Mandeville's vision of a political system which would, despite the intentions of its members, benefit the entire society was too uncompromising in its rejection of traditional Christian claims to charity for many European political economists. For the greatest of the Catholic economic theorists of the eighteenth century, Antonio Genovesi, the only solution was, in Richard Bellamy's words, 'to exploit the language of the theologian to express the new values of the merchant'. For Genovesi, too, the task was to find a mechanism which would restrain, or make beneficial, the passions. Smithian – or more exactly Mandevillian – political economy was, he claimed, too heavily dependent upon a theory of human interests which effectively eliminated the possibility that men might have other 'innate sentiments' – that they might, in fact, have non-egotistical interests – and it assumed the existence of a condition of perfect or near-perfect knowledge on the part of the agent. Rather than appeal to the interests to redress the passions, Genovesi, adapting the language of Newtonian physics, claimed that the greater passions will always control the lesser. From this it follows that the task of government is not to make it possible for men to realise their true interests, but to lead them from false to true passions. This, of course, once again made virtue central to any account of how human agents *ought* to behave. But Genovesi's understanding of virtue was, as Richard Bellamy explains, derived from Shaftesbury's belief that every man possesses a rational capacity to understand the moral order, which evolves naturally as a component of the human intellect. All men can, therefore, be said to have rational *interests*, and the separation of virtue and interest is, in

Genovesi's words, 'only hypothetically possible as in the false theories of Hobbes and Mandeville'.

Genovesi's attempt to re-write political economy in the language of Newtonian physics and Shaftesbury's Platonic moral philosophy once again made the life of *otium* and luxury the source of moral corruption. But as this critique was not merely an attempt to recover the old humanist *optimus status reipublicae*, Genovesi was compelled to detach the idea of *negotium* from the concept of a virtuous participation in an active political life, and invest it with the sense *negozio* had already acquired in eighteenth-century Italian, 'business'. The man of *negotium* in the commercial society is simply the businessman, and the 'life of endless accumulation . . . is endorsed by Genovesi as the exercise and fulfilment of our spiritual capacity'. But this activity could only be made to benefit the entire society which for Genovesi, no less than for Mandeville and Smith, was the principal concern of economic theory, by resorting to an older, predominantly Thomist, notion of charity. Wealth must, Genovesi insisted, be employed in accordance with what he called man's 'sympathetic principle'. If man is, as Shaftesbury had claimed, naturally endowed with an inclination to virtue, then he will inevitably be compelled to assist his fellow men. This did not, of course, confer upon the needy a right, since for both Shaftesbury and Genovesi inclinations replace rights, but it could clearly only be made coercive by a tacit appeal to the Thomist claim that, in necessity, every man had a right to 'another man's plenty'. Despite the novelty of his approach and the complex vocabularies he devised to sustain it, Genovesi was ultimately compelled to resort to a version of precisely that principle which the political economists in France and Scotland had attempted to replace by what they saw as a natural mechanism which would dispense with the need for both rights and with what experience had taught them – and should have taught Genovesi – was an ultimately vain belief in men's virtuous and charitable disposition towards their fellows.

V

All these languages were thought of by those who used them as in some sense 'scientific'. Whether this was understood to mean a deductive system, a *phronesis* or an *episteme*, the project, since Plato, had been to create a theory which would have the status of scientific truth. Throughout most of the Middle Ages and the Renaissance, the conceptual underpinnings for most social and political theories were heavily dependent upon either jurisprudence or theology. It was only in the seventeenth century that the notion of a 'science' of politics became detached from theology and the law and grounded in an account of the natural world and an empirical anthropology.

The modern language of the science of politics is, of course, most closely associated with the name of Hobbes. In her essay on Hobbes's translation of Thucydides, Gigliola Rossini demonstrates how Hobbes's concern to create a new scientific method, as certain as Galileo's, for the understanding of human behaviour, arose out of an earlier, and more obviously 'humanistic', concern with the proper function of history. For Hobbes's prime interest in history was its descriptive potential. History itself was not a part of philosophy, but of what he termed 'prudence', the 'original knowledge'; and this had to be distinguished from truly scientific knowledge which was 'derivative' and constituted the 'evidence of truth'. The historian's role was to provide a strictly accurate record of past events, for by so doing he would enable the student of politics to, as Rossini puts it, 'unmask the metaphysical foundations and the supposed universality of the theories of rights and civil society'. Rossini has shown how close was the link between Hobbes's later scientific and his earlier humanist writings by pointing to what, for Hobbes, remained history's single enduring merit: its ability to provide the scientific study of society with an empirical basis for its inquiries.

Throughout most of the eighteenth century Hume's celebrated claim 'that politics may be reduced to a science' was the principal objective of most social and political theorists. For most, too, from Montesquieu to Hume himself, the data used in the enterprise was predominantly historical. Even for Montesquieu, who drew on an abundance of information about contemporary societies, it was, in the end, easier to base a political theory on known facts about the past or remote, and supposedly exemplary, societies, than on the uncertain knowledge of one's own. Humean political theory amounted, in Judith Shklar's words, 'to little but maxims of good sense . . . it assumes that nothing novel will occur'.

One of the circumstances which brought a change in this perspective was precisely the need to account for something novel – to describe the behaviour of a new society: the United States of America. The new republic, though founded on Lockean and Montesquieuian ideas about political representation, lacked the means to account for its central political ritual: voting. Voting had, of course, played a central role in the discussion of classical republicanism. But in all previous republics, including the Dutch, voting had been an activity limited to the narrow body of wealthy men, designated 'citizens'. In the United States, however, as Shklar says, 'we the people' meant literally (or nearly, since women, children and slaves, not being free, were not entitled to vote) everyone. The need to account for the behaviour of this greatly enlarged political body required a language far more 'scientific' – in the sense of being more closely tied to the empirical data it sought to explain – than anything then available. Alexander Hamilton's new political science was, therefore, one which 'surveys the actual conduct of voters and their representatives'. To achieve this, Hamilton grounded it on the Baconian concern with 'irreducible facts and adequate data' which took it 'down to the last irreducible atom of social life: the voter'. The prime concern now was to discover, not how people should behave in order to achieve the best possible political arrangement; but how they will behave under specific and analysable circumstances.

Hamilton's science, indebted though it was for its theory to both Montesquieu and Condorcet, was a new departure. It was, as Shklar makes clear, in a way that no previous theory had been, a crucial part *of* a ritual. Democracies depend on what she here calls, 'consequential rituals', rituals, that is, which do have quite precise consequences – i.e., some people, but not always the same people, are elected to office and not others – but which function within the society *as* rituals. The language of modern American (and indeed modern British and German) political science is essentially the language of such rituals for, as Shklar observes, 'when you enter a ritual you are going to speak its language'. It is, or claims to be, rigorously 'scientific' because the 'democratic process' is based, as was Hamilton's science, on the assumption of the voters' ability rationally to assess their own real interests. But it also legitimates the process it describes.

Hamilton's political science was one radical departure from a widely based Enlightenment *science humaine*. Saint-Simon's was another. Like Hamilton, he too was forced to the conclusion that 'le science social' had to be developed in a direction 'wholly different from that envisaged by Condorcet' if it was going to provide a solution to the immediate problems posed by a post-revolutionary society. Like Hamilton, he saw that the older sciences, based as they were on history and the analysis of human dispositions, had to be replaced by a 'philosophy of organisation'. Saint-Simon, however, not only hoped to eradicate the political process which Hamilton was trying to understand and control, he also, by drawing heavily on the language of medicine, attempted to model an understanding of social behaviour on 'a model of the physiological system'. The consequences of this departure from traditional Enlightenment human science were considerable. For it resulted in a decisive break between the empiricism of men like Hamilton, based on the 'social mathematics' which was precisely the part of Condorcet's project Saint-Simon had rejected, and a science of society as, in Wokler's words, the study of 'what it is that persons have a mind to do, and how they ought to behave, in the light of such truths as could be established about man's nature'.

Both Saint-Simon and Alexander Hamilton wrote in recognisably modern idioms. But all the languages described in this book, however remote some of their terminology and the immediate objects of their concerns might now appear, are constitutive of one or another modern political idiom. The concern with rights, with property, with political representation, the central distinctions between 'private interest' and 'public action'[7], the search for a scientific, and predicative, understanding of social behaviour – these still determine much of our current political thinking. In their different ways, the essays in this book may help to make it clearer why we have chosen to express our social and political concerns in the languages we do.

[7] These are Albert Hirschman's terms. See *Shifting Involvements. Private Interest and Public Action* (Princeton, 1982).

I would like to thank Quentin Skinner for his comments on an earlier draft of this essay.

◁ ══ ▷

The concept of a language
and the *métier d'historien*:
some considerations on practice

J. G. A. POCOCK

What I shall attempt in this essay is an account of a practice and some of its entailments; and while one cannot verbalise a practice without offering a theory, it is my hope – seeing that we are all in some degree committed to a common practice – to stay as far as possible on this side of metatheory. I do not want to find myself affirming and defending a general theory of language and how it operates in politics or in history, still less to offer an account of my kind of historian as, himself, a historical actor or agent.[1] These are all real questions and from time to time they demand consideration; I propose, however, to let them arise, if they arise at all, out of the implications of what I shall be saying we as historians do. The *métier d'historien*, as I use the term, is primarily his craft or practice; his vocation and its significance, his experience of or action in history, are to me matters of self-discovery, to be met with in a time still to some extent our own. I shall hope, by proceeding in this way, to discover something about our shared and common discourse.

The word furnishes my starting point. The concept of a political language to me implies that what was formerly, and as a matter of convention still is, known as the history of political thought is now more accurately described as the history of political discourse. The actors in our history were of course thinking, and often thinking very hard; many of them belonged to clerisies or intelligentsias specially trained to think in various ways; but in order to give either them or their thought a history, we have to provide an activity or a

---

[1] I am aware that pronouns in the English language are biassed towards masculinity, and that no satisfactory usage yet exists for avoiding this bias. I say this in full consciousness of the presence of Judith Shklar, Caroline Robbins, Nannerl Keohane, Margaret Jacob, Joyce Appleby, Lois Schwoerer, Corinne Weston, and a great many more whose names command equality as their numbers defy tokenism.

continuity of action, made up of things being done and things
happening, of actions and performances and the conditions under
which these were enacted and performed; conditions furthermore
which were directly or indirectly modified by the actions performed
under them and upon them. We therefore suppose a field of study
made up of acts of speech, whether oral, scribal or typographical,
and of the conditions or contexts in which these acts were
performed. And in moving next, in moving immediately, to the
concept of language, we declare our belief that one of the primary
contexts in which an act of utterance is performed is that furnished by
the institutionalised mode of speech which makes it possible. For
anything to be said or written or printed, there must be a language to
say it in; the language determines what can be said in it, but is
capable of being modified by what is said in it; there is a history
formed by the interactions of *parole* and *langue*. We do not say that the
language context is the only context which gives the speech act
meaning and history, though we shall infallibly be accused of having
said that; we say only that it is a promising context with which to
begin. What consequences we have drawn upon ourselves by choosing to begin here and not somewhere else we shall discover later on.
Meanwhile, by insisting that thought must be uttered in order to
have a history, and that such a history can be viewed as the interaction of speech act and language, we have taken the first and crucial
step, though not the last – *le premier pas qui coûte* – towards constituting our history as a history of discourse.

The concept of language is both protean and subdivisible. We can
use the word 'language' to refer to one of the great ethnically
differentiated structures of human speech – English or Hopi or
Chinese – though the historian of political discourse does not usually
think of these as 'political languages' or as having a history created
by the political acts of utterance performed in them. Perhaps we
should pay more attention than we do to the fact, and its implications, that political discourse in early-modern Europe was
multilingual. It is no uncommon thing to find a treatise on politics
part in vernacular, part in Latin, part in Greek and part in Hebrew,
and we might ask whether these languages were politically differentiated. We should also pay more attention than we have done to the
phenomena of translation and ask whether the history of Hobbes's
Leviathan in English is the same as its history in Latin; the answer will
be both yes and no. But in general, languages ethnically differentiated are not the crucial categories in our study, and when we speak
of 'languages of political thought' or 'languages of politics' we have

in mind something else. The titles of the various chapters in this book indicate that we are to be concerned with idioms, rhetorics, specialised vocabularies and grammars, modes of discourse or ways of talking about politics which have been created and diffused, but, far more importantly, employed, in the political discourse of early-modern Europe. Let me pause to point out an obvious danger. We wish to study the languages in which utterances were performed, rather than the utterances which were performed in them; yet if we allow the boundaries between *parole* and *langue* to become too fluid, any utterance which long sustains an individual style may be mistaken for the language in which it was uttered. If we wish to posit a 'language', it should be possible in principle for two authors to perform in it; we are hoping to find language as context, not text.

When we speak of 'languages', therefore, we mean for the most part sub-languages: idioms, rhetorics, ways of talking about politics, distinguishable language games of which each may have its own vocabulary, rules, preconditions and implications, tone and style. An indefinite number of these may be found within a given language, and may consequently be found within a single monoglot text; for these ways of talking, while often profoundly at variance, do not typically succeed in excluding one another. While we may think of them as having the character of paradigms, in that they operate so as to structure thought and speech in certain ways and to preclude their being structured in others, we may not describe them as paradigms if the term implies that preclusion has been successfully effected. Once it became unclear whether 'paradigm' did or did not entail the latter assertion, the term became one that it was uneconomic to employ. Some languages succeed in driving out others; nevertheless political discourse is typically polyglot, the speech of Plato's cave or the confusion of tongues.

The historian of political discourse who is emerging from this account of his practice[2] spends his time learning the 'languages', idioms, rhetorics or paradigms in which such discourse has been conducted, and at the same time studying the acts of utterance which have been performed in these 'languages', or in language formed as a composite of them. It is extremely common, though it

[2] From about this point for the next five or six paragraphs and at one or two other points in the text, I draw upon material prepared for seminars conducted in the Political Science Department of the University of California at San Diego, during the spring quarter of 1983. I wish to thank Tracy Strong, Charles Natanson and others for their comments and criticism.

may not be necessary, to find that these acts in language have been
organised into texts; nearly as common, though even less necessary,
to find that these texts have authors, concerning whom information
may or may not be available from sources limited or not limited to
the texts. The historian may proceed from *langue* to *parole*, from
learning the language to ascertaining the acts of utterance which
have been performed 'in' them; after which he begins to inquire after
the effects of these acts, generally on the circumstances and
behaviour of other agents who used or were exposed to the use of
the languages, and more specifically 'on' the languages 'in' which
they were performed.

Certain consequences follow. First: the *histoire* he writes is heavily
événementielle, because he is interested in acts performed and the
contexts in and upon which they were performed. *Moyenne durée*
enters with, but is not confined to, the language context; in *longue
durée* he is interested only in so far as it gets verbalised, and thus
enters the *moyenne durée*.

Second: the history he writes is heavily textual, a matter of written
and printed utterance and response (most of the readers whom, as
we shall see, he studies are known to him because they became
authors in their turn). It is a history of discourse and performance
rather than – though, as we shall see, it does not exclude – states of
consciousness. He writes the history of *mentalités* only in so far as
these are articulated in discourse, in the utterance and response of
publicistic and polemic: i.e., at a level of relatively sophisticated
behaviour and relatively dynamic change. The pursuit of *mentalités*
(which is a noble chase) would take him deeper into *moyenne* and
towards *longue durée;* there may be elements down there which do not
surface into discourse at all; but the evidence which tells of their
existence may be of a sort best studied by some other kind of prac-
titioner. This historian is not ashamed to appeal to the division
of labour.

Third: it is also a history of rhetoric rather than grammar, of the
affective and effective content of speech rather than its structure.
This is a statement of emphasis and priority; the historian may find
himself dealing with grammar and structure; but he supposes there
to be a depth at which structures are not cognised, employed in
rhetoric or discussed in theory. At this depth there is *longue durée* but
nothing more, and he does not go down there; not because he thinks
it impossible, but because he thinks it is someone else's job. At
depths where no self-propelling organisms swim, he is not sure there
is any history, only bathyphysics; and he has his own fish to fry and

his own tales to tell – equivalents in his universe to what Alcibiades did and suffered, to what one office boy told the other office boy.

This historian is in considerable measure an archaeologist; he is engaged in uncovering the presence of various language contexts in which discourse has from time to time been conducted. I report from my own experience – and I shall elaborate on the point later – that he grows accustomed to finding many layers of such contexts within the same text, and is constantly surprised and delighted by discovering languages grown familiar from other sources in familiar texts where their presence has been neglected. Such discoveries do not always heighten his regard for the ways in which texts have been read before him. He becomes aware of the languages he discovers by an extensive reading of texts of all kinds, as a result of which he detects their presence and proceeds to 'learn' them as one 'learns' a language: i.e., by growing used to reading (but not speaking or writing) them, he comes to know what things can be uttered in them and how these things are expressed. There are important problems in interpretation and historicity which arise at this point and will have to be considered; but the central concern of this volume requires that we address ourselves first to the question of how these languages, idioms or rhetorics may be specified as historical phenomena.

If I ask myself for examples of the kind of languages I have in mind, the first to occur to me – not as privileged or paradigmatic, but as typical – might be: the language of medieval scholastic, of Renaissance emblematic, of biblical exegesis, of common law, of civil law, of classical republicanism, of commonwealth radicalism; the list is biassed by my own studies, but these move me at once to try and go beyond it. Of the items so far composing it, a number are of course highly institutional; they can be recognised at once as languages employed by specific communities in their professional discourse, as articulating their activities and the institutional practices in which they were engaged. It is important that political discourse has been conducted so largely by churchmen and lawyers, and in the modes of discourse which these were in a position to impose upon others; for clerisies do not address themselves solely to their own members, but impose their esoteric languages upon a variety of laities and lay publics, sometimes to the latter's articulate displeasure. The creation and diffusion of languages, therefore, is in large measure a matter of clerical authority; the story of how literate professionals have become involved in directing the affairs of others and have obliged others to discourse in the languages which they have evolved; but at the same time, the story of how the laities have appropriated professional idioms to unprofessional purposes, have employed idioms from other sources in such a way as to modify their effects, or have developed rhetorics of hostility to the imposition of language upon them. Along this line we catch sight of the anti-nomian use of language: of the use by the ruled of the language of the rulers in such a way as to empty it of its meanings and reverse its effects. Appropriation and expropriation are important aspects of what we have to study; I say this because I am constantly accused of denying their importance by those for whom I can never make them important enough.

It is important that the study of political language takes its depar-ture from the languages of ruling groups, which articulate their concerns and are biassed in their favour; but it is also important that the more institutionalised a language and the more public it becomes, the more it becomes available for the purposes of a diver-sity of utterants articulating a diversity of concerns. This diversifi-cation will originate within the ruling group, where there is commonly plenty of debate going on; but it may not remain con-fined within the original clerisy, profession or whatever it was. We may encounter cases where a language has been diffused beyond the original relationship of rulers to ruled by which it was created: where it is being uttered by other rulers to other subjects, by rulers uncer-tain whom they are ruling, by subjects uncertain by whom they are being ruled or on what authority, and even by revolutionaries using it in their efforts to throw off rule altogether. There are plenty of instances in early-modern Europe, even of the last supposition. The diffusion of a language may be a very different story from its creation.

The historian of political language will discover that language has a politics of its own; but to dwell upon this point, however important it may be, is to move away from the experience of the historian in discovering languages latent in the texts before him, which was what I set out to describe. Of the idioms emerging from the text, the historian has found that some are the languages of professional corporations articulating the practices which have made them powerful and their speech authoritative – and capable of being imposed on others – in society; but he will not find his experience arrested at that point. At a little distance from the case just supposed, for example, he may encounter the language of sacred or authoritative books – the Bible, the Organon, the Codex, the

Talmud, the Koran, the Six Classics – and of those who employ it in their discourse. Should he be concerned with the language activity of incorporated or accredited professional exegetes, the case will not be much altered; but he may by degrees find himself dealing instead with a network or community of men of letters, whether professional or leisured, established or *arriviste*, who employ the languages of the professional corporations without necessarily belonging to them, and are capable, first, of adapting these idioms or rhetorics to the purposes of their own discourse; second, of generating and developing idioms and rhetorics of their own in the course of pursuing it. He will now find himself dealing with idioms generated less by professional practice than by the rhetoric of discourse: with modes of discourse formulated within the discussion of particular themes and problems, or with styles of discourse perpetuating the styles of powerful and idiosyncratic authors – a Burke or a Hegel, a Leo Strauss or a Michael Oakeshott. Some of these authors will have been institutionalised as authorities serving the purposes of professional exegetes, others will not; and an author's historical significance is not measured only by his success in creating a mode of discourse – can we think of anyone who wrote in a Hobbesian idiom, at any rate in English? The point is that the historian is now dealing, not with the interlocking languages of a series of practising clerisies, but with a single though multiplex community of discourse, practising an activity which can only be characterised as rhetoric or literature; and that the language of political discourse, though we can still break it down into a multiplicity of sub-languages or idioms, must now be seen as capable of generating these idioms from within the activity of its own discourse, as well as borrowing from, or being intruded on by, idioms originating with other communities of discourse. At the beginning of the eighteenth century journalism and belles-lettres, at its end classical economics, entered powerfully into the fabric of English political discourse; but at the same time there came into being the idiom of Burke and (far more deliberately created) the idiom of Bentham, both of which – but, if you prefer, far more obviously the former – may be said to have arisen as mutations within the changing patterns of political rhetoric or discourse.

The layers of language contexts which our historian–archaeologist brings to light are thus of a very heterogeneous character. Some are languages of professional practice, which have for some reason entered into the language of politics and become idioms in which it is conducted; others are idioms, rhetorical modes or styles, which are better thought of as originating within the discourse and rhetoric of politics, as the result of moves or perforances carried out by authors and actors within it. To emphasise the former is to emphasise social structure, to stress that we are looking at speech articulated by churchmen, lawyers, humanists, professors, or perhaps the laities and occasionally the heresies defined by exclusion from one or other of these; to emphasise the latter is to emphasise discourse, to stress that we are looking at speech articulated by discursants acting within an ongoing activity of debate and discussion, rhetoric and theory, performing acts whose context is that of the discourse itself. What we mean by the creation and diffusion of political languages will vary as we adopt one or other of these highly legitimate perspectives; the social generation of languages entails one set of priorities, the rhetorical generation another. The historian–archaeologist, however, uncovering one layer after another of the languages which a text contains, finds himself obliged to adopt both; to him at least they are not categorically distinct.

We suppose these languages capable of being arranged along a scale which leads from the highly institutional and extraneous to the highly personal and idiosyncratic; though, as we shall see, these two poles are not mutually exclusive. As we near the latter pole, however, we encounter in an increasingly acute form the problem of what it is to speak of a language as an identifiable historical phenomenon. That is to say, the more we are dealing with individual styles of utterance, the creation of identifiable individuals in identifiable situations, the greater becomes the danger of confusing *parole* with *langue* and interpretation with identification. We ought not to say that we have found a new 'language', merely because we have found a highly individual style of utterance which bears its own implications and suggests its own practice; less still because we have merely found a new style in which we ourselves can read the utterances of discursants in the past and attribute modes and levels of meaning to them, for to do this is to reduce all history to a text which exists only as we can interpret it. The historian I am supposing aims to be certain, or as certain as he can be, that a 'language' or 'language context' which he claims to have discovered or uncovered existed *eigentlich*, prior to his discovery of it; he seeks means of showing that it was not merely his own invention, since he knows that *invenire* can mean both to find and to fabricate. This aim can be pursued in a number of ways.

The historian's confidence that a 'language' is not his own fabrication may increase: (a) as he can show that different authors carried out variant acts in the same language, responding to each other in it and employing it as a medium as well as a mode of discourse;   (b) as he can show that they discussed one another's use of it, devised second-order languages for criticising its use, and identified it verbally and explicitly as a language they were using (this may be called the Monsieur Jourdain test);   (c) as he can predict the implications, intimations, paradigmatic effects, problematics, etc., which the use of a given language will have entailed in specific situations, and show his predictions to have been fulfilled or, more interestingly, falsified (this may be called the experimental test);   (d) as he experiences surprise followed by pleasure at discovering a familiar language in places where he did not expect to find it (this may be called the serendipity test);   (e) as he excludes from consideration languages not available to the authors under discussion (the anachronism test).

The historian learns a language in order to read it, not to write in it. His own writings will not be composed of pastiches of the various languages he has learned, like John Barth's *The Sotweed Factor*, but of languages of interpretation, which he has developed and learned to write, each designed to bring out and articulate, in a kind of paraphrase, the assumptions, intimations, etc., explicit and implicit in one or more of the languages he has learned to read. He is engaged in a kind of dialogue with Collingwood's famous formula: he may learn another's language in order to 'rethink his thoughts', but the language in which he expresses another's thoughts after rethinking them will be the historian's and not the other's. This leaves room for both critical and historical detachment; the historian's language contains his resources for affirming both that he is adequately interpreting another's *parole* and that this *parole* was in fact being conducted in the *langue*, or in the selection and combination of *langues*, to which the historian has assigned it. This is his answer to any extremisms he may encounter about the untranslatability or unreadability of texts; he claims ability to show in what a diversity of languages a text was being written and was subsequently being read, and to distinguish between these languages and those in which it was not and could not have been written or read at a specific time.

But all this implies his ability to re-institutionalise languages: to show that what may at first sight look like highly idiosyncratic modes of utterance were already, or became subsequently, known and recognised resources of the community of discourse, 'available languages' as the jargon has it, which were used and in some measure recognised as usable by more than one actor in that community. A language must be, as a style need not, a game recognised as open to more than one player. Once we acknowledge this, however, the distinction already drawn between the social and rhetorical creation and diffusion of languages becomes more than ever crucial. If we can show that a given language originated outside the universe of political discourse, in some social or professional practice, and then entered that universe in more or less specific circumstances, it is easier to say that it possessed an institutional character, and was available for the purposes of various actors in the language game, than it is when we see a language originating within that universe, in the speech acts and rhetorical moves and strategies of the game's players; for in the latter case we face the problem of showing how the actor's moves gave rise to language institutions, and there will always be those who emphasise the uniqueness of each move to the point where the institution it was performed in and helped to form disappears. It is now being questioned[3] – I think it ought to be questioned and I am not committed to any particular answer – whether the English 'common-law mind' was in fact as monolithically insular as I suggested in *The Ancient Constitution and the Feudal Law*, published in 1957; but the effect of this criticism is to make the doctrine of the ancient constitution explicable as a good deal less of a *mentalité* and a good deal more of a move. If, as is now maintained, Englishmen of the seventeenth century were not so blinkered in their insularity as to be unaware that Roman and feudal law existed and might have enjoyed or still enjoy authority in England, then the proposition that they had never enjoyed it must have been less of an assumption and more of an assertion: an argument to which there might be a counter-argument, a paradigm to be established through the exclusion of its opposite. Sir Edward Coke, that great oracle of the law, would appear less the mouthpiece through which a *mentalité* articulated itself than a powerful advocate and successful pleader, employing speech, pen and print to induce his hearers and readers to adopt a position to which they were no doubt in many ways predisposed (it is not asserted that *mentalité* or ideology have no existence) but to which they knew but must deny that an alternative could be alleged. The speech act would become prominent in relation to the language situation.

A lot of evidence recently adduced is telling in favour of this

---

[3] A bibliography might be assembled on this point, drawn from the writings of Donald R. Kelley, G. R. Elton, Kevin Sharpe and others. I confine myself to citing Richard Tuck's *Natural Rights Theories: Their Origin and Development* (Cambridge, 1980).

revision, and I welcome it since I have no commitment to the *mentalité* type of explanation and am indeed inclined to see early-modern language situations as multilingual rather than monolithic. The problem of insularity aside, it is evident that a *mentalité* is too easily alleged if we think only of the normal operations of a language and not of the speech acts performed within and upon it; if we neglect *parole* in favour of *langue*. But somewhere in the debate over English historiography I catch sight of that powerful school of historians for whom there is no reality but that of high politics, and all historical phenomena are reducible to the moves of insiders playing at the endless adventure of oligarchical government.[4] If they were right, there would only be *parole* and never *langue*; each move's success or failure would be determined within the *durée bien moyenne* of the current state of the game, never within the more durable contexts provided by social or linguistic structures. I am concerned to argue for a presentation of the history of discourse which situates it between *parole* and *langue*, between speech act and language context; and I am stimulated by the proposed revision of my interpretation of long ago because it sharpens the perspective in which what I presented as a language can be seen in process of being modified and even established by the performance of speech acts.

But this returns us to the point at which the 'creation and diffusion of languages' must be seen going on within the activity of discourse as well as in the interactions between discourse and other social phenomena. Our historian, engaged in identifying the language contexts in which speech acts are conducted, must be able to study the creation of languages anywhere in the social context and their diffusion into the activity of political discourse; but he must also be equipped with means of showing how the performance of speech acts not merely modifies language, but leads to the creation and diffusion of new languages in our sense of the term. There is the generation of languages by the activities, practices and contexts of society; there is the generation of languages by the interactions of *langue* and *parole* in an ongoing continuity of discourse. We may consider the latter as a special case of the former, but not as its epiphenomenon once we concede that language is a continuous activity which sets its own rules and even determines the ways in

---

[4] 'The Endless Adventure' is the title of an early specimen (1912) of this genre by F. S. Oliver, concerned with English politics from Harley to Walpole. Post-Namierian practitioners include G. R. Elton (sometimes) and Maurice Cowling (rather more often).

which these rules can be changed. It is our historian's *métier* to have learned a number of languages and established them as contexts in which acts of utterance are performed; he now needs ways of understanding how the acts modify the contexts they are performed in, and how some of these modifications lead to the creation and diffusion of new languages and new contexts. Furthermore, he is typically though not necessarily engaged in studying the history of a literature: that is, a form of discourse conducted through the production of written and printed texts, which it is his endeavour to explicate as events in that history; highly complex *paroles* or acts of utterance, intelligible in terms of the *langues* from which they were drawn, of their effects upon those *langues* and upon the worlds in which they were written and uttered. To see how *paroles* of this kind modify *langue*, and how in some cases they help create and diffuse new idioms of discourse, is an important part of his endeavour.

We last saw him in the role of archaeologist, uncovering languages or idioms of discourse as so many contextual layers, of which a text might be shown to be composed so that it performed in all of them concurrently. These idioms arose from a diversity of sources and might be derived from societies and moments in history no longer presently existing (it can be an important moment in the growth of historical self-knowledge when this is found to be the case). Each was specialised for the performance of acts and the conveyance of messages peculiar to itself; but competent disputants and rhetoricians were quite capable of mixing the layers, of weaving the idioms together in a single text and a single, but complex, continuity of discourse. When this has happened, the text must be seen as performing a number of utterances simultaneously, and the historian – ceasing at this point to be an archaeologist – must ask whether it performs a unified series of acts or a plural and heterogeneous series. In several perspectives, and the historical among them, these are not mutually exclusive possibilities. We may, for example, think of the author, if a sufficiently dominant presence, as Penelope by day, weaving the idioms together in a single tapestry conveying a unified picture; but we will also do well to think of the text's readers (who need be nowhere near so sophisticated as the author) as Penelope by night, unpicking the design and reducing it to a selectivity of idioms and utterances. There are authors quite cunning enough to anticipate and exploit the diversity of reader response, but none, we suspect, who has ever anticipated all the responses which his text will elicit. Both the past and the future of a text viewed historically furnish us with grounds for emphasising the diversity and heterogeneity of the utterances it may be performing or may turn out to have performed. To the political theorist, this means that the language of politics is inherently ambivalent; as William Connolly has put the matter,[5] it consists in the utterance of essentially disputed propositions. To the historian, it means that any text may be an actor in an indefinite series of linguistic processess, of inter-actions between utterance and context. It was wise of Quentin Skinner to employ an imperfect and continuous past tense when laying down that we must know what an author 'was doing' when he published a particular text;[6] for if what he 'was doing' includes and even privileges what he intended to perform, not only may his intentions and performances have been diverse and even divergent, but what he 'would turn out to have done' may prove almost exponentially distanced from any performance he intended. History consists largely of unintended performances, and the passage from intention to performance requires both the imperfect and the conditional perfect tense.

Our historian, ceasing altogether to be an archaeologist, seeks means of showing how *parole* acted upon *langue*. We suppose him capable of showing that any text was couched and performed in a diversity of idioms, each constituting a conventional mode of utterance and exerting a paradigmatic force. From this, and from his knowledge of the historical situations and contexts in which the author was situated and to which his utterance referred, he can render a specific account of a variety of speech acts which text and author may have intended and/or performed. These acts, intended and performed in each of the text's several idioms or in all of them together, he proceeds to distinguish into the more routine – the utterance of conventions – and the more specific: the application of conventions.

When the conventions, paradigms and directives of which a political language may be thought of as composed are applied to and in political and historical circumstances other than those which it conven-tionally presupposes, two processes may be seen taking place. First, the new wine will be poured into the old bottles; the new circum-stances, and the problems in thought and action which they generate, will be assimilated to those presupposed by the old conventions, so that the latter may continue to rule them: out of the old fields must the new corn come, as Sir Edward Coke – who

[5] William E. Connolly, *The Terms of Political Discourse* (2nd edn, 1983).
[6] Quentin Skinner, *The Foundations of Modern Political Thought* (Cambridge, 1978), I, introduction.

understood this process well – liked to put it. The historian will find
this process fascinating to watch, because it highlights the presuppositions of the old language, informs him as to what sort of universe
its users were encouraged to presume they were living in, and
enables him to form judgements regarding the historical situations
in which it had been formed and was being used. He is not so
rigorous a historicist as to presuppose that the attempt to pour new
wine into old bottles is invariably a failure or productive of false
consciousness; sometimes it is and sometimes it isn't, and some
paradigms and languages display continuity in the midst of change
over lengthy periods. But needless to say, there is a process in the
contrary direction; the new circumstances generate tensions in the
old conventions, language finds itself being used in new ways,
changes occur in the language being used, and it is possible to
imagine this process leading to the creation and diffusion of new
languages – though exactly what this phrase would mean remains to
be specified. Our historian will try to study the sequences in which
such things may be seen happening, and there are two precepts
which it may be worth inserting here.

One is that the creation of new language may take place in the
attempt to maintain the old language no less than in the attempt to
change it; cases can be found in which a deliberate and conscious
stress on change, process and modernity is among the strategies of
those defending a traditional order, and it is in the logic of the
concept of tradition that this should be so. The other is that, since
the use of any language may be more or less widely diffused, the
number of actors and the diversity of their acts involved in these
processes can differ widely. Some language changes may appear as
brought about by a concurrence or consensus of speech acts
performed by so many actors, in so many language situations and
with such diverse intentions, that it is easier to think of the changes
in language as occasioned than as intended; as a product of the
heterogeneity of ends rather than as the work of identifiable leading
actors who can be shown performing innovations in *langue* by the
utterance of aggregative or disaggregative *paroles* and imposing
innovations and new language upon others. On the other hand, such
conspicuous actors do seem to occur in history; they acquire, sometimes quite rapidly, the status of authorities who are to be followed
or of adversaries who are to be rebutted; and it is not at all impossible
to imagine some kinds of language change as brought about by the
utterances performed by identifiable actors and the responses of
others not less identifiable to them. Sometimes, it is true, this image

proves to be historiographic illusion; we have been given to selecting noteworthy individuals and casting them in leading or representative roles which they did not always occupy; but if they were cast in
such roles not by historians but by those whom historians study, the
case is altered. Certainly we need means of asking whether
Machiavelli or Hobbes or Locke played the role in history which has
been conventionally assigned to him; but equally we need means of
understanding how changes in political language may be seen as
brought about by utterance and response performed by individual
actors. We need both the morphology of *langue* and the dynamics
of *parole*.

We think, then, of an individual who has something to say in and
about a highly specific and in some ways unprecedented situation,
but whose utterance is directed and constrained by the rules or conventions of the several languages available to him. The directives
imposed by these languages are at variance with the impulses and
constraints arising from the author's perceived predicament; and
these of course arise in a variety of ways. There may be something in
the situation, known or unknown or more or less known to the
utterer, which is difficult to speak of in any of the conventional ways;
or he may be in a casuistic or forensic dilemma, perhaps imposed
upon him by the speech acts of some opponent in a dispute; or his
reflection – possibly his profound and complex moral, epistemological or metaphysical reflection – on the predicament of himself
and others in or as revealed by the immediate situation may have
persuaded him that some trifling or drastic change in the conventions and presuppositions of language must be effected. We may
think – it is important to be able to think – of his *parole* as a response
to pressures imposed upon him by the *paroles* of others; but if we are
to write history in terms of the interactions of *parole* and *langue*, it is
important to see his *parole* as a response to the conventions of *langue*
which he is using and of which he is more or less aware. The players
perform speech acts according to the rules of the game; sometimes
they discuss the rules of the game and develop second-order
languages in which to do so; these have rules which may be subject to
innovation, and a change in these rules may entail a change in the
rules by which speech acts may be performed in the languages of the
first order. A change in the rules of the language game brought
about by some act of speech may be both prior and posterior to any
effect which that act performs upon any player in the game; yet all
acts are performed by players.

But we have not yet explained how such innovations may be

effected, still less how they may end in the creation and diffusion of
new languages. How an innovative speaker or author utters a *parole*
which is new is clearly hard to categorise, not only because of the
indeterminacy of the term 'new', but because of the tremendous
flexibility of language itself. Quentin Skinner has accustomed us to
speaking in terms of an author performing a 'move', and the number
and variety of possible 'moves' is as rich as the resources of rhetoric
itself; early-modern Europe was a highly rhetorical civilisation. But
such a 'move' was not only one made possible, however unexpected
by an opponent, by the rules of some game; it may also, since we are
in history, have been one which had the effect of altering the rules –
whether like William Webb Ellis picking up the ball and running
with it, or like Socrates and Thomas Hobbes suggesting that the
game was being played according to the wrong rules. We may
therefore define the verbal innovation as one which suggests, and
according to its power imposes, some change in the rules or conventions of political language: it may propose an alteration in value
signs, a treatment of that which was bad as now good or vice versa; or
it may propose to remove the discussion of a term or problem from
the language context in which it has been conventionally discussed
into some other context itself known but not hitherto considered
appropriate to this discussion. Machiavelli's employment of the
term *virtù* is an example of both kinds of 'move', and there are of
course many other kinds. Let us note that such acts suggesting rule
or paradigm innovation may be performed explicitly or implicitly,
overtly or covertly, intentionally or unintentionally, and much
depends upon *Rezeption* and reader response; the reader and interpreter may have the resources of rhetoric at his disposal too. Many
an author has found himself a more radical innovator than, or even
than, he intended to be or ever admitted he was.

    How can such innovatory *paroles* give rise to the creation of new
languages? A question we must discuss if we are prepared to consider
the process originating with specific acts by specific individuals.
There can be many ways of answering it. Let our author be perceived
as having proposed some change in the rules of a language game; it
may follow – given sufficient publicity – that the game is never the
same again, because those who wish to maintain the old rules do so
not by reiterating them as if the innovator had never existed, but by
answering him and rebutting his proposals; and since those who
answer an adversary must do so by accepting his language and
presuppositions, even as a prelude to debating and denying their
acceptability, a sufficiently resonant or scandalous innovator

necessarily succeeds in imposing new language and new rules of the language game, though often in ways not congruent with his intention. Some great innovators, like Plato or Marx, create and diffuse new languages through their success in becoming authorities; others, like Machiavelli or Hobbes, through their success in becoming adversaries, to rebut whom new languages come into being. And such authors, it must be remembered, are innovators in the contextual field as well as the textual. They suggest new modes of discourse which are perceived as having innovatory implications in language contexts other than those they initially discoursed in; they are therefore read and responded to, and their *paroles* have consequences affecting *langue*, in contexts which need not have figured in their intentions. To disclaim an intention may not be to preclude an effect.

But I am speaking here of change in language: of the creation and diffusion of new language in the abstract and singular; and once we admit the term 'creation and diffusion of languages', the use of the plural, or of the specific yet indefinite 'a language', obliges us to envisage a more concrete kind of phenomenon. Languages in this plural sense must be diffused as well as created; they must become available resources for the performance of speech acts other than those by which they were created, conventions themselves subject to innovation and change, *langues*, in short, rather than simple sequences of *paroles*. How a Machiavellian or anti-Machiavellian rhetoric became institutionalised in this sense, how it became an idiom or language available for the purposes of others besides Machiavelli and his immediate respondents (if he had any) is not an easy question to answer. There appear to be at least two ways of pursuing it. One is discursive: by 'learning a language', in the sense I sought to describe earlier, one learns to recognise it wherever it appears and to take note of its presence in a variety of texts and contexts, some of which may be very different from those in which we first saw it formulated. In this way, the historian may find himself studying the diffusion of a language throughout a widening and changing field of discourse, and reaches the point where it may be said that such a language is not merely the shared idiom of a series of disputants but an available resource diffused to the point where it was known to, and could enter the discourse of, persons engaged in discussions other than those for which it was originally intended. At this point the language has assumed a metaphoric as well as a paradigmatic role: what, it must be asked, were the effects of discussing a problem in language which originated elsewhere in social speech and suggested that it was a problem belonging to a certain family? The effects would be felt by the language as well as by the problem.

The advantage of studying diffusion and creation in this way is that it enables the historian to map the field of discourse and study action and change taking place upon it. The disadvantage is that it virtually confines him – though the field is so large that he need not sense the confinement – to the history of recorded discourse: to a history of texts and literature and intradisciplinary disputes, in which the response to an act of writing and publication is perceptible only when it is another act of writing and publication. It need not follow that the only actors in his story are publicists, though normally they will be; the languages he learns may turn up in private written discourse if any has survived – the public enters into the private – or in the written records of occasions of oral discourse in which early-modern English history, at any rate, is happily rich: parliamentary diaries, state trials, Putney debates. We are indebted to shorthand, it is worth recalling, as well as to moveable type. But the history of discourse among the literati – the history of text speaking to text – does not give us whatever history of *langue* and *parole* may have eventuated in the universe of orally transmitted language. Evidence about this is not easily come by, but it does exist; when the historian I am describing has any, he will ask such questions as how the discourse of orality may have interacted with that of typography, that of popular with that of clerical culture. If he remains a historian of literate discourse, he will concede that he is studying the speech of powerful and limited social groups; he will also claim that their discourse shows public speech in all its variability, changing under the pressures imposed by typography, controversy and high levels of self-consciousness. Within obvious limits, debate among the literati of the ruling order provides effective and illuminating criticism of that order's values, and he may elect to spend much of his time studying its history.

We begin to encounter here a further range of means for the study of the diffusion and institutionalisation of languages: the study of the material and social structures through which they have been disseminated. Here such techniques as those of *l'histoire du livre* have much to offer. To know how many copies of the *Encyclopédie* were bought when, where and if we are lucky by whom, can be made to yield a great deal of information, though it does not tell us whether, still less how, the purchasers read the book, or how they articulated their responses if they had any; it valuably reminds us that they may have bought the book with quite other ends in view. What such an approach does for the historian whose *métier* I have been describing is to heighten his awareness of the communicative spaces, fields, and structures within which political languages were created and diffused. He needs, I am going to suggest, a much better geography of political speech in early-modern Europe: a sense of the territories and boundaries within which certain languages were distributed and certain paradigms authoritative, so that the public discourse of one *pays*, state or province might entail a grammar, metaphysics and ideology like or more probably unlike that entailed by another. Of course there is a double perspective here; there were two faces to even an English Janus; political culture was international as well as regional, and we must consider what happened when Grotius was read in London or Hobbes in Leiden, Locke in Naples or Montesquieu in Philadelphia. But such problems must be dealt with not only by reflecting on one culture's history as compared with another's, but by reflecting that political discourse takes place in a variety of communicative spaces and situations. Those who read *Leviathan* in London during the 1650s encountered it in the world of George Thomason, in the midst of a typographic and social explosion and a revolutionary crisis in speech and consciousness; those who read it in the Netherlands encountered it, for all we have yet heard to the contrary, in the different but by no means bland or neutral environment of university lecture halls where it was read and discussed in Latin (I simply do not know if there was a Dutch pamphlet discourse, as certainly there was an English, in which Hobbes played a part). This means no more than that *Leviathan* has many histories, and figures in the creation and diffusion of languages through many kinds of context.

The historian of the creation and diffusion of political languages is, as I have described him, a historian of the interactions of *parole* and *langue*; he is concerned with *parole* largely as it acts upon *langue*, as it acts to bring about changes in *langue* considered as an institutional structure of public speech available for the diverse and often conflicting purposes of many actors in a universe of discourse. This does not, and I think it never will, altogether satisfy those whose demand upon the historian of *parole* is that it shall be shown acting from, in and upon a highly specific situation composed of social relations and historical acts. But we must beware the fallacy of demanding the immediate where the mediate must suffice. Speech acts upon people; texts act upon readers; but this action is performed sometimes synchronously, through the fairly immediate responses of the hearers and readers, sometimes diachronously, through the *parole*'s efficacy in bringing them to accept change in the usages, the rules and the perceived or implicit entailments of *langue*. In studying the creation and diffusion of languages, we are committed to processes which have to be viewed diachronously, however much they are made up of performances synchronously occurring. Languages are powerful mediatory structures, and to act in and upon them is to act upon people immediately perhaps, but by changing their means of mediation, which is often done indirectly and takes time. Certainly we must study changes in speech as they produce changes in practice, but there is always an interval in time sufficient to produce heterogeneity in effect.

PART I

2

The history of the word *politicus*
in early-modern Europe

NICOLAI RUBINSTEIN

The history of the word *politicus* in early-modern Europe begins in
the thirteenth century; as in other instances, the origins of modern
political language have to be sought in the late Middle Ages. John of
Salisbury had already used the term in the *Policraticus* to denote the
institutions of the State;[1] in his *Didascalicon*, Hugh of St Victor
divides the practical art alternatively into solitary, private, and
public, and into 'ethicam, oeconomicam et politicam';[2] but *politicus*
and other words with the same root definitively entered medieval
political language after the middle of that century as the result of the
translation of Aristotle's *Politics* and, to a lesser extent, of his
Nicomachean Ethics.[3] Albert the Great criticises the civilian lawyers
who wrongly call themselves *politici*, although they are ignorant of
the *ars politica*;[4] and Brunetto Latini draws on a translation of the

---

[1] Cf. *Policraticus*, V.2, ed. C. C. I. Webb (Oxford, 1909), I, p. 282: 'Sequuntur
eiusdem policicae constitutionis capitula in libello qui inscribitur Institutio
Traiani.' Cf. also IV.2, I, p. 237: 'secundum quam [*scil.* legem] decet vivere omnes
qui in policicae rei universitate versantur'.

[2] *Didascalicon de studio legendi*, II.19, ed. C. Buttimer (Washington, D.C., 1939), p.37:
'Practica [ars] dividitur in solitariam, privatam et publicam; vel aliter, in ethicam,
oeconomicam et politicam; vel aliter, in moralem et dispensativam et civilem.'

[3] Robert Grosseteste translates *Ethics* 1116a16 as follows: 'Dicuntur autem et alie
[virtutes] secundum quinque modos. Primum quidem politica'; 1134a25: 'Quod
queritur est et simpliciter iustum et politicum iustum.' *Aristoteles latinus*, XXVI.1–3,
fasc. 3, ed. R. A. Gauthier (Leiden–Brussels, 1972), pp. 193, 240. On the date of
Grosseteste's translation – between 1240 and 1247 – cf. D. A. Callus, 'The date of
Grosseteste's translations and commentaries on Pseudo-Dionysius and the
Nicomachean Ethics', *Recherches de théologie ancienne et médiévale*, XIV (1947).
101–9.

[4] Cf. his commentary on the *Ethics*, *Ethicorum Lib. X*, lib.x, tract. iii, c.3, in *Opera
omnia*, ed A. Borgnet, VII (Paris, 1891), p.639: 'Politica autem repromittunt
quidam sophistice dicere, cum tamen nullus eorum per doctrinam suam aliquid
politicorum possit agere ... Adhuc autem alli per tales sermones collectos, nullos
faciunt politicos ... Sophistas autem hic vocamus, non qui decipiunt locis

41

Ethics when defining, in his *Trésor*, the 'gouvernment des cités' as 'politique';[5] but it was William of Moerbeke's translation of the *Politics*, used first by St Thomas Aquinas and then by all Aristotelian political writers until the fifteenth century, which introduced *politicus*, and its Latin equivalent *civilis*, into the language of Western political thought.[6]

In the *Politics*, the adjective *politikos* shares with the other derivatives from *polis* a variety of meanings. The word could relate to the *polis* – the city or State – [7] to its constitution,[8] and to one of the three 'true' constitutions, that is the constitution in which the many rule with a view to the common interest.[9] With the first meaning, *politikos* is also used as a noun to denote the statesman or, more broadly, the man who, in contrast to the master who exercises authority over slaves, does so over equals who are by nature free.[10] This is the meaning which attaches to *politikos* in one of the opening statements of the *Politics*, in which Aristotle criticizes those who, like Plato in the *Politicus*,[11] do not recognise any difference in essence, but only one of degree, between a statesman, a monarch, and a master of a household.[12] William of Moerbeke gave this passage a different slant by substituting the neutral for the masculine gender, *politicum* for *politicus*, the 'political regime' for the 'political man': 'quicumque quidem igitur existimant politicum et regale et yconomicum et despoticum idem, non bene dicunt'.[13] Another derivative of *polis* is

---

sophisticis, sed ab imitatione sophistarum copiose ab apparente sapientia, qui seipsos vocant politicos, cum nesciant quae sit ars politica ... et repromittunt docere politica, cum artis et virtutis politicae penitus sunt expertes.' See G. Fioravanti, '*Politiae orientalium et aegyptorum*: Alberto Magno e la *Politica* aristotelica', *Annali della Scuola Normale Superiore di Pisa*, Classe di lettere e filosofia, s. 3, IX (1979), 210–15.

5   *Li Livres dou Tresor*, III.73.1, ed. F. J. Carmody (Berkeley-Los Angeles, 1948), p. 391: 'dist que son livre defineroit en politique, c'est à dire des governemens des cités, ki est la plus noble et la plus haute science ... selonc ce que Aristotles prueve en son livre'.Cf. Grosseteste's translation of *Ethics* 1094a26–7 (p. 142): 'Videbitur autem principalissime et maxime architectonice esse. Talis [*scil.* disciplina] utique, et civilis apparet.'

6   See V. Sellin, article 'Politik' in *Geschichtliche Grundbegriffe*, IV (Stuttgart, 1978), pp. 802–6. The word *politicus* was also used by schoolmen to distinguish the different parts of philosophy: see Vincent of Beauvais, *Speculum doctrinale*, I.18 (Douai, 1624), col. 17: 'Haec dividitur in theoricam et practicam. Practica est moralis philosophia ... quae ab antiquis solet dividi in monasticam, oeconomicam, et politicam; quae divisio datur penes habitus diversos, quibus mediantibus homo regit seipsum, vel propriam familiam, vel civitatem totam.'   7   E.g., *Politics* 1260b27–8.   8   *Politics* 1269a10.

9   *Politics* 1294b1.   10   *Politics* 1274b36.   11   Cf. Plato, *Politicus* 258a8.

12   *Politics* 1252a7–9.

13   I quote Moerbeke's translation from the text ed. in St Thomas Aquinas, *Opera omnia, cura et studio Fratrum Praedicatorum*, XLVIII (*Sententia libri Politicorum*) (Rome, 1971), p. A71.

politeia, which can signify the constitution in general,[14] or the constitution under which the many rule with a view to the common good. In this narrow sense, Aristotle's definition of *politeia* reads as follows: 'when the masses govern the state for the common interest, the government is called by the generic name common to all constitutions – a politeia'.[15] William of Moerbeke translates: 'quando autem multitudo ad commune conferens vivit, vocatur communi nomine omnium politiarum politia'.[16] By rendering in his translation of *Politics*, I.i.2, *politikon* as a neutral noun, as the 'political regime' rather than as the 'political man' or statesman, he gave the word, in the context of this passage, a meaning that was not intended by Aristotle; and by thus distinguishing that regime from the monarchical one, he provided republican, and later constitutionalist, theory with a fundamental argument. This argument was authoritatively clarified by Aquinas in his *Commentary* on the *Politics*, and further elaborated by Giles of Rome in his *De regimine principum*.

In the same passage, Aristotle refers to the distinction between the monarch, 'who has sole authority', and the *politikos*, who 'exercises his authority in conformity with the principles of the art of statesmanship', as one who rules and is ruled in turn. In William of Moerbeke's translation, this distinction accordingly relates to the monarchical and 'political' regimes, the 'regale' being the regime 'quando quidem ipse preest' (when one and the same person exercises authority), the 'politicum' when, 'secundum sermones discipline', the person who does so is 'secundum partem principans et subiectus' (partly ruler and partly subject).[17] Aquinas comments: 'when one and the same person exercises authority *simpliciter* and in every respect, the regime is called royal';[18] but when he does so partly, 'according to the laws posited by the political discipline,' 'est regimen politicum'.[19] What precisely does *disciplina politica* stand for?

---

[14] *Politics* 1276a15, 1279a25–8.
[15] *Politics* 1279a37–9. I follow here and elsewhere, with a few changes, the translation of Ernest Barker, *The Politics of Aristotle* (Oxford, 1946).
[16] *Opera omnia* (as n. 13) p. A203.
[17] *Ibid.*, p. A71: 'quando quidem preest regale, quando autem secundum sermones discipline talis secundum partem principans et subiectus, politicum'.
[18] *Ibid.*, p. A73: 'Quando enim ipse homo preest simpliciter et secundum omnia, dicitur regimen regale.' In his commentary on William of Moerbeke's translation of the *Politics*, Albert the Great explains this passage as follows (*Politicorum libri VIII*, in *Opera omnia*, ed. A. Borgnet, VIII (Paris, 1891), p. 8): 'Rex enim est principatum tenens super gentem propria potestate.'
[19] *Opera omnia* p. A73: 'Quando autem preest secundum sermones disciplinales, id est secundum leges positas per disciplinam politicam, est regimen politicum: quasi secundum partem principetur, quantum ad ea scilicet que eius potestati subsunt, et secundum partem sit subiectus quantum ad ea in quibus subicitur legi.'

At the beginning of his comment on Aristotle's argument in *Politics*, I.i.2, Aquinas gives a slightly different definition of the *regimen politicum*: it is the regime in which 'the one who exercises authority has his powers confined by some laws of the State'.[20] Giles of Rome expanded Aquinas's comment in his immensely popular *On the Government of Princes*, which he wrote in *c.* 1280; the contrast is now between the *regimen regale*, in which the ruler governs 'secundum arbitrium et secundum leges quas ipse instituit' (according to the laws which he himself has made), and the *regimen politicum*, in which he governs according to the laws 'which the citizens have made'.[21] Accordingly, 'praeesse politice' means, unlike 'praeesse regaliter', to govern 'non totaliter nec simpliciter, sed secundum quasdam conventiones et pacta' (not totally and simply, but on the ground of some agreements and covenants).[22]

Giles of Rome, like Aquinas before him, relates the *regimen politicum* to republics.[23] It was in keeping with this definition of the *regimen politicum* that the continuator of Aquinas's *On the Government of Princes*, Tolomeo of Lucca, devoted, around 1310, the whole of Book IV of that work to the discussion of the 'dominium plurium' (the rule of the many), 'quod communi nomine politicum appellamus' (which we call by its usual name political), monarchy having been treated in the preceding books.[24] This regime, he adds, is called *politicum* or *politia*, 'a πόλις, quod est pluralitas, sive civitas', and it exists in cities,

---

[20] *Ibid.*, p. A72: 'quando ille qui preest habet potestatem coartatam secundum aliquas leges civitatis'. Albert the Great, *loc. cit.*, explains *disciplina* more precisely by 'legibus et plebiscitis et statutis communitatis', but, unlike Aquinas, fails to understand the meaning of 'secundum partem principans et subiectus' (cf. n. 17), on which he comments: 'secundum partem, hoc est, secundum particularem cititatem, et subiectus regi, qui eum in parte suae sollicitudinis constituit, hunc dicunt esse Politicum'. This is a good example of the difficulties Moerbeke's translation was liable to present to commentators of the *Politics*.

[21] Aegidius Colonna, *De regimine principum*, II.i.14 (Rome, 1607), p. 260: 'Civitas autem ... duplici regimine regi potest, politico scilicet et regali. Dicitur autem quis praeesse regali dominio, cum praeest secundum arbitrium et secundum leges, quas ipse instituit. Sed tunc praeest regimine politico, quando non praeest secundum arbitrium, nec secundum leges quas ipse instituit, sed secundum eas quas cives instituerunt.'

[22] *Ibid.*, p. 261. We find the same definition in John of Paris's *De regia potestate et papali* (1302–3), cap. 17, ed. F. Bleienstein (Stuttgart, 1969), p. 161: 'principatus tunc solum dicitur regalis quando aliquis praeest secundum leges quas ipsemet instituit; cum vero praeest non secundum arbitrium suum nec secundum leges quas ipse instituit sed quas cives instituerunt, dicitur principatus civilis vel politicus et non regalis'.

[23] *De regimine principum*, p. 260: 'cum leges non instituuntur a principante sed a civibus, illud regimen non est denominandum ab ipso regnante et principante, sed magis ab ipsa politia et ab ipsis civibus'.

[24] St Thomas Aquinas, *De regimine principum ad regem Cypri*, IV.1, ed. J. Mathis, 2nd edn (Turin–Rome, 1948), p. 66.

'as we see especially (*maxime*) in Italy'.[25] In the *regimen politicum*, the governors, *rectores*, are restricted by the laws of the city,[26] while in States ruled by monarchs, the laws are 'hidden in their breasts', so that – according to that other maxim of Roman law – 'the will of the prince has the power of law'.[27] Moreover, the *rectores* owe their power to the people which elects them for limited terms of office: for 'in the polity, the governors must be appointed in turn'.[28] Tolomeo of Lucca builds on the foundation of Aquinas's interpretation of the Aristotelian concept of the *politeia* a republican theory which, while broadly conforming to its basic assumptions, only distantly follows the text of the *Politics*.[29] On the other hand, it is closely related to the political institutions of the city republics of Italy, where the *regimen politicum* 'maxime viget', just as it 'once flourished in Athens'.[30]

By the beginning of the fourteenth century, the word *politicus*, and its Latin and Italian equivalents *civilis* and *civile*,[31] had been squarely pre-empted for the republican regime. As a constitutional term, its principal features were the institutional restraints to which the government was subjected, and the popular source of its authority. Thus Bartolus of Sassoferrato states, around 1350, in his *De regimine civitatis*, that after the expulsion of the kings the Romans had set up a 'modus regendi per populum', a popular regime, 'and Aristotle calls this regime *politiam seu politicum*, but we call it a *regimen ad populum*, that is when such a regime is good and those who govern consider, above all else, the common good'.[32] Early in the following century,

---

25 *Ibid.*: '... quia hoc regimen proprie ad civitates pertinet, ut in partibus Italiae maxime videmus, et olim viguit apud Athenas'.
26 *Ibid.*: 'legibus astringuntur rectores politici'. Cf. II.8, p. 27: 'Politicus [principatus est] quidem, quando regio, sive provincia, sive civitas, sive castrum, per unum vel plures regitur secundum ipsorum statuta, ut in regionibus contingit Italiae'; IV.8, p. 76: '[rectores] iudicant secundum leges eis traditas, quibus sunt per iuramenta astricti'.
27 *Ibid.*, IV.1, p. 66: 'in ipsorum pectore sunt leges reconditae ... et pro lege habetur quod principi placet, sicut iura gentium tradunt'. Cf. *Codex*, 6.23.19.1: 'Omnia iura in scrinio [pectoris] principis' (on the diffusion of this maxim, quoted by Tolomeo of Lucca also in II.8, p. 28, see E. Kantorowicz, *The King's Two Bodies* (Princeton, N. J., 1957), p. 28, n. 15); *Dig.*, I.4.1: 'Quod principi placuit legis habet vigorem.'
28 *De regimine principum*, IV.8, p. 76: 'Assumendi igitur sunt rectores vicissim in politia, sive consules, sive magistratus vocentur, sive quocumque alio nomine.' Cf. IV.1, p. 66: in the *dominium politicum* appointment to office 'electivus est in quocumque hominis genere, non per naturae originem, ut de regibus accidit'.
29 On Tolomeo of Lucca's republicanism, see Charles T. Davis, 'Ptolemy of Lucca and the Roman republic', *Proceedings of the American Philosophical Society*, CXVIII (1974), 47ff.; reprinted in *Dante's Italy* (Philadelphia, 1984), pp. 285ff.
30 *De regimine principum*, IV.8, p. 76, and above, n. 25.   31 See below, p. 46.
32 Ed. D. Quaglioni, *Politica e diritto nel Trecento italiano* (Florence, 1983), p. 150: 'et istud regimen vocat Aristoteles politiam seu politicum. Nos autem vocamus regimen ad populum, et hoc quando tale regimen bonum est et per regentes consideratur bonum commune principaliter ...'

Lorenzo de' Monaci, in describing the Venetian constitution as a mixed constitution, accounts for its stability by the fact that each of its component elements was subject to the laws of the republic; and 'indeed, where the laws rule, there is a good polity, and *politicum* is nothing but what is good'.[33] Shortly afterwards, the Florentine Giovanni Cavalcanti contrasted the 'ordine del vivere politico' of his city with the ascendancy of one pre-eminent citizen;[34] and as late as 1470, Lorenzo de' Medici, who in fact had inherited such an ascendancy from his father and grandfather, insisted that he would use the authority to which he had just succeeded in the way Cosimo had done, 'cum più civilità si potesse' (by resorting, as much as possible, to constitutional methods).[35]

At the same time, the derivatives from *polis* continued to be used in the wider sense as relating to the State in general, and this remained in Italy, as well as in France, the normal usage until the end of the fifteenth century, with *civilis, civile, civil* often taking the place of *politicus, politico, politique*. Even before William of Moerbeke's translation of the *Politics*, the first translators of the *Ethics* had used *civilis* as an alternative to *politicus, civilitas* to *politeia*;[36] Moerbeke, having, in *Politics*, I.i, first translated *politikos* with *politicus*,[37] renders *zoon politikon* with *animal civile*;[38] and Albertus Magnus, when explaining

---

[33] *Chronicon de rebus Venetis*, in L. Muratori, *Rerum Italicarum Scriptores*, VIII, Appendix (Venice, 1758), pp. 276–7: 'subiecta est suis institutis et legibus; ubi vero leges principantur, est vera politia, et politicum non est nisi quod bonum est'. See A. Pertusi, 'Gli inizi della storiografia umanistica nel Quattrocento', in *La storiografia veneziana fino al secolo XVI: aspetti e problemi*, ed. A. Pertusi (Florence, 1970), pp. 278–9. On the dependence of Lorenzo de'Monaci's account of the Venetian constitution on Henry of Rimini's description of it, of around 1300, see D. Robey and J. Law, 'The Venetian myth and the "De republica veneta" of Pier Paolo Vergerio', *Rinascimento*, 2nd s., XV (1975), 12–13; cf. *ibid.*, 54–5.

[34] *Istorie fiorentine*, V.5, ed. G. di Pino (Milan, [1945]), p. 145: 'coloro che non istavano contenti agli ordini del vivere politico, l'avevano eletto per lo più solenne uomo della città'. Cavalcanti is referring to Giovanni de' Medici.

[35] Quoted in my *The Government of Florence under the Medici (1434–1494)* (Oxford, 1968), p. 178, n. 5.

[36] Cf., e.g., the *Translatio antiquior* of the beginning of the thirteenth century, in *Aristoteles latinus*, XXVI.1–3, fasc. 2, ed. R. A. Gauthier (Leiden–Brussels, 1972), p.66, and Grosseteste's translation of *Ethics* 1094a26–7, (as n.3) p.142. Grosseteste explains elsewhere that 'Politeia dicitur a polis, quod est civitas. Pro quo nomine translatores ponunt hoc nomen urbanitas vel civilitas' (quoted by Gauthier in his introduction, *ibid.*, fasc. 1 (Leiden–Brussels, 1974), p. clxxxvii).

[37] See above, p. 42.

[38] *Politics* 1253a2–3; *Opera omnia*, p. A77: 'ex hiis igitur manifestum, quod ... homo natura civile animal est'. Aquinas paraphrases this sentence as follows: 'sequitur quod homo sit animal naturaliter civile' (*Sententia libri Politicorum*, *ibid.*, p. A78). Elsewhere he calls man 'animal sociale et politicum' (*De regimine principum*, I.1, as n. 24, p. 1: 'naturale autem est homini ut sit animal sociale et politicum') or 'naturaliter animal sociale' (*In decem libros Aristotelis ad Nichomachum expositio*, lectio I, ed. R. M. Spiazzi (Turin, 1964), p. 3; *Summa theologiae*, Ia, qu.96, art. 4, but also

why the cardinal virtues are called *politicae*, equates this term with *civiles*: 'Politicae vero, idest civiles, dicuntur.'[39] Dante cites Aristotle in stating that 'l'uomo è animale civile' and, in applying the Aristotelian concept of the polity to mankind, inquires into the end 'totius humane civilitatis'.[40] Nicole Oresme, in translating, in 1371–7, William of Moerbeke's version of the *Politics* into French, renders *politikos* with *politique* or *civil*,[41] but reserves the former for the *regimen politicum*.[42] Civil law provided yet another approach to the equivalence of *politicus* and *civilis*. Baldus applied the Aristotelian concept of man as a political animal to the question of citizenship; when discussing the nature of the *populus*, he states that man may be

'secundum suam naturam. . .animal politicum' (*ibid.*, Ia IIae, qu. 61, art.5). It has been suggested that Aquinas made a distinction between *politicus*, 'im Sinne der institutionell ausgeprägten Herrschaftsordnung', and *civilis*, as referring to man as a social being (Sellin, as n. 6, p. 803), but the distinction appears to be between *politicum* and *sociale* rather than between *politicum* and *civile* (see, in fact, *ibid.*: 'Thomas wollte mit der Unterscheidung von "sociale" und "politicum" offensichtlich zwei Aspekte auseinanderhalten, die in der Formulierung des Aristoteles gleichzeitig intendiert waren'). Such a distinction was, however, made later by Fortescue, when he stated, in his *De natura legis naturae*, that 'dominium vizi super uxorem suam yconomicum, et sociale vel civile veteres nominabant . . .civile dominium quasi dominium dicitur sociale, quale vir quisque habet super uxorem suam' (II.46, in *The Works of Sir John Fortescue*, ed. Thomas Lord Clermont (London, 1869), I, p. 164; see also below, p.50). In fact, William of Moerbeke renders *politikos*, as applied by Aristotle to the relationship between husband and wife, with *politicus*, as does Aquinas: *Politics* 1259a39ff. (p. A112): 'et enim mulieri preesse et natis tanquam liberis . . . non eodem autem modo principatus, set mulieri quidem politice, natis autem regaliter'; Aquinas comments (*ibid.*, p. A113): 'vir principatur mulieri politico principatu'.

[39] *De bono*, tr. I, qu. vi, art. 2, sol., in *Opera omnia*, XXVIII (Münster, 1951), p. 80. Hugh of St Victor had similarly rendered *politikos* with *civilis*, as deriving from *polis* and *civitas* respectively (*Didascalicon de studio legendi*, II.19, as n. 2, pp. 37–8: 'Practica [ars] dividitur in solitariam, privatam et publicam. . .eademque publica, politica atque civilis . . . polis Graece, Latine civitas dicitur: inde politica dicta est, id est, civilis.' Did Hugh know Cicero's definition of political philosophy in the *De finibus bonorum et malorum*, IV.ii.5, where he says that by the Peripatetics and the members of the Academy 'eum locum [*scil.* philosophiae] quem civilem recte appellaturi videmur (Graeci πολιτικόν) graviter et copiose esse tractatum'?

[40] *Convivio*, IV.xxvii.3, ed. G. Busnelli and G. Vandelli, 2nd edn (Florence, 1964), II, p. 339; *Monarchia*, I.iii.1, ed. P. G. Ricci (Milan, 1965), p. 139.

[41] *Le Livres de Politiques d'Aristote*, ed. A. D. Menut, *Transactions of the American Philos. Soc.*, n.s., LX, pt 6 (1970). He follows William of Moerbeke in translating, in *Politics*, I.ii, *politicus* with *politique*, and *civilis* with *civil*: 'homme est chose civile par nature' (p.48). See also below, n. 42.

[42] *Ibid.*, p.45, translating *Politics* 1252a7–9 (see above, p. 42): 'Et quicunques gens cuident que princey ou gouvernement politique et royale ou gouvernment yconomique et despotique soient une meisme gouvernment, ils ne dient pas bien. . . Car quant un homme a la souveraine presidence, ce est princey royal; mes quant il gouverne selon les paroles de la discipline, ce est à dire selon les lais de la cité et il est en partie tenant princey et en partie subject sous le roy, adonques ce est princey politique'; p. 58 (*Politics* 1255b16–18): 'Par les choses devant mises appert que despotique et politique ne sont pas un meisme princey . . . Car prince politique est de frans ou sus frans, et princey despotique est de sers.'

considered 'quoddam corpus civile seu politicum';[43] elsewhere, he
quotes that concept in William of Moerbeke's translation as
paraphrased by Aquinas – 'homo naturaliter est animal civile' – but
then goes on to observe that law in its turn must be similar to the
homo civilis. Law is 'civil' in the Aristotelian sense, but it is also 'civil'
in the sense that, in the terminology of Roman law, enacted law is
part of the *ius civile*.[44]

In the following century, the Florentine humanist Matteo
Palmieri uses, in his *De vita civile*, *civile* in the broad sense of the word,
as in 'uso civile' and 'corpo civile'.[45] But the word could now also be
used with a new and more specific meaning. Palmieri, like other
Florentine humanists of the early Quattrocento, considered the *vita
civile* a condition of human perfection.[46] The retranslated moral and
political works of Aristotle, which they studied with fresh interest,
provided them with an authoritative confirmation of the all-
importance of civic values. In the *Politics*, *politikos* could also signify,
as a noun, the man who actively participates in public life, or the
statesman. In Palmieri's view, this meaning of the word, in its
vernacular equivalent, admirably fitted the social structure of
Florentine government in his time. In addressing his treatise on
education and public duties to the *civili*,[47] he does not address himself to the Florentine citizens in general, but effectively to those
among them who were eligible to the highest offices of the republic
and who were thus able to participate in government and decision-
making. His *De vita civile* is a moral and educational tract for the
citizens who constituted the political class of fifteenth-century
Florence, the *cittadini del reggimento*.[48]

It does not provide an analysis of the Florentine constitution; and
Palmieri does not use the word *civile* in the constitutionalist sense.
The same is true of other Florentine humanists. When Coluccio

43 *Ad Cod.*, 7.53.5, quoted by J. P. Canning, 'A fourteenth-century contribution to
   the theory of citizenship: political man and the problem of created citizenship in
   the thought of Baldus de Ubaldis', in *Authority and Power: Studies on Medieval Law and
   Government presented to Walter Ullmann*, ed. B. Tierney and P. Linehan (Cambridge,
   1980), p. 200: 'quoddam corpus civile seu politicum . . . et hoc si consideretur in
   preeminentia. Sed si consideratur in congregatione tunc homo naturaliter
   efficeretur politicus.'   44 *Ibid.*, pp. 202–3.
45 *Vita civile*, ed. G. Belloni (Florence, 1982), pp. 92, 98. Cf. also p. 13 ('civili
   costumi') and p. 95 ('compagnia civile').
46 See E. Garin, *L'umanesimo italiano* (Bari, 1952), pp. 56ff.; H. Baron, *The Crisis of the
   Early Italian Renaissance*, 2nd edn (Princeton, N. J., 1966), pp. 7, 466.
47 *Vita civile*, p. 7: 'Disposto dunque a monstrare l'approvata vita de' civili virtuosi coi
   quali più volti s'è vivuto et potre' vivere in terra, composi questa opera in nella
   quale Agnolo Pandolfino . . . spone l'ordine et virtuoso vivere degli approvati
   civili . . .'
48 See G. Brucker, *The Civic World of Early Renaissance Florence* (Princeton, N. J., 1977),
   ch. 5.

Salutati and Lionardo Bruni contrast the Florentine republican regime with despotic states, they stree its *libertas* and *aequalitas* and its *status popularis*, its popular regime, not its *regimen politicum*.[49] It was not until the very end of the fifteenth century that Tolomeo of Lucca's republican doctrine of the *regimen politicum* came again into its own. In his *Trattato circa il reggimento di Firenze*, Savonarola contrasts, in applying Tolomeo's definition to Florence, the tyrannical rule of Lorenzo de' Medici with the 'governo civile', which, he insists, is 'ottimo nella città di Firenze'.[50] Savonarola wrote his treatise about three years after the expulsion of the Medici and the establishment of a republican regime in Florence in 1494.[51] Like Tolomeo of Lucca, he did not doubt that the *regimen politicum*, that is the *governo civile*, was identical with republican government. The Great Council which formed the basis of the new republican regime was 'il signore della città'; in other words, it represented the sovereignty of the people.[52] Savonarola wanted to provide doctrinal arguments – derived, he thought, from St Thomas[53] – for the republican restoration of Florence. About thirty years earlier, Sir John Fortescue had applied the term *politicus* to monarchical regimes, and had thus given a new twist to its meaning which was in sharp contrast to traditional usage. His distinction between *dominium regale* and *dominium regale et politicum* opens a new chapter in the history of the word.[54]

Fortescue asserts that he owed the concept of *dominium regale et politicum* to Aquinas and Giles of Rome.[55] In fact, neither Aquinas's

---

[49] See my 'Florentine constitutionalism and Medici ascendancy in the fifteenth century', in *Florentine Studies*, ed. N. Rubinstein (London, 1968), pp. 446ff.

[50] *Trattato circa el reggimento e governo della città* di Firenze, I.3, ed. L. Firpo, in Savonarola, *Prediche sopra Aggeo* (Rome, 1965), p. 450. See D. Weinstein, *Savonarola and Florence: Prophecy and Patriotism in the Renaissance* (Princeton, N. J., 1970), ch. 9   [51] On the date of composition, see Firpo, in *Trattato*, pp. 519–21.

[52] *Trattato*, III.1, p. 474: 'non è dubbio che questo è il signore della città'.

[53] See Weinstein, p. 290.

[54] On the question of the originality of Fortescue's terminology, see S. B. Chrimes (ed.), Sir John Fortescue, *De laudibus legum Anglie* (Cambridge,1942), introduction, pp. xciv–xcv, and especially F. Gilbert, 'Sir John Fortescue's "Dominium regale et politicum"', *Medievalia et Humanistica*, fasc. 2 (1944), 88–94. J. Burns, 'Fortescue and the political theory of *Dominium*', *Historical Journal*, XXVIII (1985), 777–97.

[55] *De natura legis naturae*, I.26, (as n. 38) p. 88: 'Quare si bonum sit omni populo legibus regi in quas ipsi assentiunt, necessario confitebitur regimen regis qui hujusmodi legibus regit populum suum, quod regimen politicum appellatur, a potentia descendere, sicut et ab hujusmodi regis voluntate.
Et quod bonum sit hujusmodi legibus populum regulari, Sanctus Thomas in primo libro Tractatus sui prenotati apertissime docuisse videtur ... Quare finaliter ibidem optare videtur ut . . . sic temperetur ejus potestas ut in tirannidem defacili declinare non possit.' *The Governance of England*, ch.1, ed. Ch. Plummer (Oxford, 1885), p.109: 'Ther bith ij kyndes of kyngdomes, of the wich that on is a lordship callid in laten *dominium regale*, and that other is callid *dominium politicum et*

and Tolomeo's nor Giles of Rome's treatise applied the term *politicus* to the *regnum*; both Tolomeo of Lucca and Giles of Rome insist on the fundamental distinction between the *regimen regale* and the *regimen politicum*.[56] In his *De natura legis naturae*, where Fortescue introduces the new concept for the first time, he correctly states that Giles of Rome based that distinction on the difference in the source of the laws by which the ruler governs: in one case it is the prince himself, in the other the people.[57] However, Fortescue adds, there is also a third kind of *dominium*, which is not less praiseworthy; it is called *politicum et regale*.[58] He claims for that *dominium* too the authority of Aquinas; no doubt he was thinking of Book III of the *De regimine principum*, in which Ptolemy of Lucca argues that the ancient Roman Empire conformed in some respects to the *dominium regale*, in others to the *regimen politicum*.[59] But a great distance separated Ptolemy's analysis of the constitution of the Roman Empire, placed, according to him, 'halfway between the political and royal regimes', 'medium ... inter politicum et regale', from Fortescue's combination of *politicum* and *regale* in a *regnum*.[60]

Fortescue clarified and elaborated the meaning of that combination in two later works, composed between 1468 and 1476, his *De laudibus legum Anglie* and *The Governance of England*.[61] The king who rules *politice* may not, like the one ruling *principatu regali*, change laws without the assent of the people, nor burden it against its will with taxes;[62] even his power itself derives from the people, 'potestatem a

regale... This diuersite is wel taught bi Seynt Thomas, in his boke wich he wrote *ad regem Cipri de regemine principum*. But yet it is more openly tredid in a boke callid *compendium moralis philosophie*, and sumwhat bi Giles in his boke *de regemine principum*.' Cf. Plummer, *ibid.*, pp. 171–7.   [56]   See above, pp. 44–5.

[57]   *De natura legis naturae*, I.16, p. 77: in his *De regimine principum*, 'Egidius Romanus ... ait, quod ille preest dominio regali qui preest secundum leges quas ipsemet statuit, et secundum arbitrium suum; sed dominio politico preest qui secundum leges quas cives instituerunt eis dominatur.'

[58]   *Ibid.*: 'Sed et tertium esse dominium non minus his dignitate et laude, quod politicum et regale nominatur, nedum experientia et veterum historiis edocemur, sed et dicti Sancti Thomae doctrina edoctum esse cognoscimus ...'

[59]   *De regimine principum*, III.12, (as n. 24) p. 53: 'medium tenet inter politicum et regale'; III.20, p. 61: 'videnda est comparatio imperialis dominii ad regale et politicum: quia, ut ex dictis apparet, convenit cum utroque et cum politico quidem quantum ad tria'. Like the consuls and dictators, 'qui politice regebant populum', Roman emperors 'assumebantur per viam electionis'; those who were elected were 'non semper de genere nobili'; and their 'dominium non transibat in posteros'. See Chrimes and Gilbert, as n. 54.

[60]   For a somewhat different interpretation, see Gilbert, pp. 92–3.

[61]   See nn. 38 and 54.

[62]   *De laudibus legum Anglie*, ch. 9, p. 24: 'Si regali tantum ipse preesset eis, leges regni sui mutare ille posset, tallagia quoque et cetera onera eis imponere ipsis inconsultis ... Sed longe aliter potest rex politice imperans genti sue, quia nec leges ipse sine subditorum assensu mutare poterit, nec subiectum populum renitentem onerare imposicionibus peregrinis ...'

populo effluxam ipse habet', and he may not rule it by any other power.[63] Fortescue thus adopts Aquinas's and Giles of Rome's distinction between the *regimen regale* and the *regimen politicum* as based on the difference in the source of the laws, but applies that distinction not to monarchies and republics, but to two different kinds of monarchy: 'the first kynge mey rule his peple bi suche lawes as he makyth hym self . . . The secounde kynge may not rule his peple bi other lawes than such as thai assenten unto.'[64] He explains the existence of these two kinds of monarchical government in historical terms. The *dominum regale* resulted, in the earliest times, from the subjection of peoples by 'men excelling in power, greedy of dignity and glory';[65] the *dominium regale et politicum* emerged when the people constituted itself as a 'body politic', a *corpus politicum*, and elected a king, who was to rule it 'by suche lawes as thai all wolde assent unto'.[66] For 'just as the head of the body physical is unable to change its nerves. . .so a king who is head of the body politic (*corporis politici*) is unable to change the laws of that body, or to deprive that same people of their own substance uninvited or against their wills'.[67] It will be seen that Fortescue operates here both the broader and the narrower connotation of *politicus*, shifting almost imperceptibly from the first to the second: the 'incorporation' of the people as a body politic leads to the establishment of a monarchy, and thus to a *dominium regale*, which is however limited by the laws of that body and owes its authority to it, and is consequently a *dominium politicum* as well as *regale*.

Fortescue believed this regime to be greatly superior to the *dominium regale tantum*. He saw it realised in his own time in English kingship under the Lancastrians, which he considered a constitutional monarchy,[68] and contrasted it with what he described as the oppressive rule of the *regimen regale tantum*, the absolute monarchy, of the French king.[69] He was the first to apply the Thomist–Aristotelian notion of *politicus*, in the sense of government

[63] *Ibid.*, ch. 13, p. 32: 'Habes, ex hoc iam, princeps, institucionis regni politici formam': the king is established 'ad tutelam' of the laws of his subjects and of their bodies and goods, 'et ad hanc potestatem a populo effluxam ipse habet, quo ei non licet potestate alia suo populo dominari'.[64] *The Governance of England*, ch.1, p.109.
[65] *De laudibus*, ch. 12, p. 29; cf. *The Governance*, ch. 2.
[66] *Ibid.* Cf. *De laudibus*, ch. 13, pp. 30–3. In this way, the 'regnum Anglie', which Brutus and his Trojans brought to that country, 'in dominium politicum et regale prorupit' (p. 32).
[67] *Ibid.*, pp. 31, 33. I quote from Chrimes's translation of this work.
[68] *De natura legis naturae*, I.16, p. 77: 'In regno namque Angliae sine Trium statuum Regni illius consensu leges non condunt, nec subsidia imponunt subditis suis . . . Numquid tunc hoc dominium politicum . . . dici possit, verum etiam et regale dominium nominari mereatur . . .'   [69] *The Governance of England*, ch. 3.

'secundum leges civitatis', to kingship, and base on it a theory of constitutional monarchy.[70] About forty years later, it was the turn of a Frenchman, Claude de Seyssel, to describe the same French monarchy which Fortescue had condemned as absolutist, as a mixed constitution, and as such 'si politique qu'elle est toute aliénée de la Tyrannie'.[71] In his *La Monarchie de France*, he calls one of the three bridles, *freins*, 'par lesquels la puissance absolue des rois de France est réglée', 'la Police':[72] 'c'est à savoir de plusieurs Ordonnances qui ont été faites par les Rois mêmes, et après confirmées et approuvées de temps en temps, lesquelles tendent à la conservation du royaume en universel et particulier'.[73] Seyssel also uses the terms *politique*, *police*, in the broad sense of political;[74] but it is the constitutionalist connotation which he gives to these terms which rank him, with Fortescue, as one of the innovators of modern political language. The third was Machiavelli.

Machiavelli, like Savonarola before him, calls the true republican regime *vivere civile*,[75] or, more emphatically, *vero vivere libero e civile*.[76] He also uses for it the term *politico*. Thus when discussing, in his *Discourses* on Livy, the 'riordinare una città al vivere politico',[77] he emphasises the difficulties 'nelle città corrotte, a mantenervi una republica'.[78] Of the constitution of Sparta and Venice he says that,

[70] For a different interpretation, see R. W. K. Hinton, 'English constitutional doctrines from the fifteenth century to the seventeenth: I. English constitutional theories from Sir John Fortescue to Sir John Eliot', *E.H.R.*, LXXV (1960), 410–25.

[71] 'Prohème en la translation de l'Histoire d'Appien alexandrin', in *La Monarchie de France et deux autres fragments politiques*, ed. J. Poujol (Paris, 1961), p.79: 'je la treuve si raisonnable et si politique qu'elle est toute aliénée de la Tyrannie'. On the 'empire français' possessing a mixed constitution, cf. p. 80. On the date of the *Prohème* ('vers 1510'), *ibid.*, p. 75.

[72] *La Monarchie de France*, I.8, (as n. 71) p. 115. On the date of composition (*c.* 1515), *ibid.*, p. 16; the work was first printed in 1519 (p. 91). [73] I.11, p. 119.

[74] E.g., I.1, p. 103: 'il y a trois sortes et manières de régime politique', monarchy, aristocracy, and democracy, 'qui est l'état populaire'; cf. the *Prohème*, *ibid.*, p. 99; 'je n'ai écrit chose en particulier que ne puisse prouver par raison politique'; 'le gouvernement ... monarchique est le meilleur entre les autres politiques'.

[75] Cf., eg., *Discorsi sopra la prima deca di Tito Livio*, I.9, ed. S. Bertelli (Milan, 1960), p. 154: after the expulsion of the Tarquins, the Romans replaced the king with two annual consuls, 'il che testifica tutti gli ordini primi di quella città essere stati più conformi a uno vivere civile e libero che a uno assoluto e tirannico'; I.7, p. 148: 'Francesco Valori era come principe della città; il quale sendo guidicato ... uomo che volesse ... transcendere il vivere civile ...'

[76] *Storie fiorentine*, III.5, ed. P. Carli (Florence, 1927), I, p. 142: in an invective against Florentine faction strife, a speaker demands the annulment of 'quelli ordini che sono delle sette nutritori ... prendendo quelli che al vero vivere libero e civile sono conformi'.

[77] *Discorsi*, I.18, p. 182. In conclusion, he emphasises 'la difficultà o impossibilità che è nelle città corrotte' of achieving this, that is 'a mantenervi una republica o a crearvela di nuovo'. [78] *Ibid.*; cf. I.55, p. 256.

'potendosi tenere la cosa bilanciata in questo modo. . .e' sarebbe il vero vivere politico'.[79] But occasionally he extends the meaning of *civile* or *politico* to encompass not only republics but also kingdoms. Not only a city but also a province can be made into a *vivere politico*;[80] on the other hand, in parts of Italy, such as Naples and Lombardy, 'non è mai surta alcuna republica nè alcuno vivero politico';[81] and, most incisively, in chapter 25 of Book I: 'E questo. . .debbe osservare colui che vuole ordinare uno vivere politico, o per via di republica o di regno', in contrast to the 'potestà assoluta, la quale dagli autori è chiamata tirannide'.[82] Like Fortescue's *dominium politicum, il vivere politico* or *civile* stands for constitutional government. But while Fortescue referred *dominium politicum* solely to the English, Seyssel *la police* to the French monarchy, Machiavelli's *vivere politico* encompasses both republics and monarchies. Although he argued, throughout the *Discourses*, for the superiority of republics over monarchies, he firmly believed that a constitutional order could be achieved by either. The one contemporary monarchy which represented such an order was, according to him, that of France. The principal feature of a *vivere politico* was that it was 'regolato dalle leggi'[83] and by 'ordini', by laws and institutional arrangements;[84] and the French monarchy corresponded to this model. The kingdom of France 'vive sotto le leggi e sotto gli ordini più che alcuno altro regno.' Delle quali leggi ed ordini ne sono mantenitori i parlamenti.'[85] Machiavelli's notion of France as a constitutional monarchy reminds one of Seyssel's. He cannot have read *La Monarchie de France* when he composed the *Discourses*,[86] but he may well have become acquainted with French constitutional thinking during his travels in France between 1500 and 1510. It was in keeping with the distortions his thought was subjected to after his death that his critics ignored his concept of the *vivere politico* and concentrated on the sinister interpretation of Machiavellian policy.

The ambivalence which the terms 'policy' and its derivatives

[79] *Ibid.*, I.6, p. 145.
[80] *Ibid.*, II, proem, p. 272: 'E vedesi una città o una provincia essere ordinata al vivere politico da qualche uomo eccellente.'   [81] *Ibid.*, I.55, p. 256.
[82] *Ibid.*, p. 193. This is repeated, at the opening of the following chapter, with *civile* substituted for *politico* (*ibid.*): 'Qualunque diventa principe o d'una littà o d'uno stato. . .e non si volga o per via di regno o di republica alla vita civile . . .'   [83] Cf. *ibid.*, I.58, p. 265.
[84] See J.H. Whitfield, 'On Machiavelli's use of *ordini, Italian Studies*, X(1955), 19–39, reprinted in *Discourses on Machiavelli* (Cambridge, 1969), pp. 141–62.
[85] *Discorsi*, III.1, p.383; cf. I.58, p.262: 'il quale regno è moderato più dalle leggi che alcuno altro regno di che ne' nostri tempi si abbia notizia'.
[86] See above, n. 72. Cf. Poujol (as n. 71), p. 36, and I. Cervelli, *Machiavelli e la crisi dello stato veneziano* (Naples, 1974), pp. 241ff.

acquired in the course of the sixteenth century was largely due to the impact of Machiavelli, and of anti-Machiavellism, on political thought. In Elizabethan England, 'policy' and 'politic' came to be generally used as denoting cunning, and altogether amoral conduct based on expediency, deceitfulness – especially after the Massacre of St Bartholomew, which was believed by Protestants to have been the work of Machiavellians at the French court.[87] 'Am I politic? Am I subtle? Am I a Machiavel?', asks the Host in *The Merry Wives of Windsor*; and the First Stranger in *Timon of Athens* asserts: 'Men must learn now with pity to dispense: / For policy sits above conscience.'[88] But amoral conduct was not the only ground on which the terms could be used with a pejorative meaning.

Ever since the revivial of Aristotelian political philosophy in the thirteenth century, *politicus* and its equivalents had remained linked to the notion of the science of politics, as 'the most sovereign of the sciences'.[89] Aquinas considered the 'scientia politica' to be 'inter omnes scientias practicas . . . principaliorem'.[90] Fifteenth-century humanists, who were now able to read Plato's as well as Aristotle's works on politics, agreed with this high valuation of political science: thus Lauro Quirini stated that the *doctrina politica* was 'excellentior . . . multoque nobilior' than other sciences.[91] For Machiavelli and Guicciardini, the 'scrittori della civiltà', or the 'politici', were identical, for all practical purposes, with the ancient political philosophers.[92] This was no longer the case later in the century. Bodin declares in 1566 that Machiavelli was the first to revive the political science since antiquity: 'primus . . . post annos mille circiter ac ducentos . . . de republica scripsit';[93] Guillaume de la Perrière, in his *Miroir politique* (1555), cites Plato as the first, Machiavelli as the last of the writers on 'l'art de doctrine politique'.[94] The appearance of Machiavelli as innovator of political doctrine underlines the emphasis on the secular connotation of that doctrine. As such, it came to be connected with prudence. 'Icelle nostre

[87] See N. Orsini, ' "Policy": or the language of Elizabethan Machiavellianism', *Journal of the Warburg and Courtauld Institutes*, IX (1946), 122–34.
[88] III. i.92–3; III. i.88–9. See Ch. Morris, 'Shakespeare's politics', *Historical Journal*, VIII (1965).   [89] *Nicom. Ethics*, I.ii.4–5.
[90] *Sententia libri Politicorum*, Prologus (as n. 13), p. A70.
[91] *De republica*, dedication to Francesco Foscari, ed. C. Seno and G. Ravegnani in *Lauro Quirini umanista*, ed. V. Branca (Florence, 1977), p. 123.
[92] Machiavelli, *Discorsi*, I.28, p. 196; Francesco Guicciardini, *Ricordi*, ed. R. Spongano (Florence, 1951), p. 246 (A109; B132): 'vorrei che questi politici m'avessino dichiarato'.
[93] *Methodus ad facilem historiarum cognitionem*, ed. P. Mesnard (Paris, 1951), p. 167.
[94] (Lyon, 1555), pp. 12–13: 'Et de nostre temps en langue Tuscane, Macchiavegli secretaire et citoyen de Florence'.

raison', writes Guillaume Budé around 1519 in *De l'institution du prince,* 'favorise la prudence civile, qui est plus politicque et introduicte sur les façons de la police, que sur l'ordre des moeurs, qu'on appelle morale'.[95] It came also to be understood as political craft. This may have been what Gabriel Harvey had in mind when he described, in 1573, Machiavelli as 'the great master and founder of policy'.[96] Calvin had emphasised, in 1536, in his *Institution de la religion chrestienne,* that 'il y a double régime en l'homme. L'un est spirituel ... L'autre est politic ou civil, par lequel l'homme est apprins des offices d'humanité et civilité.'[97] The distinction between the religious and the political sphere, though understood here in terms of harmonious coexistence, gave way, in the course of the century, to conflicts which led to yet another twist in the meaning of the word *politicus.*

Michel de l'Hôpital calls the Romans 'les plus sages policiens du monde';[98] Rabelais describes Numa Pompilius as 'juste, politic et philosophe';[99] for the lawyer François Baudouin (1559), it was the jurist who represented the 'homo politicus'.[100] But during the Wars of Religion, and especially after the Massacre of St Bartholomew, *politique* was increasingly used in a derogatory sense, to describe the men who, in the search for peace and unity, were ready to compromise on religious matters.[101] Thus the chancellor l'Hôpital could be condemned as 'l'auteur et le patron de l'erreur politique';[102] de Thou writes later, in his *History of his Time* (1604–7), that the word *politicus* was first 'in odium tractum' as the name of those who were aiming at a peace that reconciled religion with public utility.[103] But

[95] (Paris, 1547), p. 19.
[96] Quoted in C. Morris, 'Machiavelli's reputation in Tudor England', *Il Pensiero Politico,* II (1969), 419.
[97] Ed. J. Pannier, IV (Paris, 1939), p. 146–7 (ch. 14: 'De la liberté chrestienne;').
[98] *Harangues,* in Michel l'Hospital, *Oeuvres complè*tes (Paris, 1824–6), I, p. 398.
[99] *Le Tiers livre,* ch. 1, ed. M. A. Screech (Geneva, 1964), p. 26.
[100] D. R. Kelley, " 'Murd'rous Machiavel" in France: a post mortem', *Political Science Quarterly,* LXXXV (1970), 558.
[101] See D. R. Kelley, *François Hotman: A Revolutionary's Ordeal* (Princeton, N. J., 1973), pp. 174, 251.
[102] Anon., *Description du politique de notre temps* (1588), cit. G. Weill, *Les Théories sur le pouvoir royal en France pendant les guerres de religion* (Paris, 1891), p. 133, n. 1.
[103] J. A. de Thou, *Historiae sui temporis* (Paris, 1606), II, p. 450 (a.a. 1568): 'Tunc primum Politici nomen in odium tractum in monumentis rerum nostrarum video, in quod postea concionatores grassante licentia supra modum debacchati sunt, optimates pacis, qua religio et publica securitas continentur, studiosos eo notantes.' Cf. Pierre de l'Estoile, *Mémoires-Journaux,* I(1574–80) (Paris, 1875), p. 83 (July 1575): 'ce jour, arrivèrent nouvelles de Poictiers et quelques autres villes faillies per les mal contents du Poictou et publicains, qu'on appeloit, pour ce qu'ils s'aidoient du prétexte du bien publiq', where *politiques* is equated with *publicains.*

at the same time, the Moderates, mostly Catholic, who shared these aims, appropriated the term for themselves by giving it a positive meaning. According to what François Hotman writes to a friend in 1574, for them the word stood for a programme which went beyond the religious question. 'They have taken the name of *politiques* [*politici*] and ... demand the restoration of the ancient constitution through the convocation of the Estates General.'[104] With all its new ambivalence, *politicus* had preserved its constitutionalist meaning.

[104] Quoted by Kelley (as n. 100), pp. 551–2.

3

◁ ═══════════════════════════════════════ ▷

Civil science in the Renaissance:
the problem of interpretation

DONALD KELLEY

'Interpretation', like its modern descendant 'Criticism', has often come under attack by champions of authorship and authority. From Petrarch to Susan Sontag, authors have taken stands 'against interpretation as a way of protecting the creative process from scholastic instrusions and distortions – and even, as in current 'deconstructionist' criticism, from usurpation of the authorial role.[1] Both sides are certainly aware that the struggle is in part political (even on that lowest level of interpretation, which is translation: 'traduttore, traditore'); for it centres on the meaning, hence control of the social effects, of the work in question.

This time-honoured war between authors and critics has a striking (and much more political) counterpart in the field of law, which has paralleled (and often overlapped) Western literary history. From Justinian, who gave shape to the European legal tradition, to Napoleon, who reshaped it for the modern world, 'authorities' and 'interpreters' have been at odds, if not sword's point; for here the prize is the political and social control embodied in the law and in the attendant authority to define and to apply it – in effect sovereign power.[2] *Cuius interpretatio, eius legislatio.* Both of these emperors,

---

[1] *Against Interpretation and other Essays* (New York, 1967), and cf. Jonathan Culler, *The Pursuit of Signs* (Ithaca, 1981).

[2] G. G. Archi, 'Interpretatio iuris – interpretatio legis – interpretatio legum', *Zeitschrift der Savigny-Stiftung für Rechtsgeschichte, Römische Abteilung,* C (1970), 1–49; F. Pringsheim, 'Justinian's prohibition of commentaries to the Digest', *Gesammelte Abhandlungen,* II (Heidelberg, 1961), 85–106; J. Charmont and A. Chausse, 'Les interprètes du code civil', in *Le Code civil 1804–1904, livre du centenaire* (Paris, 1904), II, pp. 131–72; Helmut Coing, *Die juristischen Auslegungsmethoden und die Lehren der allgemeinen Hermeneutik* (Cologne, 1959); *Archives de Philosophie du Droit,* XVII (1972), 'L'interprétation dans le droit'; Ronald Dworkin, 'Law as interpretation', in *The Politics of Interpretation,* ed. W. Mitchell (Chicago, 1983), pp. 249–70; and D. R. Kelley, 'Hermes, Clio, Themis: historical interpretation and legal hermeneutics', in *History, Law and the Human Sciences* (London, 1984), with further bibliography.

therefore, strictly forbade any 'interpretation' at all. Their efforts
were in vain, of course; and the logomachy still goes on – critics
versus authors, interpreters versus legislators, judiciary versus
executive, perhaps even practitioners of civil disobedience versus
government. What Justinian called 'the vain discourse of posterity',
Napoleon the 'murder' of his code, Mark Twain the leavings of 'the
most degraded trade' and Harold Bloom a 'map of misreading', has
progressively obscured the Word that Was in the Beginning. It has
also, of course, called for further 'interpretation'.

   'Civil science' is the name given by medieval jurists to Roman
jurisprudence in the posthumous form it assumed after the twelfth-
century revival of ancient learning. Although bound to ancient legal
'authority', European civil science – *sanctissima civilis scientia*, as
Sebastian Brant called it – was in fact the product of what jurists as
well as philosophers and theologians came to call 'hermeneutics' (*ars
hermeneutica* is the phrase used by Leibniz in his youthful essay on
jurisprudence),[3] which was to say the theory and practice of
'interpretation'. How this came about was explained by Johannes
Oldendorp in his *Interpretatio privilegii duplicis* of 1543, a commentary
on the Emperor Frederick Barbarossa's constitution *Habita* of 1159,
which bestowed the right of interpreting civil law on authorised
doctores legum.[4] The 'double grounds' for this privilege were pedagogical
utility and religious propriety; that is, the need to make ancient ideas
intelligible to beginning students and to reconcile them with
Christian truth. Thus, from being a punishable crime (*pena falsitatis*),
interpretation was transformed into a major rubric of medieval and
modern jurisprudence, spawning not only endless justifications of
interpretation but also a new methodological and philosophical
genre devoted to legal hermeneutics.

   The chief source of inspiration came from the classical texts of
civil law itself, especially from that fragmentary monument, the
Digest, which was a highly edited and poorly organised anthology of
over a millennium of ancient jurisprudence. For interpretation the
loci classici were the first three titles of Book I (on the theory of law,
the origin of law and the chief sources of law) and titles sixteen and
seventeen of the last, the fiftieth, book (on the meaning of words and
on the various rules of law).[5] The motto of legal interpretation – the

---

[3] See below at note 53.
[4] *Interpretatio privilegii duplicis, quod Friderichus primus, omnium Imperii ordinum consensu,
     summa aequitatis ratione motus, concessit bonarum literarum studiosis* (n. p., 1543); cf. *MGH,
     Constitutiones*, I. 249. Baldus, *Super Digesto veteri commentarii* (n. p., 1535), fol. 3r.
[5] *Digest* (ed. Mommsen-Krueger), I and L, 16–17; and see the invaluable Fritz Schulz,
     History of Roman Legal Science (Oxford, 1953).

license for judges and bane of legislators for centuries – was the formula of Celsus, preserved in title three of Book I, that 'understanding laws means knowing not merely their words but their force and effect' (*vim et potestas*). This meant above all the 'will' (*voluntas*) of the prince, though necessarily as construed by the magistrate.

The oldest school of medieval civilians was that of the glossators, whose work was summed up in Accursius's great *Glossa ordinaria*, assembled around 1265, covering all the major texts of civil law, including the Digest, Institutes and Code, together with a collection of medieval imperial law called the *Consuetudines feudorum*.[6] Traditionally, *glossa* meant explanation of a single word; and for the most part the glossators avoided going beyond the literal meaning of terms and so violating Justinian's ban on interpretation, although they were in fact capable of textual emendation on an elementary level. They were also aware of the role of judicial opinion; and in a legendary debate the glossator Azo, opposing his colleague Lothair and offending the Emperor Henry VI, commented that the *imperium* itself (the so-called *merum imperium*) might be exercised not only by the emperor but also by magistrates.[7] To this extent the loophole of 'interpretation' – and the conflict of judiciary and legislature – was already opened by the thirteenth century.

This loophole (and the attendant conflict) became wider in the work of their successors, the post-glossators, or commentators, who no longer pretended to stick to the absolute letter of the law, and who introduced a variety of philosophical and literary devices in order to accommodate – the more technical term was to 'extend' – the ancient legal canon to modern conditions and demands.[8] In fact these scholastic jurists, called 'Bartolists' after their most famous (and authoritative) representative, departed so far from textual tradition that, by the fifteenth century, a humanist reaction had set in, calling for a return to the sources. In trying to reconstruct the 'historical sense' of texts legal humanists were not only following classical precedent but also anticipating the modern debate over

---

6 The best bibliographical guide to the extraordinarily rich and diversified literature on European legal science is Helmut Coing (ed.), *Handbuch der Quellen und Literatur der neueren Europäischen Privatrechtsgeschichte*, I and II (Munich, 1973–5); also Walter Ullmann, *Law and Politics in the Middle Ages* (Ithaca, 1975).

7 M. P. Gilmore, *Argument from Roman Law in Political Thought 1200–1600* (Cambridge, Mass., 1941).

8 On the problem of interpretation, see especially Ennio Cortese, *La norma giuridica* (Milan, 1962–4), and Vicenzo Piano Mortari, 'Il problema dell'"interpretatio iuris" nei commentatori', *Annali di storia del diritto*, I (1958), 29–109. There is a vast literature on individual authors.

'intentionality'; for they were literally trying to read the 'mind' or 'intention' of the original author, which was assumed to coincide with the 'meaning' of the law (*mens, voluntas* or *sententia* were terms applied indifferently to both).[9] This literal- or literary-minded sort of 'criticism' was marginal, however, to the main thrust of professional jurisprudence, which continued to be towards 'extensive' interpretation.

The tendency towards *extensio interpretiva* began with the 'ultramontane' (especially the French) commentators of the later thirteenth century, most notably Jacques de Révigny and Pierre Belleperche, who were deeply suspicious of the Italian Gloss and could not in any event accept the absolute authority of 'the emperor's law' for the French monarchy. So they became committed to the search not merely for legislative intention (*mens legum*) but rather for the underlying, or overarching, 'reason' and justice in a particular law. 'Not the intention of the law-giver but the rationale of the law' (*nec ex mente sed ex ratione*) was Jacques' formula, and Pierre went even further in the direction of judicial discretion (*nec ex mente sed ex interpretatione*).[10]

The fashion set by these 'moderns', as they were called, was followed in Italy (whose relations with the Emperor were also ambivalent at best). The pioneering figure was Dante's friend Cino da Pistoia, who had studied with the French commentators. Taking as his motto 'all novelty is pleasing' (*omnia nova placent*), Cino claimed the right to a contrary opinion even though (as he put it) all the doctors disagreed.[11] His disciples Bartolus and Baldus, champions of the Italian city-states so neglected by the emperors, extended his fondness for novelty into an elaborate theory of interpretation, with 'reason' gaining precedence over 'authority' in many ways, especially political. Their *extensiones*, naturally, were designed to benefit not the French monarch but the Italian *civitas*, which belonged to the modern law of nations (*novissimum ius gentium*) and which, like any corporation, could give itself a head. 'The city [*civitas*]

[9] W. K. Wimsatt, *The Verbal Icon* (Louisville, 1954), p. 37. The confusion between the meaning of a text and that of an author is illustrated by a passage in a famous eighteenth-century work by C. H. Wolff, *Principes du droit de la nature et des gens*, trans. M. Formey (Amsterdam, 1968), p. 321: 'Interpréter, c'est déterminer le sens qu'on a voulu attacher à certains signes. On appelle ce sens, l'*esprit* de celui qui a parlé, ou fourni ces signes. Ainsi l'*Interprétation*, c'est la découverte, ou du moins l'exposition quelconque de l'esprit indiqué par certaines paroles, ou par certains signes.'

[10] Révigny, *Lectura super Codice* (Paris, n. d.), on *Code*, I.14.5; Belleperche, *In libros Institutionum... commentarii* (n. p., n. d.), on *Institutes*, I.1.3; and see E. Meijers, *Etudes d'histoire du droit*, III (Leiden, 1966).

[11] *In Codicem... doctissima Commentaria* (Frankfurt, 1578), fol. lr.

is itself the prince' is Bartolus's famous formula of civic independence, whose spirit 'civic humanists' might share even while deplor-
ing the implied anachronism. This attitude of Bartolus, Baldus and
others, transcending particular political crises of the Renaissance,
reflects an attitude which I like to call 'civil humanism'.

In general, Bartolus and his colleagues preferred the most
straightforward sort of interpretation, which rested on 'propriety'
(*proprietas*, which is basically, according to Quintilian, calling things
by their right names). After this they might resort to etymology, or
'allusion', which of course referred to the philosophical or speculative, not the historical variety, but even then only if it did not
contradict the definition. Bartolus admitted degrees of 'latitude' in
interpretation and the use of analogy (*similia ad similium*); but the
major devices were furnished by the requirements of reason and
equity.[12] Following the lead of Cino and his French masters, Bartolus
tended to identify rationality (*ratio*) not only with intention (*mens*)
but also with liberal interpretation (*extensio*). Beyond that he could
also invoke 'natural law' and the 'law of nations', which was itself
based, as Gaius had said, on 'natural reason'. The utility of these
appeals may be appreciated by noting that the 'rules of law' declared
both 'actions' and 'peoples' to be subjected finally not to civil law
but, as Baldus had said, to the law of nations.[13]

'Civil science' was reshaped by humanism in several ways from the
later fifteenth century. First and most conspicuous was the application of philological and historical methods of criticism to the texts
(including Greek passages) of Roman law.[14] The attendant conflict
between the *mores italicus* and *gallicus* – in effect legal scholasticism
versus legal humanism – created more heat than light, since practitioners of the science of law, no less than those of the science of
theology, had no intention of submitting to the authority of the
lower arts, including the 'historical sense' required by grammar and
the 'eloquence' which rhetoric sometimes seemed to prize above

---

[12] Bartolus, *In primam [Digesti] veteri partem Commentaria* (Turin, 1574), fol. 16rff. and
(on the 'rules of law') 248rff.; Baldus, *Super Digesto veteri*, fol. 4v. And see Norbert
Horn, *Aequitas in den Lehren des Baldus* (Cologne, 1968).

[13] Commenting on *Digest*, I.1.1, Baldus makes the point in the form of a syllogism:
'Populi sunt de iure gentium, ergo regimen populi est de iure gentium. Sed
regimen non potest esse sine legibus et statutis, ergo eo ipso quod populus habet
esse, habet per consequens regimen in suo esse, sicut omne animal regitur a suo
proprio spiritu et anima.' See also Cino da Pistoia, *Super Codice et Digesto veteri lectura*
(Lyon, 1547), fol. 4r, and Baldus, *Super Digesto veteri*, fol. 10r; and C. Karsten, *Die
Lehre von Vertrag bei den italienischen Juristen des Mittelalters* (Rostok, 1882).

[14] See now Hans Troje, *Graeca leguntur* (Cologne, 1971), and D. R. Kelley, 'Civil
science in the Renaissance: jurisprudence Italian style', in *History, Law and the
Human Sciences*.

justice. Humanists could claim indeed to be more faithful to the 'intention' of the original law-giver (and thus to respect Justinian's ban), but old-fashioned jurists rejected this with their own claims to serve the higher aims of the law.

In the end the influence of humanism on legal interpretation was significant but, in conceptual terms, marginal. Within the professional tradition the consequences may best be seen in Andrea Alciato's great commentary of 1520 on the Digest title *De verborum significatione*. Going beyond Bartolism, yet rejecting the literary excesses of mere 'grammarians' like Valla, Alciato distinguished four modes of interpretation, beginning with the literal, which was to say linguistic, 'propriety' tied ideally to the will and intention of the author, though in case of doubt recourse might also be had to definition or etymology.[15] The second type of interpretation was improper (*improprietas* was the term), though this did not necessarily mean error, since it might rest on a convention or 'fiction' which did not produce misunderstanding (such as the use of foreign terms). Third was interpretation according to common usage (*ex usu*), which was permissible, though undesirable, given the tendency of vulgar language to degenerate into 'abuse'. 'What is common usage today', Alciato remarked, 'cannot be presumed to have been so formerly.' Last of all came *extensio*, and here Alciato discussed a wide range of means and conditions and ways of pushing interpretation beyond propriety and custom. Besides the conventional extensions made through analogy, through the application of rules (*regulariter*) and through invocation of natural law and 'equity' (*epieikeia*), Alciato devoted one whole book to literary extensions, that is to say, proverbs (supplementing the 'adages' of Alciato's older friend, Erasmus), figures and tropes, from metaphor to irony. Technically, of course, these were 'improper' but they were essential since the law, like the Bible as interpreted by Erasmus, was 'literature' as well as 'science'.

Another area in which civil science and humanism overlapped was the art of rhetoric, which became the basis for the so-called 'new logic' associated with Rudolph Agricola, Philip Melanchthon and especially Peter Ramus (though in fact the apparatus of Aristotelian dialectic was never wholly rejected or replaced). The convergence

---

[15] *De verborum significatione* (Lyon, 1536); and see Hans Troje, 'Alciats Methode der Kommentierung des "Corpus iuris civilis" ', in A. Buck & O. Herding (eds.), *Der Kommentar in der Renaissance* (Godesberg, 1975); and Guido Kisch, *Erasmus und die Jurisprudenz seiner Zeit* (Basel, 1960).

between 'topical' logic and legal interpretation in the fifteenth century produced a new genre devoted to the theory and practice of *extensio* of authoritative legal text. In a stream of monographs from Nicolas Everardus's *Topica legalia* (1516) to Leibniz's *Nova methodus iurisprudentiae* (1667) and beyond, jurists sought a proper 'method' of law through rational reorganisation. In treatises by Oldendorp, Bartolommeo Cepolo, Costantino Rogerio, Pietro Andrea Gammaro, Claudius Cantiuncula, Johannes Apel, Matteo Gribaldi and Christopher Hegendorph, legal hermeneutics came into its own.[16] In the context of the general sixteenth-century pursuit of a true 'Method', these champions of *interpretatio extensiva* continued the search for the 'inner meaning', or inherent 'reason' of laws.[17] But the goal of interpretation always remained the common good; and as Oldendorp warned, legal error not only undermined justice, it also produced social and political corruption (*error corrumpit politicis ordines et introducit confusionem poenitendam*).[18]

As the method of civil science was developed by treatises devoted to legal 'method' and the theory of 'extension', so its vocabulary was fixed by another new genre. This was the tradition of juridical lexicography, which was basically an 'extension' of the Digest title *De verborum significatione*, and which, like the parallel works of Valla and Erasmus, treated not merely the individual words (*paroles*), according to the Saussurean distinction, but also the common language (*langue*) of juridical discourse. As Barnabé Brisson wrote in his great dictionary, 'Since the meaning of texts is obscure, we must have recourse to the proper usage [*proprietas*] of the word, and what and whom is referred to, and we must explain and extract the sense

---

[16] The major collections are in Nicolas Reusner, *Cynosura juris* (Speier, 1588), and *Variorum opuscula ad cultiorem jurisprudentiam adsequendam pertinentia* (Pisa, 1769); and see also Piano Mortari, *Ricerche sulla teoria dell'interpretazione del diritto nel secolo XVI* (Milan, 1956), and *Diritto, logica, metodo nel secolo XVI* (Naples, 1978); Cesare Vasoli, 'La dialettica umanistica e la metodologia giuridica nel secolo XVI', in *La formazione storica del diritto moderno in Europa* (Florence, 1977), I, pp. 237–79; Gerhard Otte, *Dialektik und Jurisprudenz* (Frankfurt, 1971); Theodor Vieweg, *Topik und Jurisprudenz* (Munich, 1975); Aldo Mazzacane, *Scienza, logica e ideologia nella giurisprudenza tedesca del sec. XVI* (Milan, 1971); Georges Kalinowski, 'La Logique et son histoire', *Archives de Philosophie du Droit*, XXVII (1982), 275–89; and Norbert Bobbio, *L'analogia nella logica del diritto* (Turin, 1938), as well as various works by Guido Kisch, Rodolph Stintzing, *Geschichte der deutschen Rechtswissenschaft*, I (Munich, 1880), and the old classic of C. H. Eckhardt, *Hermeneutica Iuris* (Pisa, 1750).

[17] Stephanus Fredericus, *De interpretatione legum*, in *Tractatus universi juris* (Venice, 1584), I, fol. 210r., quotes the famous preference of St Paul for the life-giving spirit over the deadening letter. Various more or less elementary rules or 'canons' of interpretation are given by Hegendorph, *Epitomi tyrocinii iuris civilis* (in Spiegel, *Lexicon*), and Oldendorp, *De copia verborum et rerum in iure civili* (Lyon, 1543).

[18] *De duplici verborum, et rerum significatione* (Venice, 1557), fol. 7r.

of what they say.'[19] It is significant that this lexicographical development occurred just during the heroic age of modern philology and
the emergence of 'Criticism' in a modern sense, which had the effect
of reinforcing ties with ancient legal science.

  Roman law has commonly been identified with authoritarian
attitudes, but there is obviously more to it than the gross formulas of
absolutism. In order to find its deeper 'meaning', we must look
behind the political rhetoric and into the structure, conceptual-
isations and terminology of 'civil science'. From the beginning and
perhaps prehistorically, civil law has been fundamentally anthropocentric, presuming and unfolding from the thinking – or at least
the wilful and responsible – subject. 'All our law', as Gaius put it, 'has
to do with persons, things and actions.'[20] This ancient legal
trichotomy seems to correspond directly with the general structure
of Indo-European languages (subject, object, verb) and to presume a
condition of (self-) consciousness, which in these terms distinguishes 'personality' from 'reality' through 'action'. *Personalitas,
realitas, actio* – these are the rudimentary categories of psychology
and speech as well as social custom and law, the connection being
established by predication in some sense, which is to say human
judgement. Absolutely central is the factor of will (*voluntas*), which
defines the individual in civil society (as in discourse) and which also
reflects the relationship between the law and the law-maker.

  In this connection it is interesting to pursue a bit further the
interaction of language and law in the social arena defined by the
Gaian triad. Law is basically a product of 'action' in the sense not
only that politically it was expressed in 'acts of law' expressing
sovereign will, but also that particular law in the first instance was
created by individual appeals for justice (*legis actiones* was the technical phrase).[21] Civil science seems to contain a rudimentary sort of
'action theory' whose field seems to correspond, in terms of structural linguistics, to language (*langue*) as individual acts to words
(*paroles*). For interpreters of the law, words were in a sense socialised

---

[19] *De verborum significatione* (Halle, 1743), preface. And see Jacob Spiegel, *Lexicon juris
   civilis* (Basel, 1539); Oldendorp, *De copia verborum et rerum in iure civili* (Lyon, 1546);
   Hotman, *Novus commentarius de verbis iuris* (Basel, 1563); and P. C. Brederode,
   Thesaurus dictionum et sententiarum ex Bartoli a Saxoferrato operibus (Frankfurt, 1660);
   also Guido Kisch, 'Juridical lexicography and the reception of Roman law',
   Forschungen zur Rechts- und Sozialgeschichte des Mittelalters (Sigmaringen, 1980).
[20] *Digest*, I.5.3; and see D. R. Kelley, 'Gaius Noster: substructures of Western social
   thought', in *History, Law and the Human Sciences*, and the literature there cited.
[21] It was proverbial that, as Claude de Seyssel wrote, *Speculum Feudorum* (Basel, 1566),
   p. 4, civil science 'non in speculatione sed in actione consistit'. In general, see
   Riccardo Orestano, *Azione, diritto soggettivo, persone giuridiche* (Bologna, 1978).

– or actions verbalised? – and the two were assumed to be translatable.[22] What is more, practising jurists had to judge reality as well as legal principle (*de facto* as well as *de iure*) conditions, and so – long anticipating the development of the seventeenth century – were tied to the logic of probability. These considerations underline the special meaning of the title which the civil scientist gained in the Renaissance: he was *Iuris Interpres*, critic both of words and things, judge both of persons and actions, and pretender still to the ancient monopoly of 'true philosophy'.[23]

Could the jurist then usurp the function of the legislator? A very good question, said Bonifacius Amerbach.[24] The official answer was, of course, no. As Alberico de Rosate repeated in the fourteenth century, 'the author of a law should be its interpreter' (*legis auctor debet esse interpres*).[25] And yet if the judge was obliged to construe statutes *strici iuris*, he nonetheless also had to apply them and resolve problems. Here the premise – one might better say the fiction – of the identity of the word and the spirit of a law was most useful, since 'propriety' in principle pertained only to the latter. If there could be no exception to the law, remarked Bartolus, there might well be to its words, and he spoke even of 'irrational statutes'. In any case, considerations of justice and that most pliable concept of equity (Aristotelian *epieikeia*) could never be ignored, and like Bartolus, Alberico admitted the necessity of 'extensive' interpretation in criminal cases. 'The statutes demand decapitation of murderers, but are madmen or infants decapitated?' he asked. 'Certainly not,' because of their age or because, in the case of *furiosi*, their condition is punishment enough.

Probably the most obvious judicial limitation on, or even alternative to, legislative sovereignty was the other major source of law, arising from the will not of the prince but of the people. This refers

---

[22] Conceptually, the intersection of ideas of language and of action comes in the notion of custom, especially in the mutual pattern of change and process of obsolescence (*desuetudo*), which is reflected in the medieval (and indeed Justinian) formula 'Hodie'. Odofredus, *Lecutra super Codice* (Lyon, 1552), fol. 3r, 'mutata est hodie consuetudo' and 'leges per desuetudine possunt tolli'; and Placentinus, *Summa Codicis* (Mainz, 1536), p. 17, 'hodie nec populus Romanus nec Senatus'. See also Emilio Albertario, 'Hodie', *Studi di diritto romano*, VI (Milan, 1953), 125–42.

[23] Developed further in my 'Homo politicus: the perfect jurist as Rennaissance man', forthcoming in *The Journal of the Warburg and Courtauld Institutes*.

[24] *Defensio interpretum iuris*, in Guido Kisch, *Humanismus und Jurisprudenz* (Basel, 1955), p. 82.

[25] In *Tractatus de statutis, diversorum autorum et j. c. in Europa praestantissimorum* (Frankfurt, 1608), p. 10; relevant works by Baldus and others are also collected in this anthology.

not only to the belief that, according to the legendary *lex regia*, the
Roman Populus was the original source of sovereignty (*maiestas*) but
more importantly to the medieval interpretation that a people never
lost its right to make laws for itself, notably in its customs, which
indeed 'represented' its spirit or mind. 'Consuetudo', as Bartolus put
it, 'repraesentat mentem populi.'[26] The mighty force of custom had
been recognised in classical jurisprudence, which regarded it (in a
famous formula of Paulus) as 'the best interpreter of law' (*optima enim
est legum interpres consuetudo*). Medieval civil science went further and
attributed to custom the power to make and even abrogate law:
'Consuetudo', wrote Azo, 'conditrix legis, abrogatrix et inter-
pretatrix.'[27] Part of its force arose from the fact that custom was born
of 'natural reason', according to Gaius, and was, in the more famous
Aristotelian formula, a kind of 'second nature' (*altera natura*). In any
case, *consuetudo* brought popular culture into the tradition of legal
interpretation.

Guardians of the ancient legal canon, civil scientists were also
masters of social and political thought; and it is fascinating to see
them giving shape and meaning to their world through linguistic and
hermeneutical virtuosity. On many levels their vocation was to
'civil'-ise: they thought and judged 'civilly' (*civiliter* meant 'according
to the *ius civile*', as *regulariter* meant 'according to the *regulae antiqui
iuris*' and *communaliter* meant 'according to consensus').[28] They were
agents of 'civility' (*civilitas* being equivalent to sociability and even
'civilisation'). Like the humanists but earlier and more professionally,
'civilian' jurists sought to bring the urbanity of the *civitas* and the
activism of the *civis* to late medieval society. Drawing upon Greek
political philosophy as well as Roman legal science, they were led in
many ways to 'think big' – to extend their horizons and to distinguish
larger social and political patterns, assessing the nature and
behaviour of collectivities and institutions as well as individuals.
They developed – that is, they inherited and 'extended' – a massive
vocabulary and conceptual apparatus designed to comprehend the

[26] *Commentaria*, fol. 16r; and Ullmann, 'De Bartoli sententia: concilium repraesentat
mentem populi', in *Bartolo da Sassoferrato* (Milan, 1962), II, pp. 707–33.
[27] Azo, *Summa Codicis* (Venice, 1566), on Code, 8.52, and Odofredus, *Lectura super
Codice* (Lyon, 1552); cf. Accursius on *Digest*, I.3.37; and Walter Ullmann, *The
Medieval Idea of Law as Represented by Lucas de Penna* (London, 1946), p. 62. See also
the extended commentaries of François Connan, *Commentarii juris civilis* (Paris,
1553), fol. 43r, and Conrad Lagus, *Methodus iuris utriusque traditio* (Lyon, 1566),
p. 18.
[28] Alciato, *De verborum significatione*, p. 20, defining 'interpretatio civiliter' as 'secundum
ius interpretari'. 'Homo natura civile est' was William of Moerbeke's rendering of
Aristotle's 'political animal' (*zoon politikon*); see pp. 46–7 above.

wide range of social groupings and political forces that agitated the city and countryside of Europe.

Through the conceptual efforts of jurists, then, social groups were literally personified (accommodated, that is, to the first Gaian rubric of *personalitas*); and the world was peopled by corporate entities, *personae fictae*, endowed with personalities, hence with liberties, status and responsibilities before the law.[29] Thus was created an extended family of socialising and communalising concepts and terms drawn from antiquity and given modern form. Legal 'bodies' (*corpus* being the most general term) materialised, were described, defended and manipulated by jurists – and sometimes were criticised by juridical nominalists who could not accept the paradox (variant of the 'holist fallacy') that a group could be composed of individuals and yet be itself an individual without parts. Such was the meaning, for example, of the term *universitas*, which had Ciceronian and Augustinian connotations. Jurists separated such corporate concepts from the more general rubrics of genus and species and distinguished them from each other – *societas* being ordinarily a secular organisation formed for a particular purpose, for example, while a *collegium* signified nothing more than the accident of living together. There were of course many classes of such corporate entities, ecclesiastical, municipal, academic and artisanal; and many intricate permutations and combinations. The history of corporatism, still dominated by the spirit if not interpretations of Otto Gierke, has been usefully extended in several recent works, most notably those of Pierre Michaud-Quantin and Anthony Black, but invites further exploration.[30]

If civil science possessed a language of sociability, it developed also a 'language of power', emanating from the arena of 'public law' and largely neglected by feudal custom and virtually inarticulate in feudal monarchy (except in such para-legal devices as 'distraint'). Political forms, too, had to be constructed, or accounted for, and of course legitimised; and in this connection a large variety of political entities and forces were identified and analysed. Many of the political questions of the Renaissance had been disputed for generations by jurists, 'ultramontanes' as well as 'citramontanes', canonists as well as civilians; but new methods and historical context gave these issues new meaning and in some cases new urgency in times of civic,

---

[29] P. W. Duff, *Personality in Roman Private Law* (Cambridge, 1938), and Grossi (ed.), *Quaderni fiorentini* (1983), on the topic of juridical personality.

[30] Michaud-Quantin, *Universitas, expression du mouvement communitaire dans le moyen âge latin* (Paris, 1970), and *Etudes sur le vocabulaire philosophique du moyen âge* (Paris, 1970); and Black, *Guilds and Civil Society* (Ithaca, 1984).

national and international crisis from the fifteenth century. At the same time the legal profession itself, extending its influence from the academy to the forum, had become massively and inextricably entangled in the political as well as social and economic activities of European states, and had come to establish a certain monopoly over (at least official) political discourse. The political realm, too, experienced what a legal historian has called 'the triumph of the professionals'.[31]

How did the 'civil scientists' discuss political questions within the conventions of their 'antique–modern' discourse? In the first place we should notice the fundamental, though not always articulated assumption of the primacy of written culture, in the sense not only that 'written law' (*ius scriptum*, virtually identified with the *ius civile*) was prior to custom but that custom (even while continuing to be defined as *ius non scriptum*) was assimilated into written culture. Typography magnified the difference between scribal and oral culture, and the 'authority of the written word' became proverbial.[32] Long identified with the art of oratory in terms of education and purpose, lawyers distinguished themselves by becoming the masters and (in many respects) the slaves of print culture, along with its proliferation of records and litigation, which were the subjects of endless celebrations or laments. Modern political thought, or 'public law', was in many ways a creature of the modern world of 'publicity'.

The central assumption of medieval and modern civilians was always the status of their discipline as a 'science' (*scientia*) because it treated matters in terms of cause and effect.[33] The basic hermeneutical premise of Bartolism was that 'knowing was understanding through causes', and indeed there were no grounds for discourse at all without a 'cause' in the technically legal sense; for according to a much discussed maxim, all consequences cease when the cause ceases (*cessante causa, cessat effectus*).[34] *Causa* was an extraordinarily

---

[31] John P. Dawson, *A History of Lay Judges* (Cambridge, Mass., 1960), p. 69.

[32] This is one of the few facets of the problem not treated by Elizabeth Eisenstein in her widely discussed book on printing as an agent of historical change. More generally, see the provocative work of Brian Stock, *The Influence of Literacy* (Princeton, 1983).

[33] Jean Coras, *De iure civili in artem redigendo*, in *Tractatus universi juris*, I, fol. 62v, poses the classic question whether jurisprudence is *ars* or *scientia*.

[34] Baldus, *Super Digesto veteri*, fol. 4r, and Coras, *De iuris arte libellus* (Paris, 1560). On the concept of 'cause', see André Tiraqueau in *Tractatus varii* (Lyon, 1574); see also Cortese, *La norma giuridica*, index, and A. London Fell, *Origins of Legislative Sovereignty and the Legislative State* '(1984); and in general, Robert MacIver, *Social Causation* (Boston, 1942), and Quentin Skinner, ' "Social meaning" and the explanation of social action', in Patrick Gardiner (ed.), *The Philosophy of History* (New York, 1974), pp. 106–26.

complex and often confusing term, possessing connotations not only social, in the sense of a position to be defended or grounds for judgement ('just cause'), but also natural, and specifically Aristotelian. According to the famous fourfold scheme of Aristotle, the people, or in recent times the prince, represented the 'efficient cause'; the texts of the laws the 'material cause'; the extension of law from individuals to society in general the 'formal cause'; and justice or public utility the 'final cause'. All legislative and judicial activity was carried on within this teleological framework.

In the discussion of political questions, the professional 'duplicity' of civil scientists – the habit and requirement of *duplex interpretatio* – was reflected in various conceptual polarities, which have been analysed by Pietro Costa from the standpoint of structural semantics, of the vocabulary of political thought.[35] *Imperium* and *iurisdictio*, *potestas* and *auctoritas*, *princeps* and *populus*: these are a few of the dualities which inform the arguments of medieval and Renaissance jurists in their various political engagements, not including the recurrent controversies between secular and ecclesiastical institutions. They are not the 'ascending' and 'descending' themes inferred by Walter Ullmann, nor the confrontation between *rex* and *iudex*, nor the opposition of rulership and constitutionalism, nor yet that between absolute and ordinary power (recently surveyed by Francis Oakley).[36] They are rather manifestations of conflicting appeals to 'power' and socialised conceptions of 'legitimacy'. The tension between these political and legal lines of thought are preserved in the modern concept of 'sovereignty' and attendant notions of resistance. Nor have legal or political philosophers been able to reconcile or to transcend them.

In this connection a word needs to be said about 'civic humanism' (a phrase which might have been rendered 'bourgeois humanism' if someone other than Hans Baron had established the English equivalent of the original *Burgerhumanismus*). Civic humanism has been a topic of much debate and no little exaggeration in recent years, partly because scholars have allowed humanist rhetoric to drown out, and in important ways to discredit, the comparatively pedestrian work of more professional scholars. Political posturing and propagandising by humanists as well as their more conspicuous participation in contemporary issues have in many ways overshadowed the contributions of jurists to social and political thought. Yet as historians used to notice, civil scientists like Bartolus and

---

[35] *Iurisdictio: semantica del potere politico nella pubblicistica medievale (1100–1400)* (Milan, 1969).
[36] *Omnipotence, Covenant and Order* (Ithaca, 1984).

Baldus possessed not only technical legal expertise but also the values and goals of a new *civiltà*, including a commitment to the ideals of citizenship and the *vita activa*, a favourable attitude towards republican 'liberty', and even towards resistance to tyranny, although the arguments remained decorously, rigorously and classically legal.[37] Like late scholastic theology (as defended by Heiko Oberman), scholastic jurisprudence from the fifteenth century enjoyed not a 'waning' but a 'harvest time', reaped in political terms by city-states and national monarchies as well as by empire and church.

Some of the most crucial problems of interpretation occurred in the confrontations and conflicts between rival national traditions, since Roman law was technically the 'emperor's law' and to this extent unwelcome in the realms of kingdoms which 'recognised no superior in temporal things', according to the adaptable canonist formula. The issue arose in commentaries on the title in the Code, 'Cunctos populos', which suggested that the emperor was 'lord' of the whole world (*dominus mundi*).[38] This was rejected by French, Spanish, English and some Italian jurists, who invoked another popular formula, that their king was 'emperor in his kingdom' (*rex imperator in regno suo*). French legists used this principle during the rivalry between Francis I and Charles of Spain in the imperial election campaign in 1519, as in effect did Thomas Cromwell, defending Henry VIII's statutory break with Rome.[39] In general the French king had, from the thirteenth century (if not, arguably, from Carolingian times), accumulated his own 'regalian rights', which were interpreted by royal legists partly in terms of, partly in opposition to, civil law, and which furnished the material for a larger theory of 'sovereignty' (*maiestas*), expressed most famously in the *Republic* of Jean Bodin.

[37] See, e.g., *L'opera di Baldo* (Perugia, 1901); also Peter Riesenberg, 'Civism and Roman law in fourteenth-century society', *Explorations in Economic History*, VIII (1969–70), 237–54, and J. P. Canning, 'A fourteenth-century contribution to the theory of citizenship: political man and the problem of created citizenship in the thought of Baldus de Ubaldis', *Authority and Power*, ed. Brian Tierney and Peter Linehan (Cambridge, 1980), pp. 197–212, and his forthcoming book on Baldus, as well as the old work of C. N. S. Woolf on Bartolus (Cambridge, 1913). Reference here is to Hans Baron's *Crisis of the Early Italian Renaissance* and the massive literature it has inspired, and to Oberman, *The Harvest of Medieval Theology* (Cambridge, Mass., 1963).
[38] Belleperche, *In aliquot Cod. leges* (Frankfurt, 1571), p. 8, a passage which, according to Baldus, Bartolus published as his own (see *Dictionnaire de biographie française*); also Alberico de Rosate, *Super Codice* (Lyon, 1545), fol. 7r, and Giason del Maino, *In primam Codicem partem Commentaria* (Venice, 1579), fol. 2v.
[39] In the famous opening lines of the Act of Appeals, 1533; the formula also adorns the *Siete Partidas*.

The fundamental dilemma of civil science was surviving and adapting itself to a large variety of expanding and jostling national traditions; and it is in this connection that we encounter one of the central problems of 'interpretation'. I refer to translation in the literal sense of expressing in civilian terms the various local, provincial and national customs of Europe. In a very basic sense this entailed the comparative study of law, for example, in the interpretation of municipal statutes in Italy and in the enterprises of certain national jurists setting out variously (depending on their immediate purpose) to establish analogies, common denominators or contrasts between civil law and native customs or legislation. Although commentators on French *coutumes* from the time of Beaumanoir had at least inadvertently had to Romanise (later to de-Romanise) provincial customs, the pioneer of comparative law was the first of Alciato's French disciples, Eguinaire Baron, who composed a series of 'bipartite commentaries' on the texts of Roman law in order to suggest the corresponding French institutions (*roy* and *princeps*, *Parlement* and *Senatus*, *Chancelier* and *Praetor*, *interpretatio* and *practiquer les lois*, and so on).[40] This was the sort of 'interpretation' carried on by Etienne Pasquier's *Interprétation des Institutes de Justinian* (which began as a translation but ended as a critical, comparative commentary) and, in England, by William Fulbeke's *Parallele or Conference of the Civil Law, the Canon Law, and the Common Law of this Realm of England*. And other examples could be cited for Germany, Italy and Spain.

In the context of what Piano Mortari has called 'juridical nationalism', such comparisons commonly became invidious. Protestant jurists in particular deplored the supposed rigidity and absolutist character of Romanism. In France the model was the 'anti-Tribonianist' critique of François Hotman, who came to believe that the influence of Roman law was irrelevant, if not pernicious, and more generally that law, like language, should be in agreement with the character and 'humours' of a people. The English counterpart was the professional chauvinism of common lawyers like John Fortescue and Edward Coke. 'Upon the text of the civil laws', declared Coke, 'there be so many glosses and interpretations, and again upon these so many Commentaries, and all these written by Doctors of equal degree and authority, and therein so many diversities of opinions, as they rather do increase than resolve doubts and

[40] See D. R. Kelley, 'Civil science in the Renaissance: jurisprudence in the French manner', and 'History, English law and the Renaissance', in *History, Law and the Human Sciences*.

uncertainties, and the professors of that noble Science say, That it is like a Sea full of waves.'[41]

By contrast, common law, regarded since Bracton as a species of custom, affected to stand apart from interpretation. So it was, too, with English statutes which had to be kept and observed, according to a fourteenth-century statute roll, 'without addition or fraude, by covin, evasion, art or contrivance, "ou par interprétation des paroles" '.[42] Not *ius dare* but *ius dicere* was the way Bacon aphorised it. The practical result, however, was often to give authorial voice to the judge: (not *rex* but, in Coke's rephrasing) *iudex est lex loquens*; and Coke indeed claimed to speak for the true meaning not only of the statutes, the yearbooks and the law reports but also for the 'immemorial custom' of England – and this even as he took a classic stand 'against interpretation'.[43]

In various ways civil science in the Renaissance began to drift away from its ancient moorings. Increasingly, jurists worked within the confines not of the *ius civile* (the *ius proprium* of ancient Rome) but rather of the 'law of nations' (the *ius gentium*, or *ius naturale gentium*) which accommodated 'peoples' and 'actions' never envisaged by Caesar or Justinian or even by Irnerius and Accursius. Concerning the 'status of men', for example, there were various changes brought by modern times, wrote Alberico de Rosate, which were not treated by ancient law.[44] The 'law of nations' also involved questions of international commerce and especially war, which itself stemmed ultimately from disagreement about words – 'from those possessive pronouns "mine" and "thine" ', as Alberico de Rosate wrote (*ab istis pronomibus meum et tuum*).[45] This was the so-called 'secondary law of nations', which was produced not (as the primary form) by 'right reason', according to Hugues Doneau, but by 'necessity' (which proverbially 'knew no law') and indeed the actions – the history – of peoples since the beginning of civil society.[46] With these issues we enter the (legally) uncharted realm of 'public utility': as Pierre Ayrault wrote, 'in republics one has sometimes to consider not only

[41]   *The Second Part of the Institute of the Laws of England* (London, 1671), proem.
[42]   T. F. T. Plucknett, *Statutes and their Interpretation in the First Half of the Fourteenth Century* (Cambridge, 1922), p. 49; cf. Bacon, 'On judicature'.
[43]   See J. G. A. Pocock's *Ancient Constitution and the Feudal Law* (new edition forthcoming).
[44]   *Commentarii super Digesto veteri* (Lyon, 1545), fol. 44v: 'secundum moderna tempora varii sunt status hominis de quibus hoc titulo [I.3] non tractatur . . . quia status hominis sub perpetuo motu consistit'.
[45]   *Ibid.*, fol. 14v; and cf. Walter Ullmann, *The Medieval Idea of Law*, p. 47.
[46]   *Opera omnia* (Lucca, 1762), I, p. 48.

what is just in itself but also what is needed for the state'.[47] We leave the realm of juridical discourse for contingencies of social actions and reasoning of state.

So it was that civil scientists came often to work under the rubric not of law but rather of 'custom', and this offered new resources for the process of interpretation, since *consuetudo* marked the intersection between fact and law (might and right, as some would infer). It marked, too, the entry into the forum of oral culture and social memory. 'It is enough for the profe of a custom (as I have credibly heard)', wrote John Cowell, 'if two or more can depose that they heard their father say, that it was a custome all their time and that their fathers heard their fathers also say, that it was likewise a custome in their time.'[48]

In France the actual writing down or redaction of a custom required the agreement of the local estates, after which 'interpretation' had the same restrictions as for 'written' (that is, civil) law. Yet this by no means stemmed the flow of interpretations. Pasquier's friend Antoine Loisel, also a member of the French school, turned his attention from Roman law to native customs and tried to find the 'spirit' of such customary law not only in medieval legal texts but also in literature, proverbs and oral tradition. Loisel's *Institutes coutumières* was in effect a pioneering treatise on the anthropology of law, later recognised as an anticipation of the work of the nineteenth-century historical school of law.[49] Politically, the implication of such works was to suggest the priority of judicial 'interpretation' – in effect as an act of popular mind-reading – to the Romano-Byzantine model of legislation, hence to the primacy of princely 'will'. This was another attempt by critics, in a way, to gain parity with authorial initiative by asserting the popular as the truly authorial 'will' – and themselves, of course, as its spokesmen.

Not only the practice but also the theory of interpretation – legal hermeneutics – was introduced into European customary law. In France, Paul Challine published in 1666 a quasi-Cartesian 'method for the interpretation of the customs of France'. While forbidding the addition of words and demanding that customs be construed in their own terms (*se doivent expliquer par elles-mêmes*), Challine requires the interpreter to determine the 'motive or intention' of the law; he

[47] *De l'Ordre et instruction judiciaire, dont les anciens Grecs et Romains ont usé en accusations publiques. Conferé a l'usage de nostre France* (Paris, 1576), fol. 22.
[48] *The Interpreter* (London, 1607).
[49] Michel Reulos, *Etude sur l'esprit, les sources et la méthode des Institutes coutumières d'Antoine Loisel* (Paris, 1935).

allows laws to be overridden by non-usage; and he provides for supplementing them, when 'defective', by a variety of devices, including recourse to royal ordinances, nearby customs, what he calls 'the general spirit of French custom' (expressed best in the *coutume* of Paris) and finally what he calls 'the reason of Roman law' (that is, whatever French lawyers may find useful).[50] What started as a loophole in civil law has obviously become a great portal of critical and creative interpretation.

But the greatest portal of them all, short of the executive justice of the Queen of Hearts, was 'natural law', whose spirit was conveyed by the texts of civil law and magnified by the new philosophy of the seventeenth century that put all, at least all convention, in doubt.[51] Of course the language and ideas of the *ius naturale* were embedded in civil science. It was commonplace in customary as well as civil and canon law, for example, that 'by nature all men are free', as Nicholas Bohier quoted from the *coutume* of Bourges.[52] But not until the age of what Gierke called 'antique–modern' political thought were such abstract notions taken seriously as a way of reforming jurisprudence. As Leibniz hoped to find a 'new method of jurisprudence' appropriate to this sort of naturalism, so Jean Domat tried to reformulate civil law in purely 'natural' terms; Hobbes affirmed the superiority of 'natural reason' to the 'artificial' and obscurantist variety practised by Coke, invoking the old hermeneutical rule which subordinated what he called the 'Grammatical construction of the letter' to the 'Intention' of a law – by which he meant, of course, its rationality as determined by the Philosopher (if not the Sovereign).[53]

There is no doubt that the first aim of 'jusnaturalism' was to take still another stand 'against interpretation'; and in the eighteenth century political absolutism and the codification movement reinforced such pretensions, as indeed did invocations of 'natural

---

[50] *Methode générale pour l'intelligence des coutumes de France* (Paris, 1666).
[51] The classic work of Otto Gierke, *Natural Law and the Theory of Society*, trans. Ernest Barker (Cambridge, 1934) has never been superseded; but see Georges Gurvitch, *L'Idée du droit social* (Paris, 1932), and Otto Wilhelm Krause, *Naturrechtlicher des sechszehnten Jahrhunderts* (Frankfurt, 1982).
[52] *Consuetudines Biturcensis* (Paris, 1543), fol. 1r: 'Haec consuetudo comprobetur iure naturali quod omnes homines nascuntur liberi'; and cf. Coras, *In titulum Pandectarum de justitia et jure* (Lyon, 1568), p. 299. See *Digest*, I.5.
[53] Leibniz, *Nova methodus discendae docendaeque jurisprudentiae* (Frankfurt, 1667); Domat, *Les Loix civiles dans leur ordre naturel* (Luxemburg, 1702); and Hobbes, *A Dialogue between a Philosopher and a Student of the Common Laws of England* (1661), ed. J. Cropsey (Chicago, 1971), p. 97. And cf. Peter Stein, *Regulae Iuris, From Juristic Rules to Legal Maxims* (Edinburgh, 1966).

liberty' and 'absolute property'.[54] Yet in practice the appeal to naked reason – to a 'natural law' that is metahistorical and metalinguistic as well as metatextual – was an invitation to the most 'extensive' of all interpretation. For purposes of interpretation, the *ius naturale* was more flexible even than *consuetudo*, to the extent at least that it tended to liberate judgements from legal convention, and to transform the ancient legal maxims into juridical counterparts of Descartes' 'clear and distinct ideas'; and in this sense it fundamentally changed the style of modern political and social thought.

But this vision of 'perfect jurisprudence' could remain intact only on the level of theory, and in fact civil science was never successfully 'naturalised'. It could not escape what has been called 'the horizon-structure of experience', that is, its anthropocentric orientation; nor could it avoid practical involvements; and despite claims to treat human matters in terms of 'cause and effect', the idea of *causa* was permeated with questions of value and motive. Far from being an exercise in pure reason, jurisprudence involves a certain kind of 'prejudging' (*praeiudicium* being one of the conventional topics of civil science, according to Cantiuncula's analysis).[55] This is not 'prejudice' in the 'prejudiced' (that is, prejorative) Enlightenment sense, however, but rather in the hermeneutical sense of what Gadamer, and Heidegger before him, called the 'fore-structure of knowledge', which is one of the conditions of 'social meaning' and indeed communication. And as Gadamer has also pointed out, *praeiudicium* originally (and 'civilly') referred not to a false judgement but rather to a legal precedent or provisional verdict before a final judgement – on the basis of that 'experience of tradition' essential to human science.

Nor, despite resemblances between what jurists called 'inductive interpretation' and empiricism, can jurisprudence be assimilated to Baconian natural science. 'Since laws vary', wrote Gammaro in his

---

[54] E. Meynial, 'Notes sur la formation du domain divisé (domain direct et domain utile) du XII au XIVe siècle dans les romanistes', *Mélanges Fitting* (Montpellier, 1908), II, pp. 409–61 and Paolo Grossi, *Le situazioni reali nell'esperanza giuridica medievale* (Padua, 1968).

[55] Cantiuncula, *Topica legalia* (Basel, 1545). Cf. Gadamer, *Truth and Method*, trans. G. Barden and J. Cumming (New York, 1975), pp. 238, 289; and see Gunther Buck, 'The structure of hermeneutical experience and the problem of tradition', *New Literary History*, X (1978), 31–47. The commonest criticism of Gadamer, espècially by Jurgen Habermas, is the neglect of the social dimension; but this is conspicuously not true of legal hermeneutics; and Gadamer agrees that philosophical attention to this connection might further deflect such criticisms.

treatise on *extensio*, 'the interpretation of law is obviously bound to contingencies.'[56] As Ian Hacking has recently pointed out, jurisprudence rests not on pure reason but rather on a 'logic for contingencies'. This could only mean probable judgement, which (as Claudius Cantiuncula admitted in his pioneering treatise of 1520) was all that argument from precedent (*praeiudicium*) permitted. And this was precisely the position taken by Leibniz, one of the founders of the logic of probability, in his discussion of the old theory of legal interpretation (*ars hermeneutica* he called it). In the long as well as the short run, then, *civilis scientia* remained a human not a hard science – part of the 'moral' rather than the 'natural' world, as Hotman wrote, or according to the ancient and currently fashionable distinction, a form of *phronesis* not *episteme*.[57] For legal (as for social) judgement, pure logic must be subordinate to practical reason, rational consistency to human values (good or bad), explanation to interpretation, and universal to 'local knowledge'.

An extraordinary illustration of the vitality of Renaissance civil science appears in the work of Giambattista Vico, the first version of whose 'new science' was expressed in terms of Roman law. Beginning with the humanist *ars interpretationis*, with all of its emphasis on historical context and avoidance of anachronism, Vico went on to devise ways of 'divining' antiquity and interpreting primitive culture, especially through ingenious extensions of the old technique of etymology. Out of custom came civilised law, according to Vico, and out of the pre-historical principles of lordship, liberty and self-defense came all the civil institutions of the modern age, including the concept of sovereignty (*summum imperium*).[58] Like Bodin, Vico expanded his horizons from civil law to the law – and the historical 'world' – of nations. Among the several faces of Vico's final 'new science' we find not only a 'natural law of nations' but a 'philosophy of authority', in effect Vico's way of realising the old claim of civil science to be, as he repeated, *vera philosophia*.

But the old-fashioned wisdom of civil science was in many ways out of step with the intellectual fashions of the Enlightenment,

---

[56] *Topica legalia*, p. 7: 'Sed legis interpretatio est de contingentibus, quia leges variantur'; and cf. *De extensionibus*, in *Tractatus universi juris*, XVIII, fol. 248v: 'Interpretatio iuris non est scientia.' See also Pierre Ayrault, *Rerum ab omni antiquitate iudicarum Pandectae* (Geneva, 1677). In general, see Hacking, *The Emergence of Probability* (Cambridge, 1975), p. 86; Alessandro Giuliani, 'The influence of rhetoric on the law of evidence and pleading', *The Juridical Review*, LXII (1969), 216–51; Lawrence Manley, *Convention 1500–1750* (Cambridge, Mass., 1980); Richard J. Bernstein, *Beyond Objectivism and Relativism* (Philadelphia, 1984).
[57] *Jurisconsultus* (Basel, 1559), p. 11.
[58] See D. R. Kelley, 'Vico's road', in *History, Law and the Human Sciences*.

which was anything but a great age of interpretation. Then legislative reform and the great movement for codification overshadowed judicial remedies. Voltaire's famous advice to burn old laws and make new ones was taken seriously even by jurists, and the Revolution called up visions of a society without legal machinery. 'No more courts!' cried the former advocate Adrien Duport, addressing the committee for judicial reform at a high point of populist enthusiasm. 'No more judges!'[59] At one point Napoleon himself expressed the hope that lawyers could be done away with; and of course he tried to prohibit any tinkering with, or academic criticism of, his great 'Code of the French People', as it was originally called.[60] His hopes were dashed in the most massive way. Within a generation the Civil Code recapitulated the same evolutionary pattern – cautiously literal glosses, increasingly 'extensive' commentaries and freewheeling revisions – that it took the civil law almost five centuries to pass through.

In fact the early nineteenth century saw an extraordinary revival of hermeneutics not only in theology and philosophy but also in jurisprudence. Paralleling the famous work of Schleiermacher and Ast were the theories of legal interpretation hammered out by champions of the rival philosophical and historical schools, centreing in particular on the famous debate between Thibaut and Savigny, and in the wake of that the much more destructive criticism of renegade jurists like Marx and Proudhon (for whom civil law and its modern incarnation, the Code Napoléon, represented the soon-to-be-superseded Old Testament of social thought).[61]

In the past century the legal tradition has produced a variety of schools of interpretation – positivist, formalist, sociological, not to speak of fascist, communist and other more or less blatantly political varieties – and through the work of Hans Georg Gadamer and Emilio Betti legal interpretation has contributed to the recent upsurge of philosophical hermeneutics, in which the metalegal structure of civil science is preserved. In particular Gadamer has pointed out that the category of 'thing' as well as that of 'person' must, to be meaningful, be interpreted in a social sense.[62] In other words, *res* must be

[59] *Archives parlementaires*, XII, 570.
[60] Cf. Cocczius, *Code Fréderic, ou corps de droit pour les états de sa majesté le Roi de Prusse*, tr. from German (1751), xviii: 'Et afin que les Particuliers n'ayent pas occasion d'en corrumpre les Loix par les Interprétations données de leur propre autorité, le Roi a défendu sous sévères peines de faire des Commentaires, soit sur tout le Droit du Pays, soit sur quelqu'une de ses parties. Par la même raison il a défendu aux Professeurs qui instruisent la jeunesse . . .' etc.
[61] D. R. Kelley, *Historians and the Law in Postrevolutionary France* (Princeton, 1984).
[62] *Truth and Method*, p. 289, and *Philosophical Hermeneutics*, trans. D. Linge (Berkeley, 1976), pp. 69–81.

understood not according to the old Cartesian duality (*res extensa, res cogitans*) or to the Kantian *Ding an sich*, but rather as the *res* of civil law, which represents an extension as well as an object of consciousness, desire and sociability (or belligerence) – which is to say, of personality, action and politics.

In any case, criticism and critical theory, interpretation and the theory of interpretation, are all alive and well; and the struggle for the authority to give, preserve, correct, control and extend meaning goes on in law as in literature and philosophy. The old formula traditionally applied to the king seems much more appropriate for the process of criticism – which indeed 'never dies'. Authors and legislators to the contrary notwithstanding, 'the problem of interpretation' is still with us – though some critics will probably disagree.

4

◁ ═══════════════════════════════════════ ▷

Dispossessing the barbarian: the language of Spanish Thomism and the debate over the property rights of the American Indians

ANTHONY PAGDEN

I

In 1537 the Spanish Dominican Francisco de Vitoria, Prime Professor of Theology at the University of Salamanca, delivered a lecture entitled *De indis* whose purpose was, he declared, to discover 'by what right the barbarians' – by which he meant the American Indians – 'had come under the rule of the Spaniards'.[1] For although, he professed, the conscience of the Spanish kings and their advisors was of itself sufficient guarantee that everything 'had been well-done', all men are compelled to consult the wisest and best-informed persons they can find before reaching a decision on any issue where matters of conscience are involved.

Vitoria's *relectio* belongs to a tradition of ritual legitimation which the Castilian crown had, since the later Middle Ages, regularly enacted when confronted by uncertain moral issues. The conclusions which the crown's advisors reached on these occasions were frequently ignored since, as Vitoria himself observed, kings were, of necessity, pragmatic beings compelled to 'think from hand to mouth'.[2] But the declarations issued by the theologians and jurists on crown policy formed an important part of the ideological armature of what, after the defeat of the *comunero* revolt in 1520, has some claims to being the first early-modern nation state. With the accession of Philip II, that state had, effectively, secured the consensus of its own political nation. Unlike France, and even England, it had, therefore, no further need to assert its own legitimacy against particular and faction interests, and its principal ideological concern

[1] Francisco de Vitoria, *De indis recenter inventis*. I have used the edition in Teofilo Urdanoz (ed.), *Obras de Francisco de Vitoria* (Madrid, 1960), pp. 643–4.
[2] Quoted in Anthony Pagden, *The Fall of Natural Man: The American Indian and the Origins of Comparative Ethnology* (Cambridge, 1982), p. 28.

became instead its self-appointed role as the guardian of universal Christendom. In order to safeguard this role, it was crucial that the crown was seen to act on all occasions in strict accordance with Christian ethico-political principles. The task of the theologians and jurists under Habsburg rule was to establish just what those principles were.

The legitimacy of the conquests had consequently been a subject of debate ever since the New World was discovered to be truly new and inhabited by non-Christian peoples living in what, to European eyes, were remarkably un-civil, 'barbarian' societies. Vitoria's *relectio* was, however, the most detailed and far-reaching discussion of the subject. It was also the first to claim that 'the affair of the Indies', as it had come to be called, was a question neither of the limits of papal jurisdiction, nor of Roman law, but of the law of nature, the *ius naturae*, and that the issue was consequently one not of juridic but of *natural* rights. What was at issue in the prolonged debates over the conquest of the Americas was not the Castilian crown's sovereignty in America (no one, not even Bartolomé de las Casas, the 'Apostle to the Indians' and the most radical defender of their interests, denied that) it was the nature of the rights and, in particular, rights of property, which that sovereignty entailed.

Vitoria and his pupils, and the pupils of his pupils down to the generation of the Jesuits Luís de Molina (1535–1600) and Francisco Suárez (1548–1617), have come to be called 'The School of Salamanca', although the Italian term 'seconda scholastica' is a better description. Their project was to create a moral philosophy based upon an Aristotelian and Thomist interpretation of the law of nature. Central to that project was an understanding of what we refer to loosely as 'property', but which, in the language of natural jurisprudence, was called *dominium* or more exactly in this case *dominium rerum*. By the terms of the social contract, men had renounced their primitive freedom in exchange for the security and the possibility of moral understanding which only civil society could provide; but they retained certain natural and hence inalienable rights of which *dominium* is the most fundamental. During the seventeenth century, the application of the term was successfully limited, by Grotius and then Pufendorf, to private property.[3] But for the scholastics, men could be said to have *dominium* over not only their private property,

---

[3] James Tully, *A Discourse on Property: John Locke and his Adversaries* (Cambridge, 1980), p. 69; and see Richard Tuck, *Natural Rights Theories: Their Origin and Development* (Cambridge, 1979), pp. 58–81. I am greatly indebted to this book for my discussion of *dominium*.

their goods (*bona*), but also over their actions, their liberty and even –
with certain important qualifications – their own bodies. *Dominium*
described the relationship which held together the three parts of the
triad into which the Roman jurist Gaius had divided the natural
world: persons, things and actions.[4]

Civil society was, by definition, a society based upon property, and
property relations were what constituted the basis for all exchanges
between men within society. It might, therefore, be argued that if, in
objective fact, a society possessed no such relationships, and hence
could not be described as a civil community, its individual members
could make no claims to *dominium rerum* when confronted by invaders
attempting to seize their lands. This, the jurist Palacios Rubios had
claimed in 1513, provided one justification for the Spanish occupation of the Caribbean islands.[5] For the theologians, however, such
arguments were deficient. All rights were natural whether they were
exercised in social practice or not. The conquest of America could
only be made legitimate by demonstrating that the native popu-
lations had forfeited these rights by their own actions. And this, as
we shall see, had to be done without endangering the claim that all
rights were the products of God's laws and not of God's grace.

The definition of the term *dominium* had itself been the subject of a
prolonged debate for which, in the end, Grotius's reductive solution
was the only satisfactory one. Most of the Spanish schoolmen,
however, operated until important changes were introduced by
Suárez and Molina in the seventeenth century, with the definition
provided by Domingo de Soto in his *De iustitia et iure* of 1556.
'*Dominium*', he said, 'is a faculty and a right (*facultas et ius*) which one
has over anything to use it for his own benefit by any means which is
permitted by law.' But since the Thomists upheld the distinction in
Roman law between *dominium* and mere possession, he went on,
'*dominium* is to be distinguished from possession, use or usufruct . . .
for *dominium* is not simply the ability to use something and take its
produce, but to alienate it, give it away, sell it or neglect it'.[6] As
Richard Tuck has pointed out, the phrase 'by any means which is
permitted by law' presented considerable difficulties because with

---

[4] Paolo Rossi, 'La proprietá nel sistema privatistico della seconda scolastica', in
Paolo Grossi (ed.), *La seconda scolastica nella formazione del diritto privato* (Milan, 1972),
pp. 117–222.

[5] Juan López de Palacios Rubios, 'Libellus de insulanis quas vulgus Indias apelat', in
S. Zavala, *De las islas del Mar Océano* (Mexico, 1954), p. 27.

[6] *De iustitia et iure* (Salamanca, 1556), p. 280 and cf. F. J. Brufau Prats, 'El
pensamiento político de Domingo de Soto', *Acta salamanticensis*, IV (1960),
pp. 280–4.

that qualification it was hard to see what distinguished Soto's account of usufruct from the *dominium utile* which Accursius – and Aquinas– had granted to the user as distinct from the *dominium directum* possessed by the superior lord, but whose existence the Spanish Thomists vigorously denied.[7] The qualification had, however, important consequences for the arguments over the rights of the Amerindians because it was introduced by Soto precisely to deal with the problem of the rights of children before the age of reason; for children clearly do have *dominium* even if they cannot be allowed to exercise it – a condition in which, as we shall see, the Indians might be said to be.

II

Before 1539, the Castilian crown's principal claim to *dominium* in America had rested on the Bulls of Donation made by Alexander VI in 1493. These had granted to Ferdinand and Isabella sovereignty over all the lands inhabited by non-Christians they might discover in the Atlantic. Since, however, the power to make such donations rested on the papal assumption of temporal authority over both Christians and pagans – an assumption which only the Canonists were willing to endorse – the Bulls provided very shaky grounds indeed for conquest. Once they had been detached from their Caesaro–papal claims they only imposed upon the Castilian crown a duty, the duty to evangelise; but they could not confer upon it a corresponding right.[8] Vitoria, therefore, set the Bulls aside and turned his attention to those arguments for *dominium* which could be expressed in a language of natural rights.

It was clear, he said, from all that he had heard, that before the arrival of the Spaniards, the Indians had been 'in public, private and pacific possession of their things'.[9] There were, therefore, only four possible grounds for claiming that they did not, at the time of the conquest, also enjoy *dominium* over them: either because they were sinners, or because they were infidels, or because they were *insensati* (i.e., animals) or idiots (*amentes*). Only the first three of these had any

[7] *Natural Rights Theories*, pp. 48–9.
[8] *De indis*, pp. 682–5. Vitoria also considered, and rejected, the claims of the emperor to universal *dominium* (pp. 666–75) and the right by virtue of discovery (pp. 684–5). On this last claim he observed that it would only be valid if the Indians were not, prior to the discovery, 'private and public owners of their things' which, as he goes on to show, they were. The rejection of the universalist ambitions of both the papacy and the empire is repeated by all of Vitoria's followers. See, e.g. Soto, *De iustitia et iure*, p. 241.   [9] *De indis*, pp. 650–1.

direct bearing on the case of the Indians, since the mad are a special case whose rights can only be considered under the positive law, which clearly cannot apply to the Indians.

The first claim – that the Indians had forfeited their natural rights by reason of their sins – invoked an old heresy associated with Wycliff and Huss which had now been revived by 'the modern heretics', that 'no-one can have civil *dominium* if he is in a state of mortal sin'.[10] It was central to Vitoria's whole project to refute the claim of these 'modern heretics' that the authority of a prince depended not upon God's laws but upon God's grace, and the subsequent argument that if any prince fell from grace he might legitimately be deposed by his subjects or by another more godly ruler. The Thomists' attack on the arguments which the crown's apologists had hitherto used to legitimate the occupation of America and those used, as we shall see, by such men as Juan Ginés de Sepúlveda and a number of canon lawyers, came ultimately back to this. For, in the end, Vitoria and his successors were far less concerned with the particulars of the American case than they were with the opportunities it provided for a refutation of Lutheran and, later, Calvinist theories of sovereignty.

The accepted refutation of Wycliff's thesis provided by the Gersonian nominalists Pierre d'Ailly and Jean Almain depended – in Vitoria's somewhat schematised account of it – on the case of a sinner on the edge of starvation. If such a man does not have *dominium rerum* he cannot even possess the bread he needs to eat in order to stay alive. He is thus faced with an impossible moral choice: in order not to die voluntarily, which would be to commit one kind of mortal sin, he is compelled to commit another, theft. Since it is clearly impossible that God should have placed any of his creatures in such a position it follows that *dominium* must be independent of grace.[11]

This account of *dominium* implied, however, a theory of unlimited rights which, in effect, denied the Thomists' claim that *in extremis* all the necessities of life reverted to their common state, that every man may take what he truly *needs* from 'another man's plenty' without being guilty of theft.[12] It also obscured what, for Vitoria, was the

[10] *De indis*, pp. 651–2.   [11] *De indis*, pp. 652–5.
[12] *Summa theologiae* Ia.IIae. q.66 a.7, Anthony Parel, 'Aquinas' theory of property', in A. Parel and T. Flanagan (eds.), *Theories of Property: Aristotle to the Present* (Calgary, 1879), pp. 89–111. For a discussion of this point, see Istvan Hont and Michael Ignatieff, 'Needs and justice in the wealth of nations: an introductory essay', in Istvan Hont and Michael Ignatieff (eds.), *Wealth and Virtue: The Shaping of Political Economy in the Scottish Enlightenment* (Cambridge, 1983), pp. 28–9.

main argument against Wycliff's thesis, namely that *dominium*
derives from the fact that man is a rational being made in God's
image, and that he cannot lose that characteristic of himself through
sin. The Sun, he said, quoting Matthew 5.45, shines on both the just
and the unjust. And if this is the case then *dominium* is inalienable
since, by Vitoria's own account, no act, however irrational it might
seem, can be anything other than a temporary aberration. There
may, of course, be certain acts which are so deviant as to suggest that
their agents are not, in fact, men at all. As Locke was to argue, slavery
was an option only for a man who had violated the law of nature and
thus shown himself to be not a man but a beast.[13] But, in Vitoria's
view at least, the Indians were not guilty of such acts. If, as he
explained, neither their supposed cannibalism nor the practice of
human sacrifice could deprive them of *dominium* then neither could
their paganism.

This left Vitoria with the last two claims. Truly irrational beings do
not have *dominium* since this is a right (*ius*) and rights can only be held
by those creatures who are capable of receiving injury. Since, for
Vitoria, *ius* could only be defined objectively as 'that which is allowed
under law', creatures who were incapable of receiving injury clearly
could not be subject to laws and and could not thus be the
object of rights.

The definition of *dominium* as natural to man by virtue of his
rationality, which is what makes him an object of justice, raised for
Vitoria what seemed to be a potential threat to any definition of
dominium which made it a natural right independent of possession:
namely the status of children. Children, claimed Vitoria, have
dominium, 'which is nothing other than a right to use something
according to its proper use'[14] because unlike, say, lions, they can be
said to suffer injury; and because in law their goods are held independently from those of their tutors. But, as they cannot make
contracts, they own these goods only as their inheritance.[15] The legal
concept of inheritance can also, he implied, be transferred to a
consideration of infantile psychology, for however irrational
children may seem to be – and they are, he claimed in another lecture
on the limits of human obligation, truly un-rational – [16] their reason
is potential (just as their goods are potentially theirs) and since

---

[13] *The Two Treatises on Government*, ed. Peter Laslett (Cambridge, 1970), p. 292, and see
     Tully, *A Discourse on Property*, p. 114.
[14] *De indis*, p. 661, 'dominium nihil aliud est quam ius utendi re in usum suum'.
[15] *De indis*, pp. 663–4.
[16] 'De eo ad quod tenetur homo cum primum venit ad usum rationis', in *Obras de
     Francisco de Vitoria*, pp. 1307–8.

'nature never fails in what is necessary', that potential cannot ever fail to become actual. As we shall see, this observation offered a powerful analogy with the condition of the Indian.

Having thus rejected all these categories as possible grounds for denying the Indians *dominium* before the arrival of the Spaniards, Vitoria introduced what was to prove the most contentious claim of all. In 1510 the Scottish Dominican John Major had suggested that the Indians were the 'natural slaves' described by Aristotle in Books I and III of the *Politics*. [17] This had seemed to some to offer an objective proof that they had never had any property rights even in their pre-contact state for, both by the terms of Aristotle's psychology and in law, *servus* is the antithesis of *dominus*. Nor did the undeniable fact that the Indians had been legally 'free' in their own societies necessarily make them any the less slaves since, as Vitoria pointed out, a slave does require a master in order to be a slave. [18] The theory of natural slavery is also predicated upon the claim that such slaves are men who do not *possess* but have only a share in the faculty of deliberation and who, though they might be capable of understanding, are not capable of practical wisdom (*phronesis*). Since, therefore, such creatures lack free will, they cannot have any subjective right to *dominium* either.

But even if the American Indians appeared to be 'very little different from brute animals who are incapable of ruling themselves' they did, in fact, have 'a certain rational order in their affairs'. They lived in cities, had a recognised form of marriage, magistrates, rulers, laws, industry and commerce, 'all of which', as Vitoria observed, 'require the use of reason'. [19] This is a simplified version of Aristotle's requirements for civil life and it is clear that no people who fulfil them can be described as society-less and hence rights-less beings. At the very end of his lecture, however, Vitoria reconsidered this argument. Indian communities, he now claimed, possessed only the minimal requirements for social life. They had, for instance, no knowledge of the liberal arts, no proper agriculture, no true artisans. Theirs were societies in which no true *nobilitas* – in the Aristotelian and Thomist sense of the word – could exist and in which it would therefore be impossible to live a life of true *optium*. [20] But if the Indians do, in fact, live 'almost like beasts and wild animals' this is not because they belong by innate disposition to a state of semi-

[17] For a more detailed discussion of the theory of natural slavery, see Pagden, *The Fall of Natural Man*, pp. 27–56.   [18] *De indis*, p. 651.   [19] *De indis*, pp. 664–5.
[20] *De indis*, pp. 723–5. For the argument that the highest moral life is one of *otium*, or pacific contemplation, see pp. 127–8 below.

rationality, but because their 'poor and barbarous education' has rendered them incapable of fully rational behaviour. Since the cause of their cultural condition is to be found in the state of their education, then they may be, not natural slaves, but some kind of natural children and, like all children, heirs to a state of true reason. By the terms of Soto's definition of *dominium* they may be said to be in full possession of their rights without being able to exercise them. The Castilian crown might thus claim a right to hold the Indians, and their lands, in tutelage until they have reached the age of reason. The acceptance by any civil prince of such peoples 'into his care' might even, Vitoria concluded, be considered an act of charity.[21]

None of these arguments, of course, could provide the Castilian crown with *dominium* in America. In place of claims which made a direct appeal to either the natural or the civil law, Vitoria therefore substituted three based on the law of nations, the *ius gentium*. This was, by the definition given in the *Institutes* (1.2.1), 'that which is constituted by natural reason among men'. Just what this implied was a subject of much debate, but Vitoria took it on this occasion to be that which is 'of the natural law or derives from the natural law' and which, consequently, like the natural law, cannot be modified in any way by human agency.[22]

Under the *ius gentium*, the Spaniards possessed what he called the 'right of society and natural communication'.[23] Seas, shores and harbours are necessary for man's survival as a civil being and they have, therefore, by the common accord of all men, been exempted from the original division of property. It had always, Vitoria claimed, been an objective right in law that no man could be forbidden to land on any stretch of beach, no matter to whom it actually belonged, which is why Aeneas had rightly described the ancient kings of Latium as 'barbari' when they refused him anchorage. This right to travel, the *ius peregrinandi*, therefore, gave the Spaniards right of access to the Indies. There was also, under the heading of *communicatio*, an implied right to trade. As the Spaniards had come to America, or so Vitoria claimed, as ambassadors (*legati*) and traders, they had to be treated with respect and be permitted to trade with all those who wished to trade with them. And since this was a right under the law of nations, it could only (at least by the terms of Vitoria's present definition) be changed by the consensus of the

---

[21] *De indis*, p. 725.
[22] *De indis*, p. 706. The Spanish Thomists generally held the *ius gentium* to be a form of positive law, see e.g., Francisco de Vitoria, *Commentarios a la Secunda secundae de Santo Tomás*, ed. Vicente Beltrán de Heredia, III, pp. 8–9.   [23] *De indis*, pp. 705–6.

entire human community, not by the will of an individual ruler.[24] Vitoria also claimed that the *ius gentium* granted the Spaniards the right (the *ius predicandi*) to preach their religion without interference – although it did not compel anyone to accept it – and that it permitted them to wage a just war against any tyrant 'in defence of the innocent'.

In the first two of these cases – the *ius peregrinandi* and the *ius predicandi* – the Spaniards could enforce their rights if opposed because any attempt to deprive a man of his natural rights constitutes an injury. The vindication of injuries constitutes a just war, and ultimately it was only by means of such a war that the Spaniards could legitimate their presence in America.[25] By the terms of such a war the belligerent acquires the status of a judge with respect to his opponents and he may, therefore, appropriate their private property (their *bona* and usually only their moveable goods) as he sees fit.[26] Similarly, the victor acquires authority over the vanquished in order to defend himself against any future injuries, and prisoners taken in a just war may legitimately be enslaved. But in no other case may the enemy be deprived of his *dominium rerum*. In circumstances, however, where the offence is very great – and this might apply to the Indians – or where the enemy seems to be incapable of arriving at a peaceful solution, it is possible to depose ruling princes, to *tollere principem* or *mutare principatum*.[27] The Spaniards might then be able to send 'ministers' to protect their future interests and to depose troublesome local rulers should the need arise.

Vitoria's third title, the 'defence of the innocent', is even more limited in its application. The Spaniards may not, he insisted, make war on the Indians because of their supposed crimes against nature, since all nations are guilty of such crimes. If a prince has no right to invade the territory of another in order to punish cases of 'simple fornication' – since no nation on earth is free of that sin – no prince can punish another for cannibalism or sodomy.[28] For the Thomists, crimes against nature do not admit of degrees, since such crimes are offences against God not man, and only God can punish them. To suggest that any prince however godly, even the emperor himself, could act as *flagellum dei* was to fall, once again, into the Lutheran error of supposing that *dominium* is conferred by God's grace, not God's law.

---

[24] *De indis*, pp. 707–14. [25] *De indis*, pp. 715–21.
[26] Francisco de Vitoria, *Relectio de iure belli*, ed. L. Pereña *et al.* (Madrid, 1981), pp. 187–99. [27] *Relectio de iure belli*, p. 200. [28] *De indis*, pp. 698–9.

Vitoria had thus left the Castilian crown with a slender claim to *dominium iurisdictionis* in America but no property rights whatsoever. And, of course, the rights the crown might claim under the *ius gentium* would only be valid if the Indians had indeed 'injured' the Spaniards. If, however, as seemed to be the case, 'these barbarians have not given any reason for a just war, nor wish voluntarily to accept Christian princes, the expeditions must cease'. In the end, all that remained was the starkly objective claim that, since the Spaniards were already there, any attempt to abandon the colonies would only result in 'a great prejudice and detriment to the interests of [our] princes which would be intolerable'.[29]

III

Over the next three decades all of Vitoria's pupils re-described parts of these arguments in their own lectures on the subject of *dominium*. Perhaps the most important of these, partly because it is among the most radical, at least as far as its implications are concerned, partly because its author was later involved in the most widely publicised debate on the subject, was delivered by the Dominican theologian Melchor Cano in 1546. The Indians, Cano argued, may only be said not to possess *dominium* if they can be shown to be irrational beings. Since they clearly are not simpletons (*stulti*) the only possible argument is that they are 'slaves by nature'.[30] But this theory is, he claimed, incoherent, not only because – as Vitoria himself had argued elsewhere – no man who merely had a share in the faculty of reason could properly be described as a man,[31] but because slavery could, by definition, only be a category in law. Aristotle's mistake had been to confuse a legal classification with a psychological disposition. Since the accepted definition of slavery given in Roman law (Digest 1.1.4) was 'someone who has been deprived of his liberty contrary to nature', there could evidently be no such creature as a *natural* slave. This confusion had, furthermore, been made in the interest of the parochial claim that Athenians were the wisest of all living creatures. And even if we understand Aristotle only to be stating the general principle that the wise should always rule the foolish,

---

[29] *De indis*, p. 725.
[30] Melchor Cano, 'De dominio indorum', Biblioteca Vaticana MS Lat. 4648, fol. 30r.
[31] For a discussion of this argument, see Pagden, *The Fall of Natural Man*, pp. 57–97.

this, although it might indubitably be the case, cannot confer *dominium*, since *dominium* does not derive from wisdom any more than it does from grace. *Dominium iurisdictionis* derives from the will of the community and *dominium rerum*, of course, from the natural law.[32]

It may, of course, still be the case, as Vitoria had argued, that the Indians really are like children in need of education. But even if this were so, the Christians would not be entitled to 'take them into their care' if, in order to do so, they had to conquer them first, since any act whose purpose is to secure the utility of another is, as Vitoria had rightly suspected, a precept of charity, and no precept of charity can involve coercion. The position of the Castilian crown was thus, Cano concluded, analogous only to that of the beggar to whom alms may be due but who is not empowered to extract them.[33]

Cano also rejected Vitoria's other claims. The title 'society and natural communication' does not, he claimed, provide a right of entry to another's territory because even if the *ius gentium* is of the natural law, it can only be so in the third degree and is consequently, like any code which relies upon an interpretation of the natural law, subject to abrogation and alteration. Like Vitoria himself on other occasions, Cano could not really accept the *ius gentium* as anything other than a positive law. For it was, he pointed out, clearly absurd to suggest that there could exist a law of nations which might forbid a prince from controlling the movement of foreigners over his lands. Such a law would prevent the king of Spain from denying entry to the French, which would be contrary to actual practice and in violation of the positive law of Castile. Furthermore, even if it were the case that merchants and travellers might claim the right of free access under the law of nations, the Spaniards had clearly not presented themselves to the Indians as such. They had gone to America as conquerors. 'We would not', he concluded drily, 'be prepared to describe Alexander the Great as a "traveller" '.[34]

This left only the *ius predicandi* and the right to defend the innocent. These Cano was prepared to accept, but he made it clear that they did not have the power to confer property rights upon any secular prince. The Castilian crown's rights in the Indies were, by the terms of Cano's argument, severely limited to political sovereignty. It clearly did not possess rights of *dominium rerum* in America any more than it did in Naples or Aragon. The Indians were, as Las Casas was to insist time and again, free subjects of the Castilian crown, and their

---

[32] 'De dominio indorum', fols. 30r–31v.   [33] 'De dominio indorum', fol. 39r.
[34] 'De dominio indorum', fol. 39v.

property – including both their land and, more polemically, what lay beneath it –[35] remained their own.

IV

By the middle of the century, this modified version of Vitoria's argument was widely accepted by all the Thomists. They may not quite, as Dr Johnson supposed, have given it 'as their opinion that it was not lawful'[36] to deprive the Indians of their property, but they had come perilously close. And the changing tone of the legislation governing the crown's relationship with both the colonists and the Indians in the years after 1540 suggests that they voiced their views to some effect in the influential circles where they moved. In 1550, however, both Soto and Cano, together with Las Casas and a number of lesser figures, were confronted by a quite different set of arguments over the property rights of the American Indians. These were set out in a short dialogue, entitled *Democrates secundus*, by Juan Ginés de Sepúlveda, one of the Emperor's chaplains, and his official historian.[37] Sepúlveda stridently denied that the Indians had been capable of *dominium* before the arrival of the Europeans. John Major, says Democrates, Sepúlveda's mouthpiece in the dialogue, had rightly claimed that as these peoples had had no rulers, no laws, they might legitimately be appropriated by the first civil man to reach their shores. For Sepúlveda (as, in this case, for Major) and for most Roman lawyers and their humanist commentators, all property relations are the product of civil society. They constitute, that is, objective not subjective rights.[38]

To the Thomists, Sepúlveda seemed, by this claim, to have recast the whole issue in the language of humanist jurisprudence. Worse still, in order to make good his claim that not merely the Taino and the Arawak of the Caribbean, but also the Mexican and the Inca, were pre-social men, Sepúlveda was committed to a far starker read-

---

[35] Most of the Thomists rejected any claims that the Indians were not the rightful owners of the gold and silver mined on their lands. See, e.g. Soto, *De iustitia et iure*, p. 424, who argued that the Spaniards had no more right to mine for precious metals in America than the French had to come looking for buried treasure in Spain. And see Bartolomé de las Casas, *Tratado de las doce dudas*, in *Biblioteca de autores Españoles*, Cx, p. 523, who insisted that to deny this was 'to fall into the heresy of Huss'.

[36] Quoted in *Boswell's Life of Johnson*, ed. G. B. Hill (Oxford, 1934), I, p.45.

[37] For a discussion of this text and its reception by Cano, Soto and Bartolomé de Carranza, see Pagden, *The Fall of Natural Man*, pp. 109–18.

[38] *Democrates segundo, o de las justas causas de la guerra contra los indios*, ed. Angel Losada (Madrid, 1951), pp. 83–6.

ing of Aristotle's theory of natural slavery than any previous author
had been. The Indians, he claimed, were evidently not civil beings
since they consistently violated the law of nature. To the objection
of the speaker in the dialogue (a mild-mannered German called
Leopoldus who speaks throughout in the language of political
Aristotelianism) that all men violate the law of nature and that in
many societies such crimes are not even proscribed by civil law,
Democrates replies that a man may perform certain unnatural acts *as
an individual* and still retain his humanity. What he may not do is to
set up 'laws and institutions' which are contrary to nature. Single
individuals frequently, even in Christian societies, falter in their
understanding of the law of nature. But if the consensus of the entire
community, which is the only means of knowing the precepts of that
law, is itself at fault, then it is clear that this cannot have been arrived
at by a collectivity of rational beings. The 'crimes committed against
human society' by such creatures therefore constituted, as the
Canonists had always insisted, grounds for a just war in which the
vanquished might be deprived of all their rights, including their
liberty, their *dominium corporis suis*.[39]

Sepúlveda was extremely proud of what he believed to be his
discovery of the weakness in the Thomists' rejection of the argument that 'crime against nature' constituted legitimate grounds for
depriving a man of his natural rights. Leopoldus, however, objects
that Mexican society, even if guilty of such crimes, has any number
of other features characteristic of civil communities. Certainly,
replies Democrates, for the Indians obviously possess some power
of understanding; even natural slaves are men, not 'bears or
monkeys'. But the communities they have created are not like those
of 'truly civil beings'. For there are, he points out, many forms of
natural association among animals which share some of the features
of a true society but which are clearly not in any sense civil ones. A
closer look at the Indian world would, he concludes, reveal that it
was really not much better organised than a colony of bees or
ants.[40]

Before the arrival of the Spaniards, the Indians had, Sepúlveda
conceded, been lords in their own lands, they had enjoyed, that is,
imperium under the terms of the law of nations which grants rights of
occupancy to the first settler. But, he insisted, not only was *imperium*
not *dominium*, any claim made under the *ius gentium* may be abrogated
since it was, as the humanists had maintained, a positive, not a

---

[39] *Democrates segundo*, p. 97.   [40] *Democrates segundo*, p. 36.

natural law. The Castilian crown's claims to *dominium* in America rest, however, on the dictate of the natural law which grants *dominium* to all those who are civil beings over all those who are not.[41]

It might, however, be argued that, under the new civil regime created by the Spaniards, the Indians could still retain their use rights over their lands and, more importantly, over their gold and silver. To this Democrates replies that God gave property to man for his use, but since use, unlike *dominium*, is limited, man may not *abuse* it. The Indians have clearly abused their property, cannibalism and human sacrifice being the most grisly violations of those limited use rights which men have over their own bodies. More importantly, they had only used their gold and silver for idolatrous ends. Like the Egyptians, then, they may be said to have forfeited whatever rights they had had over these metals because, in Augustine's words, 'they were sacriligeous and made ill-use of their gold'.[42] Furthermore, since no Indian society had had a monetary economy, no Indian could be said to have exercised any rights over any precious metal. These were, therefore, still a common part of Adam's patrimony, to which the Spaniards had a high moral claim by having traded metals which had been useless in the ancient Indian world for such useful things as iron, European agricultural techniques, horses, donkeys, goats, pigs, sheep, and so on.[43] For Sepúlveda, as for such eighteenth-century natural-law theorists as Wattell who, in the generation after Grotius and Pufendorf, rewrote the language of iusnaturalism in a more fully humanistic idiom, *dominium* could only exist if it were exercised. The cultivation of the land allotted by God to man is not, as Wattell claimed, merely useful: it is an obligation 'imposée à l'homme par la nature'.[44] Any people who failed to fulfil that obligation could have no claim against other more industrious nations who occupied and cultivated its lands. It followed, therefore, that the Christians might, in Democrates' words, take possession, 'by private and public law', of all Indian goods. The Indians' historical relationship to their property may now, he concluded, be likened to that of a man who has been deprived of his goods by the court but granted the *ius utendi* until sentence has been formally promulgated by a judge. The arrival of the Spaniards, directed to America by divine providence, constituted that promulgation.[45]

---

[41] *Democrates segundo*, pp. 79–83.
[42] *Democrates segundo*, pp. 87–90, citing *Contra Faustum*, Bk XXII, cap. 7.
[43] *Democrates segundo*, pp. 78–9.
[44] M. de Wattell, *Le Droit de gens ou principe de la loi naturelle* (Paris, 1820), I, p. 113.
[45] *Democrates segundo*, pp. 90–1.

Sepúlveda's argument, couched as it was in the language of a humanist jurisprudence which restricted all rights – and rights of property in particular – to the members of civil societies, met with fierce opposition from the Salamanca theologians. Their hostility to his work was, so Cano told Sepúlveda, based on the fact that his doctrines were unsound, that he was ignorant of what Vitoria had written on the subject and that he seemed to know more about history and philosophy than he did about theology.[46] In part, as Sepúlveda himself recognised, this was the reaction of a professional intellectual coterie to interference from an outsider. But Cano's increasingly acrimonious correspondence with Sepúlveda makes it clear that the Thomists were concerned by two other issues. In the first place, Sepúlveda's objective (and conceptually somewhat confused) use of *ius* had allowed him to translate concepts from the positive into the natural law. In the second, his reliance on the Canonists' defence of the thesis that no man who has committed crimes against nature may possess *dominium* seemed, once again, to open the way to an ultimately Lutheran definition of sovereignty.

The most sustained attempt to meet Sepúlveda's arguments on these issues came in a series of lectures given between 1560 and 1563 by Juan de la Peña, a pupil of Soto and a close friend of Las Casas.[47] Peña began, as Cano and others had before him, by dismissing the theory of natural slavery. It was, he claimed, not only inapplicable, as Cano had argued, it was also incoherent. For if it were possible for there to exist whole races of partially rational men capable of performing some, but not all, of the actions of civil beings, this would seriously threaten the doctrine of the perfectibility of man and the unity of the whole species, both of which have been guaranteed by divine revelation. If natural slaves do exist, they must be very rare beasts indeed, and they must *be* beasts. Peña was willing to concede the minor premise – that the wise should always rule the less wise – but the fact remains, he said – *factum tenet* – that in no actual society is this ever the case.[48]

If the Indians are rational men they have *dominium rerum*, since 'the foundation of *dominium* is that man is a rational creature',[49] and no act

---

[46] *Jo. Genesius doctor theologus Melchiori Cano doctori theo* in *Joannis Genesii Sepulvedae cordubensis opera* (Madrid, 1780), III, pp. 34–5, and see Pagden, *The Fall of Natural Man*, pp. 110–13.

[47] *De bello contra insulanos* and *De libertate indorum contra Sepulvedam*, parts of a commentary on the *Secunda secundae* of Aquinas and printed in *De bello contra insulanos*, ed. L. Pereña *et al.* (Madrid, 1982), pp. 136–393.

[48] *De bello contra insulanos*, pp. 245–9. Like Cano, Peña also accused Sepúlveda of being 'mediocriter in theologia exercitatus' (*Ibid.*, p. 213).

[49] *De bello contra insulanos*, pp. 146–7.

they might perform can, *of itself*, deprive them of that right. The manifest errors of their society before the arrival of the Spaniards, like the errors of all non-Christian societies, were, Peña insisted, merely probable. They were, that is, the kind of errors into which any individual might fall if he were deprived of proper guidance, the kind of guidance which, in the end, only a Christian civil society can provide. But a man who is in error is still in full possession of all his natural rights. Sepúlveda's claim that only civil men could enjoy *dominium* (the assumption which underwrites all Roman legal thinking on the subject) is merely the legislative norm of a tyranny, and may ultimately prove to be as parochial as Aristotle's assumption that all those who are not Athenians are natural slaves.[50]

Sepúlveda's claim that the Indians had also forfeited their use rights in the lands they occupied was similarly false. Use rights were, Peña pointed out, not *dominia* and thus came under not the natural but the civil law. From this it clearly followed that whatever misuse the Indians might have made of their property could only be punished by those who enjoyed civil jurisdiction over them. Since, however, they had had *dominium* before the arrival of the Spaniards and were guilty of no offence 'in respect of another republic', they could not be punished under a new regime – even supposing that regime to be a legitimate one, which, in this case, was by no means certain – for crimes committed under another. If they were in fact unworthy (*indigni*) of *dominia*, then it was up to *their* judges to deprive them of such rights and not the Spaniards, 'who have no authority over them'.[51] Far, therefore, from being, as Sepúlveda had suggested, under sentence of confiscation, the Indians were now in the position of persons from whom a judge has taken far more than the law allows and, like all such persons, they were entitled to restitution.[52] And, Peña concluded, if that was the case, then in order to press their claims for restitution, the Indians were perfectly within *their* rights to make war on the Spaniards.

Like Cano before him, Peña was willing to accept that the Spaniards could make just war on the Indians, and thereby deprive them of their rights, in defence of innocent parties. This, at least, would provide a legitimate reason among Christian princes. Henry VIII of England, whose *respublica* was, because of the offences he had caused its citizens, already in disarray, might legitimately be attacked

[50] *De bello contra insulanos*, pp. 247–9.
[51] *De bello contra insulanos*, p. 261.
[52] *De bello contra insulanos*, p. 239. Soto had come to much the same conclusion with regard to the Africans enslaved by the Portuguese, *De iustitia et iure*, p. 289.

in order to prevent further collapse.[53] Similarly, it was legitimate for
the Spaniards to prevent such tribes as the Caribs from eating each
other by force. It was, however, by no means clear that the Mexicans
– who did not eat their subjects – had sufficiently offended a large
enough number of their people to warrant European interference.
The Aztec kings had only been accused of one major violation of the
rights of their citizens: human sacrifice. But from what Peña had
heard (and this must have been a piece of information given him by
Las Casas), this was, in fact, only a ritualised mode of execution.

In the end it was impossible for Peña, faced as he was by the need
to refute Sepúlveda, to find sufficient grounds in any of Vitoria's
original titles to deny the American Indians their natural property
rights. The only title which could escape careful scrutiny in the light
of an increasingly detailed body of ethnographic information was
the *ius predicandi*, the right to preach. But, as Vitoria himself had
recognised, this only gave the Spaniards the right to be heard.

The obvious conclusion, and it had been obvious now for some
time, was that if the consequences of these arguments were going to
be taken seriously, the Spaniards had to withdraw and return to the
Indians all that they had taken from them. Although this was never
considered as a real possibility because, as Vitoria had observed, it
would be intolerable in practice, it was at one point widely believed
in the colonies themselves that Charles V intended to 'abandon the
Indies' to satisfy his conscience. The only possible argument which
could preserve both Indian rights and the Spanish claim to, if not
dominium rerum, at least *dominium iurisdictionis*, was the claim by Las
Casas in 1554 that 'the only title which Your Majesty has is this: that
all, or the greater part of, the Indians wish voluntarily to be your
vassals and hold it an honour to be so'.[54] But this, of course, did not
mean that the Indians had thereby voluntarily forfeited their natural
rights, for it is obviously in no man's power to do that, nor that they
were any the less due for restitution of their goods, and their

---

[53] In the interests of peace, which required the recovery of the well-ordered society,
   otherwise legitimate princes might be deprived of their goods (*bona*) and, if they
   continued to be unfit to rule, of their *dominium*. See, e.g., Francisco Suárez,
   Disputatio XII: de bello, in *Opus de triplici virtute theologica: fide spe et charitate* (Paris,
   1621), p. 819.
[54] 'Sobre el título del dominio del rey de España sobre las personas y tierras de los
   indios', in *De regia potestate*, ed. L. Pereña *et al.* (Madrid, 1969), pp. 171 f. Vitoria himself had discussed this point in *De indis* (pp. 721–2). Just as the French had elected
   Pipin, so the Indians might 'elect' Charles V, since every *respublica* 'may constitute
   its own *dominium* with the consensus of the majority'. But he recognised that it
   would prove impossible in fact to discover what the consensus of the majority
   was.

liberties, even the liberty of self-government. For, by the terms of this formulation, the rights which the crown now had in the Indies were similar, not to those it had over the people of Castile, but to those it had in Milan. The Indian chieftains, like the Dukes of Milan, ruled over polities which were, in all respects, 'perfect republics', and their subjects were consequently free men with full *dominium* under their own laws. Philip II could no more parcel out the Amerindians to his Castilian subjects than he could give away the Milanese to the French.[55]

It followed from this, Las Casas wrote in 1555 to the Archbishop of Toledo, Bartolomé de Carranza, who had been fighting the Council of the Indies on his behalf, that the colonists must abandon the Indies, leaving only 'the universal principate of the King of Castile'. A limited number of soldiers should remain to protect the missionaries, and once restitution had been made, the crown might begin to trade for the precious metals it required.[56] Under this description, America resembled less the Duchy of Milan than a Portuguese factory in India, an analogy which Vitoria himself had drawn at the very end of *De indis*, pointing out that there was no evidence to suggest that the crown of Portugal had acquired any less through licit trade than the Castilian crown had through illicit occupation.[57]

V

With the death in 1566 of Las Casas, who had done so much to keep it alive, the debate over the rights of the Indians lost much of its immediate force. The rapid decline of the Indian population itself and the collapse of the missionary ambition, which Las Casas had shared, to create a New Jerusalem in the New World, greatly reduced the urgency of the whole issue. The Castilian crown's own concerns with political legitimacy were now focused on the Netherlands and Italy, where the issues – despite attempts by both Netherlanders and Neapolitans to turn Las Casas's arguments to

---

[54] *De regia potestate*, pp. 33–9, 83–5. This treatise, which was printed in Frankfurt in 1571, was the last Las Casas wrote. It relies heavily on the arguments of the work of the fourteenth-century jurist Lucas da Penna and consequently proposes a strongly contractualist account of government which contrasts markedly with the weaker versions proposed by the Thomists in which political authority is said, in, e.g. Suárez's formulation, to be held by the people only *in fieri* and not *in conservari*. (*Defensio fidei catholicae et apostolicae adversus anglicanae sectae errores* (Coimbra, 1613), p. 225.)

[56] 'Carta al maestro fray Bartolomé de Miranda sobre la perpetuidad de las ecomiendas', in *De regia potestate*, pp. 441–5.   [57] *De indis*, p. 275.

their own advantage – were quite unlike those which had applied in America. When in 1631 the jurist Juan de Solórzano y Pereira attempted to write what was, in effect, a history of the whole debate, the nature of the Vitorian project, the over-arching concern to refute the Lutheran account of *dominium*, had become invisible. In Solórzano's view, the entire debate had, from the moment Vitoria delivered his famous lecture, simply been couched in the wrong language. The Castilian crown's claims to *dominium* had derived, in the first instance, from Alexander VI's Bulls of Donation. But ever since Vitoria had cast doubt on these by denying the pope any degree of temporal power, the entire issue had been conducted in the vocabulary of natural rights. The point which had, therefore, escaped all the natural-law theorists was that even if the Bulls were invalid – and Solórzano seems inclined to accept that they were – neither Ferdinand nor Isabella were aware of this. As no less a person than Cardinal Bellarmine had pointed out, the Catholic Monarchs had believed in good faith that the pope had conferred full *dominium* upon the crown, and the crown had, therefore, behaved in good conscience of acting as it did. What Solórzano was now arguing, by recasting the whole debate in the language of Roman jurisprudence, was that if the crown had come into possession of the Indies by what it believed to be a legitimate right, then it could claim *dominium* by virtue of subsequent occupation. It was, as Solórzano pointed out, precisely this argument which had traditionally been used to legitimate the Roman conquests retrospectively. 'Even a tyranny', wrote Solórzano, and in this respect the Roman Empire was a tyranny, 'becomes in time a perfect and legitimate monarchy.'[58] Time, the Spaniards' historical presence, is then the sufficient condition of *dominium*, for it is the objective condition which confers legal rights; and, in the end, it is legal, not natural rights, which are under debate. A similar acceptance of an historical basis for rights was, as he pointed out, the only claim made by the other European maritime state to *dominium* over the seas closest to its shores. No one (except the wretched and heretical Grotius) denied the right of Alexander III to grant *dominium* over the Adriatic to Venice, or the right of the

---

[58] *Politica indiana sacada en lengua castellana de los dos tomos del derecho i govierno municipal de las Indias* (1648) in *Biblioteca de autores Españoles*, CCLII, p. 108. The argument which underpins this claim is set out by Vitoria himself in the prolegomenon to *De indis* (pp. 643–8). If someone, after due consultation with 'the most learned doctors', is convinced that an act is legitimate, then he cannot be held guilty of any offence, even if those doctors subsequently prove to be wrong. What Vitoria was not claiming, however, was that an illicit act performed in good faith could render the consequences of that act legitimate, particularly once it was recognised that the act itself had been illicit.

Genoese to the Ligurian Sea. Turn, he told his readers, to John Selden's *Mare clausum*, where you will find arguments which will do quite as well for Spanish claims to rights in the lands of America, as they do for the English king's claims to the North Sea and the North Atlantic.[59] Selden, of course, was writing in the terms of the language of 'modern' iusnaturalism (described here by Richard Tuck), a language in which objective conditions play a far larger role than they did for the Spanish Thomists. But the terms of that discourse were already beginning to look by the 1630s distincly unwieldy and outmoded. As Solórzano concluded, the whole issue to which Vitoria and his pupils had addressed themselves was now only of 'antiquarian interest' and was raised, when at all, only by 'certain heretics out of envy of our nation'.[60]

[59] *Politica indiana*, p. 114. On Selden's *Mare clausum*, see Richard Tuck, *Natural Rights Theories*, pp. 86–7.
[60] *Politica indiana*, pp. 112–13.

An earlier version of this essay was read as a paper at a conference on the Roman Law held at the Warburg Institute and at the Social and Political Theory Seminar at Cambridge. I am grateful to those present, and in particular to John Dunn, Quentin Skinner, Geoffrey Hawthorn and Istvan Hont, for their comments and suggestions.

5

The 'modern' theory of natural law

RICHARD TUCK

It is a familiar observation that the late eighteenth century in Europe witnessed one of the greatest revolutions which has ever occurred in the writing of philosophy. The novelty of the views of Kant and his followers was obvious to contemporaries, and has been a truism in the historiography of philosophy to this day. What is not so familiar is that the writing of the *history* of philosophy was transformed at the same time, and that it has remained in its new form ever since. In order to vindicate his own philosophy, Kant was located by both himself and his successors in a new version of the history of philosophy, sweeping away what had been commonplaces for more than a century. The transformation was most complete in the area of modern moral philosophy, for there not only did an old interpretation vanish, but so did a complete cast of characters. Given Kant's own views, this was understandable, but the survival of the post-Kantian history into our own time has proved a great barrier to a genuine understanding of the pre-Kantian writers. What I want to do in this essay is outline the history of recent moral philosophy which Kant rejected and seek to understand why it seems to the men of the Enlightenment to be such a powerful and obvious account of their origins.

The character of the revolution is best appreciated by contrasting two works written within fifty years of each other, the second edition of Johann Jakob Brucker's *Historia critica philosophiae* (1766; the first edition was 1742–4) and Johann Gottlieb Buhle's *Geschicte der neuern Philosophie* (1802). Both were vast compendiums written by professors at German universities to help their students find their way through the philosophy courses; both were also seized on by the wider European audience of their time as the best syntheses available of the history of philosophy. But both their overall structure and their specific content are startlingly different.

Brucker's main conviction was that 'eclectic' philosophy was characteristic of the modern world. Although the dogmatic schools of antiquity did have modern representatives, the purest strain of philosophical thinking since the Renaissance was represented by the man who respects no ancient authorities but 'diligently investigates the nature and properties of the objects which come under his observation, that he may from these deduce clear principles, and arrive at certain knowledge'.[1] This stress on *certainty* was, as we shall see, an important element in this history. Bacon, according to Brucker, was the first philosopher fully to exhibit this eclectic character, for he was the first (apparently) who knowingly repudiated all the philosophical schools of antiquity. Because eclectic philosophy does not admit of division into schools, Brucker argued, the history of post-Baconian philosophy should be written in terms of the areas of inquiry rather than the substantive positions taken up, and he therefore tried to write the history of modern 'moral and political philosophy' as a whole.

In this history, the first modern writer is Montaigne, closely followed by Pierre Charron, for they were undogmatic investigators, though they lacked the ability to put together a new and persuasive system. That honour fell to Hugo Grotius, who was the main hero of Brucker's account – a hero both because in his *De iure belli ac pacis* (1625) he produced a genuinely *new* system of ethics which was not simply a defence of one of the ethical theories of antiquity, and because of his *open* eclecticism. 'His eclectic spirit clearly appears, in the general maxim which he lays down concerning antient systems; that, "as there never was any sect so enlightened, as to be entirely destitute of truth." '[2] Grotius was followed closely by John Selden, Thomas Hobbes and above all Samuel Pufendorf, with whose *De iure naturae et gentium* (1672) Brucker ends his story, disclaiming any intention of carrying it down to his own time.

If we then move on to Buhle's *Geschicte der neuern Philosophie*, we find a wholly different account. Gone, first of all, is the attempt to write the history of modern moral philosophy as a whole; instead, modern philosophy is characterised in every area by the opposition of two schools described, in a terminology unknown to Brucker, as

---

[1] Jacob Brucker, *Historia critica philosophiae*, IV.2 (Leipzig, 1766), p. 4. The translation is from William Enfield, *The History of Philosophy . . . drawn up from Brucker's Historia Critica Philosophiae* II (London, 1819), p. 469, which in this passage is a literal rendering of Brucker. The standard account of this Enlightenment historiography is Giovanni Santinello, *Storia delle storie generali della filosofia* (Brescia, 1980–   ).

[2] Brucker, *Historia*, p. 00; Enfield, *History*, p. 543.

'realists' and 'idealists', that is of course 'empiricists' and 'rationalists', the labels which have bedevilled the history of philosophy ever since. Grotius, the lynch-pin of Brucker's account of the modern history of ethics, is treated with dramatic contempt: his *De iure belli ac pacis* is 'ordinarily regarded as a system of natural law, which it is not, nor could it be, according to the object which the author set himself' – which was simply to write an analysis of international law.[3] To do so, Grotius had to outline the fundamental principles of natural law, but 'the principles which serve him as a point of departure are for the most part vague, inexact and without precision; for he presents the rights of men and of peoples against one another, now as general maxims of reason, now as features of social necessity, and sometimes as the customs of civil societies, to such an extent that the science of natural law has neither firm foundations nor any systematic unity in his work.'[4] Not only was his philosophy unsatisfactory: Buhle even argued that Grotius was temperamentally and intellectually ill-equipped to act as ambassador for the Queen of Sweden, the post Grotius held for more than a decade at Paris.[5]

It is Buhle's account which we find, in effect, in all subsequent general works on the history of philosophy: Grotius and Pufendorf have never re-emerged to take up places of honour in the history of modern moral philosophy. If they are mentioned, it is as late examples of scholasticism, and their *modernity*, which so impressed Brucker, is not taken at all seriously. (One example: Alasdair MacIntyre in *A Short History of Ethics* mentions Grotius's 'later development of Aquinas' view of natural law into a law for the nations'.)[6] The way in which international lawyers at the end of the nineteenth century rediscovered the scholastic writers on the laws of war, and placed both Grotius and Pufendorf in that tradition, helped to underwrite this view of them.

And yet, Brucker's history was far more than a piece of his own idiosyncracy. He was merely stating in very conventional terms a history of modern ethics which was a commonplace in his time, though he integrated it into a defence of 'electicism' which was,

[3] Johann Gottlieb Buhle, *Geschicte der neuern Philosophie*, III (Göttingen, 1802), p. 329; *Histoire de la philosophie moderne*, trans. A. J. L. Jourdan, III (Paris, 1816), p. 283.
[4] Buhle, *Geschicte*, p. 332, *Histoire*, p. 285.
[5] Buhle, *Geschicte*, p. 328n, *Histoire*, p. 282n.
[6] Alasdair MacIntyre, *A Short History of Ethics* (London, 1967), p. 120. That is the sum total of his discussion of Grotius; Pufendorf is not mentioned at all.

perhaps, more unusual.[7] The origins of this history lie in the late seventeenth century, and it received a comprehensive exposition at the very beginning of the eighteenth century. The first sketch of it is to be found in the preface to the first edition of Pufendorf's *De iure naturae et gentium* itself, in 1672: in the preface, he described Grotius as 'the first person to make our age value the study of natural law', and observed that his successors were Hobbes (in whose work, despite many errors, there is 'much of infinite value') and Selden.[8]

This sketch, like the rest of the work, came under fierce attack in the next six years, and in 1678 Pufendorf answered his critics and provided a justification and expansion of this history, in a volume entitled *Specimen contoversiarum circa ius naturale ipsi nuper motarum*. Most of the attacks on the *De iure naturae et gentium* had come from the pens of German Protestants; foremost among them were two colleagues of Pufendorf at Lund University in Sweden, Nikolaus Beckmann, professor of Roman Law (who later converted to Catholicism) and Josua Schwartz, professor of Theology. They were joined by Friedrich Gesen, the Lutheran minister of Gardelegen near Magdeburg, Valentin Velthem, professor of Theology at Jena, and Valentin Alberti, professor of Theology at Leipzig.[9]

Although these Lutheran worthies had a variety of elaborate arguments to make against Pufendorf, their central claim was that he was in effect a Hobbesian, and that he had therefore departed from the metaphysical and theological orthodoxy of the Protestant church. To establish this, they seized on two distinctive features of Pufendorf's theory. One was Pufendorf's argument that no human action is *in itself* either good or bad: actions do not exhibit inherent moral properties comparable to their physical properties, but instead have their moral qualities 'inputed' to them by the application to them of a rule devised by some agent or group of agents. His critics took this strong ethical anti-realism to be comparable to Hobbes's anti-realism, and to be in direct conflict with the truths of Aristotelianism (as indeed it was). The second feature of Pufendorf's ideas which disturbed the Lutherans was his claim that the principles

---

[7]   A good example of the commonplace character of this history in the eighteenth century is provided by its incorporation in a characteristic work of the *salons*, Alexandre Savérien's *Histoire des philosophes modernes* (3rd edn, Paris, 1773, II, pp. 79ff. for Grotius).

[8]   Samuel Pufendorf, *De iure naturae et gentium* (Lund, 1672), sig. b4v ff.

[9]   A full discussion of this controversy is to be found in Fiammetta Palladini, *Discussioni seicentesche su Samuel Pufendorf* (Bologna, 1978). I am indebted to Istvan Hont for my introduction to this invaluable work.

of the law of nature can all be interpreted as means towards the end of the preservation of 'society', as this too seemed to them to be comparable to Hobbes's account of the laws of nature. Although they recognised that this latter claim was one which had also been made by Grotius, the Lutherans tended to argue that Grotius was fundamentally orthodox by virtue of his denial of the former claim; and both Velthem and Alberti in fact produced their own commentaries on Grotius to make this point.

The history which was implicit in these Lutheran critiques of Pufendorf was in some ways closer to the post-Kantian one. Velthem praised the 'prince of moralists' Aquinas and the 'father of metaphysics' Suárez, and saw Grotius as in some sense their successor; Hobbes was outside this realist tradition, and there was a fundamental break between his work and Grotius's.[10] To answer these critiques, Pufendorf once again stressed his rival history, which cut Grotius off from his predecessors and linked him both to Hobbes and to Pufendorf himself. In some ways this looks like a scramble for the authority of Grotius, but there was no particular reason why Pufendorf should have felt obliged to wrest it from his opponents – he had after all been quite critical of Grotius (and, indeed, of Hobbes) in *De iure naturae et gentium*. Pufendorf's account is more plausibly read as a genuine attempt to place himself in what he took to be his theoretical context, and to cast doubt on his opponents' understanding of recent intellectual history.

The first chapter of the *Specimen* is entitled 'The origin and development of the study of natural law', and it starts from the assertion that 'in fact, there was no one before *Hugo Grotius* who accurately distinguished the laws of nature from positive law, and put them in proper order'.[11] The New Testament contained the foundations of the law of nature, but it could not be used as the fundamental text in the study of the law, for it also contained much that non-Christians would not accept– and the essence of the laws of nature was that all men actually recognised their force. The classical writers were also deficient; it is true that 'among the various sects of ancient philosophy, the Stoics made some claims which, somewhat emended, would apparently have been easily developed into a body of natural jurisprudence; but they were neglected, and only the

---

[10] Samuel Pufendorf, *Specimen controversiarum circa jus naturale ipsi nuper motarum* (Uppsala, 1678), p. 26. For the problem of which work of Velthem's is quoted here, see Palladini, *Discussioni.*, p. 200, n.3.   [11] Pufendorf, *Specimen*, p. 1.

dogmas of Aristotle admitted to the schools'.[12] His objection to
Aristotle's moral theory was its *localism*: 'his *Ethics*, which deals with
the principles of human action, apparently contains scarcely anything
other than the duties of a citizen in some Greek *polis*. Just as in his
Politics, he seems mainly to have had in view the practices of his own
Greek states, and to have put a special value on their liberty; which is
a grave defect in a study intended to serve the interests of the whole
human race.'[13]

Not until Grotius did anyone produce a work uncontaminated by
the theories of earlier writers.[14] Pufendorf even conjectured that it
had been inspired 'by what the most perceptive *Bacon*, once
Chancellor of England, declared about the advancement of learning',[15] an association with Bacon which he was the first to make. His
remarks represent a very early use of Bacon as a symbol of anti-
scholastic enlightenment, at least outside the peculiar circles of the
mid-seventeenth-century enthusiastics for a technological utopia
who have been studied by Charles Webster; like Pufendorf's whole
interpretation, this use of Bacon became a standard feature of
histories of philosophy before Buhle, as we saw in the case of
Brucker. Grotius was the model for all students of the laws of nature;
though, in a sideswipe at Velthem and Alberti, Pufendorf warned
against treating *De iure belli ac pacis* as a text in need of scholastic
commentaries – in the end Grotius would become like Aristotle,
buried beneath pedantry and casuistry.[16]

Although Grotius made the breakthrough into a modern science
of natural law, Pufendorf was fairly critical of some of his views, and
in particular of his claim that the laws of nature are equivalent to laws
of *logic*, comparable to the proposition that twice two is four.
Pufendorf of course denied just this in his *De iure naturae et gentium*,
and he repeated his denial in the *Specimen*. But he also acknowledged
that 'it can happen, that someone who goes wrong on some general
issue, can get particular matters absolutely right. Though it should
not make his definition any the less faulty, there are a vast number of
questions which Grotius answers correctly.'[17] In other words,
Pufendorf believed that while the *superstructure* of Grotius's theory
was correct, its *foundations* were in need of modification. In the
Specimen he failed to give a clear explanation of *why* he approved of
the superstructure, other than some references to Grotius's use of

---

[12]   *Ibid.*, p. 8.   [13]   *Ibid.*, p. 9.
[14]   'Accinxit porro sese *Grotius* ad moliendum opus, in quo nulla priorum vestigia
       ipsum regebant.' *Ibid.*, p. 10.
[15]   *Ibid.*, p. 9.   [16]   *Ibid.*, p. 11; cf. also pp. 86–9.   [17]   *Ibid.*, p. 169.

the principle of 'sociability'. But it is fairly clear from his argument in the *De iure naturae et gentium* that he took the common ground between Grotius and himself to be, as his Lutheran opponents perceived, the idea that the laws of nature consisted of rules concerning the *preservation of individuals*.

The crucial passage in the *De iure naturae et gentium* is Book II, chapter 3.11:

It is an easy Matter to discover the Foundation of Natural Law. Man is an Animal extremely desirous of his own Preservation, of himself expos'd to many Wants, unable to secure his own Safety and Maintenance, without the Assistance of his Fellows, and capable of returning the Kindness by the Furtherance of mutual Good: But then he is often malicious, insolent, and easily provok'd, and as powerful in effecting Mischief, as he is ready in designing it. Now that such a Creature may be preserv'd and supported, and may enjoy the good Things attending his Condition of Life, it is necessary that he be *social*; that is, that he unite himself to those of his own Species, and in such a Manner regulate his Behaviour towards them, as they may have no fair Reason to do him Harm, but rather incline to promote his Interests, and to secure his Rights and Concerns. This then will appear a |*recte* the?] fundamental Law of Nature, *Every Man ought, as far as in him lies, to promote and preserve a peaceful Sociableness with others.*[18]

This, as we shall see later, is more or less identical to Grotius's theory about the content of the laws of nature. Both Pufendorf and Grotius believed that what was *right* (*honestum*), was so because it was fundamentally *profitable* (*utile*) to an individual in need of protection from his fellow men, and both quoted with approval those passages of Cicero where he associated the right and the profitable (though Cicero did not believe that *utilitas* was logically prior to *honestas*). It was because Pufendorf believed this, that he could also speak of Hobbes with such approval, and bracket his name with Grotius's.

His disagreement with Grotius came over the question of whether a belief that some course of action was profitable (in this general sense) was *in itself* sufficient to induce a belief in an agent that the course of action was morally obligatory. Grotius apparently believed that it was, and that an accurate assessment of social realities was enough to give rise to knowledge of an obligatory moral law. Pufendorf, on the other hand, observed that men can often act quite knowingly against their own interests, and that therefore knowledge of what is in our interests cannot be sufficient to make us believe we are under an *obligation* to perform the actions.

---

[18] Samuel Pufendorf, *The Law of Nature and Nations*, ed. Jean Barbeyrac, trans. Basil Kennet (London, 1749) p. 134.

To make these Dictates of Reason obtain the Power and Dignity of Laws, it
is necessary to call in a much higher Principle to our Assistance. For altho'
the Usefulness and Expediency of them be clearly apparent, yet this bare
Consideration could never bring so strong a Tie on Mens Minds, but that
they would recede from these Rules, whenever a Man was pleas'd either to
neglect his own Advantage, or to pursue it by some different Means, which
he judg'd more proper, and more likely to succeed. Neither can the will of
any Person be so strongly bound by his own bare Resolution, as to hinder
him from acting quite contrary, whenever the Humour takes him.[19]

This 'higher principle' upon which Pufendorf called was the will of
God; it was only because all men believed in a God who had power
over them, that they felt obliged to do something which they might
not otherwise choose to do. His criticism of Grotius (and Hobbes) in
this area is forceful and perceptive. But the crucial point to stress at
the moment is that the criticism did not take him as far away from
Grotius and Hobbes as one might have expected, if one considered
only these foundational matters. Pufendorf believed that we determine what it is that God wills us to do, by considering what is in our
best, long-term *interests*: we know that God wishes us to be preserved,
and therefore we know that we are obliged to do whatever is
necessary for our preservation. We need no beliefs which a rational
and self-controlled atheist could not also possess, in order to determine the content of the laws of nature; and Pufendorf always
emphasised that the content of the laws was the important issue, and
that there was no point to the kind of trivial propositions which his
Lutheran opponents believed to be foundational to a moral theory,
such as 'what is morally right is to be performed'.[20] As Pufendorf
said, the problem was to determine what *was* morally right; and his
answer to this question suggests that the Lutherans who accused
Pufendorf of a kind of Hobbism had seen a genuine and important
feature of his theory.

Having argued that Grotius represented a fundamental break with
all previous theories of natural law, Pufendorf went on to outline the
developments in the subject after 1625. The principal followers of
Grotius, Pufendorf argued, were John Selden and Thomas Hobbes.
Both shared Grotius's basic approach, and in particular his hostility
to scholasticism; but both had grave deficiencies. Selden 'did not
deduce the law of nature from some principle whose force all nations
would recognise', but from a specifically *Jewish* source, albeit one
supposedly promulgated to all mankind, namely the *Praecepta*

[19] *Ibid.*, p. 141.   [20] See his remarks in the *Specimen*, p. 123.

noachidarum.[21] Hobbes tried to construct a mathematical model of the laws of nature, but what he developed was in fact the old Epicurean hypothesis (possibly, Pufendorf conjectured, because his great friend Gassendi had tried to do the same in physics).[22] Nevertheless, he was a man of great intellect, and he had forced his opponents to think very carefully about fundamental features of the law of nature. The last person to figure in Pufendorf's historical sketch was another Englishman, Richard Cumberland, who had published his *De legibus naturae* in the same year as Pufendorf's *De iure naturae et gentium*. Pufendorf recorded his delight at finding that someone else had independently discovered many of the same points (particularly in opposition to Hobbes) which he himself had thought of, and in the second edition of the *De iure naturae et gentium* he incorporated extensive references to Cumberland.[23]

In its broad outlines, Pufendorf's sketch was to go through almost unaltered into the eighteenth-century textbooks. Only one thing needed to be added to this account of modern moral philosophy in order to turn it into precisely the history which Brucker put forward. As we saw, alongside Bacon and Grotius, Brucker put Montaigne and Charron: the modern moral science, in his eyes, began as a response to ethical *scepticism*. Although in some ways this was indeed assumed by Pufendorf, it is not at all explicit in his work; the writer who put it at the centre of the history of morality was the French Protestant philosopher Jean Barbeyrac. At the beginning of the eighteenth century he undertook to place the ideas of the modern natural-law school before as wide a public as possible. His great editions of Grotius and Pufendorf, and their translations into French and English, flooded both Europe and the New World, and represented in themselves virtually an encyclopaedia of modern political thought. To the 1709 edition of his Pufendorf he appended a history of ethics, which was translated into English as *An Historical and Critical Account of the Science of Morality*, and which sets out more or less completely the history which was to be repeated by Brucker. According to Barbeyrac, the writers of antiquity and the Middle Ages all failed to produce an adequate scientific ethics; the Stoics and Cicero (whom Barbeyrac took to be a 'moderate Academic', i.e., sceptic) came nearest, but even they were deficient in a number of crucial respects. Not until Grotius 'broke the ice' after the long domination of Aristotle did a new and truly scientific ethics appear.[24]

---

[21] *Ibid.*, p. 3.   [22] *Ibid.*, p. 12.
[23] *Ibid.*, p. 13.   [24] Pufendorf, *The Law of Nature and Nations*, pp. 63, 67.

But in addition to recapitulating Pufendorf's views about the unity and identity of the new school (Grotius's followers, Barbeyrac said, being Selden, Hobbes, Cumberland, Pufendorf and now Locke), Barbeyrac explained just what Grotius had done that was so significant.

Barbeyrac's *Account* begins with some sections of general philosophical reflection, in which he sought to establish that there could be a demonstrable moral science. He was very clear where the chief objection to this programme lay, and what was wrong with the objection.

Some have, for a long Time, believ'd, and, even at this Day, many do maintain, that Morality is a science very uncertain, and wherein scarce any Thing, beyond Probabilities, is to be found: But it is solely for want of due Examination into the Nature of Things, that this false Notion has prevail'd.[25]

As examples of the objection, he singled out particularly the works of Montaigne and Charron, though he also referred to the views of the sceptics of antiquity (notably Carneades), and to the writings of his own contemporary Pierre Bayle.[26] It was the distinctiveness of its answer to this scepticism which in Barbeyrac's eyes made the *De iure belli ac pacis* the foundational text of the modern natural-law school.

What led Barbeyrac to stress the importance of scepticism as a background for the Grotian moral science was clearly the activity of Bayle, who during the 1680s and 1690s published a wide variety of essays defending Pyrrhonian scepticism. This activity culminated in his famous *Dictionnaire historique et critique* of 1697, in which the articles on the sceptics of antiquity (notably, again, Carneades) are miniature treatises on the desirability of their ideas. Bayle even sought to some extent to appropriate the leaders of the modern natural-law school for his own enterprise – the articles on both Grotius and Hobbes (especially the latter) are full of praise for their subjects, particularly on account of their religious beliefs.[27] By 1709 it seemed to Barbeyrac that scepticism was as flourishing as it had been in the time of Montaigne, and he emphasised accordingly that Grotius and his followers had been explicit and well-judged *opponents* of scepticism.

[25] *Ibid.*, p. 5.
[26] *Ibid.*, pp. 5–8 (Montaigne and Charron), p. 9 (Bayle) and p. 56 (Bayle compared to Carneades).
[27] Pierre Bayle, *The Dictionary Historical and Critical*, ed. P. Des Maiseaux (London, 1734–8), II, pp. 325 ff. (Carneades), III, pp. 241 ff. (Grotius) and 467 ff. (Hobbes).

The obvious question to ask about Barbeyrac's belief that the modern natural-law school developed as a reply to scepticism is, how far was that belief shared by Grotius and Pufendorf themselves? In fact, Grotius in the *Prolegomena* to *De iure belli ac pacis* did signal quite clearly that his main intention was to answer the sceptic. He remarked,

> since it would be a vain Undertaking to treat of Right, if there is really no such thing; it will be necessary, in order to shew the Usefulness of the Work, and to establish it on solid Foundations, to confute here in a few Words so dangerous an Error. And that we may not engage with a Multitude at once, let us assign them an Advocate. And who more proper for this purpose than *Carneades* . . .? This Man having undertaken to dispute against Justice, that kind of it, especially, which is the Subject of this Treatise, found no Argument stronger than this. Laws (says he) were instituted by Men for the sake of Interest; and hence it is that they are different, not only in different Countries, according to the Diversity of their Manners; but often in the same Country, according to the Times. As to that which is called NATURAL RIGHT, it is a mere Chimera.[28]

The use of Carneades as the principal spokesman for the position which Grotius was about to attack was, I think, unprecedented in any work on the laws of nature. The medieval and sixteenth-century scholastics had never put their theories in this kind of context: their intention had always ostensibly been to interpret the ethical theories either of Aristotle or Aquinas, neither of whom saw the refutation of scepticism as their prime task. After Grotius, however, the fragments of Carneades's discussion of justice (which had been embedded in a lost work by Cicero, and had been preserved only in extracts from that work in the Christian father Lactantius)[29] became part of the standard repertoire of modern discussions of natural law. It is fairly clear that the fragments had become far more than curiosities of the history of ancient philosophy through their new association with the sophisticated and comprehensive scepticism of the late-sixteenth-century writers, and that for 'Carneades' one should in effect read 'Montaigne' or 'Charron'.

Grotius's reply to the sceptic was, as Pufendorf perceived, to stress the importance of *self-interest*. To understand the force of this, we have to consider the character of contemporary scepticism. The first point to stress is that for Montaigne and Charron, as for the ancient sceptics, the force of their scepticism in ethical matters came simply from their apprehension of the truth of moral relativism – in

---

[28] Hugo Grotius, *The Rights of War and Peace*, ed. Jean Barbeyrac, trans. anon. (London, 1738), pp. xiv–xv. [29] Lactantius, *The Divine Institutes*.

the most famous passage in Montaigne, 'what truth is that, which these mountains bound, and is a lie in the world beyond?'[30] It thus had a different basis from their scepticism in general epistemological matters, for that rested primarily upon the illusory character of sense experience. It is true that in each case no *criterion* was available with which to distinguish true from false belief, and the sceptic thus had to suspend judgement; but if a *criterion* had become available in the physical sciences, this would have been no remedy for the moral sciences, as no true account of the material world will necessarily resolve fundamental moral disagreement. There was thus an *empirical* basis to the sceptical doubt in the area of morality: it arose from an observation about the beliefs and practices to be found in different human societies, and not from any general considerations about the nature of ethical thinking.

The second point which must be made is that the sceptic did not merely register his disbelief in all scientific propositions. Scepticism (again both in antiquity and sixteenth-century France) underpinned a way of life: the sceptic still had *some* principles to live by. His main goal was a life of *ataraxia* or *apatheia*, free from the disturbance caused by emotions based on beliefs, including beliefs about the virtues and vices. The one thing which he did not exclude from this life was, however, the simple desire for self-preservation, for it was precisely to preserve oneself that the sceptical sage recommended *ataraxia*. The flight from the world which the sceptic advocated had as its objective the preservation of the individual from the emotional and – often – the physical harm consequent upon an engagement in public life. At this point in the writings of the post-Renaissance sceptics (and maybe also in those of Carneades himself), scepticism reached out to hold hands with Stoicism, for the Stoics too had argued that man's primary desire was to preserve himself. They had also argued that principles of justice would be compatible with this, something which Carneades ridiculed in the passage which Grotius quoted, and it is noteworthy that although both Montaigne and Charron exhibited a great respect for and interest in the Stoic arguments, they were unwilling to pick up the Stoic defence of justice.[31]

Grotius's great idea seems to have been that the sceptic could be

---

[30]   Michel de Montaigne, *Essayes*, trans. J. Florio, ed. J. I. M. Stewart (London, n.d.), p. 524.
[31]   See Myles Burnyeat, 'Can the sceptic live his scepticism', in *Doubt and Dogmatism*, ed. Malcolm Schofield, Myles Burnyeat and Jonathan Barnes (Oxford, 1980), pp. 20–53.

answered once the full implications of his acceptance of the principle of self-preservation had been thought out. The argument is in fact set out most clearly in his early work, *De iure praedae* (which he composed in 1604/5, and which remained largely in manuscript), though it is presented in a much more detailed form in *De iure belli ac pacis*. In *De iure praedae* he argued that

since God fashioned creation and willed its existence, every individual part thereof has received from Him certain natural properties whereby that existence may be preserved and each part guided for its own good, in conformity, one might say, with the fundamental law inherent in its origin. From this fact the old poets and philosophers have rightly deduced that love, whose primary force and action are directed to self-interest, is the first principle of the whole natural order. Consequently, Horace should not be censured for saying, in imitation of the Academics [i.e., the Academic sceptics, headed in the second century B.C. by Carneades], that expediency might perhaps be called the mother of justice and equity.[32]

Thus the two primary laws of nature, he asserted, were '*It shall be permissible to defend one's own life and to shun that which threatens to prove injurious*' and '*It shall be permissible to acquire for oneself and to retain those things which are useful for life.*' 'On this point the Stoics, Epicureans and Peripatetics are in complete agreement, and apparently even the Academics have entertained no doubt.'[33]

As the last remark shows, Grotius presented these laws in what would later be regarded as an 'eclectic' manner, as principles which all men would accept, and which all societies would acknowledge. In part, this involved a simple observation of human societies: Grotius's contention was that no society had been or could be found in which *this* moral principle was denied, though many other moral principles, e.g., of the Aristotelian kind, were frequently disregarded. The moral relativist had therefore jumped to too pessimistic a conclusion. Grotius argued the same about the next two laws of nature, which he presented as secondary to the principle of self-preservation, but equally universal – '*Let no one inflict injury upon his fellow*' and '*Let no one seize possession of that which has been taken into the possession of another.*'[34] These bans on *wanton* injury of another human being were also principles which no man or group of men would deny, though they would at the same time concede that injury to another in the cause of self-preservation might be justified (this is the door which led fairly directly to Hobbes). Grotius's explanation of why all these laws were universal was essentially that they were

[32] Hugo Grotius, *De iure praedae commentarius*, I, trans. G. L. Williams (Oxford, 1950), p. 9.   [33] *Ibid.*, pp. 10–11.   [34] *Ibid.*, p. 13.

functionally necessary for social existence: no society could be imagined in which they were systematically flouted. But the persuasiveness of his case came as much from his deployment of empirical evidence about social practices as from this functionalist explanation.

In the *De iure praedae*, this account of the *content* of the laws of nature in terms of self-preservation is associated with what might be called a 'voluntarist' theory of their *form*. Grotius argued that 'What God has shown to be His Will, that is law . . . The act of commanding is a function of power, and primary power over all things pertains to God, in the sense that power over his own handiwork pertains to the artificer and power over inferiors, to their superiors.' He even asserted, in dramatic contrast to what he was to say in *De iure belli ac pacis*, that 'a given thing is just because God wills it, rather than that God wills the thing because it is just'.[35] But, like Pufendorf later, he believed that we can determine what it is that God wills for mankind, not by consulting Scripture or what seems intuitively obvious, but by considering what must be done if a man, made as God has made him, is to be preserved from his fellow men. The *De iure praedae* would in fact have met many of the objections which Pufendorf and Barbeyrac levelled at the *De iure belli ac pacis*; ironically, it remained locked away in the house of the De Groot family, and was not made public until 1864.

However, during the twenty years after he wrote *De iure praedae* Grotius abandoned this theory about the form of the laws of nature, and in *De iure belli ac pacis* produced instead the notorious claim that the laws would bind mankind, 'though we should even grant, what without the greatest Wickedness cannot be granted, that there is no God, or that he takes no Care of human Affairs'. The laws of nature, Grotius now argued, could only be ascribed to God in the sense that 'it was his Pleasure that these Principles should be in us'.[36] Despite this, Grotius's account of the *content* of the laws in 1625 was very close to what it had been twenty years earlier. In Book I he argued that 'the first impression of nature' is 'that Instinct whereby every Animal seeks its own Preservation, and loves its Condition, and whatever tends to maintain it'.[37] This instinct may be governed by rational reflection on the needs of society, but social life itself is to a great extent the product of man's necessity: 'Right Reason, and the Nature of Society, . . . does not prohibit all Manner of Violence, but only that which is repugnant to Society, that is, which invades

[35] *Ibid.*, p. 8. [36] Grotius, *The Rights of War and Peace*, p. xix. [37] *Ibid.*, p. 24.

another's Right: For the Design of Society is, that every one should quietly enjoy his own, with the Help, and by the united Force of the whole Community.'[38] These are the two principles of *De iure praedae*, self-preservation and the ban on *wanton* injury.

In the *Prolegomena* to *De iure belli ac pacis*, it should be said, Grotius did emphasise more than he had done in *De iure praedae* the positive advantages of society and the universal human desire to live with his fellows, and this led him to reverse his judgement on the quotation from Horace he had endorsed in 1604/5; but he did so in a somewhat qualified way. His new position is summed up in the following passage:

> the Saying, not of Carneades only, but of others, *Interest, that Spring of Just and Right* [Horace], if we speak accurately, is not true; for the Mother of Natural Law is human Nature itself, which, though even the Necessity of our Circumstances should not require it, would of itself create in us a mutual Desire of Society: . . . But to the Law of Nature Profit is annexed: For the Author of Nature was pleased, that every Man in particular should be weak of himself, and in Want of many Things necessary for living Commodiously, to the End we might more eagerly affect Society.[39]

The substantial continuity of Grotius's most powerful and original idea (particularly in the body of his text), despite a radical change in his view of the laws' foundations, is a striking illustration of the fact that foundational issues are not the most important ones in this history. What is important is the continued attempt to integrate the laws of nature into a system based on the principle of self-preservation; beyond that, there was scope for a great deal of disagreement (even, as we have just seen, within one person's own intellectual career) about how to interpret the system as a whole, and how to explain the obligatory character of the laws. We could draw a rather strict analogy with contemporary natural science: Galilean physics provided a new and integrated system, but left a substantial opening for philosophical discussion about its metaphysical basis.

If a concern with Carneades, and a commitment to refute what he had said by using the principle of self-preservation, are the *leitmotivs* of the modern natural-law school, then both Pufendorf and Hobbes do indeed amply qualify for membership. Pufendorf devoted two sections of the chapter in which he discussed the general character of the law of nature to a discussion of Carneades's argument that 'there's no such Thing as natural Law, but that all Law first arose from the Convenience and the Profit of particular States', and he

---

[38] *Ibid.*, pp. 25–6.   [39] *Ibid.*, p. xx.

refuted it (as we have seen) by deductions from the principle of self-preservation.[40] Hobbes, of course, thought more deeply about just these issues than any other seventeenth-century philosopher; but he too seems to have had contemporary scepticism largely in mind. A particularly striking example is the well-known passage of *Leviathan* in which he remarked,

The Foole hath sayd in his heart, there is no such thing as Justice; and sometimes also with his tongue; seriously alleaging, that every mans conservation, and contentment, being committed to his own care, there could be no reason, why every man might not do what he thought conduced thereunto: and therefore also to make, or not make; keep, or not keep Covenants, was not against Reason, when it conduced to ones benefit.[41]

This looks very much as if Hobbes had in mind the same observation of Carneades which Grotius also attacked, that 'either there is no justice; or, if there is such a thing, it is the greatest foolishness, since one will harm oneself while consulting the interests of other people' (*aut nullam esse iustitiam; aut, si sit aliqua, summam esse stultitiam, quoniam sibi noceret alienis commodis consulens*).[42] Mersenne in fact recommended Hobbes's *De cive* to Sorbière as the ideal refutation of scepticism.[43] The particular character of the refutation of scepticism in both Pufendorf and Hobbes (and, indeed, in Grotius himself) left them, however, open to the charge that they were sceptics of a kind themselves: for they refuted the sceptic by employing one of his own ideas, that the fundamental principle of human conduct was the desire for self-preservation. Hobbes was continually attacked for endorsing this sceptical proposition, and when Pufendorf's opponents accused him of Hobbism, they often joined this to an accusation of moral scepticism – Friedrich Gesen, for example, alleged that Pufendorf was in fact a new Carneades.[44] Although Barbeyrac may have overstressed the singlemindedness with which his heroes combatted contemporary scepticism, it is clear enough that this was indeed a crucially important element in their enterprise, and that many of their differences from earlier natural-law theories can best be understood in this context. It is also clear that post-Kantian writers have misrepresented their strategy because they have forgotten the original point of their ideas. Grotius and his successors were responding to a straightforward pre-Humean moral

---

[40] Pufendorf, *The Law of Nature and Nations*, p. 125.
[41] Thomas Hobbes, *Leviathan*, ed. C. B. Macpherson (Harmondsworth, 1968), p. 203.   [42] Lactantius, *Opera omnia*, I, ed. S. Brandt (Vienna, 1890), p. 449.
[43] Thomas Hobbes, *De Cive: The Latin Version*, ed. Howard Warrender (Oxford, 1983), p. 86.   [44] Palladini, *Discussioni*, p. 177.

scepticism, which simply pointed to the multiplicity of beliefs and practices around the world, and concluded that there were no common moral beliefs and hence nothing stable upon which to build a universal ethics. Part of their response consisted equally simply in demonstrating that there were actually at least two universal moral beliefs (the right of self-preservation and the ban on wanton injury), and that this minimalist ethics could be used as the basis for a universal moral science. There was therefore a substantial element of descriptive ethical sociology in their works, since that was the battleground chosen by their opponents. When Hume (and also, it should be said, Rousseau, though in a much more allusive fashion) pointed out that no information of *that* kind could possibly be relevant to the construction of a *moral* theory, theirs was a new kind of scepticism, which no earlier writer had had to deal with.

I hope to deal in another context with the eighteenth-century criticisms of the modern moral science; here, my purpose is simply to consider its general character, and its relationship to its predecessors and competitors. In particular, recognising the centrality of the arguments against scepticism for the modern natural lawyers helps us to understand Pufendorf's and Barbeyrac's sense that there was a fundamental division between the ancient or medieval natural-law writers and the modern ones, and it also helps us see the *humanist* roots of the latter. When the particular antisceptical point of the modern school was forgotten, it was easy to see it as merely an extension of the long medieval tradition of natural-law theory, and wholly distinct from the humanist mode of political theorising (in which, it was always clear, the notion of 'natural law' played a very small part). But as we have seen, Pufendorf and his followers believed strongly in an absolute break between the medieval moral philosophy willprove unsatisfactory: no major work of ethics devoted *explicitly* to refuting the sceptic survives from utterly different in their eyes from the genuinely 'modern' writers.

The explanation of this is that if one is principally alert to the problem of moral scepticism, then it is true that both ancient and medieval moral philosophy will prove unsatisfactory: no major work of ethics devoted *explicitly* to refuting the sceptic survives from antiquity (though it is clear that there were some), and medieval natural-law thinking is conspicuous by its lack of awareness that full-blooded moral scepticism was an intellectual possibility. The Ockhamists, who of course exhibited a scepticism about the realist basis for a demonstrative moral science, never denied that such a science was possible. The simple deduction which Montaigne and Charron made from the observed fact of radical moral disagreement, that perhaps there could *be* no universal standard of right and wrong, was something to which men at the beginning of the seventeenth century had to think up their own response.

The men who were most likely to think up such a response were men trained in a humanist manner. Elements of scepticism had been present from the early Renaissance, in the work of people such as Valla, and we have already seen the importance of a detailed knowledge of the ancient sceptical texts for sixteenth-century sceptics. Montaigne simply saw very clearly the implications of many things which earlier humanists had argued. A sensitivity to the force of these ideas, and therefore a desire to confront them in a sympathetic manner, was going to be found at the end of the sixteenth century among humanists themselves rather than among contemporary natural lawyers trained in a scholastic style. The biographies of Grotius or Hobbes are indeed strikingly different from that of Suárez: both the former were brought up largely on the humanist texts, and both displayed all the interests and abilities of the humanist. They each wrote poetry, both in their vernaculars and in Latin; throughout their lives they also wrote history, and retained an interest in literary and textual criticism as well as philosophy. Grotius was of course internationally famous for his precocious humanist talents. While not ignorant of medieval and contemporary scholastic writers, the context in which they employed that knowledge was always shaped largely by their humanist concerns.

This obvious fact about their biographies has not carried much weight with many recent writers (including, I should confess, myself in an earlier work.)[45] This is largely because the modern moral scientists used extensively the terminology of *natural law*, and it is almost a defining characteristic of the humanist political theorist that he did not. It is true that Grotius and his followers broke decisively with the humanist view of politics and ethics as *practical* subjects (in the Aristotelian sense, i.e., not deductive systems, 'sciences' or *epistemes*); their refutation of scepticism allowed them to reinstate the idea that the study of men's actions could be 'scientific', and to this extent they did resemble contemporary scholastics. But the scholastic writer in both the Middle Ages and the sixteenth century believed that it was possible to put Aristotle's ethics, or a similar account of the classical virtues, on a theoretical and scientific

---

[45] Richard Tuck, *Natural Rights Theories* (Cambridge, 1979), p. 176.

foundation, while the modern natural lawyers saw clearly that this was impossible: in their eyes, the sceptical critique of such ethical theories was overwhelming.

The sympathy which these writers retained for many features of humanist and even sceptical moral theories comes out in many important aspects of their work. It is a familiar fact, for example, that the seventeenth-century natural-law writers stressed the distinction between a state of nature and civil society to a degree far beyond any medieval author. This was because they shared the sceptics' sense that most familiar moral beliefs and practices were the product of specific circumstances and histories, and differed from place to place; their history was the history of civil societies. But the minimalist core of universal moral principles was not part of that story, and could be used to describe (speculatively) what life would be like without the superadditions of civility. It could also be used for the same reason to describe relations between different civil societies, the first use to which it was in fact put, in the writings of Grotius.

But perhaps the most important way in which the modern moral science preserved something of the outlook of the late-sixteenth-century sceptical humanist is in the deep *pluralism* inherent in it. The function of the new moral science was not crudely to rebut scepticism but to *transcend* it: to use what the sceptic himself believed as the basis for an anti-sceptical science. Thus the multiplicity of possible beliefs and customs to which the relativist pointed was not to be denied, or treated as evidence for human irrationality, but (in general) to be endorsed and absorbed into the new theory. As Grotius said plainly, 'there are several Ways of Living, some better than others, and every one may chuse what he pleases of all those Sorts'. [46] All the writers in this tradition, including even Hobbes, saw it as part of their duty to defend a relatively pluralist intellectual and aesthetic culture against its enemies – notably the Calvinist and Catholic churches. This aspect of Pufendorf's work was another reason for the hostility levelled at him by the Lutheran clergy.

It would, I think, be impossible to overestimate the importance to these writers of their sense that large areas of life needed defending from fanatics, that is, from people who believed in more extensive universal moral obligations than those contained in the minimalist core. In a way, they all wished to see the world made safe for the sceptic; the irony was that scepticism itself could not show how the world

[46] Grotius, *The Rights of War and Peace*, p. 64.

was to be made safe, for it could not in principle show why the fanatic was *wrong* in holding his moral beliefs and acting upon them, however violently. We can see the character of this ambition clearly if we contrast the fortunes of both scepticism and what we might call 'post-scepticism' in the United Provinces and in France. The fact that the wars of religion had been fought to a stalemate across Europe, and that henceforward politicians in most major European countries were going to have to live with fundamental and irreconcilable ideological divisions within their states, undoubtedly fostered a kind of disengaged and sceptical attitude in the leaders of many states by the beginning of the seventeenth century. 'To know nothing is the surest faith' remarked Jan van Oldenbarnevelt, Advocate-General of the United Provinces and the patron of the young Grotius; 'in matters of state the weakest are always wrong' observed Cardinal Richelieu of France, ironically enough to Grotius *à propos* of the fall and execution of Oldenbarnevelt.[47] Richelieu helped the so-called *libertins érudits* and contributed to the sceptical culture which was so prominent in seventeenth-century France; there, the power of the state protected such ideas and to some extent even based itself upon them. In the United Provinces, on the other hand, the execution of Oldenbarnevelt and the exile of Grotius were dramatic illustrations of the fact that disengaged and pluralist politicians were themselves vulnerable to the attacks of fanatics. It is no accident that in France (as Professor Keohane has shown) the kind of post-sceptical moral science I have been discussing hardly developed;[48] it was Holland and England above all where it was invented, two countries where in the first half of the seventeenth century the power of the state was threatened or broken by religious dogmatists. Nor is it an accident that so many of these modern natural-law writers turned to a powerful and – in our terms – illiberal state to protect intellectual freedoms from mistaken or dogmatic philosophers arrayed in churches. Pufendorf too fits into this picture, for one of his principal concerns apart from his natural jurisprudence was an analysis of the German constitution in the wake of the destructive religious wars of the mid-century, in which he pleaded for strong and effective states in Germany to prevent such a catastrophe being repeated.

This deeper understanding of the humanist roots of the modern

---

[47] Jan den Tex, *Oldenbarnevelt*, I (Cambridge, 1973), p. 7; Grotius, *Briefwisseling*, II, ed. P.C. Molhuysen (The Hague, 1936), p. 448.
[48] Nannerl Keohane, *Philosophy and the State in France* (Princeton, 1980), p. 122.

moral science is merely one example of the kind of insight which is available to us once the post-Kantian history of morality is replaced with the pre-Kantian one. The moral theories of the late-seventeenth- and eighteenth-century natural lawyers constituted in many ways the most important language of politics and ethics in Europe, influential over a huge area and in a wide variety of disciplines. Their essential unity has been fractured and their character misunderstood for the last two centuries; but if we allow ourselves to be guided by the 'history of morality' which they themselves inspired, we can recover a truer sense of what they represented. Not the least important consequence of this is then that we can put into a proper perspective the invention at the end of the eighteenth century of the political and ethical theories by which in one way or another we all still live.

PART II

A version of the following essay on More's *Utopia* was delivered as a lecture at the Warburg Institute on 18 June 1986 in memory of Charles Schmitt (1933–86) and in honour of his contributions to Renaissance studies.

6

◁ ═══════════════════════════════════════ ▷

Sir Thomas More's *Utopia* and
the language of Renaissance humanism

QUENTIN SKINNER

Almost everything about More's *Utopia* is debatable, but at least the general subject-matter of the book is not in doubt. More announces his theme on the title page, which reads: *De optimo reipublicae statu deque nova insula Utopia.*[1] His concern, that is, is not merely or even primarily with the new island of Utopia; it is with 'the best state of a commonwealth'.

To say that this is More's concern is at once to raise what has always been seen as the main interpretative puzzle about his book. Does he intend us to take the description of Utopia in Book II as an account of a commonwealth in its best state? Are we intended to share and ratify the almost unbounded enthusiasm that Raphael Hythloday, the traveller to Utopia, displays for that island and its way of life?

Until recently More's interpreters tended to answer in the affirmative. One theory has been that More aimed to picture the best state that reason can hope to establish in the absence of revelation.[2] Another suggestion has been that he not only sought to portray a perfectly virtuous commonwealth, but wished at the same time to convey that, in spite of their heathenism, the Utopians are more truly and genuinely Christian than the nominally Christian states of western Europe.[3] While disagreeing on the extent to which More

---

[1]   Thomas More, 'Utopia', in *The Complete Works of St. Thomas More*, IV, ed. E. Surtz and J. H. Hexter (London, 1965), p. cxcv.

[2]   This interpretation was originally propounded in R. W. Chambers, *Thomas More* (London, 1935) and has since been adopted by a considerable number of scholars. For a list, see the bibliography in Q. Skinner, *The Foundations of Modern Political Thought*, I: *The Renaissance* (Cambridge, 1978), p. 257n.

[3]   This is J. H. Hexter's thesis, originally put forward in *More's 'Utopia': The Biography of an Idea* (New York, 1952), p. 57 and fully developed in the Introduction to Thomas More, *Utopia*, in *Complete Works*, IV, pp. lxviii–lxxvi. See also Q. Skinner, 'More's Utopia', *Past and Present*, XXXVIII (1967), 153–68 for a discussion, and Skinner, *Foundations of Modern Political Thought*, I, pp. 255–62 for a broad endorsement.

holds up Utopia as an ideal, both schools of thought accept that Utopia must in some sense be regarded as an ideal commonwealth.

Of late, however, the best scholarship on *Utopia* has instead laid all its emphasis on the doubts and equivocations in More's text. Some commentators have stressed the inherently ambiguous character of the dialogue form that More chooses to employ;[4] others have underlined the points at which he seems to criticise his own analysis of the 'best state',[5] and even to treat it as a futile theory which is doomed to 'get nowhere'.[6] From several different perspectives, scholars have thus converged on the suggestion that (as Bradshaw puts it) More must be taken to be expressing 'serious reservations about the ideal system' which Hythloday describes.[7] More's final aim (in Allen's words) must have been to leave us 'with an ambivalent and puzzled view' about Utopian life as a whole.[8]

There can be no doubt that this new approach has added significantly to our understanding of More's text, especially by insisting on the implications of the fact that the figure of More in the dialogue disagrees with Hythloday at several important points.[9] Nevertheless, the new orthodoxy seems to me to embody an unacceptable view of More's basic purposes. I shall accordingly try in what follows to restate the case for saying that, for all the ironies and ambiguities in More's text, his main aim was to challenge his readers at least to consider seriously whether Utopia may not represent the best state of a commonwealth.

[4] See especially D. M. Bevington, 'The dialogue in *Utopia*: two sides to the question', *Studies in Philology*, LVIII (1961), 496–509; E. Surtz, Introduction to Thomas More, *Utopia*, in *Complete Works*, IV, pp. cxxxiv–cxlvii. For a discussion of the problems posed by More's use of the dialogue form, see also G. M. Logan, *The Meaning of More's 'Utopia'* (Princeton, 1983), esp. pp. 121–3 and references.

[5] Logan, *ibid.*, even goes so far as to claim that *Utopia* is less a discussion of More's views about the best state than a critical analysis of the classical and Renaissance literature on that theme. See especially pp. 257–62 for a summary of his case.

[6] For this phrase, see D. Fenlon, 'England and Europe: *Utopia* and its aftermath', *Transactions of the Royal Historical Society*, XXV (1975), 115–35, at p. 124.

[7] B. Bradshaw, 'More on Utopia', *The Historical Journal*, XXIV (1981), 1–27, p. 25. I must emphasise, however, that although I disagree with much of what Bradshaw says, I am deeply indebted to his article. It seems to me a brilliant contribution, and has forced me to reconsider my own interpretation of More's text at several crucial points.

[8] See W. S. Allen, 'The tone of More's farewell to *Utopia*: a reply to J. H. Hexter', *Moreana*, XIII (1976), 108–18, p. 118.

[9] R. S. Sylvester, 'Si Hythlodaeo credimus: vision and revision in Thomas More's *Utopia*', *Soundings*, LI (1968), pp. 272–89, especially emphasises this point. See also Logan, *Meaning of More's 'Utopia'*, pp. 4–6 and references.

Otium and *Negotium*

More's handling of the theme of the *optimus status reipublicae* undoubtedly contains many unusual and puzzling elements. But it is
important to note at the outset that there was nothing unusual about
More's decision to consider that particular theme. More's text is
sometimes approached as if he introduced a completely new topic
into Renaissance political thought.[10] But in fact the question of what
constitutes the best state of a commonwealth was a standard subject
of debate throughout the era of the Renaissance. We find the question being raised by a number of scholastic political philosophers in
the wake of Aristotle's discussion in the *Politics*.[11] And we find the
same question being raised, and the same phraseology used, by an
even wider range of so-called 'humanist' political writers – that is, by
writers whose primary intellectual allegiances were owed to the
studia humanitatis, and hence to the moral and political philosophy of
Rome rather than Greece.[12]

This in turn suggests a way of approaching the complexities of
More's text. If *Utopia* is an instance of a familiar genre of Renaissance
political theory, it may be best to begin not with More's text itself
but rather with some attempt to indicate the assumptions and conventions characteristic of the genre as a whole.[13] Beginning in this

[10] See for example J. C. Davis, *Utopia and the Ideal Society* (Cambridge, 1981), pp. 43, 61
and Bradshaw, 'More on Utopia', p. 18.
[11] For a scholastic discussion of the fruits of different forms of government as either
optimi or *pessimi*, see for example Marsilius of Padua, *Defensor pacis*, ed. C. W. Previté-
Orton (Cambridge, 1928), I.1.2 and I.1.4, pp. 2–3.
[12] Among the most influential Roman political writers, Seneca uses the phrase in *De
beneficiis*, where he tells us (II.20.2) that a city is in its best state under the rule of a
just king ('optimus civitatis status sub rege iusto sit'). Cicero repeatedly uses the
phrase, mentioning in his *Tusculan Disputations* (II.11.27) that Plato inquired into
the question of the best state of a commonwealth ('optimum rei publicae statum
exquireret') and adding in *De finibus* (V.4.11) that Aristotle also asked about it ('qui
esset optimus rei publicae status'). Drawing on such sources, the humanist political
writers of *Quattrocento* Italy frequently employed the same phrase as well as debating the same general theme. Finally, the Erasmian humanists also speak in the same
terms. Erasmus himself compares the *pessimus* with the *optimus status reipublicae* in his
Institutio Christiani principis (see Desiderius Erasmus, *Institutio Christiani principis*, ed.
O. Herding in *Opera Omnia*, pt IV, vol. I (Amsterdam, 1974), pp. 95–219, at pp. 162,
194); Starkey examines the question at considerable length in his *Dialogue* (see
T. Starkey, *A Dialogue between Reginald Pole & Thomas Lupset*, ed. K. M. Burton
(Cambridge, 1948), especially the summary at p. 63).
[13] For the contrasting suggestion that More's purposes are fully revealed 'by the
guidance which he provides for the reader in the text itself', see Bradshaw, 'More
on Utopia', p. 18.

way, we may eventually be able to gain some sense of More's own basic purposes. For we may be able to see how far he is accepting and reiterating common assumptions, or perhaps rephrasing and reworking them, or perhaps criticising and repudiating them altogether in order to attain a new perspective on a familiar theme.[14] It is this approach which I shall now attempt to put to work.

I

Among political theorists of the Renaissance, whether scholastic or humanist in allegiance, there was little debate about what constitutes the *optimus status reipublicae*. A state will be in its best state, it was widely agreed, if and only if two claims can appropriately be made about it. One is that its laws are just, and thereby serve to promote the common good of its citizens. The other is that its citizens are in consequence able to pursue their own happiness, 'living and living well' in the manner most befitting the nature and dignity of man.[15]

As soon as writers of this period turn, however, to ask how these conditions can be brought about, large differences of opinion begin to emerge. Among these, the most basic concerned the form of government that needs to be set up if a commonwealth is to have any chance of attaining and remaining in its best state. One widely held belief was that the only sure method is to assign all the affairs of the *res publica* to a wise guardian, a *Pater patriae*. His duty is to take upon himself all the burdens of the *vita activa*, leaving everyone else free to pursue their own higher purposes and so attain their happiness. This was the view of the earliest generation of self-styled humanists, including Petrarch himself in his last political testament,[16] and of such younger contemporaries as Pier Paolo Vergerio and Giovanni da Ravenna, both of whom lived and wrote – as did Petrarch in the closing years of his life – under the patronage of the Carrara lords of Padua in the final decades of the fourteenth century.[17]

---

[14] For a general defence of this approach, see Q. Skinner, 'Some problems in the analysis of political thought and action', *Political Theory*, II (1974), 277–303.

[15] This was the standard scholastic viewpoint. See for example Marsilius of Padua on the need for the law to promote the *commune conferens*, thereby allowing each citizen *vivere et bene vivere*, in *Defensor pacis*, I, esp. chs. 4 and 5, pp. 11–21. The same assumptions recur among the Erasmian humanists of More's own day. See for example Starkey, *Dialogue*, esp. pp. 61–65. This was also More's own viewpoint in *Utopia*. See More, *Complete Works*, IV, esp. pp. 236, 238, 240.

[16] This was composed in the form of a letter to Francesco da Carrara in 1373. See Francesco Petrarcha, *Opera omnia* (Basel, 1554), pp. 419–35.

[17] For biographical and bibliographical details on Vergerio, see D. Robey 'P. P.

It was the belief of all these writers that, as Giovanni expresses it, 'the government of a single individual is always to be preferred, even when the person in question is only a moderately good man'.[18] One of his grounds for this belief is that 'where one person is in complete control, everyone else is able to pursue his own affairs in an untroubled way, and remains entirely free from public business'.[19] One reason for supposing this to be a highly desirable state of affairs is that a life of *otium*, of freedom from public duty, is indispensable for the achievement of our highest ends and hence our greatest happiness.[20] But a further reason derives from the fact that the alternative, the life of *negotium* as lived by courtiers, public servants and advisers to princes, is said to be inherently corrupt. 'No life is more miserable, more uncertain, more self-deceiving.'[21] Flattery takes the place of truth, while approval is constantly sought for the most disgraceful policies, including violations of peace and betrayals of trust.[22] The moral is said to be obvious: 'if you wish to remain pious, just, a respecter of truthfulness and innocence, remove yourself from the life of the court'.[23]

These commitments remained an enduring element in humanist political theory, and became increasingly popular after Ficino's translations in the 1480s made Plato's political doctrines widely available for the first time. We find the ideal of the philosopher–king being espoused even by a number of Florentine humanists in this period.[24] The connected suggestion that, under any less perfect system, the philosopher must remain aloof from politics recurs even more prominently among northern humanists in the opening decades of the sixteenth century.

Vergerio the Elder: republicanism and civic values in the work of an early humanist', *Past and Present*, LVIII (1973), 3–37, esp. pp. 8–9, 20–1; on Giovanni see B. J. Kohl, Introduction to Giovanni di Conversino da Ravenna, *Dragmalogia de eligibili vite genere*, trans. H. L. Eaker (Lewisburg, 1980), pp. 13–46, at pp. 22–9.

[18] Giovanni da Ravenna, *Dragmalogia*, p. 106: 'Unius ... vel mediocriter boni eligibilius esse regimen arbitror.'

[19] *Ibid.*, p. 132: 'Nam ubi unus dominatur, suo quisque negotio prorsus publici securus vacat.'

[20] See especially the discussion in Giovanni da Ravenna, *Dragmalogia*, pp. 138–40.

[21] *Ibid.*, p. 166: 'nulla alia miserior, incertior ... magis suique prorsus ignara'.

[22] See *ibid.*, esp. pp. 84–8, 94–6.

[23] *Ibid.*, p. 96: 'Exeat aula qui vult esse pius, etiam qui iustus, qui vericola, qui innocens.'

[24] See for example the discussion in Bartolomeo Scala, 'De legibus et iudiciis', ed. L. Borghi, *Bibliofilia*, XLII (1940), 256–82, which opens (p. 259) with an invocation of Cosimo de' Medici as 'pater patriae noster sapientissimus civis'. For a discussion of Scala's Platonism, see A. Brown, *Bartolomeo Scala, 1430–1497, Chancellor of Florence* (Princeton, 1979), esp. pp. 310–16.

Within More's own intellectual circle, for example, we find the claim that a princely regime is always to be preferred, together with the claim that a life of *otium* is best for everyone else, both being eloquently defended. Erasmus's *Institutio principis christiani*, published in the same year as More's *Utopia*, is founded on the assumption that the only means to attain the *optimus status reipublicae* is to ensure 'that there is a prince whom everyone obeys, that the prince obeys the laws and that the laws answer to our ideals of *honestas* and equity'.[25] Similarly, More's younger contemporary, Thomas Starkey, writing his *Dialogue* between Pole and Lupset in the early 1530s, begins by presenting the related ideal of *otium* as the outlook to be expected from a fashionable humanist intellectual trained in Italy. Pole opens the discussion by announcing that he desires no part in public life. Instead he wishes to imitate 'the old and antique philosophers', who 'forsook the meddling with matters of common weals, and applied themselves to the secret studies and searching of nature'.[26] He offers two main reasons for his preference, both very familiar by this stage in the development of humanist culture. One is that the life of *negotium* inhibits us from attaining our highest ends and thereby cheats us of our fullest happiness. This is because 'the perfection of man resteth in the mind and in the chief and purest part thereof', and in consequence requires a life dedicated to *otium* and the pursuit of truth.[27] The other reason 'which hath caused many great, wise and politic men to abhor from common weals'[28] is that the life of *negotium* forces the philosopher, whose concern is with truth, into a world of compromise, hypocrisy and lies. It leaves the wise man 'nothing obtaining but only to be corrupt with like opinions as they be which meddle therewith' and is therefore to be shunned in the same way that a good man shuns the company of thieves.[29]

II

This strand of humanism was always opposed, however, by a school of thought which argued that it can never be safe or even just to entrust our happiness to others. The exponents of this position generally concluded, by contrast, that the only possible means of bringing about the *optimus status reipublicae* must be to train an active

[25] Erasmus, *Institutio Christiani principis*, p. 194: '[felicissimus est status] cum principi paretur ab omnibus atque ipse princeps paret legibus, leges autem ad archetypum aequi et honesti respondent'.
[26] Starkey, *Dialogue*, p. 23.   [27] *Ibid.*   [28] *Ibid.*, p. 36.   [29] *Ibid.*, p. 37.

citizenry and cleave to a fully participative system of republican government.

This so-called 'civic' humanism has been associated in particular with the great city-republics of Renaissance Italy, and above all with *Quattrocento* Florence.[30] But the movement was of course of much broader significance than this, and even penetrated the princely courts of northern Europe in the early years of the sixteenth century. For example, while Starkey's *Dialogue* opens with Pole's Platonist defence of *otium*, the figure of Lupset quickly replies that if anyone allows himself to be 'drawn by the sweetness of his studies' away from 'the cure of the common weal', then 'he doth manifest wrong to his country and friends, and is plain unjust and full if iniquity, as he that regardeth not his office and duty, to the which above all he is most bounden by nature'.[31]

Nor of course was this 'civic' scale of values simply a product of the Renaissance. The ideals in question, as well as the vocabulary used for expressing them, were taken more or less wholesale from the last great defenders of the Roman republic – from Livy, Sallust and above all from Cicero, whose *De officiis* furnished virtually the whole framework for civic humanist discussions of the active life.

The *De officiis* had taught in the first place that the highest aim of a good man must be to embrace the four cardinal virtues, since these are the qualities needed for the effective performance of our duties.[32] To possess these qualities is to be *honestus*, Cicero's general and most honorific term for someone who succeeds in cultivating the virtues and performing the *officia* they prescribe.[33] For Cicero, however, it was also a crucial principle that 'all the praise of *virtus* derives from action'.[34] From this he inferred that our highest earthly duty must always be to place our talents in the service of our community.[35] We must learn to recognise that 'every duty which tends to preserve society and uphold the unity of men must be given preference over any duty to forward knowledge and science'.[36] Acting on this insight, we must train ourselves to discharge with *industria* all the *officia* of war and peace.[37] We must labour for our *res publica* in everything that conduces to *honestas* and a well-ordered life.[38] We must, in short,

[30] See especially H. Baron, *The Crisis of the Early Italian Renaissance* (Princeton, 1966), esp. pp. 443–62 and J. G. A. Pocock, *The Machiavellian Moment* (Princeton, 1975), esp. pp. 83–330.   [31] Starkey, *Dialogue*, p. 22.
[32] Cicero, *De officiis*, I.4.14 to I.5.17.   [33] *Ibid.*, I.18.61.
[34] *Ibid.*, I.6.19: 'Virtutis enim laus omnis in actione consistit.'   [35] *Ibid.*, I.43.153.
[36] *Ibid.*, I.44.158: 'omne officium, quod ad coniunctionem hominum et ad societatem tuendam valet, anteponendum est illi officio, quod cognitione et scientia continetur'.   [37] *Ibid.*, I.34.122.   [38] *Ibid.*, I.34.124.

make it our principal task 'to respect, defend and preserve concord and unity within the whole community of men'.[39]

But what of the Platonist objection that this will cheat us of happiness, since it will carry us away from the life of *otium*, the way of life best suited to the nature and dignity of man? Cicero directly addresses himself to this central contention of Greek ethics in Book I of the *De officiis*, and offers an answer that was later to be endlessly cited by civic humanists of the Renaissance.

He admits that 'the noblest and greatest philosophers' have always 'withdrawn themselves from public affairs'.[40] They have held that, if you are a sage, it is essential 'that you should be able to live as you wish' (*sic vivere, ut velis*).[41] But he firmly repudiates this scale of priorities. Near the start of his discussion he roundly declares that 'it is contrary to one's duty to permit oneself to be drawn away by one's studies from taking an active part in public life'.[42] And later he reiterates the same point in far more positive terms. The life of *negotium* is not merely of more importance than that of *otium*, but also calls for greater abilities.[43] As a result it is not only 'more fruitful' as a way of life; it is also capable of bringing us greater fulfilment and happiness.[44] 'So it appears that what Plato says about philosophers is not really adequate. Although they secure one kind of justice, in that they do no positive harm, in another way they fail; for their studies prevent them from living an active life, so causing them to abandon those whom they ought to defend.'[45]

What of the further objection that the life of *negotium* will degrade the philosopher, since he will be obliged, in an imperfect world, to abandon the cause of truth in the name of playing a part and accommodating to the times? Again Cicero has a direct answer, and again it was endlessly echoed by civic humanists of the Renaissance.

The truly wise man, Cicero retorts, is someone who recognises that all the world's a stage. 'Actors select for themselves not the best plays, but those in which they are best able to accommodate their talents.'[46] The relevance of the image is that 'if a player looks to this

---

[39] *Ibid.*, I.41.149: 'communem totius generis hominum conciliationem et consociationem colere, tueri, servare debemus'.

[40] *Ibid.*, I.20.69: 'a negotiis publicis se removerint ... nobilissimi philosophi'.

[41] *Ibid.*, I.20.69.

[42] *Ibid.*, I.6.19: 'studio a rebus gerendis abduci contra officium est'.

[43] *Ibid.*, I.26.92.   [44] *Ibid.*, I.22.74–8; I.43.153 to I.45.160.

[45] *Ibid.*, I.9.28: 'Itaque videndum est, ne non satis id, quod apud Platonem est in philosophos dictum ... Nam alterum [iustitiae genus] assequuntur, ut inferenda ne cui noceant iniuria, in alterum incidunt; discendi enim studio impediti, quos tueri debent, deserunt.'

[46] *Ibid.*, I.31.114: 'Illi [scaenici] enim non optimas, sed sibi accommodatissimas fabulas eligunt.'

consideration in selecting his roles, should not a wise man look to the same consideration in his entire way of life?'[47] Surely we must recognise that 'necessity will sometimes thrust roles upon us which we do not in the least feel to be suitable'.[48] But we must recognise at the same time that our duty in such a situation is to do the best we can, 'serving with as little indecorousness as can be mustered' in the adverse circumstances.[49]

III

These debates about the form of *regimen* best suited to bringing about the *optimus status reipublicae* provide us, I suggest, with a context for understanding some at least of the complexities of More's text. In particular, they help us to make sense of what he is doing in Book I, the dialogue between Hythloday and the figure of More himself. We can now hope to recognise some of what is at stake in their argument: what orthodoxy More is questioning, what response he is offering, what exact position on the spectrum of political debate he is seeking to defend.

Like his younger contemporary Thomas Starkey, More begins by allowing a fashionably Platonist commitment to be fully stated. This is done through the figure of Hythloday. When we first encounter him, we are told that he is no ordinary traveller; rather he is a voyager in the manner of Plato, a man in search of the truth about political life.[50] After this introduction, the next fact we learn about him is that he adopts an unequivocal stance on what we have seen to be one of the major topics of debate in Renaissance moral and political philosophy: whether the truth about political life is more readily to be gleaned from Greek or from Roman sources. Hythloday 'is by no means ignorant of the Latin language', we are told, 'but he is exceptionally learned in Greek, which he has studied with far greater attention than Latin. This is because he has devoted himself completely to philosophy, and in Latin has found nothing of the least significance in that subject except for some bits of Seneca and Cicero.'[51]

---

[47] *Ibid.*, I.31.114: 'Ergo histrio hoc videbit in scaena, non videbit sapiens vir in vita?'

[48] *Ibid.*, I.31.114: 'aliquando necessitas nos ad ea detruserit, quae nostri ingenii non erunt'.

[49] *Ibid.*, I.31.114: 'ut ea . . . at quam minime indecore facere possimus'.

[50] More, *Complete Works*, IV, p. 48. This point and its significance are very well brought out in Bradshaw, 'More on Utopia', pp. 21–2.

[51] More, *Complete Works*, IV, pp. 48–50: '& latinae linguae non indoctus, & graecae

Hythloday then begins to recount what he has learnt on his
travels, at which point his interlocutors urge him to place his wisdom
at the disposal of the public by entering the service of a king.[52]
Hythloday responds in precisely the tones which, as we have seen,
Cicero had particularly associated with the admirers of Platonic
philosophy. According to Cicero, the view adopted by that greatest
of all philosophers had been that, if you are a sage, you must seek
your happiness by living as you please – *vivere, ut velis*. Hythloday
completely agrees. 'I live as I please' (*vivo ut volo*), he replies, and in
consequence live more happily (*felicior*) than a life of public service
would ever permit.[53]

When the figure of More presses him, he later offers a further–and
again a purely Platonist – reason for refusing to enter public life.
Being a philosopher, he says, 'I wish to speak the truth.'[54] If I were to
become a courtier, 'I should instead have to approve openly of the
worst possible decisions and endorse the most disgraceful decrees'.[55]
The invariable outcome of such a way of life, he insists, is that 'rather
than being able to do any good, you find yourself among colleagues
who are easily able to corrupt even the best of men before reforming
themselves'.[56] Plato was right, he concludes: he showed us 'why wise
men are right to take no part in public affairs'.[57]

Having allowed these standard arguments in favour of *otium* to be
fully laid out, however, the figure of More in the dialogue then
attacks them point by point. He does so, moreover, not merely from
the general perspective of a Ciceronian civic humanist, but in precisely the vocabulary which, as we have seen, Cicero had originally
put into currency in his defence of the active life.[58]

More first assures Hythloday that 'if only you could induce yourself not to shun the courts of princes, you would be able to do the
greatest good for the commonwealth by means of your advice'.[59] To

doctissimus (cuius ideo studiosior quam Romanae fuit, quoniam totum se addix-
    erat philosophiae: qua in re nihil quod alicuius momenti sit, praeter Senecae
    quaedam, ac Ciceronis extare latine cognovit)'. We later learn that the Utopians
    agree with these judgements: see p. 180.   [52] More, *Complete Works*, IV, p. 54.
[53] *Ibid.*, pp. 54, 56.   [54] *Ibid.*, p. 100: 'vera loqui volo'.
[55] *Ibid.*, p. 102: 'approbanda sunt aperte pessima consilia, & decretis pestilentissimis
    subscribendum est'.
[56] *Ibid.*, p. 102: 'in quo prodesse quicquam possis, in eos delatus collegas, qui vel
    optimum virum facilius corruperint, quam ipsi corrigantur'.
[57] *Ibid.*, p. 102: 'cur merito sapientes abstineant a capessenda Republica'.
[58] It is perhaps worth underlining the nature of the claim I am making at this stage,
    especially in view of the comments in Logan, *Meaning of More's 'Utopia'*, p. 84n on
    Skinner, 'More's *Utopia*'. I am claiming only that the argument presented by the
    figure of More in the dialogue is also to be found in Cicero's *De officiis* – and is also to
    be found, of course, in the writings of Cicero's numberless imitators and disciples. I
    am claiming, in short, that by More's time the argument had become part of the

this he adds in sterner tones – echoing the *De officiis* almost word for word – that 'there is in fact no greater duty than this one incumbent upon you as a good man'.[60] The Platonist objection that such a life cheats us of happiness is met with the lie direct. A life of public service 'not only constitutes the means by which you can help people both as private individuals and as members of the community, but is also the means to secure your own greater happiness'.[61] Finally, the Platonist fear that this will betray the cause of truth by forcing the philosopher to accommodate to the times is met with a strong rebuke, one that again echoes the sentiments and even the imagery of the *De officiis* almost word for word.[62] All that this betrays, More retorts, is a kind of scholasticism, whereas a wise man knows 'that there is another and more practical kind of philosophy, one that understands its place on the stage, accommodates itself to whatever play is already in hand, and seeks to discharge whatever roles are assigned to it as decorously as possible'[63] The same considerations, he goes on, 'apply equally in the case of the commonwealth and in the matter of giving advice to princes. Even if you cannot pull out evil opinions by the roots, even if you cannot manage to reform well-entrenched vices according to your own beliefs, you must never on that account desert the cause of the commonwealth.'[64]

common intellectual currency of humanist debate. I am not claiming that More took the argument directly from Cicero, or indeed from any particular source. I am not in the least interested in whether Cicero did or did not 'directly influence' More, a question that seems to me neither worth raising nor capable of being convincingly answered one way or the other.

[59] More, *Complete Works*, IV, p. 86: 'si animum inducas tuum, uti ne ab aulis principum abhorreas, in publicum posse te tuis consiliis plurimum boni conferre'.

[60] *Ibid.*, p. 86: 'quare nihil magis incumbit tuo, hoc est boni viri, officio'.

[61] *Ibid.*, p. 54: 'eam tamen ipsam esse viam, qua non aliis modo & privatim, & publice possis conducere, sed tuam quoque ipsius conditionem reddere feliciorem'. It seems a serious misunderstanding of the theory More is presenting to translate the last word (as in *Complete Works*, IV, p. 55) as 'more prosperous'. (Where More wishes to speak of living prosperously (as he does at p. 102, for example) he uses the term *prospere*.)

[62] Other humanists who also echoed Cicero's image of the world as a stage included Erasmus. See Desiderius Erasmus, *Adagia* (Basel, 1551), p. 54: Adage XCI, 'Servire scenae' opens by quoting Cicero on the need to accommodate to the times ('M. Tullius servire scenae dixit, pro eo quod est servire tempori, & rebus praesentibus sese accommodare'). Surtz makes this point in his Commentary on *Utopia* in *Complete Works*, IV, pp. 255–570, p. 372) but without mentioning the *De officiis* in this connection.

[63] More, *Complete Works*, IV, p. 98: 'est alia philosophia civilior, quae suam novit scenam, eique sese accommodans, in ea fabula quae in manibus est, suas partes concinne & cum decoro tutatur'.

[64] *Ibid.*, p. 98: 'Sic est in Republica sic in consultationibus principum. Si radicitus evelli non possint opiniones pravae, nec receptis usu vitiis mederi queas, ex animi tui sententia, non ideo tamen deserenda Respublica est.'

There are, I think, two morals to be drawn from this first part of the story. The first is that the labels 'humanist' and even 'Christian humanist' have come to be applied too loosely to More's text even in some of the best recent scholarship.[65] More's stance in the opening Book of *Utopia* is undoubtedly that of a humanist, and includes some explicit criticism of scholastic philosophy. But we cannot simply speak of Hythloday as 'the ideal type of Christian humanist';[66] nor can we say that, in defending the importance of counselling princes, More's position is 'in all respects the orthodox humanist one'.[67] The question whether philosophers ought to counsel princes was a subject of intense debate among Christian humanists; no specific answer to the question can properly be called orthodox. If we are to speak more precisely, we must recognise that what More is doing in Book I is reviving one particular set of humanist beliefs – those of a 'civic' or Ciceronian humanism – and sharply opposing them to a more fashionable and broadly Platonist outlook which was threatening to undermine the element of political commitment in the humanism of More's own time. More is restating the case for a humanist ideal to which the courts of northern Europe were proving increasingly inhospitable: the ideal of civic self-government, based on an active and politically educated citizenship.

The other moral suggested by this first part of the story concerns the relationship which has often been noted between Book I of *Utopia* and More's own personal circumstances at the time of writing it. In 1515, the year when *Utopia* was conceived, More was employed on an embassy to Flanders; in 1516, the year of its publication, he was first offered a pension by Henry VIII; in the course of 1518, after much apparent hesitation, he accepted a place on the privy council and embarked on his career at court.[68] The arguments about *otium* and *negotium* in Book I have often been seen as a dramatisation of the 'moral tension' induced by the 'temptation' to give up the ideals of humanism embodied in the figure of Hythloday in favour of just such a worldly life.[69]

---

[65] After Hexter's fundamental contribution, it no longer seems necessary to stress that *Utopia* is, of course, basically a work of Christian humanism. But it still seems to me too loose-fitting to speak of it as a work of Christian humanism *tout court*, as even the best recent discussions are content to do. See for example Bradshaw, 'More on Utopia', esp. p. 23 and Logan, *Meaning of More's 'Utopia'*, esp. pp. 235, 254.

[66] As Hexter does. See Introduction to *Complete Works*, IV, p. xcii.

[67] As Logan does. See *Meaning of More's 'Utopia'*, p. 41.

[68] See R. W. Chambers, *Thomas More* (London, 1935), pp. 111–14, 144–6, 162–3.

[69] This is how Hexter, for example, puts the point. See Introduction to *Complete Works*, IV, pp. lxxxiv, xci.

It is arguable, however, that this is to misunderstand the nature of More's humanist allegiances. So far from viewing the choice of a public career as a temptation, the figure of More in the dialogue clearly regards it, in good Ciceronian style, as the one means of fulfilling the highest *officium* of a true humanist philosopher. If we are to relate this first half of *Utopia* to More's own life, my suggestion is that More should not be seen as expressing doubts about the decision he was himself in the process of making; he should rather be seen as offering a justification for that decision as the outcome of a true understanding of the proper relationship between philosophy and public life.[70]

Vera nobilitas

I now turn to a second debate among Renaissance political theorists about the *optimus status reipublicae*. This arose within the ranks of those who agreed that the best state can only be attained if we live as active citizens within a self-governing commonwealth. The further question they raised concerns the range of attributes that citizens need to possess if they are to discharge their civic *officia* to the best effect. To phrase it in the form in which it was habitually discussed, the question is about the qualities that make a citizen best fitted to serve the common good, and in consequence most deserving of honour, esteem and praise. Or, to put it in the precise vocabulary the Renaissance writers liked to use, the question is about the qualities that go to make a truly noble citizen, a citizen of *vera nobilitas* whose conduct is worthy of honour, esteem and praise.

I

The humanists inherited an unambiguous answer to these questions from scholastic and ultimately Aristotelian sources. It became a favourite literary tactic of theirs to dramatise their doubts about this intellectual inheritance by way of writing dialogues about the concept of *vera nobilitas*, dialogues in which they counterpoised their own ideal against the more commonly accepted point of view. This genre first attained widespread popularity among the civic humanists of *Quattrocento* Florence. Buonaccorso de Montemagna's *Controversia*

---

[70] On this point see also J. Mermel, 'Preparations for a politic life: Sir Thomas More's entry into the king's service', *Journal of Medieval and Renaissance Studies*, VII (1977), 53–66; Bradshaw, 'More on Utopia', p. 24; Logan, *Meaning of More's 'Utopia'*, p. 16n.

de nobilitate (*c.* 1420) provides one of the earliest examples, while Poggio Bracciolini's *De nobilitate* (*c.* 1440) is perhaps the most celebrated. Thereafter the topic became a standard one, with many leading humanists of the second half of the *Quattrocento* contributing to the debate. For example, such well-known figures as Cristoforo Landino, Bartolomeo Sacchi and Antonio de Ferrariis all wrote dialogues on the meaning of true nobility.[71]

If we turn to the first exponents of the *studia humanitatis* in England, and thus to More's immediate intellectual background, we find the same topic being widely taken up. John Tiptoft made a translation of Buonaccorso's *Controversia* as early as the 1460s,[72] and by the start of the new century the question of *vera nobilitas* was much discussed in Erasmian humanist circles. Erasmus himself raises the issue in his *Institutio principis christiani*, and within a few years we find it recurring in such works as *Fulgens and Lucrece*, Heywood's *Gentleness and nobility*, Elyot's *Book of the Governor* and many other writings of a similar humanist character.[73]

The problem all these writers address – as Tiptoft's translation of Buonaccorso puts it – is to identify who should hold 'of right' the various 'offices of estate and worship' in the commonwealth.[74] According to the commonly accepted view, the answer is that those citizens who are noblest and worthiest to occupy such honourable positions will be those who are possessed of high lineage and ancient wealth. As Tiptoft more succinctly expresses it, the suggestion is that 'noblesse resteth in blood and riches'.[75]

Although lineage is held to be important, the defence of this position principally centred on the claim that wealth is one of the conditions of true nobility. One point on which everyone agreed was that, if wealth is indeed a criterion, it must be inherited wealth. If it is instead the product of one's own acquisitive talents, this robs one of any title to be regarded as a citizen of the highest worthiness. As Niccolò explains in Poggio's *De nobilitate*, 'I certainly cannot see what kind of nobility can be acquired by trade, for trade is judged by

---

[71] See Cristoforo Landino, *De vera nobilitate*, ed. M. Liaci (Florence, 1970); Bartolomeo Sacchi [Platina], 'De vera nobilitate', in *De vitis et gestis summorum pontificum* (Cologne, 1540), pt II, pp. 41–64; and for the treatise by Antonio de Ferrariis, *De nobilitate* (1495), see E. Savino, *Un curioso poligrafo del quattrocento* (Bari, 1941), pp. 119–23.

[72] See R. J. Mitchell, *John Tiptoft (1427–1470)* (London, 1938), p. 213.

[73] For further details about these works, see Skinner, *Foundations of Modern Political Thought*, I, pp. 236–41. For Erasmus's views, see above, n. 12 and below, nn. 90, 91, 93.

[74] John Tiptoft, *A Declamation of Nobleness*, in R. J. Mitchell, *John Tiptoft (1427–1470)* Appendix I, pp. 213–41, pp. 220, 223.

[75] Tiptoft, in Mitchell, *John Tiptoft*, p. 221.

wise men to be vile and base, and nothing that can be regarded as contemptible can be related to nobility in any way.'[76]

The positive argument purporting to connect nobility with wealth was essentially Aristotelian in character. To possess extensive riches, but without exercising the contemptible abilities required to amass them, is to be in a position to serve and benefit one's friends and community in a truly noble style of splendour and magnificence altogether denied to those who live in more modest circumstances. As Lorenzo de' Medici – the protagonist of the Aristotelian case – emphasises in Poggio's dialogue, a rich man is in a unique position, 'both in time of war and peace, whenever the spending of money is of the utmost importance, to acquire glory for himself by that means, thereby winning the nobility that arises from that source'.[77]

The underlying assumption is that wealth, far from being a hindrance to civic virtue, is one of the means to ensure its effective exercise. This had been Aristotle's contention in the *Politics*, and Aquinas had very influentially restated and developed the argument under the title *De honestate* in the *Summa theologiae*. Beginning with the claim that 'honour is due to many other things besides virtue',[78] Aquinas had declared in his *responsio* that this position is essentially correct. Some objects other than virtue are rightly honoured because, like God, they are of even greater significance than virtue itself. 'But others are rightly honoured, even though they are of lesser significance, on the grounds that they are helpful to the exercise of virtue, and these include nobility, power and wealth.'[79]

As will by now be evident, this scholastic view of true nobility rests not merely on strong beliefs about the importance of inheritance, but also on aristocratic assumptions about the proper uses of extensive wealth. As in Aristotle, an ethic of display and splendour, of liberality and magnificence, lies at the heart of the argument.[80]

---

[76] Poggio Bracciolini, 'De nobilitate', in *Oratoris et philosophi opera* (Basel, 1538), pp. 64–83, p. 70: 'At vero ex mercatura non video quae nobilitas acquiratur . . . quod vile atque abiectum sapientes arbitrati sunt . . . quod aliquo modo vituperari potest, nunquam admiscebitur cum nobilitate.'

[77] *Ibid.*, p. 77: 'bello quoque et pace, in quibus pecuniam sumptus maxime sunt necessarii, glorie acquiritur, a qua descendit nobilitas'.

[78] Aquinas, *Summa theologiae*, II.II.145: 'multis aliis debetur honor quam virtuti'.

[79] *Ibid.*, II.II.145: 'Alia vero quae sunt infra virtutem honorantur, inquantum coadjuvant ad operationem virtutis, sicut nobilitas, potentia et divitiae.'

[80] See for example Poggio, 'De nobilitate', pp. 77, 81, where the figure of Lorenzo, the protagonist of the Aristotelian point of view, insists on the indissoluble links between *nobilitas* and the capacity to display both *splendor* and *magnificentia*. It seems important to underline this point, if only because of the influential but misleading claim in Hexter, *More's 'Utopia'*, pp. 36–7, that none of More's contemporaries 'would have maintained for a moment that what mattered in a commonwealth was splendor, magnificence and majesty'.

Again, Aquinas was to prove a highly influential intermediary in the transmission of these values. As his title *De magnificentia* in the *Summa* insists, 'the achievement of anything great – from which the term 'magnificent' arises – appropriately relates to the idea of virtue, from which it follows that the term 'magnificent' denotes a virtue'.[81]

The same assumptions generally reappear in humanist dialogues about *vera nobilitas*, where they usually figure not merely as scholastic arguments but as commonly accepted beliefs. In Buonaccorso's *Controversia*, for example, the first speaker ends by explaining that his reason for treating wealth as a criterion for true nobility is that 'the chief and highest part of noblesse must rest in liberality', and that 'he paineth himself vainly to exercise liberality to other folks which hath not whereof to use it to himself'.[82] 'If you deny this view', as Lorenzo adds in Poggio's dialogue, 'you will be rejecting what is agreed about this matter by everyone.'[83]

II

Among humanist intellectuals, however, this view was in fact denied. It was challenged with a claim that soon became almost a slogan of humanist political thought: the claim that *virtus vera nobilitas est*, that the possession of virtue constitutes the only possible grounds for regarding someone as a person of true nobility.

This is not to say that the humanists in general had any quarrel with the basic assumptions about private property and its heritability that underpinned the Aristotelian and scholastic case. On the contrary, they strongly endorsed Aquinas's classic account of the indispensability of private property in any well-ordered commonwealth. Drawing once more on Aristotle, Aquinas had argued in his title *De furto et rapina* in the *Summa* that private property is not merely legitimate but essential to the satisfactory conduct of political life. One reason he gave was that, if all things are instead held in common, everyone will avoid working and in consequence help to bring about a state of gratuitous poverty. But his main contention was that, in the absence of private property, endless confusion and quarrelling will be sure to arise, a state of disorder that can never be

---

[81] Aquinas, *Summa*, II.II.134: 'operari aliquid magnum, ex quo sumitur nomen magnificentiae, proprie pertinet ad rationem virtutis. Unde magnificentia nominat virtutem.'

[82] Tiptoft, in Mitchell, *John Tiptoft*, p. 221.

[83] Poggio 'De nobilitate', p. 66: 'si negas ex his ... communi omnium sensu repugnas'.

regulated and stabilised except by recognising that some goods must be held privately and not treated as part of the common stock.[84]

The humanists found little to say about the first of these claims, although Cicero in the *De officiis* had argued that one of the prime duties of our rulers must be to ensure that there is an abundance of goods, a point he had made in the course of his own defence of private property.[85] But they firmly underlined Aquinas's second point, making it a commonplace of humanist political theory to insist that no political order can ever be maintained unless the values of 'degree, priority and place' are firmly upheld.[86] As always, Cicero's arguments in the *De officiis* furnished them with their highest authority, and on this issue Cicero had spoken with exceptional vehemence. 'What plague could ever be worse', he had written, than to favour an equal distribution of goods?[87] Those who do so 'are undermining the foundations of the commonwealth, for in the first place they are destroying harmony, which cannot possibly be sustained where money is taken from one person and given to someone else; and in the second place they are subverting equity, which will altogether collapse if it ceases to be lawful for people to hold their own goods'.[88]

Despite their endorsement of these widely accepted beliefs about the social basis of nobility, the humanists completely repudiated the related claim that the quality of nobility itself is in any way connected with lineage or inherited wealth. They permitted themselves a tone of pure amazement at the idea that ancient lineage might be supposed relevant. As Niccolò puts it in Poggio's dialogue, 'what can conceivably be thought noble about a man who merely has numerous ancestors and a long account of his family history?'[89] Erasmus in his *Institutio* was later to allow himself a similar note of surprise. He concedes that he has no wish 'to take away honour from those of high lineage, provided they are formed in the image of their ancestors and excel in those qualities that originally made them

---

[84] See Aquinas, *Summa*, II.II.66. Cf. also I.II.105, where Aristotle's *Politics* is cited on the indispensability of private property.

[85] Cicero, *De officiis*, II.21.74.

[86] On the need for 'degree' if 'order' is to be preserved, see Skinner, *Foundations of Modern Political Thought*, I, pp. 238–41 and references there.

[87] Cicero, *De officiis*, II.21.73: 'qua peste quae potest esse maior?'

[88] *Ibid.*, II.22.78: 'labefactant fundamenta rei publicae, concordiam primum, quae esse non potest, cum aliis adimuntur, aliis condonantur pecuniae, deinde aequitatem, quae tollitur omnis, si habere suum cuique non licet'.

[89] Poggio, 'De nobilitate', p. 70: '[qui enim fieri potest ut] vir. . . maioribus tantum ac stirpis origine sisus possit ullo esse pacto nobilis?'

members of the nobility'.[90] But he adds that this gives us no reason at
all 'for allowing the title of nobility' to those who merely happen to
be members of a leisured class and live a life of *iners otium*,
'sluggish idleness'.[91]

The main point the humanists make, however, is that it is even
more ridiculous to suppose that the possession of inherited wealth
can in any way entitle someone to be regarded as truly noble. Niccolò flatly declares in Poggio's dialogue that 'riches cannot in the
least ennoble us',[92] while Erasmus in the *Institutio* offers an anatomy
of true nobility which serves to underline the same point. 'There are
three forms of nobility,' he maintains, 'one of which arises from
virtue and good deeds, while the next derives from an understanding
of those studies which are *honestissimae* and the third from ancestral
portraits and long lineage, or else from the possession of wealth. But
this third and lowest degree is so low that it really amounts to nothing at all unless it has arisen out of virtue itself.'[93]

If lineage and inherited wealth are both irrelevant, what gives rise
to the quality of true nobility? Erasmus's analysis already gives the
answer, and in offering it he was able to draw on a century of civic
humanist argument. As Niccolò had declared in triumph at the end
of Poggio's dialogue, 'it is virtue that constitutes the one and only
nobility',[94] a conclusion he takes both Seneca and 'our Cicero' to
have demonstrated beyond doubt.[95] 'It is thus the judgment of wise
men', he adds, 'that nobility arises neither from a life of *otium* nor
from contemplative solitude, nor even from the possession of great
wealth; it arises exclusively from the study of virtue, a quality we are
much better able to exercise when living in cities and amid the
fellowship of mankind.'[96]

[90] Erasmus, *Institutio Christiani principis*, p. 198: 'Non quod bene natis suum honorem
detraham, si respondeant maiorum imaginibus et iis rebus praecellant, quae
primum nobilitatem pepererunt.'
[91] *Ibid.*: 'nec iners ocium [*sic*] nobilitatis titulo donandum'.
[92] Poggio, 'De nobilitate', p. 71: 'nobilitare ergo nos [opes] minime possunt'.
[93] Erasmus, *Institutio Christiani principis*, p. 146: 'tria sint nobilitatis genera: unum,
quod ex virtute recteque factis nascitur; proximum, quod ex honestissimarum dis-
ciplinarum cognitione proficiscitur; tertium, quod natalium picturis et maiorum
stemmatis aestimatur aut opibus . . . quod sic infimum est, ut nullum omnino sit,
nisi et ipsum a virtute fuerit, profectum'.
[94] Poggio, 'De nobilitate', p. 80: '[scribens] solam atque unicam virtutem nobilitatem
esse'.
[95] See Poggio, *ibid.*, citing 'noster Cicero' and quoting from Seneca, *Epistulae
morales* XLIV.
[96] *Ibid.*, p. 72: 'Non enim solitudine, aut ocio [*sic*] ignavo vel opum magnitudine, sed
virtutis studio comparandam sapientes censent . . . quam magis in urbibus &
hominum coetu exercere possumus.'

III

As before, my suggestion is that this aspect of the debate about the *optimus status reipublicae* supplies us with a context that helps to make sense of some of the further complexities of More's *Utopia*. In particular, it helps us to explain the connections between the two Books into which *Utopia* is divided, and at the same time enables us to reconsider what has always been the chief interpretative question about the book, the question of how far More intends us to admire the portrait of Utopian society sketched by Hythloday in Book II. What emerges, I suggest, if we turn to these aspects of the work – and especially to the exact vocabulary More employs – is that one of his main concerns in *Utopia* is to intervene in the precise debate we have so far been considering, the debate about the meaning of true nobility. To grasp the nature of that intervention, I shall argue, is at the same time to uncover the serious message that underlies the seemingly detached and ironic surface of his text.

Hythloday engages with the issue of *vera nobilitas* at two connected but distinguishable points. First of all, he provides us simply with a picture of what he describes as the true and the counterfeit images of nobility,[97] together with a description of the contrasting social consequences that naturally flow from espousing one or other of them.

The moment at which he draws this contrast most forcefully is in the closing pages of the book. After outlining the Utopian way of life, Hythloday ends by discussing with the figure of More the significance of the story he has told. The first claim Hythloday makes at this juncture is that, in his judgement, the Utopians have in fact attained the *optimus status reipublicae*.[98] Their laws and institutions seriously aim at the common good, as a result of which they are able to live *felicissime*, as happily as possible.[99]

How have they managed it? Hythloday answers in essentially negative terms. They have managed by not organising their society 'according to the unjust ideas of justice that prevail everywhere else'.[100] These unjust ideas take the form of 'lavishing great gifts'

---

[97] The term More uses is *fucatus*. See *Complete Works*, IV, p. 168.

[98] See More, *ibid.*, p. 236 on the Utopian hope that the *optima forma* has been achieved.

[99] See More, *ibid.*, p. 238 on how the citizens of Utopia 'seriously concern themselves with public affairs' ('serio publicum negotium agunt') and p. 244 on how, as a result, they live 'felicissime'. Cf. also p. 178.

[100] See More, *ibid.*, p. 238 comparing Utopian with 'aliarum iustitiam gentium'.

upon nobles, rich merchants and other 'so-called gentlemen'[101] who
either live a life of *otium* and 'do no work at all', or else occupy themselves with 'wholly superfluous *negotium*' that contributes nothing of
value to the commonwealth.[102] 'For this they are rewarded with a
luxurious and a splendid life.'[103] By contrast, no thanks, no benefits,
no feelings of kindness[104] are shown to those who work 'with unceas-
ing labour' at tasks 'so essential to the commonwealth that it would
not last a single year without them'.[105] 'The lives they lead are so full
of misery that the condition of beasts of burden might seem
altogether preferable.'[106]

We may say, then, that what Hythloday appears to be claiming, at
this summarising point in his argument, is that the Utopians owe
their happiness to their avoidance of mistaken beliefs about the
qualities that truly deserve to be regarded as noble and praiseworthy,
as opposed to the qualities that merely happen to be displayed by
the so-called gentry and nobility. Nor is this to put words into
Hythloday's mouth. If we turn back to the account he gives in Book
II of the Utopians' social attitudes, we find him phrasing his description in exactly these terms. The Utopians are distinguished by their
belief that to connect nobility with *splendor*, with richness of apparel
or other conspicuous displays of wealth,[107] 'such that someone will
think himself nobler if the texture of his garments is finer', is nothing but insane.[108] The Utopians 'not only think it extraordinary,
they actually detest the insanity of those who pay almost divine
honours to the rich, especially when those who do so owe the rich
nothing, are under no obligation to them, but behave towards them
in that fashion simply because they happen to be rich'.[109]

[101] See More, *ibid.*, p. 240 on how 'tanta munera' are lavished on 'generosis ut
vocant'.
[102] See More, *ibid.*, p. 238 on the otium, or else supervacuum negotium, of the nobiles
and rich merchants.
[103] *Ibid.*, p. 238: 'lautam et splendidam vitam . . . consequatur'.
[104] See More, *ibid.*, p. 240 on the lack of benignitas or beneficia, and the failure
'referre gratiam'.
[105] See More, *ibid.*, p. 238 on those who work 'assiduo labore' in such a way that is 'tam
necessario, ut sine eo ne unum quidem annum possit ulla durare Respublica'.
[106] *Ibid.*, p. 238: 'vitam adeo miseram ducunt, ut longe potior videri possit
conditio iumentorum'.
[107] See More, *ibid.*, p. 154 on the amusement caused by the 'splendor' of the foreign
'nobiles' who visited Utopia. Confronted with all their magnificence of apparel,
the Utopians 'altogether failed to pay it the least honour' ('totus ille splendor . . .
honore praetermiserunt'). Cf. also p. 166.
[108] *Ibid.*, p. 156: 'ipsum denique solem liceat intueri, aut quemquam tam insanum
esse, ut nobilior ipse sibi ob tenuioris lanae filum videatur'.
[109] *Ibid.*, p. 156: 'mirantur, ac detestantur insaniam qui divitibus illis, quibus neque
debent quicquam, neque sunt obnoxii, nullo alio respectu, quam quod divites
sunt, honores tantum non divinos impendunt'.

Rejecting this counterfeit view of nobility, the view the Utopians espouse is exactly the one we have already encountered in Cicero and his humanist disciples, and is couched in exactly the same terms. The Utopians believe that what is alone noble and deserving of honour is a willingness to labour for the common good.[110] The qualities they think of as truly noble are accordingly the qualities of virtue that are indispensable for performing such civic tasks. As a result, the laws and customs of Utopia not only forbid *otium* and require *negotium* from everyone;[111] they are also designed to ensure that the elements of civic virtue are encouraged, praised and admired above all. Thus we learn that the Utopians are all trained in virtue.[112] They are all encouraged to follow a virtuous way of life by the fact that virtue is so highly honoured in their society.[113] They are especially incited to virtue by the fact that statues of great men who have performed outstanding services to the community are erected in their marketplaces.[114] Magistrates who serve with the highest virtue are rewarded with honour and praise.[115] And the priests, who are chosen for their outstanding virtue, are regarded for that reason as persons of true *maiestas*.[116] The whole society is portrayed as one in which the quality of virtue has been made the ruling principle. It is a society in which the women, the magistrates and the heads of families are all described as possessing *honestas*,[117] the highest term of praise among Ciceronian humanists for those who attain the full range of the virtues and deploy them upon the betterment of our common life.

As a result of substituting this view of what is truly noble for the commonly accepted one, the Utopians have managed at the same time to avoid a number of baleful social consequences that stem, according to Hythloday, from accepting the counterfeit belief. Hythloday lists them when first mentioning the existence of Utopia at the end of Book I, and reiterates them when summarising his argument in the closely parallel passage at the end of Book II. One is poverty, which is unknown in Utopia, a society in which 'it has dwindled away completely', leaving 'no poor men, no beggars',[118] but 'abundance of everything for everyone'.[119] The other is social disorder, the inevitable concomitant of poverty. This too has 'perished completely' in Utopia,[120] leaving 'a people so well-

---

[110] See More, *ibid.*, pp. 130, 134.
[111] See More, *ibid.*, esp. p. 126 on the absence of 'otium' in Utopia, and the enforcement by the magistrates of the obligation of 'negotium' upon everyone.
[112] *Ibid.*, p. 184. [113] *Ibid.*, p. 192. [114] *Ibid.*, p. 192. [115] *Ibid.*, p. 196.
[116] *Ibid.*, p. 228, 230. [117] *Ibid.*, pp. 126, 188, 196. [118] *Ibid.*, pp. 238, 242.
[119] *Ibid.*, p. 102: 'rebus omnia abundent omnibus'. [120] *Ibid.*, p. 242.

ordered', according to Hythloday, 'that if you had seen them, you would say that there is no good order anywhere else'.[121]

We can summarise the entire scale of values Hythloday is describing – as he does himself when first mentioning Utopia – by saying that Utopia is a society in which *virtuti precium sit*, in which 'virtue has its reward'.[122] For it is a society in which virtue is regarded, as it ought to be, as the one quality truly deserving of honour, esteem and praise.

I am suggesting, then, that Hythloday's description of Utopia in Book II should be read as an account of the social benefits that flow from espousing the true instead of the counterfeit view of nobility. By contrast, his famous analysis of the injustices of English society in Book I forms a perfectly balanced account of the dire effects that stem from accepting the counterfeit view in its place.

That the English endorse the counterfeit view is emphatically asserted in the course of Book II, especially at the point where Hythloday compares 'what is now believed' about this question with the Utopian attitudes we have just examined. 'What is now believed is that nothing else counts as nobility' except 'being descended from a long line of ancestors who have been rich over a long period of time, especially if they have been rich in landed estates'.[123] The result is that men of high lineage and inherited wealth 'believe themselves to be noble' in the sense of being entitled to honour and respect, entitled to be met with bared heads and bent knees.[124]

Hythloday not only characterises this belief as 'sweetly insane';[125] he also treats it as the cause of all the woes afflicting English society that are analysed in Book I. Not only does he start by directing his accusations specifically against 'the great number of nobles' and their 'immense crowds of idle retainers';[126] he subsequently confines himself almost entirely to illustrating how these particular social groups have been the ruin of English society.

The most obvious consequence of their ascendancy is widespread poverty. Recognising that their title to respect depends on their capacity to live a life of *splendor* and magnificence, the nobles are

[121] *Ibid.*, p. 106: 'populum recte institutum nusquam alibi te vidisse quam illic'.
[122] *Ibid.*, p. 102.
[123] *Ibid.*, p. 168: 'quod eiusmodi maioribus nasci contigerit, quorum longa series dives (neque enim nunc aliud est nobilitas) habita sit, praesertim in praediis'.
[124] *Ibid.*, p. 168: 'ii qui nobilitatis opinione sibi blandiuntur ac plaudunt'; cf. also p. 168 on 'nudatus alterius vertex, aut curvati poplites'.
[125] *Ibid.*, p. 168: 'suaviter insaniunt'.
[126] *Ibid.*, p. 62: 'tantus est ergo nobilium numerus . . . [et] verum immensam quoque ociosorum stipatorum turbam'.

driven into 'evil greed' as the only means of satisfying their pride. [127]
'They are not content, living in *otium* and luxury, to do no good for
their community; they actually do it positive harm.' [128] To ensure the
highest profits from their lands, 'they leave no arable at all, but
enclose everything for pasture, demolishing houses, destroying
towns' and evicting tenants who are then left to starve. [129] Desperate
and gratuitous hardship is the price that others pay for their aristocratic way of life.

The other and consequential outcome is endemic social unrest.
The armies of retainers kept by the aristocracy form a serious part of
the problem, for they live in idleness, never learn any kind of trade,
devote themselves to the arts of war and 'continually make trouble
and disturb the peace'. [130] Finally, even worse disorders are caused by
those evicted from their lands and livelihoods. 'For what remains for
them, in the last resort, but to steal and then be hanged – justly, no
doubt – or else to wander and beg?' [131]

Hythloday completes this aspect of his argument when he points,
at the end of Book II, to the principles that must inevitably govern
any society founded on this view of nobility. As we have seen, to base
a society on the true view, as the Utopians do, is to make virtue its
ruling principle. By contrast, to base a society on the counterfeit
view is to ensure that its citizens cultivate the worst of the vices. Of
these the deadliest is pride, 'that serpent from hell which coils itself
round the hearts of mortal men'. [132] To connect nobility with wealth
is to place 'this chief and progenitor of all plagues' at the centre of our
social life. [133] For pride 'measures prosperity not by her own advantages, but by the disadvantages suffered by others', [134] and therefore
loves to live 'in circumstances where her happiness can shine more
brightly by comparison with their miseries'. [135] Finally, once the life
of magnificence demanded by pride becomes our highest aspiration,
the other ruling passion of our society can only be avarice. For

[127] See More, *ibid.*, p. 68 on their 'improba cupiditas'.
[128] *Ibid.*, p. 66: 'nec habentes satis, quod ociose ac laute viventes, nihil in publicum
prosint, nisi etiam obsint'.
[129] *Ibid.*, p. 66: 'aruo nihil relinquunt, omnia claudunt pascuis, demoliuntur domos,
dirvunt oppida'.
[130] See More, *ibid.*, p. 62, and cf. p. 64 on 'turbam alere, quod infestat pacem'.
[131] *Ibid.*, p. 66: 'quid restat aliud denique, quam uti furentur, & pendeant iuste scilicet,
aut vagentur atque mendicent'.
[132] *Ibid.*, p. 242: 'haec averni serpens mortalium pererrans pectora'.
[133] *Ibid.*, p. 242: 'omnium princeps parensque pestium superbia'.
[134] *Ibid.*, p. 242: 'haec non suis commodis prosperitatem, sed ex alienis metitur
incommodis'.
[135] *Ibid.*, p. 242: 'quorum miseriis praefulgeat ipsius comparata felicitas'.

everyone will then be forced to act 'with insatiable cupidity' if the demands of pride are to be adequately satisfied.[136]

So far, then, Hythloday has simply reiterated and defended a conventional humanist equation between virtue and true nobility. As I began by observing, however, his contrast between the rival views of nobility only represents one of two ways in which he engages with the debate about *vera nobilitas*. When we turn to the further claim he wishes to make, we find ourselves moving beyond the confines of humanist orthodoxy, confronting an argument at once more radical and explicitly Platonist in character.

Hythloday signals this further commitment in the form of two metaphors introduced at the end of Book I. He remarks that hitherto he has been talking about the diseases of bodies politic; he now wishes to consider 'how to return them to a healthy state'.[137] But there is no hope of such a cure, he adds, unless we can first identify the seeds of evil in social life and pluck them out by the roots.[138]

What then is the evil that needs to be rooted out? After surveying the Utopian system, Hythloday answers his own question in a single word. At the root of social injustice lies a mistaken belief about what should count as *privatus*, the realm of private as opposed to public interests. Describing Utopia as a community in which the *optimus status reipublicae* has in fact been reached, Hythloday at once adds that it is a society of which it can also be said that *nihil privati est*, there is nothing of the private about it at all.[139]

This explains why there is such a strong suspicion of privacy in Utopia. The Utopians never eat in private, but always in public halls;[140] they seem to prefer public to private worship;[141] they live in private houses, but these are kept public by virtue of a design that 'gives admission to anyone who wishes to enter';[142] and they even insist that, before marriage, the private parts of the body must be made public to the partner involved.[143]

What they have recognised above all, however, is that no community can ever hope to attain its best state unless the institution of private property, and the money economy sustaining it, are both abolished.[144] We can now see the force of Hythloday's metaphor: money, he is saying, is the root of all evil, and must be eradicated if

---

[136] *Ibid.*, p. 240: 'cum inexplebili cupiditate'.
[137] *Ibid.*, p. 104: 'ut sanentur vero atque in bonum redeant habitum'.
[138] For this image, see esp. More, *ibid.*, p. 86; cf. also p. 242.
[139] *Ibid.*, p. 238. Cf. also pp. 102, 104.
[140] *Ibid.*, pp. 128, 138.   [141] *Ibid.*, pp. 222–4, 232, 236.
[142] *Ibid.*, p. 120: 'quemvis intromittunt, ita nihil usquam privati est'.
[143] *Ibid.*, p. 188.   [144] *Ibid.*, esp. p. 102.

there is to be any prospect of serving public as opposed to private interests. As Hythloday declares at the end of Book I, this is what Plato recognised. 'As that wisest of all men easily foresaw, the one and only road to public welfare is by way of an equality of goods.'[145] Hythloday emphatically agrees, and goes on to spell out the implications of the argument. 'I am fully persuaded that no just and equal distribution of goods will ever be possible, nor will happiness ever be found in mortal affairs, until the institution of private property is totally overthrown.'[146] To put his point at its simplest and most resonant, what he is saying is that we have no hope of establishing a genuine commonwealth unless we base it on a system of common wealth.

As Book II goes on to show, this is the insight the Utopians have put into practice. As a result, Hythloday affirms at the close of his account, they not only live *felicissime*, as happily as possible; it also seems likely that their happiness will last *aeternum duratura*.[147] And the right way to translate that last phrase is surely by observing that Hythloday ends in just the way that such stories are supposed to end, by assuring us that the heroes lived happily ever after.

The *optimus status reipublicae*

Hythloday's conclusion is a sufficiently resounding one, but it still leaves us with the problem of assessing where the author of *Utopia* stands in relation to it. Are we to take it that More endorses the claim that the Utopians have succeeded in establishing a perfectly rational society? Are we even to suppose, as some commentators have lately argued, that the description of Utopia is intended as the portrait of a perfectly Christian commonwealth? Or must we conclude, as the best recent scholarship has claimed, that More's irony and indirection reflect his own deep feelings of ambiguity about the Utopian way of life?

I

If we are to reconsider these questions, we need to start by reminding ourselves of the precise topic More addresses in the book. As I

---

[145] *Ibid.*, p. 104: 'Siquidem facile praevidit homo prudentissimus, unam atque unicam illam esse viam ad salutem publicam, si rerum indicatur aequalitas.'

[146] *Ibid.*, p. 104: 'Adeo mihi certe persuadeo, res aequabili ac iusta aliqua ratione distribui, aut feliciter agi cum rebus mortalium, nisi sublata prorsus proprietate, non posse.'   [147] *Ibid.*, p. 244.

began by observing, it is surely uncontentious to say that More's basic concern is with the character of the best state of a commonwealth. But to say that this is his theme is at the same time to insist that he is not primarily concerned with a number of other distinct though closely related questions that also preoccupied Erasmian humanists at the time. He does not begin – as Erasmus does in the *Enchiridion* – by telling us that his topic will be 'the right way of life, such that, if you are instructed in it, you can attain that state of mind which is worthy of a true Christian'.[148] Nor does he announce – as, for example, Starkey does in his *Dialogue* – that his aim will be to examine the relationship between the best state of a commonwealth and the attainment of that way of life 'wherein lieth the perfection of man'.[149] More's concern, as his title page tells us, is purely and simply with the best state of a commonwealth in itself.

Once we recognise the precise focus of More's inquiry, and the need to distinguish it from other topics of debate within the Christian humanist movement, we can hope to re-examine some of the interpretations of More's text suggested by recent scholarship. In particular, we can hope to reconsider Hexter's thesis that, for all the heathenism of Utopia, it was More's intention to portray the Utopians as living a perfectly virtuous and hence a truly Christian way of life.

This interpretation cannot survive an examination of what Hythloday tells us about the place of religion in Utopian life. The chief point he makes is that, insofar as the Utopians have any shared religion, their religious beliefs are at the same time dictates of rationality. They all think it obvious that the world is governed by divine providence.[150] Likewise, they all agree 'that the soul is immortal; that it is destined by God's mercy for a life of happiness; and that there will be punishments after this present life for our crimes as well

---

[148] Erasmus, *Enchiridion militis Christiani* (Strasbourg, 1525), p. 14: 'quandam vivendi rationem [praescriberem] qua instructus, possis ad mentem Christo dignam pervenire'. This was perhaps the central question of Erasmian humanism in More's time, but it is not the question More addresses in *Utopia*. Cf. J. K. McConica, *English Humanists and Reformation Politics* (Oxford, 1965), esp. pp. 13–43, and Bradshaw, 'More on Utopia' on this aspect of the Erasmian movement.

[149] Starkey, *Dialogue*, pp. 23, 26. The discussion of this relationship, as distinct from the discussion of the perfect life in itself, was a long-established topos of humanist political thought. For a very early example, see Giovanni da Ravenna, *Dragmalogia*, pp. 164–6, telling us that 'my present concern is not with those who, released from all their passions, are transported from this temporal slime heavenwards, but only with those who are engaged in civil life' ('Sed presens intentio non de his qui, defecatis usquequaque desideriis, e ceno temporali in superna rapiuntur...sed de his qui in vita civili versantur').   [150] More, *Complete Works*, IV, p. 220.

as rewards for our virtues and good deeds'.[151] But they think that 'although these principles belong to religion, reason also leads us to the judgement that they are worthy to be believed and accepted'.[152] This makes the Utopians willing to enforce these particular principles, for they feel that to deny them 'would be to sink below the dignity of human nature.'[153] But it also leads them to acknowledge that, apart from these obvious exceptions, nothing about religion is certain and everything ought therefore to be tolerated.[154]

The first comment Hythloday offers on this outlook is that even the Utopians admit that it may not be altogether satisfactory. They recognise that moral arguments depend in part on religious premises.[155] 'They also concede without hesitation that, if religious sanctions were to be withdrawn, no one would be so foolish as not to pursue his own pleasure by fair means or foul.'[156] They think the religious principles they introduce into their own discussions about human happiness are such that 'no truer viewpoint can be attained by the processes of human reasoning alone'.[157] But they emphasise that their conclusions have been arrived at 'in the absence of a heaven-sent religion'.[158] Finally, they acknowledge that such a religion might well be able 'to inspire men with something more holy' than the beliefs they currently accept.[159]

Moreover, Hythloday himself – a fervent Christian no less than a Platonist – makes it clear that in his view the religious and in consequence the moral attitudes of the Utopians are in fact seriously flawed. He thereby introduces into his analysis a distinction familiar to classical humanists: a distinction between the optimal conduct of

---

[151] *Ibid.*, p. 160: 'Animam esse immortalem, ac dei beneficentia ad felicitatem natam, virtutibus ac bene factis nostris praemia post hanc vitam, flagitiis destinata supplicia.'

[152] *Ibid.*, p. 162: 'Haec tametsi religionis sint, ratione tamen censent ad ea credenda & concedenda perduci.' For a discussion of this issue, and valuable references, see Logan, *Meaning of More's 'Utopia'*, pp. 163–4.

[153] More, *Complete Works*, IV, p. 220: 'ab humanae naturae dignitate degeneret'.

[154] *Ibid.*, p. 220.

[155] *Ibid.*, p. 160. We are told that the Utopians 'never discuss the idea of happiness without taking their principles from religion as well as philosophy' ('Neque enim de felicitate disceptant unquam, quin principia quaedam ex religione deprompta, tum philosophia'). The translation in *Complete Works*, IV, seems seriously at fault in this passage. Cf. Skinner 'More's *Utopia*', p. 159.

[156] More, *Complete Works*, IV, p. 162: 'quibus e medio sublatis, sine ulla cunctatione pronunciant neminem esse tamen stupidum, qui non sentiat petendam sibi per fas ac nefas voluptatem'. The translation in *Complete Works*, IV, again seems at fault in this passage. Cf. also Skinner, 'More's *Utopia*', pp. 159–60 on this point.

[157] More, *Complete Works*, IV, p. 178: 'nullam investigari credunt humana ratione veriorem'.   [158] *Ibid.*, p. 178: 'caelitus immissa religio'.

[159] *Ibid.*, p. 178: 'sanctius aliquid inspiret homini'.

public affairs on the one hand and the optimal conduct of one's own individual life on the other.[160] The former he believes the Utopians have already attained; on the latter point, however, he feels that they still need to be further instructed.

Hythloday is quite explicit in the first place about the incompleteness of religious understanding in Utopia. Before his arrival the Utopians knew nothing of the Incarnation, being wholly ignorant of 'the name and the doctrine and the nature and the miracles of Christ'.[161] Even after his voyages they still lacked any access to the Sacraments or the Scriptures, thus remaining cut off from the Church's mediating powers and from any understanding of the divine positive law and the soteriological scheme outlined in the Bible.[162]

Hythloday is equally emphatic about the resulting limitations of the Utopian moral code. These derive from the one feature of Utopian life he directly criticises, namely their view of human happiness. Basing themselves on reason alone, and knowing nothing of God's purposes as disclosed in the Bible, 'they show themselves more inclined than is right'[163] to conclude that individual happiness must simply consist 'in leading as carefree and joyful a life as possible while helping others do the same'.[164] One implication of their outlook is that in certain circumstances they are ready to permit and even encourage both suicide and euthanasia. 'If someone has a disease which is not only incurable but a source of continual agony and distress',[165] then 'the priests and magistrates exhort the man'[166] either to commit suicide and 'free himself from this bitter life' or else 'voluntarily to allow others to free him from it'.[167] Such decisions are

---

[160] Cf., on this point, n. 149, above.

[161] More, *Complete Works*, IV, p. 216: 'CHRISTI nomen, doctrinam, mores, miracula'.

[162] See More, *ibid.*, pp. 180–2 on the books Hythloday subsequently took with him to Utopia: at no point did he take the Bible. A strange omission, but essential if More is to make his point about the limitations of a moral creed founded purely on reason. See also p. 218 on the fact that, similarly, Hythloday's party at no point included a priest, with the result that the Utopians still lack the sacraments.

[163] *Ibid.*, p. 160: 'at hac in re propensiores aequo videntur.' This is the sole point at which Hythloday criticises any feature of the Utopian way of life. The translation in *Complete Works*, IV, suggests a further criticism at p. 145, but only because 'aliquanto procliviores' is translated as 'somewhat too much inclined' instead of 'somewhat more inclined' as the context requires.

[164] *Ibid.*, p. 162: 'nos ut vitam quam licet minime anxiam, ac maxime laetam ducamus ipsi, caeterisque omnibus ad idem obtinendum adiutores'.

[165] *Ibid.*, p. 186: 'si non immedicabilis modo morbus sit verumetiam perpetuo vexet atque discrutiet'.

[166] *Ibid.*, p. 186: 'sacerdotes ac magistratus hortantur hominem'. It is unclear what significance, if any, should be attached to the fact that More appears to exclude women from this arrangement, unless 'homo' here means 'person'.

[167] *Ibid.*, p. 186: 'acerba illa vita . . . vel ipse semet eximat: vel ab aliis eripi se sua voluntate patiatur'.

regarded not merely as wise but as 'pious and holy', and those who take them are honoured for doing so.[168]

Given their view of human happiness, this attitude strikes the Utopians as perfectly reasonable. But it is a case in which their reliance on reason alone, without the benefit of Christian revelation, leads them seriously astray.[169] Although they have no means of knowing it, the actions they regard as pious and honourable are at once mortal sins and a negation of an important aspect of Christian soteriology. The Utopians lack any understanding of the intrinsic value of suffering, a value which – under the symbol of the Cross – is central to the soteriological scheme presented in the New Testament. At the same time they fail to recognise, as Hythloday remarks in his tirade against the English practice of hanging thieves, that 'God has not only forbidden us to kill', but 'has withdrawn from us the right to bring about our own death as well as the death of others'.[170] Although reason might incline us to allow certain exceptions – as the Utopians do in their ignorance – the divine positive law made known by God in the Mosaic Code, and renewed by Christ in the New Testament, is completely unambiguous. It simply tells us 'Thou shalt not kill.'

It cannot, then, have been More's intention, in emphasising the heathenism of Utopia, to point ironically to the fact that the heathen Utopians, 'far more than the nominal Christians of Europe, have succeeded in establishing a truly Christian commonwealth'.[171] The irony of the situation seems rather to be registered by the figure of More himself when he first tells us at the start of Book I about his conversations with Hythloday. He reports that Hythloday 'told me of many mistaken customs to be found among the newly-discovered peoples'.[172] But he adds at once that Hythloday 'also informed me of not a few customs that could well serve as examples to our own cities, nations, peoples and kingdoms, thereby enabling us to correct our own mistakes'.[173] Possessing as we do the benefits of

[168] *Ibid.*, p. 186: such acts are held to 'prudenter facturum'; they are also held to be 'pie sancteque facturum' and are regarded as 'honorificum'.
[169] On this point see also P. A. Duhamel, 'Medievalism of More's *'Utopia', Studies in Philology*, LII (1955), 99–126 and the discussion in Logan, *Meaning of More's 'Utopia'*, pp. 218–20.
[170] More, *Complete Works*, IV, p. 72: 'Deus vetuit occidi quenquam . . . deus non alienae modo, verum etiam suae cuique mortis ius ademerit.'
[171] As I previously argued myself in *Foundations of Modern Political Thought*, I, p. 233.
[172] More, *Complete Works*, IV, p. 54: 'multa apud novos illos populos adnotavit peram consulta'.
[173] *Ibid.*, p. 54: 'haud pauca recensuit, unde possint exempla sumi corrigendis harum urbium, nationum, gentium, ac regnorum erroribus idonea'.

revelation as well as reason, we ought to be able to surpass such heathern communities in all respects. The irony – and the scandal – lies in the fact that we have so much to learn from them.[174]

II

The Utopians have not attained for themselves the ideal of a perfectly Christian life. But it does not follow that they have not attained the best state of the commonwealth. Reason and revelation are both indispensable for the first, but reason alone suffices for the second, and reason is a universal possession of mankind, one common to heathens and Christians alike. It is certainly possible, therefore, that More intends us to accept that the Utopians have in fact achieved a correct view of what constitutes true nobility, have avoided the baleful consequences of espousing the counterfeit view instead, and have arrived as a result at the *optimus status reipublicae*.

As we have seen, it is certainly Hythloday's belief that this is the case. But the question, as before, is whether More intends us to endorse that belief. The answer appears to be contained in a single highly charged passage at the end of the book, a passage in which the figure of More comments directly on the lessons Hythloday has drawn from his own narrative. 'When Raphael finished his story, many things occurred to me which seemed absurdly established in the customs and laws of the people he had described.'[175] Of these, More goes on, 'the one that struck me most was the feature that constitutes the foundation of their entire social structure: their common life and mode of subsistence, based on having no money transactions at all. If this were to be established, it would overthrow all the nobility, magnificence, splendour and majesty that represent,

---

[174] Here I revert to an interpretation which, although questioned by some recent scholars, used to be widely accepted. For earlier discussions, see the references in Logan, *Meaning of More's 'Utopia'*, p. 141n. For an excellent restatement of the case, see Bradshaw 'More on Utopia', pp. 6–14. One reason for accepting the interpretation is that the point was commonly made by other Erasmian humanists. Erasmus himself notes on several occasions (for example in the Preface to his edition of Cicero, *De officiis*) the almost scandalous extent to which certain pagan authors are able to instruct us, while Ludovico Vives in *De subventione pauperum*, ed. A. Saitta (Florence, 1973), p. 27 speaks even more pointedly of 'Seneca, a pagan, teaching Christians things it would be more appropriate for him to learn from them' ('Senecam, hominem gentilem, Christianos edocentem quae illum conveniebat potius a Christianis discere').

[175] More *Complete Works*, IV, p. 244: 'Haec ubi Raphael recensuit, quanquam haud pauca mihi succurrebant, quae in eius populi moribus, legibusque perquam absurde videbantur instituta.'

according to the commonly accepted opinion, the true decorations and ornaments of a commonwealth.'[176]

This is a highly ambiguous as well as a highly charged passage. But it certainly contains one objection to Hythloday's analysis to be expected from a good Ciceronian humanist – the persona that, as we have seen, the figure of More sustains throughout the dialogue.[177] The objection More implicitly raises is in fact no different from the one we have already seen him making at the end of Book I. Philosophy, he had told Hythloday, must seek to be useful in civic life. But in order to be useful it must be willing to accommodate to the times. It must work with commonly accepted opinions and try to make them 'as little bad as possible'.[178] But, as we have seen, the most commonly accepted opinion in More's time about nobility, magnificence, splendour and majesty was that they are all connected together. It is precisely Hythloday's contention, however, that the ideal of nobility will have to be separated from these other values if the *optimus status reipublicae* is ever to be attained. More's objection is, therefore, in part a purely practical one: what is absurd about Hythloday's advocacy is the fact that it takes no account whatever of what is generally believed.[179]

It seems clear, however, that More is also offering a deeper comment on the story Hythloday has told, and the question of what further comment he wishes to make has become a subject of intense debate. Recent commentators have suggested that More's remarks must simply be taken at face value: he is criticising the absurdity of the Utopian system for failing to recognise the importance of nobility, magnificence, splendour and majesty in social life.[180] But this thesis has I think nothing to recommend it. In the first place it is not what

---

[176] *Ibid.*, p. 244: 'in eo quoque ipso maxime, quod maximum totius institutionis fundamentum est vita scilicet, victuque communi, sine ullo pecuniae commercio, qua una re funditus evertitur omnis nobilitas, magnificentia, splendor, maiestas, vera ut publica est opinio decora atque ornamenta Reipublicae'. Note the misleading impression conveyed by *Complete Works*, IV in translating 'publica opinio' as 'the estimation of the common people', p. 245.

[177] Bradshaw 'More on Utopia', pp. 25 and 27 claims that 'the role in which More casts himself in the dialogue' is that of 'the practical man of affairs'. But this seems to me to misunderstand More's views about the role of the humanist intellectual in public life. It is as a committed 'civic' humanist, not a mere man of business, that More presents himself.

[178] More, *Complete Works*, IV, p. 100: 'ut sit quam minime malum'.

[179] Here I am much influenced by the excellent discussion in Bradshaw, 'More on Utopia', pp. 25–6.

[180] For example, Bradshaw, *ibid.*, p. 25 thinks that the passage must be taken at face value as an expression of 'More's serious reservations about the ideal system which Hythloday has just outlined'. Cf. also Allen, 'The tone of More's farewell to *Utopia*', pp. 116–18 for a similar argument.

More says in the crucial passage. All he says is that the Utopian system would overthrow 'the commonly accepted opinion' of these values – the opinion that they are all indissolubly linked with each other. As I have laboured to demonstrate, however, it was one of the characteristic ambitions of humanist political theory to dissolve those very links in the name of upholding the rival opinion that true nobility derives from virtue alone. To suppose that More, at this crucial summarising point in his argument, was aligning himself with the very orthodoxy his fellow humanists were overwhelmingly concerned to attack is not merely to go beyond anything he actually says in the text; it is also to make nonsense of the fundamentally humanist allegiances he displays throughout the book.[181]

The clue to More's meaning lies instead, I suggest, in examining the implications of his argument from the point of view of his fellow humanists.[182] His argument itself (to repeat) is that if the Utopian system were to be instituted – forbidding the use of money and abolishing private property – the effect would be to overthrow the values conventionally attached to the concepts of nobility, magnificence, splendor and majesty. As I have been emphasising, however, it was precisely the ambition of More's fellow humanists to overthrow just those conventional values. The implication seems inescapable: More is pointing out that, although the Utopian system may look absurd at first sight, it provides a means of overturning those very values which, according to the humanists themselves, were standing in the way of their own equation between virtue and true nobility, and in consequence standing in the way of enabling the best state of the commonwealth to be realised.

It appears, then, that what More is doing in this crucial passage is putting a challenge to his fellow humanists, and in particular raising a doubt about the coherence of their political thought. On the one hand they liked to claim that they wanted above all to prevent inherited wealth from being treated as a criterion of true nobility. But on the other hand they continued to insist on the indispensability of private property, of hereditability and in general of 'degree, priority and place' as preconditions of any well-ordered

---

[181] For this reason, I cannot accept Surtz's claim (Surtz, *Commentary*, p. 454) that, in using the term 'nobilitas' pejoratively, More 'is emphasising the gulf between the high ideal and the accepted standard'. As I have tried to show, what he is doing is opposing a humanist standard to the commonly accepted one.

[182] Here I argue against my own previous interpretation of the passage. See *Foundations of Modern Political Thought*, I, pp. 256–9, an account endorsed in Logan, *Meaning of More's 'Utopia'*, p. 242.

society. The question we are left with at the end of *Utopia* is whether we can really have it both ways. If we are serious about the claim that virtue constitutes the only true nobility, it may be incoherent simply to endorse the usual justifications for private property. It may instead be necessary to consider the Utopian case for abolishing it in the name of ensuring that virtue alone is honoured, and that the best state of the commonwealth is thereby attained.

There is one very obvious objection, however, to supposing that this is the fundamental message More intends to leave with us at the end of *Utopia*. This is the fact that the figure of More appears throughout the book in the guise of a good Ciceronian humanist. As I have shown, that school of thought consistently and vehemently opposed the Platonist claim that the attainment of the *optimus status reipublicae* might require the abolition of private property. Moreover, when Hythloday first presents the Platonist point of view at the end of Book I, the figure of More responds in precisely the terms I have shown to be characteristic of humanist (and scholastic) theories about the indispensability of private property in any well-ordered commonwealth. 'It is quite impossible to live a satisfactory way of life', More retorts, 'where everything is held in common.'[183] One reason is that gratuitous poverty will result. 'For how can there ever be an adequate supply of goods where individuals are no longer spurred onwards by the motive of personal gain, and become sluggish through trusting to the industry of others?'[184] A further reason is that 'endless quarrelling and sedition' will be sure to arise, 'especially since the authority of magistrates and any reverence for their office will have been completely undermined'.[185]

But the point which has not been sufficiently noticed about the structure of More's *Utopia* is that Hythloday's entire contribution can – and I think should – be read as an ironic inversion of precisely these two central assumptions of scholastic as well as humanist political thought. What Hythloday shows us in Book I is that, even if you uphold the rights of private property, you do not necessarily

---

[183] More, *Complete Works*, IV, p. 106: 'ibi nunquam commode vivi posse, ubi omnia sint communia'.

[184] *Ibid.*, p. 106: 'Nam quo pacto suppetat copia rerum, unoquoque ab labore subducente se? utpote quem neque sui quaestus urget ratio, & alienae industriae fiducia reddit segnem.' As I have sought to show, these were the principal objections that scholastic and humanist political theorists alike registered about Platonic communism. It seems to me a serious anachronism to dismiss them, as Logan does, as 'ineffectual' and 'feeble'. Cf. Logan, *Meaning of More's 'Utopia'*, p. 127.

[185] More, *Complete Works*, IV, p. 106: 'necesse est perpetua caede ac seditione . . . sublata praesertim autoritate ac reverentia magistratuum'.

avoid the twin dangers of poverty and disorder. For in England, where the rights of property-holders are defended with extreme violence, the country nevertheless suffers, as we have seen, from exactly these two social diseases. By contrast, what Hythloday shows us in Book II is that, even if you abolish private property, you do not necessarily contract these social diseases at all.[186] For in Utopia, where everything is held in common, the community is nevertheless described as one in which – as Hythloday very revealingly puts it in his summary – there is no disorder, and where there is abundance of everything for everyone.

There is, moreover, a carefully contrived asymmetry between More's response to these claims at the end of Book I and his later response to exactly the same claims at the end of Book II. At the end of Book I he confidently replies by putting the standard case in favour of private property. By the end of Book II, however, his confidence has completely evaporated in the face of Hythloday's arguments. He makes no attempt to restate his earlier case,[187] but instead brings the discussion to a close by making fully explicit the two points we have seen to be implicit in his earlier comments on Hythloday's narrative.[188] On the one hand he reiterates his purely practical doubts. 'I cannot have any hope', he says, of seeing many features of the Utopian commonwealth adopted.[189] But on the other hand he leaves us to wonder whether this may not be entirely to our loss. For the book ends with More saying that 'I readily confess that there are very many features of the Utopians' commonwealth which, although I cannot have any hope of seeing, I should nevertheless like to see, realised in our own communities.'[190]

Like his fellow-humanists, More acknowledges the impracticability of seeking to abolish the institution of private property. Unlike them, however, he implies that such realism is purchased at a high price. To concede the point, he shows us, is to close off one of the means – perhaps even, Hythloday insists, 'the one and only means' – of bringing about the *optimus status reipublicae*.[191] As a result,

---

[186] But Hexter *More's 'Utopia'*, p. 42 makes a point similar to my own in relation to Book II. See also Bradshaw, 'More on Utopia', pp. 17 and 25 for valuable comments, and the summary of Hexter's discussion in Logan, *Meaning of More's 'Utopia'*, p. 128 and note.

[187] This point is excellently made in Bradshaw, *ibid.*, p. 25.

[188] There seems to me no textual warrant for Bradshaw's claim (*ibid.*, p. 26) that the dialogue is 'simply broken off' at the end.

[189] More, *Complete Works*, IV, p. 246. For the full passage, see n. 190, below.

[190] *Ibid.*, p. 246: 'ita facile confiteor permulta esse in Utopiensium republica, quae in nostris civitatibus optarim verius quam sperarim'.

[191] See More, *ibid.*, p. 104 on the 'una atque unica via' to attain this goal.

Utopia ends on a wistful and elegiac note. Doubtless we have no hope of ever living in the manner of the Utopians; but the thought we are left with is that, for all that, theirs may nevertheless be the best state of a commonwealth.

Acknowledgements.   For giving me comments on earlier drafts of this essay, I am greatly indebted to Brendan Bradshaw, John Dunn, Susan James and Richard Tuck.

Note on quotations.   When citing from Latin texts I have made my own versions in every case, even when using editions which contain facing-text translations. When quoting from sources written in English I have modernised spelling and punctuation.

◁ ═══════════════════════════════════ ▷

7

The concept of *ordre* and the language of classical republicanism in Jean-Jacques Rousseau

MAURIZIO VIROLI

I

This essay has two principal objectives. In the first place I shall offer an analysis of Rousseau's concept of 'political order', and in the second I shall attempt to show how that concept was indebted to the language of classical and modern republicanism.

The term *ordre* occupies a central place in all of Rousseau's writings, and is used to describe a wide range of different concepts.[1] There is the metaphysical order, the natural order, the moral order and – what I shall be almost wholly concerned with in this essay – the political order.[2] Rousseau uses the term in two distinct senses, both of which derive from the philosophical language of his day.[3] In the first sense it is broadly synonymous with 'harmony' or 'concord', the co-operation which must exist between the parts that make up any whole if it is to attain some common end. The antithesis of this is, of course, internal conflict, the tendency of the various parts to pursue individual and separate ends.[4] In the second sense, order is used to

---

All references to the works of Rousseau are to the edition of the *Oeuvres complètes* edited by Bernard Gagnebin and Marcel Raymond (Paris, 1959–69).

[1] See P. Burgelin, *La Philosophie de l'existence de J. J. Rousseau*, Presses Universitaires de France (Paris, 1952), pp. 411–15; J. Shklar, *Men and Citizens* (Cambridge, 1969), p. 1; R. Polin, *La Politique de la solitude* (Paris), pp. 64–71.

[2] Cf. M. Launay, *Le Vocabulaire politique de Jean-Jacques Rousseau* (Geneva–Paris, 1977), pp. 151–4.

[3] See the definitions of 'ordre' and 'désordre' in the *Dictionnaire de l'Academie Française* (Paris, 1745).

[4] Examples of the use of the term 'ordre' as harmony can be found in 'Profession de foi du Vicaire savoyard', in *Emile*, IV, pp. 578–83; *Les Rêveries du promeneur solitaire*, I, pp. 1010, 1018–19; *Rousseau juge de Jean-Jacques*, I, pp. 953–4, 959. See also A. Robinet, 'Lexicographie philosophique de l' "ordre de la nature" dans la profession de foi du Vicaire Savoyard', *Revue Internationale de Philosophie*, XXXII (1978), 238–59 and P. Bréhier, 'Lectures malebranchistes de Jean-Jacques Rousseau', *Revue Internationale de Philosophie*, I (1938), 98–120.

mean 'the just and proper disposition', the correct location, that is, of each part of any whole on a scale of values or of degrees of perfection. The antithesis of this is an unjust or incorrect scale or hierarchy in which the best are at the bottom and the worst at the top. It was, for instance, as he set out in the *Confessions*,[5] clearly contrary to the order of nature that the highest positions in a society should be occupied by those who are morally the worst of men, while the best are confined to the lower reaches. The third meaning of the term, 'order' as a synonym for 'moderation' or 'temperance', partially overlays both the notion of harmony and of just disposition. Moderation is, in fact, the distinctive feature of every man who is capable of controlling his passions. In the moderate man the passions are, therefore, in harmony with the other parts of his being, and in particular with his reason. The antithesis of moderation is the absence of any control. This concept of moderation was central to Rousseau's definition of virtue and to his understanding of the characteristics of the well-ordered community.

Rousseau's sources for this view are many,[6] but it was, perhaps, in the works of Lamy that he found what was for him the most compelling and impassioned celebration of the natural order. In Lamy's *Entretiens sur les sciences*,[7] which Rousseau claimed to have been one of his earliest 'spiritual guides', and which derived much of its inspiration from a reading of St Augustine and Cicero, he found the idea of virtue as the *ordo amoris* and the notion of order as, in Cicero's words, 'the arrangement of things in their suitable and appropriate places' (*De officis* I.xl.142). Rousseau's principal source for order as moderation is indubitably Plutarch.[8] Nature, the creation of an intelligent and benevolent God, is the model for order in the sense both of harmony and of the *suum gradum*.[9] The model for disorder, in the sense of both internal conflict and 'unjust disposition', is human society.

The *political* order is intended to supplant the disorder which pre-

[5] *Les Confessions*, I, pp. 95–6.
[6] See, for example, Shaftesbury, *An Inquiry Concerning Virtue and Merit*. Rousseau probably knew the French translation: Shaftesbury, *Philosophie morale* (Amsterdam, 1745), esp. pp. 128–30.   [7] B. Lamy, *Entretiens sur les sciences* (Paris, 1706), p. 304.
[8] *Les Oeuvres morales et meslées de Plutarque: translatées de Grec en François ... par le traducteur Jacques Amyot* (Geneva 1582), ch. 3, 'De la vertu morale', p. 32.
[9] On this point see J. Ehrard, *L'Idée de la nature en France dans la première moitié du XVIII siècle* (Paris, 1963); R. J. Howells, 'The metaphysic of nature: basic values and their application to the social philosophy of Rousseau', *Studies on Voltaire and the Seventeenth Century* LX (1968), 109–200; P. Benichou, 'Réfléxions sur l'idée de nature chez Jean-Jacques Rousseau', *Annales de la Société Jean-Jacques Rousseau* XXXVIII (1972–7), 25–40.

vails among men. This cannot, however, be modelled on the same principle which governs the natural world since this is itself the model for order. The principle is the preservation of all things. But as each individual part has a value which is relative only to the whole, it may, if necessary, be sacrificed for the good of the whole. This law, which grants superiority to the whole over any of its parts, applies, according to Rousseau, only to the natural, and not to the moral sphere.[10] In the political order the preservation of the whole cannot be obtained by the sacrifice of any of its individual parts. 'Public welfare' (*le salut publique*), Rousseau told Helvetius – in reply to his claim that, 'everything becomes legitimate, even virtuous, in the interest of the public good' – 'is nothing if all its parts are not themselves secure.'[11] It is tyranny, not the true *ordre politique*, which demands that its citizens sacrifice themselves in the interest of society as a whole.[12]

Nature is the model of harmony, but the political order can only be achieved through artifice and by observing rules which are quite different from those which obtain in the natural world. Disorder among men is clearly unnatural, but only the art of politics can reintroduce order into the human sphere. For Rousseau, as for Machiavelli, the masters of this art are the great legislators, the founding fathers of the ancient world.[13] While *les politiques modernes* seek only their own gain, these men sought only the establishment of a well-ordered political community in which every man would be compelled to live a life of *virtù*. Legislators must, therefore, be prudent men capable of ordering their laws, if they are to be at all persuasive, in accordance with the spirit of the people. But while Machiavelli's *prudente ordinatore* must have power, must, indeed, be all-powerful, Rousseau's legislator has no authority whatsoever.[14] He *knows* how to create the true political order, but he lacks the power to institute it.

For Rousseau the conflict between individuals was indissolubly linked to the very existence of society itself. In the state of nature there simply is no conflict, but neither, of course, is there any society. Once men begin to live together they become concerned with the esteem in which they are held by their fellows. Every man

---

[10] *Lettre de J.-J. Rousseau à M. De Voltaire*, 18 August 1756, IV, p. 1070.
[11] *Notes sur 'De l'esprit' d'Helvétius*, IV, p. 1126.
[12] *Economie politique*, III, p. 256.
[13] See V. Goldschmidt, *Anthropologie et politique: les principes du système de Rousseau* (Paris, 1974), p. 571.
[14] Cf. N. Machiavelli, *Discorsi intorno alla prima deca di Tito Livio*, Bk I, ch. 9, and Rousseau, *Contrat social*, Bk II, ch. 8.

seeks the approval of every other man, and each one struggles to be the most admired or the most respected. In passing from the state of nature into civil society, man's *amour de soi* is transformed into *amour propre* and the *fureur de se distinguer* becomes the prime concern in life. As a result, every man's fellows are reduced to just so many rivals in the struggle for appreciation and esteem. The 'natural history of society'[15] cannot, therefore, produce harmony and the just disposition of its parts spontaneously. The reverse is, in fact, the case since it is precisely society which creates hostility and produces moral inequalities which are wholly at variance with the laws of nature. 'Society' and 'order' are, therefore, antithetical terms, from which it would seem to follow that the recovery of order can only be achieved by exiting from society altogether, for only thus may a man hope to recover the order of nature and with it the moral and metaphysical order.[16]

In Rousseau's political theory the notion of a political order is an alternative to both disorder and solitude. At its most essential, the problem which Rousseau attempted to solve was how to make order and society compatible, how, in other words, to create a *société bien ordonnée* for individuals who pursue only their own interests.[17]

II

Plutarch, who was one of Rousseau's favourite authors, explains in his *Parallel Lives* the principle which guided Solon in drawing up the constitution of Athens. Laws, so Solon believed, have the power to prevent injustice and restrain avarice. To Anacharsis who mocked the idea that written laws might be able to control the actions of men, Solon replied that all men will respect agreements when these seem to be operating in their own interests, that in such cases it was simply more useful to respect the law than to transgress it, and on the basis of this proposition he had drafted his constitution. Subsequent history, observed Plutarch, had, however, shown Solon to be wrong and Anacharsis right.[18] Rousseau's political theory is a continuation of Solon's utopian vision, for its ambition was precisely to restrain through the law the passions which drove men to harm and offend one another. And, in order to achieve this end,

---

[15] R. Nisbet, *Social Change and History* (New York and Oxford, 1969), p. 145.
[16] *Les Rêveries du promeneur solitaire*, I: pp. 1066 and 1010.
[17] *Manuscript de Genève*, III p. 289.
[18] Plutarch, *Lives*, I (Solon), The Loeb Classical Library (Cambridge, Mass., and London, 1957), V, pp. 415–17.

the true political constitution had, like Solon's, to make justice compatible with utility and rights with interest.

For Rousseau the only hope of checking disorder is to make the law sovereign over all men, rather than, as happens in tyrannies, making certain men masters of the law. Rousseau himself said that the *Contrat social* should be read as a theory of good government based upon the principle of the sovereignty of the law, and of all modern political philosophers he is, perhaps, the one who has most insisted that the principle of liberty should be identified with the rule of law.

When Rousseau speaks of 'laws' he means the public and sovereign decrees of the General Will acting in the public interest. One can only speak of laws if these are decreed by a legitimate and sovereign authority, and if they respect the twin principles of universality and reciprocity. If, however, the authority is not legitimate or if the decree discriminates or makes exceptions, then it does not constitute a law.[19] If, that is, any law seeks to promote any particular interest at the expense of the public interest, it is void. In all of Rousseau's writings the sovereignty of the law means always the sovereignty of those laws which emanate from the General Will for the public good and the security of every citizen.[20] Only then does the sovereignty of the law become the necessary condition of liberty.

The frontispiece of the *Contrat social* carries a rubric from Virgil, 'foederis aquas dicamus leges'. But Rousseau might also have added Cicero's famous remark, 'omnes legum servi sumus uti esse liberi possumus'.[21] In a fragment entitled *Des loix* Rousseau explained how this claim should be understood. 'A man is free', he wrote, 'when he is subject to laws, not when he owes obedience to a single individual, for when that occurs he is constrained by the will of another, but in observing the law he is bound only by the General Will which is also his own.'[22]

This account of the relationship between liberty and the law is both simple and reductive. It is, as others have noted, an account only of that 'positive liberty' which derives from membership of a Sovereign Body and, as Norberto Bobbio has pointed out, to attribute to the law the power to safeguard a 'negative' liberty, would require a limitation of the meaning of the term 'law'. It is,

[19] *Contrat social*, Bk IV, ch. 1.
[20] See, for instance: *Economie politique*, III, pp. 248 and 254; *Lettres de la montagne*, III, pp. 807–8.
[21] Cf. also Titus Livy, *Ab urbe condita*, Bk II, ch. 1.   [22] *Des loix*, III, p. 492.

indeed, necessary to define as true laws only those norms which limit the individual's behaviour, with the sole purpose of allowing everyone to enjoy his own sphere of liberty safe from the possibility of interference by others.[23]

I believe, however, that Rousseau's concept of the sovereignty of the law is sufficient as a necessary condition not only for the preservation of the 'positive' but also for the enjoyment of 'negative' liberty. The passage quoted above ends with the claim that the sovereignty of the law is the guarantee that some men shall not become the slaves of others, that it is precisely their *negative* liberty which that sovereignty preserves since in becoming a slave a man is prevented from pursuing his own ends. 'The master', wrote Rousseau, 'may allow to one man what he denies to another, unless the law makes no distinction between men, and the condition of all men is the same and consequently there are neither masters nor servants.'

The principle which underpins this whole argument is that individuals can only be free if they live in a state where the laws are sovereign, if, that is, they live in a *République*.[24]

The term 'republic', as Rousseau uses it, is not intended to describe a form of government, but the nature of a political constitution whose distinctive characteristics are that 'l'intérêt public gouverne' and that 'la chose publique est quelque chose'. The antithesis to the republic is tyranny, a political constitution, that is, in which private interests rule and the public domain (*la chose publique*) is empty. Rousseau repeats verbatim Aristotle's distinction (*Politics* 1272a) between right political constitutions and corrupt ones which operate solely in the interests of their rulers.

In principle, then, a 'republic' is perfectly compatible with a monarchical form of government, provided one bears in mind that, for Rousseau, it was imperative that the prince was only the minister of the sovereign body, and only when that body comprised all the people, could it exercise legislative power. This meant, of course, that it was impossible for a monarch to rule both for the public good and in his own personal interests.[25]

We find the same apparent ambiguity in Rousseau that we do in Machiavelli, the 'modern' republican whom Rousseau probably

---

[23] N. Bobbio, *Il futuro della democrazia* (Torino, 1984), p. 156; Bobbio refers to the definitions of B. Constant, *De l'esprit de conquête* (1814), chs. 7 and 8, and I. Berlin, *Four Essays on Liberty* (London and Oxford, 1969), pp. 162–3.
[24] For the definition of 'République', see *Contrat social*, Bk II, ch. 4.
[25] *Contrat social*, Bk III, ch. 10; *Jugement sur le projet de paix perpétuelle*, III, p. 952.

most admired. In certain passages in the *Discorsi* Machiavelli speaks of political constitutions which operate for the public good but which are ruled by a king.[26] Elsewhere, however, he claims explicitly that *only* a republican government, as opposed to a monarchy or principate, is capable of upholding the public against the private good.[27]

From Machiavelli to Rousseau the definition of the republic acquired a far more general significance than it had previously had. It came to mean not 'republican government' but a political constitution in which authority is exercised *sub leges* and *per leges* and in which the common good is upheld. And if one goes beyond definitions, it is clear that Rousseau is also close to Machiavelli in the latter's claim that only a republican government can secure the public good; for in order that the laws may be sovereign, and that the common good may be upheld, it was essential that the people should exercise legislative power and elect their own magistrates. Only thus, under these conditions, would it be possible for the laws to be just and to protect the liberty of people.

The liberty of the citizens depends, according to Hobbes, on the obligation which everyone contracts at the moment of submission to the sovereign. This liberty consists, essentially, in the right to defend one's own person against any aggressor and to cause no harm to oneself. It is a liberty which exists primarily in the absence of constraint, in the freedom to buy and sell, to enter into contracts, to choose one's own home or style of life, to educate one's own children. Hobbes criticises the Greek and Roman political theorists for having created a confusion between the liberty of cities and the liberty of citizens.[28] Rousseau, on the other hand, draws upon those same writers, and their modern followers, to overthrow Hobbes's thesis and return to the identification of the liberty of the individual with the liberty of the community.

The concept of liberty, as something independent of the private will of another man, is further defined by analogy with the republican idea of the liberty of the community. Cicero had defined the liberty of the city as the antithesis of slavery and domination. This same analogy is also to be found in Machiavelli. In the first of the *Discorsi*, Machiavelli distinguishes between those 'citizens whose principle has been subordinated by another' and those 'whose principle

[26] See, for instance, *Discorsi sopra la prima deca di Tito Livio*, Bk I, ch. 9.
[27] See *Discorsi*, Bk II, ch. 2.
[28] Hobbes, *Leviathan*, in *The English Works of Thomas Hobbes* (Aalen, 1966), Part II, ch. 21.

is far from any foreign servitude and who are thus ruled according to their own free will'. In similar terms, he also distinguishes between 'free men' and those who 'depend on others'.[29] Rousseau also borrowed from this language the sense of his opposition between servitude and liberty, and he made of it the principal foundations for his doctrine of the sovereignty of the law. When Rousseau speaks of the liberty which is guaranteed by the sovereignty of the law he means the liberty of the state or of the people, but that liberty is for him also synonymous with the liberty of the individual.

In any community in which the ruler imposes his own interests against those of the general will, the greater part of the citizenry will, by being hindered by the private will of a single individual, be unable to pursue its own ends; the same occurs when the community as a whole becomes the slave of another, for the citizens of a state which is not free are also unfree if a freeman is, in Hobbes's account, he 'that in those things which by his strength and wit he is able to, is not hindered to do what he has a will to do'.[30]

For Rousseau the antithesis of the well-ordered polity was, of course, a tyranny. In the former, government is always *sub leges* and *per leges*, while in the latter it constitutes the usurpation of sovereign power for the achievement of particular and private ends.

When Rousseau speaks of tyranny as government by a ruler who places himself above the law, I would argue that the law to which he is referring is the fundamental and constitutive law of the body politic, the terms, that is, of the social contract itself.[31] Such fundamental and constitutive laws are those *conventions générales* which restrain the sovereign and which are created for this express purpose.[32] With the institution of a legitimate authority, however, there is also created a reciprocal obligation on the part of every citizen towards his sovereign, and it is this reciprocity which binds together all the members of a political community.

By the terms of the original contract, each individual submits himself to the General Will, but the latter can only direct the powers of the state for the purposes for which the political community was originally created, for the good, that is, of all and everyone.[33] The

[29] *Discorsi*, Bk I, ch. 2.
[30] Hobbes, *ibid.*; see also Q. Skinner, 'The idea of negative liberty: philosophical and historical perspectives', in R. Rorty, J. B. Scheewind, Q. Skinner, (eds.), *Philosophy in History* (Cambridge, 1984), pp. 212–13.
[31] The opposite view has been expressed by R. Derathé, *Rousseau et la science politique de son temps* (Paris, 1950), pp. 130–5.
[32] cf. *Des loix*, III, p. 491.   [33] *Contrat social*, Bk I, ch. 2.

tyrant, therefore, who exercises sovereign authority for his own ends commits a violation of the original social contract and this violation annuls the citizens' obligation to him. For this reason, Rousseau reiterates that tyranny destroys the unity of the body politic,[34] since, as we have already seen, tyranny for the citizen means a loss of his 'negative' liberty, in that he is prevented from pursuing his own interests. It is only when the sovereign deliberates by laws which compel or forbid the same thing for all people and which (as laws) exhibit no preferences, that the citizen's liberty will be assured.

The freedom which the citizenry enjoys by virtue of the law is *civil liberty*. For Rousseau, civil liberty is preferable to the liberty supposedly enjoyed by men in the state of nature. Natural liberty is apparently unlimited; but since it depends only upon the power of the individual, it is necessarily precarious and may, at any moment, be transformed into servitude. Civil liberty, however, is limited, its boundaries are set by the laws and the individual liberties of others. But civil liberty assures 'par un droit que l'union sociale rend invincible'[35] the protection of the life and property of every individual. The force of the law shelters men from the consequences of their dependence upon others, and by the force of sanctions prevents them from committing injustice.

In addition to civil liberty, Rousseau also cites as one of the benefits of the well-ordered society, *liberté morale*.[36] Unlike civil liberty, moral liberty is, by nature, wholly interior. While civil liberty is concerned with the relationship between men, moral liberty is concerned with the relationship between each individual and himself. The man who is morally free is one who is master of his own passions and who lives by a moral law which he himself provides. The morally free individual is just and moderate not because the law compels him to be so, but because he loves justice and moderation. A man may be compelled to be civilly free; but no man can be compelled to be morally free.

A morally free man is, for Rousseau, a man who is *bien ordonné*. The analogy between the microcosm of the well-ordered man and the macrocosm of the well-ordered society is an essential component of Rousseau's theory of political order. Just as in the well-ordered man individual reason rules the passions, so in the well-ordered society public reason rules the passions of men through the process of law. In both the republic and the individual, laws are not imposed by

[34] *Manuscript de Genève*, III, p. 303; *Economie politique*, III, p. 256.
[35] *Contrat social*, Bk II, ch. 4.   [36] *Contrat social*, Bk I, ch. 8.

force against men's passions and their wishes, rather the wishes themselves serve to moderate the passions with, in Plutarch's phrase, 'a discrete and salutary hand'.[37] The well-ordered republic is free because it observes its own laws and is dependent upon no one. Similarly, the well-ordered man is free because he observes the laws which he himself has set and because he is the master of his passions.

All men, whether through ambition or *amour propre*, tend to impose their own ends upon others and to seek to dominate their fellows. They, therefore, naturally seek to weaken the sovereignty of the law; but so long as the law remains sovereign the liberty of every man is equal to the liberty of every other. In the republic, wrote Rousseau, citing d'Argenson, 'everyone is perfectly free with regard to everything which is not harmful to others'.[38]

Those citizens who wish only to live secure lives and to enjoy the benefits of their own private freedom, have most to fear from a ruler who attempts to place himself above the law. The great and the powerful have, however, in Rousseau's view, no wish to see the law made sovereign since this destroys any possibility of preference and the struggle for preference and superiority is what rules their lives. When they invoke the law it is only to make themselves the arbitrators of it.[39]

The claim that the law was the principal guarantee of the peace and safety of the citizenry had already been made by Cicero. 'Laws', he wrote in the *De legibus*, 'were invented for the safety of citizens and preservation of States and the tranquility and happiness of human life' (II, V, II). But the same claim may be found in Machiavelli, and it is to Machiavelli that Rousseau's language is most obviously indebted. Not all men, said Machiavelli, love the *vivere libero* and, for this reason, 'a small number desire to be free to command, but all the others, who are infinite in number, wish only for the liberty to live in safety'.[40] The people feel protected when they see that all live under the same laws and that even kings, like the king of France, cannot rule without the law. The great (*grandi*), on the other hand, driven by their ambitions constantly to increase their power, 'create alternations' in the *vivere libero*.

As an example of those citizens who wish for the liberty provided by a sovereign body of the law, Rousseau cites the middle class formed by the artisans and merchants of Geneva.[41] The liberty which

[37] Plutarch, 'De la vertu morale' (see n. 8), p. 37.
[38] *Contrat social*, Bk IV, ch. 8.   [39] *Lettres de la montagne*, III, p. 889.
[40] *Discorsi*, Bk II, ch. 16.   [41] *Lettres de la montagne*, III, p. 889.

this group sought, above all the liberty to pursue their respective professions, to enjoy their own goods, to cultivate their domestic lives, to meet in their 'clubs' and not to be unjustly condemned, was precisely that 'private' freedom which can only be guaranteed by a sovereign law. If the city becomes 'disordered' and some are able to act over or against the law, then the citizens are no longer secure and lose the positive liberty which consists in their being members of a sovereign body, as well as their negative liberty. Under such circumstances, they might be required to fight in wars of conquest ordered by the tyrant, or compelled to pay unjust taxes, or prevented from trading as they wished, or they might be unjustly imprisoned and their women subjected to indignities; and finally all access to honour would be denied to anyone who did not wish, or did not know how, to intrigue with or flatter the tyrant.[42]

So long as the General Will remains sovereign, both the community and the individual are free; but when a particular will is imposed upon the general, both the community and the individual become enslaved. In order to preserve its liberty, the republic must act rightly (*recte*) and since the active principle in any polity is the sovereign body, that liberty will survive only so long as the sovereign body prescribes the laws. In the *Contrat social* Rousseau discussed the problem of how to ensure that the sovereign body was also 'right' (*droite*) and how to prevent the sovereign assembly from acting in the interests of one group against the interests of the republic as a whole.[43] His conclusion, however, was that there simply was no way of being certain that this could be achieved. The procedures by which a collective decision was arrived at should, he argued, vary according to the problem under discussion. Every effort should also be made to prevent factions and interest groups from forming. But, in the end, the only assurance that the General Will would remain right lay in the rectitude of the individual members of the sovereign body.

At the moment of voting, those members are not being asked to express their individual preferences; they are being asked if a certain law is, or is not, in agreement with the General Will. If all vote correctly the majority will, in Rousseau's view, constitute an expression of the General Will. But if anyone has voted in the interests of his *motifs secrets*, then the sovereign deliberation will be

---

[42] See, for instance, *Lettres de la montagne*, III, pp. 882–7; *Economie politique*, III, pp. 271–2.
[43] *Contrat social*, Bk III, ch. 3; Bk IV, chs. 1, 2 and 3.

the expression of a particular will *even if* this is accepted by the majority.[44]

The liberty of the community therefore demands that civil virtue must be sufficiently compelling to overcome not the *utilitas singolorum* but rather simple *cupiditas*, the overriding desire for honour and superiority. But the preservation of the political order does not require of the citizen that he sacrifice his private interests to the *utilitas publica*, for in a well-ordered republic private and public interests are identical. True, the immediate interests of the individual may conflict with the public interest; but the permanent and principal interests of the citizen will always be preserved by the republic so long as this is governed by laws which are just. 'The first and greatest public interest', wrote Rousseau, 'is always justice.'[45] But justice is nothing other than each citizen's right to be subjected to laws which are universally binding on all men.

The republic is clearly not a society for angels. A community composed of men without private interests or passionately held preferences 'would fall into languidness'. For, in order for there to be a political society, there had to exist even among the company of angels one Satan, and among the Apostles at least one Judas.[46] The end of the good political order is not to destroy passions and private interests, but to moderate and direct them towards those objectives which are not contrary to the public interest. The objective of the true politician is not to impose the *utilitas publica* upon the *utilitas singolorum*; it is to make the private and the public interests agree.[47] And in order to achieve this, it is necessary to curb the ambitions of the powerful and ensure that the laws guarantee to the people the expression of their own interests and safety.[48]

III

For the republic to remain well-ordered it must oppose the passion for domination with another, the love of equality and of the law. The liberty of the city will survive only so long as the citizens maintain their civic virtue. If the citizens fail to concern themselves with public affairs, or fail to comply with the duties demanded of them, then the powerful (*les grands*) and the magistrates may be able to

---

[44] *Contrat social*, Bk IV, ch. 2.   [45] *Lettres de la montagne*, III, p. 891.
[46] *Jean-Jacques Rousseau à Usteri*, 18 June 1763, in P. Usteri and L. Ritter (eds.), *Correspondance de Jean-Jacques Rousseau avec Léonard Usteri* (Geneva–Paris, 1910), pp. 73–8.   [47] *Jean-Jacques Rousseau à Christophe de Beaumont*, IV, p. 937.
[48] *Economie politique*, III, pp. 255–6.

impose their interests over the public interest and, as a consequence, the city will lose its liberty. Civic virtue, then, is crucial to the maintenance of the sovereignty of the laws. Rousseau also extended Montesquieu's claim that virtue was the principle of democratic grovernment by arguing that all well-ordered states, whether democratic or not, had to be regulated by civic virtue. Such virtue will be more or less important according to the form of government, but no legitimate constitution can operate without it.[49]

In a well-ordered republic, the virtues of the citizens are identical to those of the magistrates. As the magistrates must be just, moderate, courageous and prudent, so the citizen body must be just in its observation of the laws and its compliance with its civic duties, moderate in its pursuit of wealth and honour, prudent in its choice of magistrates and courageous in opposition to its enemies.

Such virtues are not, however, created out of a Christian love for humanity so much as out of a love of the *patria*, for the community itself. Only the love of one's *patria* is capable of inspiring courage and determination; for while Christianity teaches men the virtues of sweetness, equity, charity and indulgence, republicanism, insisted Rousseau like Machiavelli before him, taught the virtues of the citizen. He, therefore, attacked Augustine for having criticised Brutus, the most outstanding example of republican virtue, and praised Cato, the symbol 'of the energy of virtue'.[50]

Machiavelli had blamed Christianity for having weakened the love of that *vivere libero* which had been so strong in antiquity but which was now almost unknown among his contemporaries. Paganism had taught that the highest good was to be found in 'greatness of spirit and in all those things which make men strong', whereas Christianity had made 'the world feeble' and had thus given it over to 'villainous men'.[51] Rousseau repeats, almost word for word, the views of what he called the 'bon citoyen et honnête homme Machiavelli'.[52] Christianity has made men *lâches*, with no love for liberty and, without that love, they make easy prey for the first person who wishes to enslave them.[53] Liberty demands antique, not Christian virtues. 'I am wrong', he declared, 'to speak of a "Christian Republic". Each one of those words cancels out the other. Christianity teaches only servitude and dependence. Its spirit is too favourable to tyranny for tyranny not to always profit by it.'[54] A corrupt people is, as Machiavelli had explained in the *Discorsi*, unfit

[49] *Contrat social*, Bk III, ch. 4.   [50] *De la patrie*, III, p. 536.
[51] *Discorsi*, Bk II, ch. 2.   [52] *Contrat social*, III, p. 409, n. 2.
[53] *De l'honneur et de la vertu*, III, p. 506.   [54] *Contrat social*, Bk IV, ch. 8.

for liberty.[55] In the *Contrat social* and the *Considérations sur le gouvernement de Pologne* we find the same language being used.[56] Rousseau also took from his republican sources – Machiavelli and Montesquieu – both the notion that liberty cannot survive without civic virtue, and the principle that good laws will never be effective without good customs.

Machiavelli had also, as Montesquieu was to do, discussed the relationship between law and custom.[57] If the customs of a people were corrupt, he claimed in the *Discorsi*, the 'well-ordered laws' would be of no use, for 'just as good customs require good laws to sustain them, so good laws require good customs if they are to be observed'.[58] Similarly Rousseau maintained that the well-ordered (modern) republic must, like the republics of the ancient world, be able to change its customs, for all private worlds are publicly relevant and bad morals are simply bad politics.[59]

The preservation of the good political order requires of the citizens not only that they should obey their magistrates, but that they should also attend the assemblies, pay their taxes and fight against invaders. It requires, too, that the men should be sober, hard-working and temperate, and that the women should be docile, reserved and dedicated to domestic affairs. In order to ensure the preservation of good customs, it is desirable that all the citizens should know each other and that even the individual's private life should be subject to the scrutiny of the community. Rousseau also suggests that the state should create a magistrate, a censor, who, like the Consistory which Calvin had established in Geneva, would be charged with watching over the integrity of private customs. For Rousseau, a people with corrupt customs cannot be a free one. But he is also certain that good customs cannot be preserved by the force of the law.[60] The legislator must, instead, attempt to influence behaviour through laws which enhance or diminish a man's public reputation.[61]

---

[55] *Discorsi*, Bk I, ch. 16.   [56] Respectively in Bk II, ch. 8 and III, p. 954.
[57] Montesquieu, *De l'esprit des lois*, Bk XIX.   [58] *Discorsi*, Bk I, ch. 18.
[59] Jean-Jacques Rousseau, *Lettre à d'Alembert sur les spectacles* (Amsterdam, 1762), pp. 208–9.
[60] Rousseau makes this point particularly clear in the *Lettre à d'Alembert* (see n. 59), pp. 113–14; cf. also the chapter 'De la censure' in *Contrat social*, Bk IV, ch. 7.
[61] The problem of civil religion in Rousseau requires a far more detailed treatment than I am able to give it here. It should be noted, however, that the chapter on civil religion in the *Contrat social* cannot be dismissed as an incoherent appendix. For Rousseau civil religion was the means to secure the sovereignty of the laws and the unity of the body politic. In this context, it is not without significance that the first draft of the chapter on civil religion was composed on the verso of the sheet which contained the draft for the chapter on the legislator.

As many critics have noted,[62] Rousseau's political doctrines, above all his views on *moeurs*, result in a severe limitation of the private arena in favour of the public; and in this respect, the final chapter of the *Contrat social*, on 'civil religion', casts a particularly sinister shadow over the image of the well-ordered republic.

Censorship and civil religion are, for Rousseau, the means of preserving good order and liberty within the republic and for preventing the *respublica* becoming a *res privata*. Such means would, however, seem to annihilate all *res privata* and thus to deny the purpose of the republic which, for Rousseau, is to protect the liberty of individuals.

Rousseau supposes that, by nature, all men seek admiration and public esteem; and since in a corrupt state admiration and respect are, above all, attributes of wealth and power,[63] it follows that men will seek greater and greater degrees of wealth and power until they finally come to violate the laws and impose their own private interests upon the community. The well-ordered republic then collapses into a tyranny. The only means to preserve liberty is to order the republic so that admiration and public esteem are attributes of virtue, not of wealth and power. It is therefore crucial that virtue should be the only means to achieve honour. To ensure this it is necessary for the opinions – and for Rousseau opinions and customs are identical – of the citizenry to be uncorrupted, and this will only occur if the laws, and the magistrates, are just.

If, however, honours are given to men who are not virtuous, the city will not be able to remain in liberty for long. By virtue, Rousseau means civil virtue, all those actions which contribute to the public good. In this insistence that *vera nobilitas (sola) virtus est*, Rousseau is following Machiavelli who, in his turn, was repeating what Quentin Skinner here calls 'almost a slogan of humanist political thought'.[64] With the same energy as Machiavelli, Rousseau insists that honours and public offices should be given only to the most virtuous and most able citizens.[67] For if such things fall into the hands of the vicious, they will use them only for their own private advantage.

The procedure by which the magistrates are elected therefore assumes the utmost importance. In both the *Contrat social* and the *Discours sur l'inégalité*, Rousseau puts forward the same arguments

---

[62] The most influential is B. Constant, *Principes de politique* (Paris, 1957), pp. 1215, 1231.   [63] *De l'honneur et de la vertu*, III, p. 503.

[64] See p. 138 above.

[65] *Discorsi*, Bk I, ch. 16 and Bk III, ch. 25; cf. also *Dedicace au discours sur l'inégalité*, III, pp. 117–18 and 222–3.

Machiavelli had used in the *Discorsi*, namely that it is public opinion, *la voix publique*, which should decide who from among the citizen body is worthy of being entrusted with public office.[66] In a monarchy the king decides and it is therefore easy for 'small meddlers, deceivers and intriguers to rise to great positions; but it would be very hard for a sot to rise to the head of a republican government'.[67] The people, so long as they are not themselves corrupt, are far more judicious in their choice of leaders, since it is they who are the first to suffer at the hands of corrupt officials.

In Rousseau's theory, the political order thus provides the only valid reply to the moral demands of order, both as *suum gradum* and as 'harmony' and 'moderation', in the first case because virtue is rewarded by public honours and vice condemned by public shame; in the second because the various parts of the body politic will co-operate rather than seek private gains; and in the third because no one's immoderate passions are permitted to impose themselves upon the republic.

IV

This theory was, as we have seen, largely inspired by the language of classical and modern republicanism. But it is also heavily indebted to the language of the natural law. These two might, at first sight, seem incompatible. The notion of the social contract is strongly individualistic and makes an appeal to normative reasoning and a rationalistic calculus, whereas republicanism makes virtue the foundation of any political association and insists upon the centrality of the passions, and in particular of the love of *patria*. Rousseau, however, drew equally on both these traditions and the attempts by some scholars to diminish the importance of the discourse of iusnaturalism in his writings are, in my view, mistaken.[68] Rousseau was certainly a republican, perhaps one of the last, but he was also the author of the *Contrat social*.

The two languages are, however, used in different theoretical contexts. From the republican tradition he took the principal characteristics of his political order: the sovereignty of the laws, the concept of liberty, the need for virtue and love of *patria*. But when he

---

[66] *Contrat social*, Bk III, ch. 2; *Discours sur l'inégalité*, III, pp. 222–3; and *Discorsi*, Bk III, ch. 34.   [67] *Contrat social*, Bk III, ch. 6.
[68] Cf., for instance, C. E. Vaughan, *The Political Writings of Jean-Jacques Rousseau* (Cambridge, 1915) I, p. 440; J. N. Shklar, *op. cit.*, p. 167; and, to a lesser extent, R. Derathé, *op. cit.*, p. 377.

claimed that *la république* was the only political constitution to which individuals who were concerned only with their own good could rationally give their consent, he was only developing the central core of the notion of the social contract. When he criticised Hobbes and Grotius, he criticised them for being, as he saw it, incoherent, not for being contractualists.

As Rousseau explained in the *Lettres de la montagne*, it is in the interests of the individual citizen to be virtuous, since if the citizens do not interest themselves with public affairs the community will, sooner or later, lose its good order and with it its liberty, to the detriment of precisely those who had abandoned public concerns in order to pursue their private interests. The un-virtuous citizen acts, therefore, not only badly but also unwisely. One cannot, however, expect men to calculate their long-term interests in this way. For Rousseau, political virtue is a passion and cannot, therefore, be the result of calculation. For this reason, the task of the modern legislator as for the legislators of antiquity, is to instil in men's hearts the sense of belonging to a national community. This community is not created through a calculation of interests but grows up through shared habits and shared customs. And it is at this point that the language of rational choice is abandoned in favour of the language of collective identity.

All of the measures described by Rousseau to maintain order within the republic – territorial limitations, the prevention of excessive economic inequality, public reward for virtue, popular election to public office, censure and civil religion – are all means to prolong the life of the community, but they are not sufficient to prevent its ultimate dissolution. This can be delayed but it can never be avoided altogether.[69] By this 'death of the body politic' Rousseau understands the collapse of the *form* of the body politic, the collapse of legitimate government into tyranny, which is 'the natural and inevitable fate of even the best constituted governments'.[70]

In the chapter of the *Contrat social* which follows the one on the 'Mort du corps politique', Rousseau sets out the best means by which to preserve the health of the body politic and to prevent it from becoming 'disordered'. All these are intended to bring the republic back to its beginnings. The most important of them are the calling of frequent assemblies of all the people which, Rousseau believed, would have the effect of 're-establishing good order' and of reaffirming the social contract.

---

[69]   *Contrat social*, Bk III, ch. 2.   [70]   *Jugement sur la Polysnodie*, III, p. 639.

For Rousseau the republic may be said to have collapsed (and this is something quite different from a change in government) when the formal ties which bind the various members of the body politic have been violated. The same concept can also be found in Grotius and Pufendorf. 'The form of a people', wrote Grotius, 'is destroyed when it loses, either completely or in part, those common rights which unite it as a people.'[71]

When the republic dissolves, the people become a multitude. There is no longer a 'common way'; there are only individuals. A multitude may be governed by a tyrant but it does not then constitute a people. The links which bind individuals in a political society, which is an artificial moral body, are constituted by the obligation which all its members have towards their sovereign and which their sovereign has towards each one of them. A group of individuals form a people so long as they are all subject to the same laws and enjoy the same rights. And as every citizen has accepted a political obligation with respect to the General Will,[72] this obligation can be no longer binding if the sovereign will becomes a particular will.

If the magistrates favour some citizens at the expense of others, or in any other way offend the citizen body, they will have violated the obligation which they have to the fundamental laws of the state, to, that is, the social contract itself. The republic will also, of course, collapse if the magistrature is too weak to prevent certain citizens from becoming so powerful that the laws cease to be equal, or if the citizens seek to avoid their public duties in order to obtain private goods.[73] The dissolution of the republic may, therefore, be attributed to several causes. But they all consist in the submission of the laws to the will of single individuals, the subordination of the public interest by *cupiditas*.

The greatest threat to the integrity of the republic comes not, however, from the private interests of particular individuals, so much as from the factions and those *petites sociétés* which have far greater resources for imposing private over general interests. Like Machiavelli, Rousseau also claimed that it was impossible to eliminate 'threats' and private interests from the republic. The prudent legislator should, however, prevent the creation of factions and ensure that no 'small society' grows so large 'that it imposes

[71] H. Grotius, *Le Droit de la guerre et de la paix*, transl. by Jean Barbeyrac (Amsterdam, 1724), Bk III, ch. 9; see also Samuel le Baron de Pufendorf, *Le Droit de la nature et des gens* transl. from the Latin by Jean Barbeyrac (Amsterdam, 1712), Bk VIII, ch. 12.   [72] *Contrat social*, Bk I, ch. 6.   [73] *Contrat social*, Bk I, ch. 7.

itself on all the others'.[74] Factions and what Rousseau also calls 'partial societies' are a danger to a legitimate government since their members believe themselves to be more entitled than single individuals to claim preferences and privileges for themselves. For an individual there is something dishonest in 'preferring oneself to others'. But as members of 'small societies' men may come to believe that there is even some merit in attempting to impose the interests of their group upon those of the community at large.[75]

Rousseau's political theory is not, as regards its basic principles, incoherent with respect to the individualistic premises on which it is largely based. At the beginning of the *Contrat social* and above all in the *Manuscript de Genève*, Rousseau makes it explicit that his project is to devise a theory of political order taking men 'just as they are', and men 'as they are' are individuals who seek for nothing beyond their own individual good and are rarely disposed to consider the effect their actions have on humanity as a whole or even on other individuals.[76] The doctrine of the *société bien ordonnée* attempts to be the rational demonstration that it is in the interests of every single individual, as much as of the community, to live under just laws rather than to live without laws or under unjust ones.

But Rousseau also insists, time and again, that even the best-ordered society is prey to corrupting passions, to immoderation and those local interests which can, all too easily, make one forget that liberty is the common and abiding interest of each and everyone.

Ambition and the love of honour have the force of natural processes. The task of good government is not to suppress them for, as we have seen, that would lead only to the kind of society which Montesquieu had described as an Asiatic despotism, a society of men without passions or interests.[77] It is, instead, to direct those purely individual passions and interests towards the public good. Rousseau's image of the well-ordered society, therefore, bears no resemblance to the reign of liberty in those utopias which never experience crisis or dissolution. It consists, rather, in a remarkable and temporary victory over the spontaneous tendencies within human society which, sooner or later, will triumph.

The weakness of the republic consists in the fact that it is, by its very nature, a public good; but men, as Aristotle (*Politics* 1261b) knew, by nature pay more attention to their private goods than to

[74] *Contrat social*, Bk II, ch. 4.   [75] *Jugement sur la Polysnodie*, III, pp. 644–5.
[76] *Manuscript de Genève*, III, pp. 281–9.
[77] Montesquieu, *De la grandeur et de la décadence des Romains*, in *Oeuvres complètes* (1950), I, pp. 414–15.

the public welfare. Machiavelli made much the same point when he observed 'that common utility which derives from liberty (*il vivere libero*) goes unrecognised by all those who possess it'.[78] It is only, as Rousseau pointed out, when it is lost that the worth of justice and good order becomes apparent. 'Justice', he wrote in *Considérations sur le gouvernement de Pologne*, 'is, like health, a good which one enjoys without being aware of it, so that it inspires no enthusiasm, and is only appreciated once it has been lost.'[79]

Although it might be almost impossible to achieve, the republic is the only alternative to disorder. For Rousseau, to live in a well-ordered community is the principal condition for happiness and personal dignity. When men feel themselves to be in their proper place and all about them to be in its proper place, then their existence becomes *douce*.[80] By contrast it is better to live alone than to live in a disordered society, for there is no condition so onerous as the absence of liberty.

Translated by Anthony Pagden

I would like to thank Quentin Skinner for all the help and encouragement he has given me in my research, and Anthony Pagden for his comments on an earlier version of this essay.

[78] *Discorsi*, Bk I, ch. 16.
[79] *Considérations sur le gouvernement de Pologne*, III, p. 935.
[80] *Les Rêveries du promeneur solitaire*, I, p. 1075.

8

The language of seventeenth-century republicanism in the United Provinces: Dutch or European?

ECO HAITSMA MULIER

I

The Dutch Republic came into existence less as the result of a pre-conceived plan, than as a consequence of an unexpected combination of political events. As the Revolt spread and Spain responded with increasing use of force, the leading figures of the provinces of Holland and Zeeland found themselves compelled to consider (in general terms) the possibility of an independent state. But even after the States General had renounced Philip II in 1581 and declared their independence, it took a long time for these unsystematic ideas on sovereignty and the nature of the new state to be given any clear delineation.[1] Political theory in the United Provinces continued to focus on the advantages and disadvantages of monarchy. A republican theory began to be formulated only with the greatest reluctance and it took until the second half of the seventeenth century before it came to be seen as a real alternative.[2] The development of republicanism in the Netherlands during this period has not yet been adequately studied and what few studies there are suffer extensively from an evil which has long plagued Dutch historiography: a nationalist insistence on the integrity of its own past, and an insufficient consideration of the influences at work in the rest of Europe. Before, and even after, World War II the Dutch Republic was viewed as unique and deviant, so that scarcely any attempt has been made to notice similarities with developments elsewhere. The

---

[1] See the Introduction to E. H. Kossmann and A. F. Mellink (eds.), *Texts Concerning the Revolt of the Netherlands* (Cambridge, 1974).

[2] E. H. Kossmann, *Politieke theorie in het zeventiende-eeuwse Nederland* (Amsterdam, 1960).

same holds true for the treatment of political theory.[3] In an attempt
to partially redress this situation this essay will discuss the language
of Dutch republicanism, and consider which aspects of it are indebted
to republican thought in other European states, most particularly
Venice.

For long after the Revolt the principal concern of political
theorists in the Netherlands was to emphasise the legitimacy of their
rebellion against the Spanish crown. The most powerful exponent
of this attempt was Johannes Althusius, a German Calvinist living in
Emden, but whose writings belong to the mainstream of contemporary Dutch political thought. In his *Politica methodice digesta* (1603–
14) Althusius argued for the citizen's right to resistance to tyranny
and defended the, as yet uncertain, form of state the Revolt had
produced.[4] In fact that form in the United Provinces had hardly been
altered by the Revolt. Each of the seven provinces, brought together
by the Union of Utrecht (1579), had its own provincial States composed of representatives of the nobility and the cities, whose
relationship was different in every province. In the wealthy province
of Holland it was the cities which were dominant. These were ruled
by municipal councils selected from among a restricted group of
citizens. Craft guilds and militia organisations were expressly
excluded in 1581 from the council and prevented from influencing
its decisions. Delegates of the provinces regularly came together in
the States General where important decisions had to be reached by a
unanimous vote. All of these organs of government remained the
same in form after the Revolt, although their role and their authority
changed. This was also true of the powerless Council of State. The
stadholder was nominated by every province separately (although
almost everywhere he was the same prince from the House of
Orange) and had originally been intended to act as a substitute for
the sovereign. After independence, however, his position became
highly ambiguous. The provincial States considered themselves to
be sovereign powers and viewed the stadholder as their servant. The
extent to which he was able to create his own centre of power depended wholly upon the person of the prince and the support he could
muster for his ambitions. It is also significant in the present context
that a clearly defined republicanism only developed in a number of

---

[3] For these aspects of Dutch historiography, see *Rivista Storica Italiana* XCV (1983),
843–71 and the Dutch version, W. W. Mijnhardt (ed.), *Kantelend geschiedbeeld:
Nederlandse historiografie sinds 1945* (Utrecht, 1983), *passim*.

[4] E. H. Kossman, 'The development of Dutch political theory in the seventeenth
century', in J. S. Bromley and E. H. Kossmann (eds.), *Britain and the Netherlands* I
(London, 1960), pp. 91–110.

provinces, most notably Holland, which decided not to elect a stadholder in the period 1650–72.

Holland, of course, played a central role in the politics of the United Provinces. It was the most densely populated, the wealthiest and therefore financially the most powerful province in the federation. Its cities, together with the nobility, had followed the tradition of the Flemish cities in maintaining their privileges against the centralising plans of their sovereign, Philip II. After the Revolt they distanced themselves in the same way from the ambitions of the House of Orange.[5] Their regents, classically educated and tolerant in their faith, identified themselves with their own city and province, and as the province derived its prosperity largely from the sea, it felt itself to be fairly independent of the other parts of the country. Since it paid more than half the total expenses of the federation it could, if necessary, successfully oppose the wishes of the other provinces and was capable on occasions of taking unilateral decisions. There was, therefore, little sense of identification with the United Provinces as a whole.[6] Only among the orthodox Calvinists of the Reformed Church (which included some regents) could anything like such an identification be found. This closely knit group of the 'select' had seen, first in the conflict with Spain, then in that with France, the creation of a new Israel; and they looked finally to support from the House of Orange against the 'godless' regents for its founding and defence.[7] We must, therefore, look for expressions of republicanism chiefly in Holland; we must also make a distinction between the commonsense observations of several of the regents and the more speculative projects of individual theorists.

A good example of the first is Cornelis Pieterszoon Hooft, many times mayor of Amsterdam after 1578 when the city joined the Revolt, and father of the famous Dutch historian.[8] In his view it was an incontrovertible fact that states developed by a process of voluntary

[5] G. Griffiths, *Representative Government in Western Europe in the Sixteenth Century* (Oxford, 1968) pp. 494ff.; H. Wansink, 'Holland and six allies: the Republic of the Seven United Provinces', in J. S. Bromley and E. H. Kossman (eds.), *Britain and the Netherlands IV: Metropolis, Dominion and Province* ('s-Gravenhage, 1971) pp. 133–55.
[6] J. C. Boogman, 'Die Holländische Tradition in de Niederländischen Geschichte', *Westfälische Forschungen, XV (1962), 96–105.*
[7] G. Groenhuis, 'Calvinism and national consciousness: the Dutch Republic as the new Israel', in A. C. Duke and C. A. Tamse (eds.), *Britain and the Netherlands* VII: *Church and State since the Reformation* (The Hague, 1981) pp. 118–33.
[8] H. A. Enno van Gelder, *De levensbeschouwing van Cornelis Pieterszoon Hooft, burgemeester van Amsterdam 1547–1626* (Amsterdam, 1918; reprint Utrecht, 1982), pp. 133–75; and Kossmann, *Politieke theorie*, p. 11.

election. This was especially the case for the inhabitants of cities who, after they had created municipal governments, joined these together to form confederations. It is clear that in setting up this model Hooft had the Netherlands in mind. The relationship of the people to their government was expressed through a system of privileges. That did not, however, mean that the people themselves should be allowed to exercise any real influence over their rulers. Hooft believed it to be self-evident that the wealthy, or more generally the educated, were the only suitable individuals to be given any measure of executive power. These aldermen in the city government and provincial States were, however, conceived not merely as representatives but as the embodiment of the concept of 'the people' and from this they derived their authority.

In his *Memorien en adviezen*, written at the beginning of the seventeenth century, Hooft offered an extensive discussion of the advantages of a republic ruled by an aristocracy. A monarchy, he argued, was plagued by continuous uncertainty. The capriciousness of the sovereign, difficulties with the succession, the high costs and the danger of a violent death all contributed to its disadvantages. In a republic, however, there is no such uncertainty since, in the classic formulation, all republics are immortal. A regent can be replaced without difficulty, and Hooft recommended that mayors and aldermen should be appointed for only a year since a regular change of office holders would make corruption difficult. He also argued that foreigners should be banned from the government of both city and province. This last measure clearly recommended itself to the moderate mayor as a means of excluding orthodox Calvinist immigrants from Flanders, for in Hooft's republic the church was to be subordinate to the secular government. It is also not surprising, in view of what has been said about the position of Holland, that Hooft looked no further than its borders. He was of the opinion, all things considered, that Holland had the right to make independent decisions and that the States General could not compel it to do otherwise.[9] Half a century later, in 1654, the Grand Pensionary, Johan de Witt, legal advisor to the Province of Holland, composed a treatise giving his reasons for his opposition to the stadholdership, in which he repeated this last argument and spoke in similar terms as Hooft about the dangers inherent in government by a single ruler.[10]

---

[9] C. P. Hooft, *Memorien en adviezen*, I (Utrecht, 1871) and II, ed. H. A. Enno van Gelder (Utrecht, 1925), *passim*, but see esp. I pp. 154ff.

[10] J. de Witt, *Deductie ofte declaratie van de Staten van Hollandt ende West-Vrieslandt* ('s-Gravenhage, 1654), *passim*.

Despite the certainty with which Holland's optimal future state was presented, an attempt was also made to explain the exceptional Dutch form of government in terms of the available existing republican examples and the political–theoretical dimensions associated with them. At the same time suggestions for improvements were made. It is striking that the example of Switzerland was referred to frequently in the last decades of the sixteenth century, but afterwards at most only incidentally. The cantonal structure at first appeared to be a potentially attractive model for the Dutch Republic; but the defenders of the republic, most of whom came from Holland at a period of increasing prosperity, were looking for more inspiring examples. The republics of the ancient world were also considered; and the Calvinists of the Reformed Church, among others, sought inspiration in the Jewish state. Most attractive of all, however, were the republics of the city states of Italy with their long and glorious histories. To the rising republic of northern Europe, these southern European examples served as a beacon.[11]

Of the examples available, Genoa was considered unattractive as it was connected to the Spanish monarchy through financial and other ties.[12] Venice, however, was quite another matter. At the beginning of the seventeenth century the city had attracted a great deal of attention through its conflict with the Pope over the Interdict which he had placed upon the city. The Dutch Republic had later given Venice armed support, and there had for long been a resident community of Netherlandish merchants in the city. The Venetians themselves, however, were suspicious of the 'heretic rebels' of the north; while the northern republic, for its part, was very conscious of the fact that it had, as Hooft proudly put it around 1610, surpassed Venice and the other maritime cities and 'sailed them out of the seas'. Later experiences with Venice were not encouraging either and moved the pragmatic De Witt to write, in 1664, that he could not see the use of a treaty with Venice as it had not honoured its earlier obligations.[13]

Intellectually, however, the contact was intensive and cordial, and there was widespread admiration in the north for its sister republic. A point in Venice's favour was that she was believed by some to hold the balance of power in Italy; and as Hooft observed, practised a high

---

[11] For details, see my *The Myth of Venice and Dutch Republican Thought in the Seventeenth Century* (Assen, 1980), p. 64.

[12] See my 'Genova e l'Olanda nel Seicento: contatti mercantili e inspirazione politica', in R. Belvederi (ed.), *Atti del Congresso internazionale di studi storici rapporti Genova–Mediterraneo–Atlantico nell'età moderna*, V (Genoa, 1983), pp. 429–44.

[13] J. de Witt, *Brieven*, 7 vols. ('s-Gravenhage, 1723–7), I, p. 677, 3 January 1664; Hooft, *Memorien*, I, p. 236.

degree of religious toleration. Above all, however, Venetian institutions of government excited amazement and admiration.
Theorists in the Low Countries, long used to concentrating on
monarchy, directed their attention to the Doge and the measures
which ensured that he could not misuse his high position. As early as
1569 the Antwerpian physician and linguist Johannes Goropius
Becanus had claimed that the development of Antwerp was in part
due to an earlier association with Venice. Justus Lipsius also praised
the thousand-year-long stable and moderate government of Venice.
So, too, did Hooft, despite his reservations, when he came to formu-
late his objections against accepting a prince in Holland. It is evident
from such remarks that elements of what has been called the myth of
Venice were present in the Netherlands by at least the end of the
sixteenth century.[14]

This myth was not only propagated by the Venetian patriciate, it
was also taken over and proclaimed in other Italian states.
Throughout Europe during the sixteenth and seventeenth centuries
it formed part of a language of republicanism which stood in opposition to increasingly absolutist theories of government. Three
elements of this language were of importance: the myth of Venice
itself, Aristotelianism, and the works of Machiavelli. Aristotle's
Politics, as expounded by the humanists of Italian city states, was
given a strongly republican interpretation. The state was only the
sum of its parts, and citizens could only really manifest their *virtù*
through participation in the political life of the republic. Each
citizen had therefore to be able to consider not only his own
interests, but also those of the community, when making a decision
on policy. The Aristotelianism of the humanists recognised among
other things three quantitative elements in the state: the many
(democracy), the few (aristocracy), and the one (monarchy). Any
state ruled by only one element was bound to collapse either into
tyranny or ochlocracy. Only when the three forms were mixed in the
appropriate way, and when opposing forces were brought into
balance, would a stable state be able to develop. But even in a mixed
state there were still complications. One part of the mixture might
predominate, for even a monarchy could have a mixed form, or a
republic a monarchical element such as, for example, the executive
magistracy of the consuls of Rome. As far as these humanists were

---

[14] *Myth of Venice*, p. 57; Joannes Goropius Becanus, *Origines Antwerpianae sive
Cimmeriorum Becceselana novem libros complexa* (Antwerp, 1569), in which the Veneti
helped at the founding of the city of Antwerp; Justus Lipsius, *De constantia libri duo*,
3rd edn (Antwerp, 1586), I, c. 16, p. 49 and II, c. 9, p. 101.

concerned, however, a true nobility (of the blood) no longer had a role to play in that the aristocratic element in a republic was constituted by a council. In the ancient world Sparta and Rome were thought to have had a mixed form of government, of which Venice was a contemporary example. There, the authority of the Doge was indeed limited, the Senate formed the aristocratic part of the mixture and the Great Council, in which all patricians sat, was perceived as the democratic element. There was some disagreement on the role and composition of the last since some commentators claimed that only the members of the Great Council were citizens. But since, in fact, no new members had been admitted since 1297, there were others who argued that it was better to speak in terms of an aristocracy with democratic and monarchical elements. Because of this conceptual vagueness it was easier to apply the Venetian example to other constitutions elsewhere. Two authors in particular were responsible for the canonisation of the myth: the Venetian patrician Gasparo Contarini and the Florentine Donato Giannotti. The first emphasised the position of the Council of Ten which appeared to be a classic 'dictator'. Giannotti was particularly fascinated by the election procedures of nomination and balloting. Since political offices were filled by a council for a fixed period and these offices were rotated, the state was able, he claimed, to achieve the highest degree of *virtù*.

In this choir of praise Machiavelli's voice is notable only by its absence. In his *Discorsi* he praised the mixed state and particularly that of Republican Rome, but went on to argue that even the mixed state was subject to a decline which could only be hindered by the rigorous action of man. Whenever a great lawgiver first founded the state, then the legally instituted 'dictator' must supervise the proper working of the constitution. Despite his great admiration for the republic, he refused to accept without reservation the mythical picture of Venice provided by his contemporaries. The Venetian constitution prevented any expansion of territory and was dominated by what was, in fact, an aristocratic oligarchy. For Machiavelli, also, it was the 'many' in the mixed state which alone guaranteed the preservation of freedom and, contrary to the opinion of many of his contemporaries, he held that the 'people' ought to constitute the greater number. This did not, however, imply that the many were themselves in a condition to rule, only that they were the best judges of who was fit to hold office. In other words, each citizen could make autonomous decisions with reference to the general interest. The citizen was also expected to be prepared to defend his state. Whenever the defence of the state was made dependent on mercenaries, there was a danger that the interests of a specific group would limit the autonomy of the citizen. In Machiavelli's view, Venice made insufficient use of the *virtù* of its citizens by, among other things, relying too heavily on the *condottieri*.[15]

Before returning to the Dutch Republic, some attention has to be paid to relevant developments in England. The English crown had been described as a mixed monarchy at an early state of its development, and the institutions of government during the Civil War were frequently described in republican terms. The English 'classical republicans' were inspired both by the *Discorsi* and by the myth of Venice. Machiavelli provided Harrington, for instance, with the concepts of the mixed state, the great lawgiver and the constitutional 'dictator' (not one person, but a council), while from Giannotti's account of the Venetian constitution he took the great council, a senate and a Lord Strategus. In all the councils of *Oceana*, the vote is taken by ballot after the Venetian example, since the moral purpose of Harrington's optimal state was, as Mark Goldie has explained (see p. 211), to overcome the passions through the triumph of reason. Every citizen ought to be able to make his decisions independently and autonomously. To achieve this end he must own a plot of land (possession of goods was also a possibility, but of a less stable nature), and arms for his defence. There had also to be an equal division of land in the state, a 'balance' maintained through an ingenious law of inheritance. Only one category of individuals was denied the rights of citizenship, the 'servants', those whom Harrington considered to be economically (and thus morally) dependent and consequently unable to exercise civic virtue. A small cottage-owner might therefore be considered for the rights of citizenship. But although Harrington spoke of *Oceana* as democratic and 'popular', it was nevertheless the aristocracy which dominated the daily administration of the state. The senate decided which issues were to be discussed; the great council voted merely on whether to accept or to reject the senate's decisions. The senate also elected the magistrates. Harrington therefore introduced a division between the moment of debate and the final taking of a decision.[16]

In the Dutch Republic, Venice, despite criticism,[17] was largely seen in terms of the myth. The city was very old and its institutions had remained unaltered since its foundation, which was in itself a guarantee

---

[15] *Myth of Venice*, ch. 1.   [16] For Harrington, *ibid.*, and the works of J. G. A. Pocock.
[17] Y. H. Rogge, 'De reis van Isaac Vossius (1641–1645)', *Oud Holland*, XVIII (1900),

of its stability. In politics Venice was seen as the heir of Rome, but as even more admirable in that, unlike Rome, it had always been peace-loving, and had only taken up arms when threatened by tyrants. All praised the immortality of the city and the existence of the mixed state was never questioned. Moreover, the election procedures and the secret balloting guaranteed an 'equilibrium' which made poss-ible the perfect exercise of citizenship and the equality of all citizens. The works of Contarini and Giannotti were printed in the United Provinces (the latter having even been translated into Dutch) and were widely read.[18] All these themes were summarised by the jurist Graswinckel in 1634 in his defence of the myth: *Libertas Veneta*, a lengthy account of Venetian history and institutions, written in response to Spanish attacks on the city and its government, and in the writing of which he was probably given help by the Venetians themselves.[19]

It is appropriate to ask at this point whether all this praise was any-thing more than a repetition of well-known commonplaces. Certainly the language of classical republicanism, of which the myth of Venice was an embodiment, served, at times, purely rhetorical ends. But it was also incorporated into a number of political tracts as an analogy for the Dutch Republic which was already being described as a mixed state by the beginning of the seventeenth century. In this way an attempt was made to clarify the undefined and tense relationship which existed between the stadholder and the other parts of the state structure. In 1607 the diplomat Brederode from the province of Holland recommended the Venetian example as a means of solving this problem. He saw the stadholder as occupy-ing the position of the Roman constitutional 'dictator'. The aristo-cratic element was formed by a common council of all provinces, and the function of the States– the element of the many– was to enforce its decisions. Brederode described in detail the Venetian voting procedures and expressly recommended them as a means of preserv-ing the autonomy of all participants. Not only would this ensure that everyone would be equal in the council and only hold office for a short time, it would also have the more general effect of suppressing the passions. For Brederode and others, such as Paulus Busius,

3–20; and A. H. Kan, 'Nicolaas Heinsius in Italië (1646–1648)', *Onze eeuw*, XIV (1914), pt 3, 361–89 and pt 4, 57–74.
[18] *Myth of Venice*, pp. 57–61. B. Alting, *Dissertatie of men moge schryven van REPUBLYCQUEN?* (Groningen, 1648) pp. 9 and 11, and G. Hornius, *Accuratissima orbis antiqui delineatio* (Amsterdam, 1654) p. 15. Also his *Orbis politicus imperiorum, regnorum, principatuum, rerum publicarum*, 2nd edn (Leiden, 1668) pp. 114–15.
[19] *Myth of Venice*, ch. 3. *Libertas Veneta sive Venetorum in se ac suos imperandi ius, assertum contra anonymum Scrutinii scriptorem* (Leiden, 1634).

professor in the Frisian city of Franeker, the distinguishing marks of classical republicanism were the autonomy of the citizen, rotation of office and collegial government.[20]

The first unequivocal expression of republicanism, however, only appeared in the Dutch Republic after 1650 in the works of the De la Court brothers and Spinoza. Together the De la Courts wrote two political tracts, the *Politike weegschaal* (Political balance) and the *Politike discoursen* (Political discourses), which went through a large number of editions. Johan (who died in 1660) and Pieter de la Court were the sons of an immigrant from the southern Netherlands. Pieter was a cloth manufacturer in Leiden who also published work on economic themes. The *Politike weegschaal*, which was originally composed by Johan and then enlarged and refined by Pieter in 1661 and again in 1662, is clearly indebted to the language of classical republicanism.[21]

The influence of Machiavelli and the myth of Venice is apparent in the defence of the 'popular' form of the state, in the form of institutions, rotation of office and government in councils. The brothers De la Court wished to apply their theory to Holland and to the cities of Holland in particular, since, as we shall see, it was impossible for them to endorse the republicanism of C. P. Hooft, even when there were points of agreement with his interpretation.

The De la Courts associated their view of man (derived from a mistaken understanding of Cartesianism which gave it Neo-Stoic overtones) with the form of the state. Men were, they claimed, always subject to passions which reason was seldom able to dominate successfully. Only through the creation of a condition of balance could the emotions be rationally controlled. That condition could only be achieved in the state which owed its existence to the agreement or contract. The brothers seem to have taken their contractualism from Hobbes; but while in Hobbes's work man bound himself by a contract so as to allow the sovereign to maintain the natural law, the De la Courts emphatically guaranteed every citizen the possibility of exercising his individual rights within the state. The problem remained however that in monarchy and aristocracy

---

[20] P. Cz. Brederode, *Considérations d'estat sur le traité de la paix avec les serenissimes archiducz d'Austriche*, ed. Ch. Rahlenbeck (Brussels–The Hague, 1869).

[21] For the De la Courts and Spinoza, see *Myth of Venice*, chs. 4–5. P. de la Court, *Consideratien en exempelen van Staet* (Amsterdam, 1660), revised and expanded as *Consideratien van staat ofte politike weegschaal* (Amsterdam, 1662). There is a French translation of the first part of this work by M. Francès, *La Balance politique*, I (Paris, 1937). P. de la Court, *Politike discoursen* (Leiden, 1662). See also the remarks by R. Tuck, *Natural Rights Theories: Their Origin and Development* (Cambridge, 1979), pp. 139–41.

the passions of one or more persons would very likely come to dominate. In the 'popular' state, by contrast, the passions of all could be kept in balance with each other. This, they argued, was therefore the best form of state. They based their defence of this 'popular' state on Machiavelli's *Discorsi*, which made them the first in the Dutch Republic to take Machiavelli's work seriously, as it had been, tacitly at least, long banned from discussion. Machiavelli had ascribed a political role only to the citizens of a nation, not to its entire population, and the De la Courts took the same view. The 'people' had a political voice, but the *plebs* did not. At the same time, in order to strengthen the position of the States, then without a stadholder, they rejected the idea of a mixed constitution and the possibility of the division of sovereignty. The sovereign assembly of all the citizens in a city or a country must, they claimed, be given as much power as possible.

The objective of the De la Court brothers was not a state in which all inhabitants were involved, but one in which the line of division between the 'people' and the regents was not sharply drawn. They wanted both to make fully explicit the capacities of the citizens and to avoid the division of society in opposing factions. Political office was, therefore, to be held only by rich, educated and virtuous citizens, who were to be elected in an assembly of co-citizens, casting their vote autonomously. In the later editions of the *Political Balance* Pieter further diluted the popular state by adding an aristocratic element to his schema. Like Harrington, he stipulated that no one who had received poor relief, or had worked in the service of another, was entitled to citizens' rights. Such persons were, in his opinion, unlikely to be capable of independent judgement.

In the *Political Balance* there is an extensive discussion of the history and government of Venice, based on the works of Contarini and Giannotti. The De la Courts extolled the city's geographical location, its peaceableness and political stability. But they were also critical. In the first place Venice was not, in their opinion, a mixed state. It was, in fact, ruled by an aristocracy; and moreover the constitution was not so old as the Venetians claimed. Although they approved every aspect of the balloting and voting procedures, the Venetian aristocracy was too closed to fulfil the function of a sovereign assembly. Pieter, at least, preferred the republic of Genoa, made attractive to him not only by its flourishing commerce and shipping, but also by the fact that new citizens were accepted into the ruling patriciate at regular intervals on the basis of precisely determined criteria. After examing these examples, the De la Courts

came to the conclusion that the ideal republic should have a dense
population and be made prosperous through commerce and industry.
It should not be expansionist, as the Roman republic had been, and
as Machiavelli had recommended (although the De la Courts did
take over Machiavelli's idea of a citizen army). In this peace-loving
ideal state with a council open to new members, an assembly of more
than two hundred men was to be elected every year.

The emphasis on an open patriciate clearly reflects the feelings of
an eminent citizen of Leiden who had been excluded by the regents
from government of the city. At the time when the *Political Balance*
was written, the regents were becoming increasingly a restricted
group closed to all newcomers. And it was in this context that the
political and economic views of the De la Court brothers were
worked out. As textile manufacturers and merchants *en gros* there
was a great difference between them and the small domestic
producers and an even greater difference between them and the
mass of textile workers. Their education and their travels had made
them familiar with a wider European world and this had been inten-
sified through their mercantile activities and their remoteness from
the actual textile manufacturing process. In their search for markets
and increased sales they felt themselves to be unnecessarily
constrained by strict quality control and guild regulations which
were manipulated by the Leiden regents. For that reason they
argued for the abolition of these regulations and opposed the ruling
regent obligarchy – the members of which were not directly involved
in textile production and whose interests were not those of the large-
scale merchants. From the standpoint of the city government the
separation of manufacturers from the body of textile producers was
seen as a threat to the social-political balance. Both groups, however,
had an interest in encouraging population growth and in providing
for its welfare. The textile producers required a continuous supply
of labour and the regents a reasonable return from taxes. It was
clearly these circumstances in Leiden which influenced Pieter de la
Court's views as to which groups were eligible for citizenship. His
dislike of the *plebs* and his fear that the guild masters might attempt
to seize power by whipping up the masses, as had happened in
Florence and Ghent, were likewise a response to local conditions.

In the council of the optimal republic, decisions were to be taken
by secret balloting so that no parties should be allowed to develop.
Parties would, he claimed, mean the decline of the republic; for they
endangered the expression of the 'virtue' of the individual. The

council existed to ratify draft laws, to name magistrates and to pass judgements on the decisions of smaller councils. Because members could only be re-elected once, the rotation principle could be maintained. But who could effectively control a council to which everything was subordinate? The De la Court brothers believed that a constitutional 'dictatorial' power of the kind described by Machiavelli provided an answer. 'Zindicatori' or 'Fiscalen', as they called them, should see to the proper functioning of the institutions of government and because their offices also rotated there was no danger that they might abuse them. Like both Machiavelli and Harrington, the De la Courts rejected the idea of any nobility of the blood, and their ruling assembly, far from being an hereditary aristocracy, was very similar to the small council of the Italian city states.

This ideal state also operated a rudimentary separation of powers in that members of the assembly lost their voting rights while in office. Church and public religion were also subordinate to the state. Inspectors would supervise the activities of ministers, although toleration was absolutely necessary in a country which had so many international commercial relations. The question of how far these regulations could be threatened through property relationships was also considered: Harrington had argued that a disruption of the 'balance' of landownership could have serious effects on the state, and he had therefore drafted an inheritance system for *Oceana*, which would guarantee the distribution of property within what was a largely agrarian community. The De la Courts were also aware that material relationships could have far-reaching consequences for the state. The very uncertainty of commercial capital was, they argued, an advantage in that its volatility prevented too much wealth from accruing to one person. An inheritance law which provided not just for the oldest, but for all, children would further encourage distribution.

II

In his *Tractatus theologico-politicus*, and the incomplete *Tractatus politicus*, Spinoza incorporated the work of the De la Courts (and to some extent of Machiavelli) into a superior philosophical system concerned with the spiritual welfare of mankind.[22] It is not easy therefore to discuss his political writings in isolation from his

[22] B. de Spinoza, *The Political Works: The Tractatus Theologico-Politicus in Part and the Tractatus Politicus in Full*, ed. A. G. Wernham (Oxford, 1958).

metaphysics. It is also the case that until now there have been few attempts to provide an historical account of the political works, even though it is clear that Spinoza took a keen interest in the political events of his time. According to Spinoza, men in the state of nature – a condition which, like Hobbes, he characterised as the war of all against all – were, through fear, ruled always by their passions. Only in civil society is it possible, through the creation of institutions, for reason to gain control over the passions, and it is, therefore, only in civil society that men are able to identify and safely pursue their true ends. Spinoza takes as his point of departure the axiom that in order for any government to possess real power it was necessary for it to be supported by as many of its citizens as possible. For that reason he, like the De la Court brothers, rejected the mixed state. He preferred democracy, but like them he also excluded all 'servants' (and women), by which he meant all those who were not financially and socially self-sufficient, from citizenship. He was unable to complete his treatise on democracy, but he wrote at length on aristocratic rule which would permit the regular admittance of new members to the ruling elites, but, as in a democracy, would exclude all 'servants'.

The numerical relationship between the patriciate and the rest of the population was to be examined by means of an annual census and the relationship between the two groups was to be exactly the same as it had been for the De la Courts. Spinoza, however, made a distinction between two sorts of aristocratic states: one composed of a single city, such as Rome or Venice, and the other composed of several cities such as Holland.

His constitutional claims went much deeper than those of the *Political Balance*. The conceptual vocabulary and the abiding concerns of classical republicanism are immediately evident. Spinoza was also anxious about the formation of parties and viewed the guilds with their supporters in particular as a very great danger. All election procedures should, he claimed, follow the Venetian example in order to guarantee personal autonomy. Government should always be exercised through councils and all offices must rotate. He also projected a great council which would vote on initiatives from the senate. As in Harrington's scheme, daily administration lay largely with the senate, presided over by a group of consuls. Naturally there was no head of state. Instead the important figure for Spinoza was that of the now familiar constitutional 'dictator'. This council of *Syndici* ('Zindicatori' in De la Court), the size of which was determined by the number of patricians, every half-year bestowed the responsibility for daily administration on a council composed of ten men. This council of ten worked much like the Venetian Council of Ten through which the patricians were controlled, but it also performed some of the functions of the Doge who, as chairman of the Venetian Great Council and of the Senate, supervised the drafting of all legislation.

Spinoza also discussed the material aspects of life in the optimal state and like De la Court he favoured the promotion of commerce, since he believed that, as it brought people in contact with each other, it created possibilities for rational understanding. But he also claimed that in an aristocracy land ownership was of greater importance in that it was a means of binding those lacking political rights to their country.

The exceptional character of the republicanism of Spinoza and the De la Courts can be made much clearer if we compare it with the views of one of their rare republican contemporaries from the eastern province of Overijssel, the magistrate Rabod Scheels (Schelius). Scheels's *Libertas publica*, most likely written during the first war between the Dutch Republic and England (1652–4), was produced in the same years that the De la Courts were developing their political views, although the work did not appear until 1666, four years after the author's death. This 'rhetorical idyll', as his book has been called, celebrated the freedom that had supposedly characterised the Low Countries ever since the time of the Batavians at the beginning of the Christian Era. In those places, Scheels argued, where rule was concentrated in the hands of a single person, all the bad qualities of the individual (the furious beast which lives in every man) was bound to triumph, even if he were the best-intentioned of men. Under a republican government, on the other hand, where the 'people' and the 'best' ruled through participation in a lawful assembly, the citizens held each other in check; as a result reason, tranquillity and stability would be victorious.

Despite the fact that Scheels's views, by their insistence on the need to question the validity of ancient exempla and to pay due attention to the lessons of more recent history, seem to anticipate the 'querelle des anciens et des modernes', his thought was, nonetheless, strongly shaped by pre-Cartesian traditions. Although this summary may seem to make them appear distantly similar to the views of the De la Court brothers, the differences are marked. Scheels named no specific examples from among contemporary republics (although he did refer to Rome and Sparta), nor did he discuss election procedures. The language of classical republicanism does not appear in his work, nor is there any evidence of the influence of Machiavelli. Instead he endlessly reiterated the advantages of republican rule with brief references to Plato, interrupted by attacks on what he called the 'new teachers' who in his view wished only to base domination on fear and by so doing had blurred the distinction between justice and injustice. When he spoke about the blind necessity for obedience he was referring in all probability to the theories of Hobbes. It was religion which provided the moral basis for all political thought. Without it man would return to a bestial state.

The De la Courts and Spinoza could not be content with the undifferentiated and essentially providentialist republicanism of a Rabod Scheels.[23] Nor did they accept the commonsense republicanism which a regent from their own province such as Hooft had espoused at the beginning of the century, although they shared certain of Hooft's views such as his argument for toleration and a state-regulated church; and, like Hooft, the De la Courts had also stressed the need for the rotation of office holders as a means against corruption and the misuse of power. The point of departure for them all, the preference for a state where no one man could indulge in the misuse of power, was the same, although the De la Courts expressed themselves on this subject in much stronger language than Hooft. The latter preferred a fully aristocratic republic, one in which no newcomers or outsiders would be included in the government. Although the De la Courts, like Hooft, were especially concerned with Holland, and even with their own city, they were prepared to go further and incorporate elements of classic republicanism into their vision of the optimal state. They attempted, as did Spinoza, to create a balance in the state at the institutional level, and by doing so to neutralise the effect of the human passions. If their ideas on the reform of the state had been realised, then not only would the position which was filled by the stadholder have disappeared, but so, too, would that of the Grand Pensionary, the office held by Johan de Witt in this period. During the fifties and sixties this official had become too powerful and ideally a council should have taken his place. In addition, Spinoza and both the De la Courts wished for new patricians to be admitted regularly on the basis of established criteria. The regent obligarchy, to which they did not belong

[23] R. Schelius, *Libertas publica liber posthumus* (Amsterdam, 1666). Dutch translation: *Algemeene vrijheid* (Rotterdam, 1666), esp. pp. 66 and 41–2. See also Kossmann, *Politieke theorie*, pp. 32–3. The unique position of the De la Court brothers and Spinoza is also apparent from G. O. van de Klashorst, H. W. Blom and E. O. G. Haitsma Mulier, *A Bibliography of Dutch Seventeenth-Century Political Thought: An Annotated Inventory* (Amsterdam, 1986).

themselves, could only be broken open in this way. The government should also be controlled through a separate independent body; and in the States General decisions should henceforth be made by a majority of votes, so that the continuous stalemate arising from the necessity of unanimity could be eliminated.

If we now return to the question of whether or not this republicanism was Dutch or European, in inspiration it would seem that in many respects it was more European than specifically Dutch; certainly more European than any Dutch historian has yet recognised. Nevertheless there was also a definite Dutch contribution. The merger of elements of European republican thought with elements from the Dutch tradition resulted in the creation of a new language of republicanism which might have had an enriching effect on political practice, had not the declaration of war in 1672 put an end to the aspirations it embodied. The concept of the mixed state was used in 1672 to explain the position of the restored stadholder within the totality of the institutions of the state; but the myth of Venice, already modified by the De la Courts in various points, disappeared, as did all further mention of Machiavellian republicanism. The consciousness of the strength of the United Provinces and the situation in which it now found itself made this form of republicanism unattractive, while, despite certain similarities, the new state now differed considerably from the English model.[24] At the same time the government of the Dutch Republic had come, in its turn, to seem unique and even to offer an example to other nations. In seventeenth-century Italy, for instance, whenever an attempt was made to introduce changes in the state structure, the North was often invoked as a source of inspiration. But that is another story.[25]

I would like to thank Anthony Pagden for his revision of the translation of this essay.

---

[24] See my 'J. G. A. Pocock and seventeenth-century Dutch republicanism: a reconsideration', *Theoretische Geschiedenis*, IX (1982), 24–9. Also E. H. Kossmann, 'Dutch republicanism', in *L'età dei lumi: studi storici sul settecento europeo in onore di Franco Venturi*, 2 vols. (Rome, 1985), I, pp. 455–86.

[25] S. Mastellone, 'Holland as a political model in Italy in the 17th century', *Bijdragen en mededelingen betreffende de geschiedenis der Nederlanden*, XCVIII (1983), 568–82.

9

◁ ═══════════════════════════════════ ▷

The civil religion of James Harrington

MARK GOLDIE

> What has Athens to do with Jerusalem?
> Tertullian

I

The idea of a civil religion is not one which students of political theory pay much attention to today. In so far as it resonates at all, it suggests a dark and aberrant episode in the career of the modern state. In the 1940s and 1950s scholars were understandably concerned to discover the roots of totalitarian state worship. In constructing its intellectual ancestry, paternity seemed to lie with Hegel, Rousseau and Machiavelli. Hegel, it was held, had sanctified the Prussian state by embodying God in the unfolding of national history. Rousseau, in his chapter on 'Civil religion' in *The Social Contract*, had apparently married a religion of patriotism to his theory of an invincible democratic sovereignty. And Machiavelli, in the *Discourses*, had found the Christian religion inadequate in comparison with ancient Rome's ability to harness piety for the glory of the *patria*. Unavoidably, therefore, 'civil religion' came to connote a Faustian and totalitarian device to secure blind obedience to the state by the exploitation of human aspirations to spiritual fulfilment. For some commentators its aberrance lay in its violation of Augustine's Christian scepticism about temporal rule and earthly perfectibility. For others it lay in its violation of what seemed the pre-eminent achievement of modern political sensibility, the secular separation of politics and religion. It was, either way, 'a radical departure from Western tradition'.[1]

Versions of this essay were presented as papers to the Political Economy and Society conference at the King's College Research Centre, Cambridge, in 1984, at the University of Sydney and at the Australian National University, Canberra, in 1985.
[1] R. Tucker, *Philosophy and Myth in Karl Marx* (Cambridge, 1961), p. 31. The literature is considerable, but see especially Karl Popper, *The Open Society and Its Enemies* (London, 1945), and J. L. Talmon, *The Origins of Totalitarian Democracy* (1952). In the context of the present discussion, it is interesting that Talmon (pp. 10–11) finds in Harrington and the Puritan revolutionaries a glimpse of the 'totalitarian temperament'.

Perhaps the chief reason for the near invisibility of the concept of civil religion in studies of the mainstream of Western political thought is the enormous intellectual investment which political science has in the notion of the disjunction between the civil and the religious. Secularism remains as much a boast as a fact. To discover the moment at which politics became 'autonomous' and 'rational' is a constant endeavour for a profession still deeply imbued with the Enlightenment presumption that the maturity of the species consists in its ability to conduct civil life without recourse to superstition. A modern civil religion can only seem like a backsliding into barbarism. The positivist mode in the history of political thought eagerly searches the era of human adolescence, and rewards philosophers for signs of 'science', the 'modern', the 'secular'. Machiavelli (his remarks on Roman religion notwithstanding) and Hobbes are the pre-eminent bearers of this celebration of the struggle of science to emerge from the embrace of theology. It would not be difficult to document such claims in the scholarly literature. But consider instead the case of another canonical 'modern', James Harrington, the republican analyst of property and power in the mid-seventeenth century. In the scholarship of the last few decades, it is Harrington's apparent ability to conduct a political science based purely on the rational calculation of empirical human needs, and upon an analysis of the relationship between economic and political formations, which has absorbed attention.[2] Of Harrington it has been said that his aim was 'to get God out of politics'; there was a 'total lack of spiritual content' in his work, because his 'is a world of human reason'. Modern political science is about 'the retreat from God' and 'in this campaign Harrington was an important figure'.[3] The military imagery – a 'campaign' – is a popular one: a heroic freedom fighter is portrayed seizing modernity by intellectual *force majeur*. And if there still seem to be remnants of a religious preoccupation in Harrington, this is said to be because, although basically on the side of science, 'he lacked the self-confidence that would have permitted him to turn his back on divine

[2] R. H. Tawney, 'Harrington's interpretation of his age', *Proceedings of the British Academy* (1941); R. H. Tawney, 'The rise of the gentry 1558–1640', *Economic History Review*, XI (1941); C. B. Macpherson, 'Harrington's opportunity state', *Past and Present*, XVIII (1960), also in *The Political Theory of Possessive Individualism* (Oxford, 1962); F. Raab, *The English Face of Machiavelli* (London, 1964), ch. 6; W. H. Greenleaf, *Order, Empiricism and Politics: Two Traditions of English Political Thought 1500–1700* (Oxford, 1964), ch. 11; J. A. W. Gunn, *Politics and the Public Interest in the Seventeenth Century* (London, 1969), ch. 3.

[3] J. N. Shklar, 'Ideology hunting: the case of James Harrington', *American Political Science Review*, LIII (1959), p. 684; Raab, *The English Face of Machiavelli*, p. 204.

revelation'.[4] Here, surely, a Victorian Freethinker's condescension towards the immature religious past still jogs the pen.

What was, in fact, one of the most pervasive political languages of early-modern Europe, that of civil religion, has, accordingly, been systematically neglected. Civility and piety, the synthesis of which was a crucial project in early-modern thought, are peremptorily detached from each other by modern political science. In this chapter my main aim is to show how a Christian Reformist vision was integral to Harrington's construction of the just polity. But I shall first continue with some, necessarily truncated, general remarks concerning the language of civil religion, for I take the case of Harrington to be one striking instance of a much broader stream in the European political tradition.

Hegel claimed to belong to the mainstream of Protestant thought. His generation engaged in the exhilarating task of a new understanding of Christianity, in which the Greek ideal of human fulfilment in the *polis* simply *was* the freedom promised by the Gospel. The opposite of such fulfilment was popery, which alienated sanctity from citizenship. Popery was identified not merely as the name of false doctrines, but as a systematic usurpation by priests of public life. Popery was the practical embodiment of irrational political relations, and no adequate human community could be constructed on clericalist premises. When rightly construed, Hegel argued, 'religion contains the same truths as the state expresses in reality'. Historically, he claimed, Christianity had passed through three stages: opposition to the world (in the early church of Augustine and the Fathers), tutelage to the world (in medieval popery), and realisation of the world (in the modern state). 'In the Middle Ages', he wrote, 'the embodying of the divine in actual life was wanting'; it was a 'contradictory and self-alienated phase', because religion was but an 'externality'. It was so in three ways: firstly, transubstantiation was an idolatry 'bodying God in a particular material object'; secondly, 'knowledge ... [was] the exclusive possession of a class', the priests, who gave to their priesthood an external, 'outward form of ordination'; and thirdly, the clergy's 'acquisition of outward property' rendered it an economic externality. These were calamities for individual selfhood and for civil communities. The Reformation consists in annulling all of this, the 'building up of the edifice of secular relations'. The revolution of seventeenth-century England, Hegel continued, was a

---

[4] Charles Blitzer in *The Political Writings of James Harrington: Representative Selections* (New York, 1955), p. xxxiv.

part of that Reformation, because it was mounted 'in opposition to Catholic externality'. The revolution was a crucial moment in the struggle of *imperium* against *sacerdotium*, a struggle which the modern 'German' world resolves, and the resolution of which is the keynote of the modern state. Hegel's injunction that 'man must therefore venerate the state as a secular deity' was not an unholy rupture in the history of European political languages. It was a Protestant catechism. And, as we shall see, Harrington best exemplifies Hegel's account of the English Revolution.[5]

Hegel's political thought was both secular and Lutheran. It is not of course inapt to speak of the emergence of secular political theory: the mistake is to speak disjunctively. For secularisation was an evangelical pursuit, it was the working out of a central idea in the thought of the Reformers, the 'priesthood of all believers'. Where the medieval church hypostatised priesthood in a particular class, the Reformers universalised it. Where the 'false religion' of medieval popery invested the means of sanctification in particular persons, practices and material objects, 'true religion' discovered sanctification in the conduct of ordinary human relations. The Reformers' notion of popery became a complex one, referring to all of the means by which human flourishing, both material and spiritual, was prevented. Crucially, the Reformers asserted the sanctity of civil sovereignty. The medieval church fused spiritual and civil life in the *imperium* of the papacy. This, for the Reformers, constituted a world turned upside down; the supremacy of the civil community would be a world righted. The theory of the modern state is a retort to the claim of the medieval popes to be *dominus mundi*, lord of the world. In most political philosophy between Dante and Hegel, the primary drama of Christendom was the liberation of the prince and the patriot from the priest. As Sir Robert Molesworth expressed it in the 1690s, in a manifesto which was to be much admired throughout the Enlightenment, 'the character of priest will give place to that of true patriot'.[6] From at least the time that the Joachites in the thirteenth century first identified the pope as Antichrist, the priests began to be seen as impediments to Christian prospering, and Godly people began to seek their fulfilment not in the church-state, but in the state-church. In a world of popes and powerful clergies, the power of the Reformed state, of the Christian

[5] *The Philosophy of History*, ed. C. J. Friedrich (New York, 1956), pp. 343–4, 378–81, 422–4, 435; *The Philosophy of Right*, ed. T. M. Knox (Oxford, 1967), paras. 259–60, 270, 272 Addition, 285.   [6] *An Account of Denmark* (London, 1694), sig.b3r.

Prince, was a necessary guarantor of the priesthood of all. The concept of the Christian Prince, whether in the form of the Divine Right of Kings, or translated into the corporate body of the republic, was integral to the development of the idea of the self-sufficiency of the secular commonwealth. The considerable stress in modern scholarship on the emergence of the rights of private religious experience and of toleration in the Reformed tradition obscures the degree to which Reformed thought remained Erastian, and continued to be a theory about the civil state's embodiment of 'true religion'. One important strand of this idea lay in millenarian thought, the application to human history of the prophecies of the Books of Daniel and the Apocalypse. The Godly state's historic role is in the overthrow of Antichrist, in preparation for Christ's second coming. A rich vein of scholarship since the 1960s has explored millenarian beliefs in the formation of the statehood of Protestant England[7] and America.[8] But we have yet to discover just how central the idea of civil religion was for such canonical moderns as Hobbes, Harrington and Locke. Who now reads the third and fourth books of *Leviathan*?[9] Nor has the exploration extended into the mainstream of Enlightenment thought, which, I suspect, will turn out to be not predominantly an atheism in revolt against Christianity, but rather a further unfolding of the programme of Christian Reformers.

For Harrington, and for Hobbes and Locke, as much as for Hegel, the mission of the state, of the Godly Prince, was to realise in the commonwealth the religion which, in its corrupt medieval form, had held all commonwealths under its tutelage. The superstitions of the medieval church were seen to be reflections of the impingement of clericalism upon ordinary life; conversely, true religion had a necessary relationship with the right ordering of the commonwealth. For instance, Locke's exclusion of papists from toleration, too often seen as a quaint reminder of anti-Catholic prejudice lurking in an otherwise canonically liberal and secular mind, is an intrinsic outcome of the Lutheran conception of the state. Papists are not

---

[7] W. Lamont, *Godly Rule: Politics and Religion 1603–60* (London, 1969); P. Toon (ed.), *Puritans, the Millennium and the Future of Israel: Puritan Eschatology 1600–1660* (Cambridge, 1970); E. L. Tuveson, *Millennium and Utopia* (Gloucester, Massachusetts, 1972); P. Christianson, *Reformers and Babylon* (Toronto, 1978); K. Firth, *The Apocalyptic Tradition in Reformation Britain 1530–1645* (Oxford, 1979).

[8] R. E. Richey and D. G. Jones (eds.), *American Civil Religion* (New York, 1974); C. Cherry, *God's New Israel* (Englewood Cliffs, 1971); E. Tuveson, *Redeemer Nation: The Idea of America's Millennial Role* (Chicago, 1968).

[9] But see J. G. A. Pocock, 'Time, history and eschatology in the thought of Thomas Hobbes' in *Politics, Language and Time* (London, 1971).

patriots: that they have recommended the assassination of temporal sovereigns was the logical outcome of the clerical *imperium*. (Hegel similarly remarked upon the Catholic doctrine of the 'assassination of sovereigns', for in Roman Catholicism, 'it is nothing singular for the conscience to be found in opposition to the laws of the state'.)[10] In this sense, Locke does not advocate just the liberal privatisation of religion, but has a doctrine of civil religion. Similarly, we find Rousseau, in his chapter on civil religion, acknowledging an affinity with Hobbes, in a poignant phrase: 'Of all Christian authors, the philosopher Hobbes is the only one who dared to propose reuniting the two heads of the eagle', the civil and the spiritual.[11] All these philosophers agreed that a religion which sunders a person's existence as a citizen is false religion, it is popery, or priestcraft. It was, as we shall see, Harrington who first coined the word 'priestcraft', and who provided one of the best expressions of the view that the priest is the antinomy of the patriot, and that the Christian religion must, literally, be repatriated.

The philosophical task of repatriating Christianity was not of course conducted only in terms of the teaching of Scripture. Christian political thought has always been eclectic, drawing upon the secular languages of Graeco-Roman culture. Scriptural texts have characteristically been turned into aphoristic expressions of secular juridical arguments. Aquinas married Scripture to Aristotle, and the medieval lawyer popes fused Christ's commission to Peter with Roman Law doctrines of *imperium*. Reformed political thought redeployed this eclecticism on behalf of the laity and the civil state. In the first instance, it redeployed the Roman Law idea of the *imperator*, which the papacy had assumed to itself. In the Marsilian and Lutheran Godly Prince, the imperial theme provided the secularising dynamic of the Reformation: the vicegerency of Christ on earth lies in the temporal state, and in the state's personification in the Prince. This is the point of the famous declaration of the English Reformation, 'this realm of England is an empire'.[12] This secular eschatology achieved its best historical expression in Foxe's *Book of Martyrs* and its best juridical expression in Books III and IV of Hobbes's *Leviathan*.

The type of Christian–classical eclecticism which concerns us here

---

[10] Locke, *A Letter Concerning Toleration* (Indianapolis, 1983), p. 50; Hegel, *The Philosophy of History*, pp. 423–4.

[11] *The Social Contract* (Harmondsworth, 1968), p. 180.

[12] See W. Ullmann, 'This realm of England is an empire', *Journal of Ecclesiastical History*, XXX (1979).

is the civic republican ideal, so prominent in Renaissance Italy, in Augustan England, and in Romantic Germany. J. G. A. Pocock has emphasised the importance of classical republican sensibility in early-modern political thought, and he has dubbed Harrington England's 'premier civic humanist'.[13] In spite of Pocock's disinterment of the civil theology which Harrington interweaves into his humanist republicanism, Harrington's energetic classicising and thoroughgoing Machiavellianism are generally taken to be strikingly different modes of political understanding from the Christian providential. Yet it is crucial for Harrington that his citizen of England's New Rome is also a saint of the New Jerusalem.[14]

One outcome of recognising Harrington's thought to be of this character is to close the gap between him and his radical puritan contemporaries. It tends to be supposed that puritan zealotry was at odds with the 'rational' and 'secular' politics of Harrington and Hobbes – that in puritan thought Grace overwhelmed Nature, and in the 'moderns' Nature obliterated Grace.[15] It is true that puritan thought frequently slid towards a doctrine of the dictatorship of the Elect, as the means of imposing divine will on civil government. But wherever puritan thought leaned towards acceptance of the possibility of universal salvation and hence of universal priesthood, or to the Socinian idea that Christ was God-in-humanity, then puritanism became as intensely secular and naturalistic as it was Biblical and Apocalyptic. The puritans saw the English revolution as a striving to fulfil the priesthood of all believers, as a driving out of the popery of 'Prelatical' and Presbyterian clericalism, as an abolition of the tyranny of the religion which monopolised Christ's gifts in separated priesthoods and rigidly imposed formularies. As the Leveller Richard Overton wrote in 1646, every person was 'by nature . . . a king, priest and prophet'; those whom we *call* kings and priests

---

[13] J. G. A. Pocock (ed.), *The Political Works of James Harrington* (Cambridge, 1977), p. 15.

[14] My account of Harrington is much indebted to Pocock's work: see especially ch. 5 of his Introduction to Harrington's *Works*. Also: 'Post-Puritan England and the problem of the Enlightenment' in P. Zagorin (ed.), *Culture and Politics from Puritanism to the Enlightenment* (Berkeley, 1980); 'Contexts for the study of James Harrington', *Il Pensiero Politico*, XI (1978); 'Political thought in the Cromwellian interregnum' in *W. P. Morrell: A Tribute*, ed. G. A. Wood and P. S. O'Connor (Dunedin, 1973); *The Machiavellian Moment* (Princeton, 1975), ch. 11. For a critique of his approach, and hence one from which I dissent, see J. C. Davis, 'Pocock's Harrington: grace, nature and art in the classical republicanism of James Harrington', *Historical Journal*, XXIV (1981).

[15] An early exception in Harrington scholarship was J. W. Gough, 'Harrington and contemporary thought', *Political Science Quarterly*, XLV (1930).

are but servants and surrogates, appointed by 'commission, and free consent'.[16] A puritan clergyman wrote in 1659 that 'the Godliness of these times hath abolished the distinction of church and state, of civil and ecclesiastical jurisdiction, and taken away the distinction of clergy and laity'.[17] Perhaps the most conspicuous parallels are between Harrington and Gerrard Winstanley, the Digger.[18] Both sought a vision of Christian fulfilment in the perfection of secular human relations; both were Platonic, Socinian, Apocalyptic and anticlerical. And both were English counterparts of the German mystic Jacob Boehme, who is acknowledged to be a significant step along the Platonist–Lutheran path which led to the civil religion of Hegel and Feuerbach.[19] The puritans of the 1650s were, moreover, like Harrington, as deeply imbued with classical republican ideas as with Hebraic and Apocalyptic ones, with Machiavelli as well as Moses. This is patent in John Milton and Algernon Sidney, and is hardly less prominent in Marchamont Nedham, Henry Neville, and Andrew Marvell.[20] The republicans took themselves to be building Athens as well as Jerusalem; they were 'saints and statesmen' whose house was both 'a senate and a temple'.[21] As one contemporary remarked, 'The design of the English' was 'to make a republic on the model of that of the Hebrews, before they had their kings, and on that of Sparta, of Rome, and of Venice'.[22]

This synthesis of Athens and Jerusalem had precedents wherever humanist and Christian Reformist values met. In Savonarola's

[16] Qu. W. Haller, *Liberty and Reformation in the Puritan Revolution* (New York, 1963), p. 281.
[17] L. Du Moulin, *Proposals and Reasons* (London, 1659), p. 37. For other examples, see John Owen, *Works*, ed. W. H. Gould (London, 1967), XIII, p. 21; William Penn, *Works* (London, 1726) I, pp. 180–1, 188, 775, 781–2.
[18] Some have suggested that Winstanley's writings influenced Harrington; others doubt this, for lack of evidence. Both were, at any rate, reworking available ideas in similar circumstances. The historiography on Winstanley mirrors that on Harrington. Juretic, in 'The revolutionizing of Gerard Winstanley', *Journal of the History of Ideas*, XXXVI (1975), argues that Winstanley became a 'modern', overthrew the religious incubus, and emerged rational and secular. This view has rightly been criticised by L. Mulligan, J. K. Graham and J. Richards, in 'Winstanley: a case for the man as he said he was', *Journal of Ecclesiastical History*, XXVIII (1977).
[19] M. W. Wartofsky, *Feuerbach* (Cambridge, 1977), pp. 74–6; L. Kolakowski, *Main Currents in Marxism* (Oxford, 1981), pp. 36–7.
[20] B. Worden, 'Classical republicanism and the puritan revolution' in H. Lloyd Jones, V. Pearl, and B. Worden (eds.), *History and Imagination: Essays in Honour of H. R. Trevor Roper* (London, 1981).
[21] Saltmarsh in 1644, quoted in L. Solt, *Saints in Arms: Puritanism and Democracy in Cromwell's Army* (Stanford, 1959), p. 75.
[22] Bibliothèque Nationale, MS Fr.23254, 'Lantiniana', p. 99. I am grateful to Jonathan Scott for this reference.

revolution in Florence in the 1490s there was Apocalyptic talk of an
end of Babylon, and of Florence as God's civic agent in transforming
the church. Neo-Platonist philosophers quickly offered their
intellectual services. In Giovani Nesi's *Oracle of a New Age* (1496), a
vision of a Platonic republic is fused with the New Jerusalem.[23] But
much the most influential precedent for Harrington's generation
was the Venice of Paulo Sarpi. The famous struggle in 1606–7
between the papal *imperium* and Venice's claim to sovereign
Christian pastorship produced a host of books in which the
Venetians mingled the languages of Christian Reform, ancient
republicanism, and imperial sovereignty. The Catholic Sarpi was
congenial to English puritans, who cited him as an authority on the
democratic congregationalism of the early church, and on the
history of priestly and popish usurpations.[24] Sarpi's *History of the
Council of Trent* included, in its English editions, extracts from
Guicciardini's history, which furthered the fusion of Renaissance
classicism and puritan polemic. In Cromwellian England other
works by Venetian propagandists were translated and published:
Trajano Boccalini, whom Harrington was fond of, and Paulo
Paruta.[25]

In understanding the high-flown, utopian and sometimes mystical
tone of Harrington's portrayal of the Godly republic, it is important
to recall the fact that ranged against the Reformed states were the
exceptionally Promethean and threatening claims of the Counter-
Reformation papacy and its Spanish ally. Harrington's language is a
Protestant mirror of Catholic hyperbole. In papalist propaganda,
ideas of Roman *imperium*, of Hebrew theocracy, of the Platonic
philosopher–king, and of Christ's commission to Peter mingled in
quite extraordinary reveries on behalf of the pope as the universal
emperor–priest–philosopher. A strong element in this rhetoric was a
Catholic Machiavellianism which was not above using Machiavelli's
vaunting of Rome's pagan patriotic religion as a model for a
portrayal of Christianity as the patriotic religion of the Bishop of
Rome's *imperium*.[26] The genre began with Botero's *Reason of State*

[23] D. Weinstein, 'Millenarianism in a civic setting: the Savonarola movement in
Florence', in S. L. Thrupp (ed.), *Millennial Dreams in Action* (The Hague, 1962).
[24] For instance, Owen, *Works*, XIII, p. 330; and Sir Roger Twysden's *Historical Vindication of the Church of England* (1657).
[25] Paruta, *Politick Discourses* (1657) and *The History of Venice* (1658); Boccalini,
I ragguagli di Parnasso (1657).
[26] W. Bouwsma, *Venice and the Defence of Republican Liberty* (Berkeley, 1968), p. 468;
F. Meinecke, *Machiavellism* (London, 1957), ch. 4.

(1589), and was most influential in the writings of Tomasso Campanella.[27] Protestant philosophers turned these claims on their head, or, rather, turned them right side up. The Lutheran Platonist utopias of north Germany, such as J. V. Andraea's *Christianopolis* (1619), are, in this task of inversion, at one with Harrington's *Oceana*.[28]

In seventeenth-century Britain, Protestant perceptions of an aggrandising papacy and of its militant allies, first Spain and later France, ensured that not only absolutist and Royalist, but also republican and Whig political thought would be deeply imbued with a sense of the necessity of the power of the civil state as the bastion of 'true religion'. The Godly Prince of the Marsilian, Lutheran and Hobbesian tradition becomes translated into the patriot of civic humanist and Whig thought. In Whig England, the Erastian imperial theme and the theme of Christian liberty moved forward together. The ideal of Christian liberty needed the idea of the Godly civil *imperium*. This was why a republican like Harrington offered praise (as Rousseau later did) for Hobbes's civil religion: they all agreed that the civil commonwealth was the high priest. In the righteous patriotism of Whig England and emergent America, liberal yet imperial, there are distinct echoes of Harrington's vision. It is to his version of the retort to the priestly *imperium* that we must now turn.

II

James Harrington (1611–77) wrote books for only a brief span.[29] His most famous work, *Oceana* (1656), was followed by a series of large and small works which expanded and reiterated his arguments. He fell silent a few weeks before the Restoration of Charles II. *Oceana*, being a scheme for an 'immortal commonwealth', included recommendations for the settlement of religion. Much as Harrington resented Cromwell's Protectorate as a bar to a true republic, he did

[27] Campanella's *Discourse Touching the Spanish Monarchy* was published in English in 1654, and again in 1660 as *Advice to the King of Spain*. Ironically, Richard Baxter, who abhorred republicanism, thought that Harrington, by weakening the English state, pandered to Campanella's schemes for bringing England under universal Spanish monarchy: W. M. Lamont, *Richard Baxter and the Millennium* (London, 1979), pp. 189–93.
[28] See F. Yates, *The Rosicrucian Enlightenment* (London, 1972); C. Webster, *The Great Instauration* (London, 1975).
[29] Page references to Harrington's writings are given in parentheses in the text, and refer to J. G. A. Pocock's edition of *The Works of James Harrington* (Cambridge, 1977).

not much quarrel with Cromwell's management of the church. The wide ambit of toleration under the Protector was unprecedented, and separatist sects flourished. Yet Cromwell's state did not abolish the Established Church, with its endowed ministry and controversial tithes. It kept up an inspectorate of the clergy, the Committee of Triers and Ejectors, which ensured against excesses of vice and heresy among parochial incumbents. Cromwell's church was a judicious marriage of congregationalist Independency and Erastian centralism. So was Harrington's proposed church. In Oceana the parishes, decimalised into exactly ten thousand, were to be the republic's basic units, the locus of elections, taxation, and the militia (214–26). There would be a national directory of public worship and a state Council of Religion. But as well as this degree of centrally imposed uniformity, parish ministers would be subject to electoral approval by their parishioners, and 'gathered congregations' independent of the national church were to be permitted, provided they chose ministers who were not 'Popish, Jewish, nor idolatrous'. Tithes would continue, and livings would be increased to £100 per year (214–17, 251, 680–1).

This is, superficially, an imperfect compromise, which recognised a plurality of sects and consciences, and yet still genuflected in the direction of the Marsilian, Lutheran, Hookerian nationalisation of the *respublica Christiana*. It is tempting to identify Harrington as having failed, unlike Locke, to arrive at a modern liberal conception of the privacy of religion and its dissociation from the state. Yet for Harrington, and his Augustan Whig successors, 'true religion' remained a business of state. In a world of Counter-Reformation popery, an aggressive Spain or France, entrenched priestly castes, and fanatical sectarian zeal, the Reformed civil state was the bastion of uncorrupt religion, the executive arm of the Elect nation. Whig and 'Country' hostility to central state power would be tempered by a doctrine of the Godly commonwealth's duty to restrain both the anarchy of private 'enthusiasm' and the tyranny of popish priests. Harrington held that the powers of the Council of Religion in Oceana would obviate both the ignorant zeal of self-proclaimed 'gifted men' and the corrupt self-interest of the clergy. He constantly insists that 'national religion' and 'private conscience' stand together: Erastianism and Independency harmonised (185, 204, 251, 681, 752, 767, 845).

As an Erastian Independent, Harrington met with the wrath of those two energetic parties of clergymen who had in turn exasperated English gentlemen in the 1630s and 1640s, the 'Prelatists' of the Laudian school, and the Presbyterians of the Genevan discipline. The Civil War generated extraordinary assaults on the clerical estate, but divines were voluble in their own defence. Harrington was attacked by Henry Ferne, Doctor of Divinity and Archdeacon of Leicester; Matthew Wren, son of Laud's hated colleague Bishop Wren; Peter Heylyn, Laud's hagiographer and self-appointed vicar on earth after the archbishop's execution in 1645; and Richard Baxter, doyen of the Presbyterian divines. Ferne protested that 'Mr Harrington hath taken up a very great unkindness for the clergy' (466). Wren accused him of an 'underhand. . . correspondence' with Hobbes's ecclesiology.[30] The effect of these clerical attacks was to bring religious matters nearer to centre-stage in Harrington's writings after *Oceana*. He responded to Ferne in a brief tract, *Pian Piano* (1657). He defended Hobbes's ecclesiastical doctrines in the lengthy Book II of *The Prerogative of Popular Government* (1658), against two of Hobbes's adversaries, Henry Hammond, the most systematic contemporary vindicator of Anglicanism, and Lazarus Seaman, Presbyterian Master of Peterhouse, Cambridge. In Book II of *The Art of Lawgiving* (1659) he expounded the ecclesiastical structure of the commonwealth of Israel. In these writings, the clergy, who in *Oceana* seem junior partners of the crown and nobility in Harrington's famous depiction of the feudal or 'Gothic' polity, now become altogether more obtrusive. The clergy were also cast as the paradigm of civic corruption, the chief enemies of secular as well as spiritual liberty. In 1659, in the tense months before the Restoration, Harrington wrote, in Miltonic vein, that the objection which 'the Prelatical and Presbyterian sects have against popular government is that as to religion it will trust every man unto his own liberty'. If the king is restored, he warned, the priests will restore civil and spiritual intolerance (736; cf. 749–50).

What churchmen most disliked about Harrington was his aggressively secular analysis of the Christian polity. Indeed, the idea of a Christian polity as a new dispensation supervening upon Hebrew and pagan systems all but disappears. 'The political bodies or civil governments of Christians or saints can be no other, for the frame, than such as have been the political bodies or civil governments of the Israelites or of the heathens' (776). This doctrine might, he granted, be thought 'scandalous', especially when applied to the government of the church itself and to the nature of

---

[30] See James Cotton, 'Harrington and Hobbes', *Journal of the History of Ideas*, XLII (1981).

priesthood. But jurisdiction, including that of priests, is not a question of religion as such, but 'a political thing', part of 'policy'. Even priesthood was a human artifice, having no divine charisma attached to it, and its nature does not differ from that in the 'churches or commonwealths of the Jews or of the heathens'. Hence the ecclesiastical practices of pagan Rome as well as of Mosaic Israel could provide prescriptions for Christian churches (519). Like Marsilius, Luther and Sarpi before him, Harrington's reading of the Scriptural text 'My kingdom is not of this world' allowed him to subject all the externals of religion to the vicissitudes of human history.

The extent of Harrington's urge to syncretise the Graeco-Roman *polis* with the Hebraic and Christian Apocalyptic is breathtaking. It is unprecedented in England, but had roots in Italian Renaissance thought. Like Machiavelli, Harrington treats Moses as but one of a class of great lawgivers, 'Moses, Lycurgus, Solon, etc'. The models of good commonwealths are 'Israel, Athens, Lacedaemon or Rome' (421, 545). Moses, he says, instituted a commonwealth with the advice of Jethro the heathen Midianite. Machiavelli, patron of modern politics, follows Moses: he has 'trodden in his steps' (177, 392–3; cf. 210, 496). King Solomon and Machiavelli provide the epigraphs for *The Prerogative of Popular Government* (389).[31] A quotation from Tacitus's *Germania* is interpolated into one from Ecclesiastes, and follows immediately one from Plato (169). And, somewhat in the manner of Dante, for whom the pagan poet Virgil was prophetic of Christ's coming, Harrington leans heavily on the fact that St Paul was a citizen of Rome, who 'claimeth the right of a Roman', and so by extension we may 'suppose him to have been a citizen of Athens' (385, 537). Pauline Christianity teaches the reconstruction of the Athenian polity.

This syncretism also permitted a systematic use of the categories of classical political analysis in examining Christian ecclesiastical government. Aristotle, Cicero, and other canonical ancients, together with their Renaissance emulators, Machiavelli, Guicciardini, Giannotti, and Contarini (to name those Harrington cites), all discerned three pure forms of regime: monarchy, aristocracy, and democracy. For Harrington, types of church government were not matters of special providence, but reducible to these classical forms, to 'natural prudence'. Thus, wherever the papacy ruled, there was ecclesiastical monarchy; where bishops or presbyters ruled, there was aristocracy; where the laity ruled, there was democracy.

[31] Writing against Harrington, Richard Baxter sneered, 'Machiavelli be become a puritan to him': *A Holy Commonwealth* (London, 1659), p. 235.

Harrington assimilates the classical notion of historical cycles – the
rise and fall of regimes, passing through phases of monarchy, aristocracy and democracy – to the Christian linear timescale in which the
Creation, the Israelites, and the Incarnation are inimitable steps
towards the millenial Second Coming. He demonstrates at length
that the civil and ecclesiastical regimes of both the Israelite and
Christian worlds have passed through the successive classical stages.
Mosaic democratic congregationalism was usurped upon by an
obligarchic Sanhedrin ('the Presbyterian party' among the Jews),
and later by the monarchic pretensions of the High Priest Hillel, 'the
first papacy' (262, 384, 534–5). Christ came as a Reformer, to restore
the lay liberty which the Jews had lost. Harrington implicitly casts
Christ's mission as a proto-Lutheran revolt against papalism. The
overthrow of priestly power is the essence of Christ's purpose.
The grand cycle of Christendom, in turn, moved from the pure
congregationalism of Apostolic times, to the oligarchy of the
prelates, to the nadir of papal tyranny, and now, in the long process
of Reformation, Christ's new faithful are restoring Apostolic purity.
Protestants reform popery as Christ reformed the Jews.

   Moreover, for Harrington, patterns of ecclesiastical government
were intimately bound up with those of the civil. There cannot be a
free republic without lay supremacy in the church. And conversely,
under the old 'Gothic' polity, now gone from England, the lord
bishops, like the lords temporal, were the natural allies of monarchy.
Monarchy is inimical to Christ, and only a free republic is Christian.[32]
Harrington noted that just when the Emperor Tiberius was murdering the liberty of Ciceronian Rome, Pontius Pilate, the imperial
governor in Judea, was murdering Christ (186). This apparently
hyperbolic analogy in fact did no more than invert the claims of
monarchists: Dante had taken the coincidence of Christ's birth and
the rise of Caesarian imperialism to be a providential sanctification
of empire; Richard Hooker agreed that this coincidence 'doth seem
by the special providence of God';[33] and the Cavaliers in the 1650s
placed a crown of thorns upon images of the martyred Charles I to

[32] A similar point of view was strongly asserted in Holland by the De Witt party which
argued that the rise of Orangist monarchy would also give rise to clericalism and
intolerance. See P. De La Court, *The True Interest and Political Maxims of Holland*
(1702), pp. 6, 39–40, 58–65, 377–88, 403–7, 482–3. Grotius's writings on behalf of
the republic were also committed to the claim that Holland reproduced the
Hebrew commonwealth: *De republica emendanda*. Molesworth took a similar view:
'republics . . . keep their ecclesiastics in their due bounds' (*Account of Denmark*, sig.
b8 r–v).

[33] Dante, *Monarchy*, Bk.II, ch. 11; Hooker, *The Laws of Ecclesiastical Polity*, Bk VII,
ch. 8, para. 7.

signify the Puritans' conjoint murder of *imperium* and piety. Harrington constantly reiterated his belief in the undifferentiated identity of civil liberty and Christian liberty (185–6, 764–7). Oceana was the rebirth of Athens and Jerusalem. 'The liberty of Rome' was 'first discovered unto mankind by God himself in the fabric of the commonwealth of Israel' (161). Oceana is to God the Son as Israel was to God the Father: 'the Kingdom of God the Father was a commonwealth, so shall be the Kingdom of God the Son'. The just commonwealth simply *is* 'the kingdom of Christ' (332). As Lord Archon (the Legislator of Oceana) eulogises out of the Song of Solomon, in his last speech for the modelling of Oceana, it is 'the rose of Sharon, and the lily of the valley . . . queen of earth . . . holy spouse of Jesus' (333).

Underlying this Hebraic civic humanism there was a strong undercurrent of Platonic metaphysics. God is manifest in nature, and nature in turn impresses on humankind the existence of God. 'A natural man . . . is by the continued miracle of nature convinced that the world had a creator, and so comes to believe in that which is supernatural, whence it is that all nations have had some religion' (543; cf. 837–8). It follows that atheism is irrational and abhorrent and that all the world's religions share particles of a single truth, although expressed in culturally diverse ways (765–6). For Harrington, knowledge is the apprehension of divine reality; reason is the pursuit of that knowledge. The soul is the image of God, its light is reason.

Modern commentators who suppose that Harrington's rationalism consists in the utilitarian calculus of interests are mistaken.[34] Oceana will be without 'any kind of private interest or partiality' (253); it will embody 'public reason' (678–9). Practical reason is not the servant of the passions, it is the striving to bring forth the forms of reason in the matter of the world, to make actual the rational. The life of reason is the life of 'virtue and the freedom of soul'; to follow caprice is to be ungodly, to live the life of 'vice and bondage of sin' (169). Just as 'the liberty of a man consist in the empire of his reason' so 'the liberty of a commonwealth consisteth in the empire of her laws' (170). The task of practical reason cannot be sundered into private and public. 'As the form of a man is the image of God, so the form of a government is the image of man' (837). 'Government is no other than the soul of a nation or city'; it is reason 'brought forth' and made into 'virtue' (170). Hence it is that 'the soul of government,

---

[34] See, for instance, Greenleaf, *Order, Empiricism and Politics*, ch. 11, esp. pp. 233, 243; Gunn, *Politics and the Public Interest*, ch. 3, esp. pp. 139–40, 151.

as the true and perfect image of the soul of man, is every whit as necessarily religious as rational', and that 'the highest earthly felicity that a people can ask, or God can give, is an equal and well-ordered commonwealth' (838, 778). Harrington's Socinian and pantheist tendencies lead him to regard the Son of God as the image or symbol of humanity's Godlike nature. The just state, like the virtuous individual, is the incandescence of the divine in the world.[35]

III

Harrington's Oceana was not to be; Cromwell did not bring forth the Athenian Jerusalem. Much of the interest in Harrington's work lies not in its prescriptions but in its diagnostics, in the pathology of civic corruption rather than in the anatomy of civic virtue. After the collapse of the utopian hopes of the 1650s, the language of civic humanism would, in the Augustan age, largely serve polemically against the venality and self-serving of those in public office. An undue emphasis by historians on the deployment of civic humanist categories in secular politics has hidden the salience of its use also in the critique of priests, the public office holders of the church.

In identifying priests as a paradigm of civic corruption, Harrington has a crucial importance, for he made a remarkable contribution to the English language. So far as I am aware, the word 'priestcraft', that characteristic term in Enlightenment demonology, does not occur earlier than his tract *Pian Piano*, dated 3 January 1657.[36] The term betokens the self-aggrandising practices of priestly castes. False religion was not only a matter of mistaken dogmas, but of the political, economic and cultural characteristics of the priestly profession *tout court*. It was best undone not by engaging in theological dogmatics about catechisms, but by an exposure of the corrupt material practices of the divines, for mistaken doctrines could be shown to have their origins in particular political and social formations. The analysis of 'popery' in Protestant discourse had long included elements of such an exposure – the mercenary origins of

[35] On Harrington's Platonism, see W. G. Diamond, 'Natural philosophy and Harrington's political thought', *Journal of the History of Philosophy*, XVI (1978). See also Blair Worden's discussion of Sidney's Platonism: 'The commonwealth kidney of Algernon Sidney', *Journal of British Studies*, XXIV (1985), pp. 25–6. Comparison with the Platonism of Winstanley and Penn would also be instructive.

[36] The credit for noticing that this seems to be the first usage belongs to my student Justin Champion. The OED's first example is the opening line of Dryden's *Absolom and Achitophel* (1681). The word is rare until the 1690s, when it suddenly becomes commonplace.

the doctrine of purgatory is the classic case. 'Popery' came to be almost synonymous with greedy clericalism, which is why the term was readily attached by their enemies to clergies of all denominations. Winstanley provides an extreme case of the analysis of all property relations in terms of 'popery' or 'Antichrist'. But the word 'popery' retained its associations with Rome, and so, when Protestant clericalism, in the forms of Laudianism and Presbyterianism, impressed itself on English radicals, a new, generic term was needed. Harrington's coinage of 'priestcraft' is a significant step towards the addition of sociology to soteriology in the critique of the material forms of religious life.

Civic humanist analysis again made deep incursions into the religious realm, since true and false religion stand in the same relation as civic virtue and corruption. Corruption or tyranny (following the classical convention) arises where a private or group 'partial' interest displaces or distorts the public interest. The life of reason is uncoerced; tyranny is a coerced bondage to the passions and interests of a ruling faction. Tyranny occurs in religious as well as in civil life. The priestly faction coerces with its inquisitions and spiritual courts; it enslaves the mind with superstitions. 'Religion is not naturally subservient to any corrupt or worldly interest, for which cause, to bring it into subjection to interest, it must be coercive. Where religion is coercive, or in subjection to interest, there it is not, or will not long continue to be the true religion' (845). Absolute monarchies punish heretics with the stake, limited monarchies coerce with limited severity, free commonwealths have liberty of conscience (703).

False religion betrays human nature and alienates humankind from the divine essence. 'If our religion be anything else but a vain boast, scratching and defacing human nature or reason, which, being the image of God, makes it a kind of murder . . .' (333). This alienation is not only a spiritual bondage to superstition, but is externalised in the power of the priesthood. When religion is perverted to serve the interest of a class, then there is civil bondage too. The priesthood of all believers becomes the priestcraft of a particular class. And since the practice of universal lay priesthood is identical with the practice of civic virtue, the 'divines' can be said directly to be the negation of the 'patriot' (703). This is the motif which Sir Robert Molesworth later took up, in his hope that 'the character of priest will give place to that of true patriot'. This would, he thought, come about if education were given 'to philosophers instead of priests'. In the modern world the philosopher replaces the theologian, and the patriot citizen replaces the priest.[37] Harrington insisted on the state's duty to educate its citizens, for ignorance enervates the spirit of a people and makes them prey to the priests (679, 846). 'Interest and ignorance' are the twin pillars of priestcraft, and in Oceana 'neither the interest of the learned, nor the ignorance of the unlearned can corrupt religion' (386; cf. 251, 308, 679).

The baleful hegemony of the clergy in Judaic and Christian societies rested, Harrington held, upon both ideological and economic power. He set about unmasking both these pillars of clericalism. Like his contemporaries, he understood there to be three varieties of clericalism: papistical, prelatical, and presbyterial. Like Hobbes, the Erastians and the Independents, he was struck by the similarities between these clericalisms: this insight gave them their tone of sceptical urbanity when compared with the arcane furies of Roman, Anglican and Presbyterian divines, who were chiefly struck by their mutual differences. All three parties insisted that the office of priesthood had a distinct character, that God intended the charisma of the sacramental or pastoral office to be passed from priest to priest, by the laying-on of hands which is performed at the ceremony of ordination. These '*iure divino*' doctrines, of Petrine, Apostolic and Presbyterial succession, were variant readings of Christ's delivery of the Keys of Heaven to the church, and His promise to be with His church until the end of time. It was true that in England (as elsewhere) the lay appointment of bishops and parish ministers was long established. But the ceremony of the imposition of hands remained. The king, the squire or the borough corporation might elect a particular person to fill a benefice, but they do not *make* priests. The clericalists distinguished the substance of priesthood from the accidents of secular election. Upon this distinction was built the edifice of Divine Right episcopalianism and Presbyterianism after the Reformation – and of Anglo-Catholic views in modern times. As Harrington noted, 'that election and ordination be distinct things is to divines of so great importance that, losing this hold, they lose all' (540).[38]

Harrington, and all the radicals, repudiated these doctrines of priesthood. They were devices for sustaining the power of a usurping class; the clergy had turned the church into a private fief, monopol-

---

[37] *Account of Denmark*, sig.b3r.
[38] Compare Penn's splenetic account of how the priests destroy universal priesthood by 'their clink clank of extraordinary ordination. A priest, a God on earth, a man that has the Keys of heaven and hell; do as he says or be damned!': *Works*, I, p. 782.

ising the mediation of God to humankind. The insistence that only the gnostic magic of the laying-on of hands could transubstantiate laymen into priests was, he thought, a hideous parody of the true nature of the church. A true church was a spiritual republic, a priesthood of all believers, candidly and equally seeking to follow the Word. The Keys were left to all believers. This did not mean that in Oceana there would be no clerical profession. But it did mean that the clergy must understand themselves to be civil servants, functionally and not mysteriously differentiated from other Christians. Everyone is a priest, but they are ministers. The study of the Apostolic church showed that ordination had its origin in popular election. The procedure had been democratic not charismatic, and so it would be in Oceana.

Harrington's denial of *iure divino* priestly claims, together with his accusation that such claims are ways of turning the church into a private fief, placed him alongside Hobbes, and was the occasion of his devising the word 'priestcraft'. Henry Ferne charged that what *Oceana* 'said in relation to the church, or religion in the point of government, ordination, excommunication, had better beseemed *Leviathan*' (370). Harrington retorted, 'now wherever the clergy have gained this point, namely that they are the Catholic Church, or that it is unlawful for gentlemen, either in their private capacity to discourse, or in their public to propose, as well in the matter of church as state government, neither government nor religion have failed to degenerate into mere priestcraft' (372).

For Harrington, then, ordination was the crux. He had nothing to say about the eucharist, baptism, or grace, but about this he had much to say. The brief sketch in *Pian Piano* became a long disquisition in *The Prerogative of Popular Government*, although his scholarship in the matter he granted to be derived from the century's chief Erastian philosophers, Hugo Grotius in his *De imperio summarum potestatum circa sacra* (1647), and John Selden in his *De synedriis* (1652–4) (520, 531). It was easy to see, thought Harrington, that clerical pretensions, for all the charismatic talk about the laying-on of hands, simply amounted to an assertion of clerical monarchy or aristocracy against lay Christian democracy. The Greek word for election by the citizenry is *chirotonia* and the word for ordination is *chirothesia*. 'If the *chirotonia* be election by many, and the *chirothesia* be election by one or by the few, the whole difference between popular and monarchical government falls upon these two words; and so the question will be whether the Scriptures were intended more for the advantage of a [papal] prince, of an [episcopal] hierarchy or

[Calvinist] presbytery, than of the people' (538). Harrington's answer is unequivocal: the doctrine of *chirothesia* was an 'invention' of the priests, an 'innovation', a 'whim of their own', a 'cheating of the people of the right of electing their magistrates' (384). Its rankest version is in the pope who 'continues by his *chirothesia*' to hold 'absolute monarchical power (537).

Much depended upon the interpretation of Acts 14:23. The Apostles Paul and Barnabas travelled Asia Minor spreading the Gospel and establishing pastors. In most Protestant Bibles the Greek is rendered such that the elders are said to be created 'by suffrages in every congregation', or 'by the advice of the assemblies', or 'by the holding up of hands' (559). In the face of this text, the standard clerical response was to distinguish substance and accident, and thereby downplay popular participation. The Presbyterian divine Lazarus Seamen said: 'Be it granted . . . that Paul and Barnabas made elders by the consent of the people; their consent is one thing and their power another.' The Anglican Hammond was more forthright: 'election . . . was permitted by the Apostles unto the multitude, and therefore the same may be allowed, always provided that the . . . constituting be reserved unto the pastors, or ordained doctors and preachers' (541–2).[39] The electoral procedure was said to be merely a gracious concession of the priests, and not of the essence. Harrington did not think it surprising to discover that the prelatical translators of the King James Authorised Version had quietly suppressed a vital phrase, lest their flock be misled. In this version Acts 14:23 merely says Paul and Barnabas 'ordained them elders in every church' – the phrase 'by the holding up of hands' has disappeared (384, 559). This 'episcopal correction' was an execrable piece of clerical fraudulence, this 'impiety in divines to corrupt the Scriptures'. Harrington tells Ferne, who defended it, 'you must needs sin . . . but what is that to interest? If this place [phrase] be restored, ordination is restored unto the people; and so, divines losing it, there is an end of priestcraft' (384). For the second and last time, Harrington uses the word.

Harrington's sense of the power and disingenuousness of learned divines prompted a concern for university reform. He did not share the anti-intellectual iconoclasm of those Puritans who held that Scriptural meaning is transparent to all honest readers, for he was acutely aware of the scholarly problems and opportunities for deceit in translating Greek and Hebrew texts. He was a good Erasmian in

---

[39] Compare Hooker, *Ecclesiastical Polity*, Bk VII, ch. 14, paras. 5–8.

believing that the injunction to 'search the Scriptures' (John 5:39) was a philological one. There would be learned divines in the universities of Oceana, but they will have no worldly temptation to do other than disinterestedly engage in 'a right application of reason unto Scripture' (217–8, 251, 307, 679).[40]

If *chirothesia* was a fabrication, what then was the true account of the choosing of priests, of *chirotonia?* Classical republicanism here made its final inroad, for Harrington argued that the Apostles readily adopted the Graeco-Roman political practices they found around them. The political forms of Asia Minor and of Crete were those of Rome and Athens, a fact which St Paul, as a Roman citizen, was especially aware. Harrington demonstrated, from the historians Suidas, Pliny and Strabo, that despite the supervention of the Caesars upon the Ciceronian republic, the eastern provinces 'remained each particular city under her ancient form of popular government' (514; cf. 506–16). These cities were Aristotelian gentry republics. They settled matters in assemblies. The word *ecclesia*, translated in English Bibles as 'church' or 'congregation', simply meant the civil assembly of the citizens. Or, to put it the other way about, at Athens and Sparta 'the church or assembly of the people' made laws and chose magistrates (177). The 'genius of the Roman Commonwealth' was that all matters proceeded 'by the advice of the senate and the *chirotonia* of the people' (507). St Paul in Asia Minor and Titus in Crete followed the 'Roman genius'. It was not to be imagined that Paul would tell Athenian-spirited people that whereas 'your political assemblies have been hitherto called *ecclesiae*; this word must lose the ancient sense and be no more understood but of spiritual consistories, and so whereas it hath been of a popular, it must henceforth be of an aristocratical or presbyterian signification' (538). Nor could it be supposed that Titus would get away with telling the citizens of 'the most ancient and most excellent commonwealth' in history, Crete, 'know ye that on whomever I lay my hands, the same is in all spiritual affairs or matter of church government to be obeyed by you'. Such a clerical tyranny would have needed an army to uphold it, but 'what army did Paul leave with Titus?'. Paul was no Philip of Macedon, planting tyrants in every city (553–4).

These Apostolic borrowings from the *polis* allowed Harrington to use Roman religious forms as guides for the proper management of a Christian church. In ancient Rome, 'in like manner with the civil

---

[40] For Harrington's influence on educational ideas, see Peter Jones, 'The Scottish professoriate and the polite academy 1720–46', in I. Hont and M. Ignatieff (eds.), *Wealth and Virtue* (Cambridge, 1983).

magistracy were the priests created . . . for the *pontifex maximus*, the *rex sacrificulus*, and the *flamines* were all ordained by the suffrage of the people . . . the latter of which, being no more than parish priests, had no other ordination than by their parishes' (518–9; cf. 437). Civic and religious life were in harmony and were a mutual strength. In place of Machiavelli's famous indictment of Christianity as of less civic value that the Roman religion, Harrington insinuated that the Roman and Christian religions, when properly understood, were identical. The 'citizen–priest' of old Rome was the model of the Christian patriot. This use of the Roman model seemed more plausible when Harrington added the claim that Israel itself was a *polis*. Under Moses, Roman light had shone, since the Mosaic polity replicated by divine revelation what the Greeks and Romans knew by natural reason (178, 601). The 'civil congregation' of Israel was '*ecclesia Dei*' (383). Moses was both magistrate and priest 'till he consecrated Aaron and conferred the priesthood upon the Levites' (437). The Hebrew senate, or Sanhedrin, was elective; the whole people partook in civil and religious decisions (175–7, 262, 534). Only in later times did the Levites become corrupt, forget their origins in civic utility, and erect a *jure divino* oligarchy, and eventually, in Hillel, a 'papacy', with its papistical oral tradition, the factitious arcana of the Talmud, foisted upon the simple Word of Scripture. The Elohim of Israel gave way to the Cabala of corrupt Jewry (384–5, 615, 645–9). St Paul was the ambassador of Rome to the corrupted Jews, bringing the light of Roman liberty to reform the clerical darkness into which the Jews had fallen. Paul the Roman carried forward Christ's dissolution of Jewish priestcraft – Harrington the Roman carried forward the Protestant Reformers' dissolution of popish priestcraft. As John Toland remarked when he published Harrington's *Works* in 1700, he acted 'like Paul at Athens'.[41] The church, for Harrington, was the people gathered, it was the essence of civic life. Priestcraft, on the contrary, alienated saint from citizen, soul from body, church from state, an alienation historically embodied in the differentiation of, and struggle between, priests and laity. The rebuilding of Athens–Jerusalem is the trascendance of that struggle. Consequently, anticlericalism was the means of sanctification, it was a sacrament.

IV

We have seen that Harrington holds that *chirothesia* is, as we should now say, an 'ideology': it is a doctrine which masquerades as

[41] *Works* (1700), p. xviii.

transcendentally true, whilst underhand serving the aspirations and interests of a class. It is a pillar of priestcraft. The other pillar which he explores is the way in which modern priestcraft became economically entrenched in the feudal or 'Gothic' regime. Modern scholarship has paid great attention to Harrington's analysis of the relationship between economic and political life – the 'foundations and superstructures' in his own phrase (602, 762) – and to his effort to explain the Civil War in terms of structural change. As early as 1700, Toland remarked on Harrington's originality: 'that empire follows the balance of property, whether lodged in one, in a few, or in many hands, he was the first that ever made out; and is a noble discovery ... the foundation of all politics'.[42] Harrington argued that the collapse of monarchy in the 1640s was the natural outcome of a change in the 'balance' of property: the demise of the feudal aristocracy's landed 'overbalance' had weakened the crown, because the nobility had been a vital support of monarchy (195–203). Now that England had become a federation of gentry landholders, the only viable regime was a 'popular government', a gentry republic, since the art of politics was 'the skill of raising such superstructures of government as are natural to the known foundations' (202; cf. 405).

Modern accounts of Harrington's political economy have not noticed the weight he gives to the church. He did not only look to landholding and arms as the supports of Gothic monarchies, but also to the clergy. The feudal nobility provided arms, the clergy provided superstition, the 'goods of fortune' and 'the goods of the mind'. In part the medieval church functioned in the same way as the nobility, for it held a considerable proportion of the land, about one third. Hence the clergy formed an Estate in the Gothic constitution. It is indicative of Harrington's relativism that he thought it an 'absurdity' to deny that the clergy were then an Estate, since they were so 'weighty in the balance' (195; cf. 846). The same situation obtained still in France, where the lands were shared between the church and nobility (436). The popish clergy was thus 'deeply rooted in the greatest monarchies of Christendom ... by virtue of their lands' (537).

Harrington thought it no coincidence that superstitious religion reaches its apogee under the feudal regime. 'The people are led into superstition', wherein they are 'to believe no otherwise than is believed by my Lord Bishop or Goodman Presbyter' (186). Private opinions were punished as heresies, and the doctrine of *chirothesia*

---

[42] *Ibid.*

became paramount. With the halter of ignorant credulity about their necks the people were led into civil tyranny, for priests and crown served mutual ends. 'By planting a religious order in the earth [the land] . . . religion hath been brought to serve worldly ends.' The clergy became 'great counsellors unto kings' (438; cf. 846). Harrington went on to sketch a formula which Whigs would later frequently reiterate: that the Divine Right of Kings was a clerical doctrine offered to kings as a *quid pro quo* for the king's defence of clerical revenues and powers.[43] It is a 'profound' popish maxim that 'there is no making use of princes without being necessary unto them' (537). Scholarship and theology conspired to conjure up monarchical charisma, 'creating a reverence in the people and bearing an awe upon the prince', which in turn 'preserveth the clergy, that else, being unarmed, became a certain prey unto the king or the people' (537). Divine Right monarchy is itself a *chirothesia*, a manufactured charisma by which the people are excluded (848–9). The clergy are likely to be 'a more steady pillar' to thrones than the lay nobility because the latter have the resources of the sword, which renders them more independent (563). 'Herein lies the arcanum or secret of that antipathy which is between a clergy and a popular government, and of that sympathy which is between the mitre and the crown.' King James I had been quite right to say, 'No bishop, no king' (563; cf. 846).

King James, however, perceived only the superstructure and did not see the crumbling foundations of crown and church. In England a vital change had occurred. It was a 'natural revolution' which 'happeneth by commerce, as when a government erected upon one balance, that for example of a nobility or a clergy, through the decay of their estates comes to alter unto another balance' (405–6). Henry VII sequestered noble lands and curtailed retainers, 'the yeomanry or middle people' were 'hereby incredibly advanced' (606). Then 'in the reign of the succeeding king were abbeys (than which nothing more dwarfs the people) demolished' (607; cf. 198). Of course, 'a change that happens in the revolution of one hundred and forty years is not sudden', but inexorably England had been 'changing from aristocratical to popular'. In consequence this revolution will, 'since the aristocratical balance of the clergy is gone, shake the yoke of the priest' (382; cf.497). An end to priestcraft was not, therefore, just a pious hope, for it could be shown that history had buried it.

[43] See, for instance, Molesworth, *Account of Denmark*, sig.b7v; Sir William Temple, *Works* (London, 1720), I, p. 10.

V

There is no space here to explore the influence of Harrington on the eighteenth-century Whig conception of the British state as a bastion against priestcraft. The sanguine utopianism and Platonic metaphysics of the 1650s disappeared, but a civic humanist version of the Reformation persisted. The impact of Hobbes, Sarpi, Machiavelli and others would also have to be considered. So too would the development of a distinctly commercialist (and, one is tempted to say, proto-Weberian) account of how Protestant states are more prosperous than priestly ones, a line of inquiry which runs from Sir William Petty (who was deeply indebted to both Hobbes and Harrington) to Adam Smith. It is a large story that has yet to be told.[44] Its gist can be given in the lapidary form of the jibe of a High Churchman in 1709 who said that Whigs believed that people should be excommunicated for not being patriots.[45]

I shall, however, glance at the work of Henry Neville, Harrington's close associate, whom John Aubrey suggests had a hand in composing *Oceana*.[46] Neville helped carry forward the civic humanist idiom into the Augustan era, and provided brilliant epitomes of his master's civil religion. Neville also helps make links with the canonical theorists of civil religion, Machiavelli and Hegel. In 1675 Neville published an English edition of the *Works of Machiavelli*. He included a putative letter of Machiavelli to Zanobius Buondelmonte, dated 1 April 1537 – April Fool's day, ten years after Machiavelli's death. It is Neville's own encapsulation of Harringtonianism. In it, Machiavelli vindicates himself from, *inter alia*, the charge of irreligion. He insists that he is a good Christian, but hostile to popes, who 'have wholly defaced and spoiled Christian religion, and made it a worldly and heathenish thing', and who have 'deformed the face of government in Europe, destroying all the good principles, and morality left us by the heathens themselves'. He goes on to rehearse Harrington's Lutheran points about priesthood: *cleros* properly means all believers, the Elect, the church. 'The most hellish of all the innovations brought in by the popes . . . is the clergy . . . set apart and separated from the rest of mankind . . . by a human ceremony called by a divine name, viz. ordination.' Thus did this

[44] I have briefly discussed the economic theme in 'Sir Peter Pett, sceptical toryism and the science of toleration in the 1680s', in *Persecution and Toleration* (Studies in Church History, XXI), ed. W. Sheils (Oxford, 1984).
[45] W. Oldisworth, *Dialogue* (London, 1709), pp. 215–16.
[46] Aubrey, *Brief Lives* (Harmondsworth, 1972), pp. 283–5.

class, in the Gothic polity, make themselves 'a third Estate . . . by their temporalities'. The clergy is a 'united corporation against the purity of religion and the interest of mankind'. Machiavelli's peroration looks to the day when 'God shall inspire Christian Princes and states' to throw down 'execrable . . . priestcraft', rescue the 'poor enslaved' laity, and restore the 'true original Christian faith'. The 'conjunction or spell of their new invented ordination' makes the priests 'so sacred and holy that they have nothing . . . of humanity in them'. When the priesthood of all believers is restored, then humanity and the *civitas* can return from exile.[47]

Neville returned to these themes in his main work, *Plato redivivus* (1681), which was included with later editions of his *Works of Machiavelli*, and which belongs to the period of the Exclusion Crisis and of Locke's *Two Treatises*. The book attempts to apply Harringtonianism to the circumstances of the Restored monarchy. Neither crown nor church, he warns, can now wield their Gothic power, since their economic foundation is gone. But the crown, if divested of its prerogatives, might make a satisfactory Doge or president, and the clergy, divested of popish claptrap, might make tolerable pastors. 'Our barbarous ancestors' had succumbed to the priestly plan 'to get riches and power', and the priests had acquired 'no less . . . than a third part of the lands'. But that land was now gone, and the 'present state is incompatible with the empire of the priests'. The clergy as a special class had been an invention of the Gothic reign of Antichrist, for 'in Apostolic times . . . we hear nothing of clergy'. In 'Antichrist's reign' the church taught that the 'spell or charm' of ordination would 'metamorphose a poor lay idiot, into a heavenly creature'. It was as idolatrous a doctrine as that of transubstantiation; for to reify God's presence in a particular person was as much a denial of true religion as to do so in a physical object. Similarly, to lock up wealth and land in a particular class was a denial of the well-being of the whole *civitas*, it was the despotism of poverty.[48] All these facets of popery, or priestcraft, annulled and alienated the sanctification which 'true religion' knows to be implicit in all rational human secular relations. Popery cannot realise the modern state.

---

[47] Machiavelli, *Works* (1675), sigs. xxx2v–xxxx1r. The letter was several times reprinted in 1689 and after: these later, modified editions were possibly the work of the Whig politician Thomas, Lord Wharton. See Raab, *The English Face of Machiavelli*, pp. 219–20, and Appendix B; and C. Robbins (ed.), *Two English Republican Tracts* (Cambridge, 1969), p. 15.

[48] Robbins, *Two English Republican Tracts*, pp. 115–19, 133, 145, 153–5.

PART III

10

<hr/>

Liberty, luxury and the pursuit of happiness

M. M. GOLDSMITH

The existence of 'civic humanism' as a common form of British political thought in the eighteenth century is well established. It began as a Country Whig ideology in the 1670s, justifying opposition to the attempt by the monarch and his ministers to introduce popery and absolutism. It was deployed again by 'old Whigs' and their Tory allies at the end of the century in the controversy over a 'standing army' which allegedly would endanger liberty and the constitution. In the 1720s, John Trenchard, a prominent old Whig participant in that controversy, collaborated with Thomas Gordon to warn of the dangers of stock jobbing and moneyed men to British liberty. Then, Bolingbroke utilised their views as well as exploiting other elements of the civic humanist tradition to denounce the corruption of Walpole's regime. The Scottish enlightenment thinkers faced some of the problems posed by civic humanism: David Hume's critique of 'vulgar Whiggism' and Adam Smith's account of the unintended benefits of self-interested activity were a response to civic humanist themes. Subsequently these ideas filtered into the thought of reformers and radicals at the end of the century. But before then, they had helped inspire a colonial rebellion in the New World against the corruption and tyranny of the old.[1]

<hr/>

[1] See J. G. A. Pocock, *The Machiavellian Moment: Florentine Political Thought and the Atlantic Republican Tradition* (Princeton, NJ, Princeton University Press, 1975) and his essays in *Politics, Language and Time: Essays on Political Thought and History* (London, Methuen, 1971); Caroline Robbins, *The Eighteenth-Century Commonwealthman: Studies in the Transmission, Development and Circumstances of English Political Thought from the Restoration of Charles II until the War with the Thirteen Colonies* (Cambridge, Mass., Harvard University Press, 1959); Lois G. Schwoerer, '*No Standing Armies!': The Anti-Army Ideology in Seventeenth-Century England* (Baltimore and London, John Hopkins University Press, 1974); Isaac Kramnick, *Bolingbroke and his Circle: The Politics of Nostalgia in the Age of Walpole* (Cambridge, Mass., Harvard University Press, 1968); H. T. Dickinson, *Liberty and Property: Political Ideology in Eighteenth-Century Britain*

Civic humanism had a number of distinctive characteristics. It held that political activity was essential for self-fulfilment but that naturally human beings would selfishly pursue their own interests and pleasures. However, it was possible to train and discipline them into good citizens, active in public affairs and motivated by public spirit to seek the benefit of the commonwealth rather than personal advantage. A good society would have laws and institutions by which liberty would be maintained and the citizens imbued with public spirit and engaged in public service.

Certain characteristics were necessary for the persons composing the citizen body. The citizenry were naturally to be male and of age. Naturally too they had to be free; therefore they could not legally be slaves nor could they be socially so placed as to be dependent upon the will of others. Independence required the possession of property. Aristotle had favoured a 'polity' whose citizens possessed modest plots of land, as opposed to a democracy of city-dwelling craftsmen, or worse still, labourers and sailors. Like Aristotle's citizens, James Harrington's freeholders combined ownership of property with the performance of military functions. Since 'power followed property', only where property was widespread would the general good be the object of those (the many) who possessed power. Harrington believed that, in England, property had passed to the people and consequently that a popular republic or common-wealth was the only stable constitution available for England.[2]

Like Harrington, Niccolò Machiavelli was an author frequently cited in the eighteenth century. Machiavelli too had advocated (at least in his *Discourses on the First Ten Books of Titus Livy*) a popular republic; he had expressed distrust of the nobility whereas Harrington claimed to have discovered a method of balancing the two classes.[3] However it was possible to prefer a more aristocratic republic – following the example of another authoritative exponent of this tradition, Algernon Sidney, martyr as well as hero of the republican cause.[4] Authors utilising elements of civic humanist

(London, Weidenfeld and Nicolson, 1977); Iain Hampsher-Monk, 'Civic humanism and parliamentary reform: the case of the Society of the Friends of the People', *Journal of British Studies*, XVIII (1979), 68–89; Bernard Bailyn, *The Ideological Origins of the American Revolution* (Cambridge, Mass., Harvard University Press, 1967).

[2] See *The Political Writings of James Harrington*, ed. J. G. A. Pocock (Cambridge, Cambridge University Press, 1977).

[3] See Niccolò Machiavelli, *The Chief Works and Others*, ed. Allan Gilbert, 3 vols. (Durham, NC, Duke University Press, 1965).

[4] See Algernon Sidney, *Discourses on Government*, 3rd edn (London, 1751).

thought might differ in their opinions of what counted as independence – or, what sort and how much property was needed to provide a suitable base for civic activity. But whether or not a special role was provided for a noble class, the classical noble virtues were to be inculcated: courage, for the performance of military functions; justice, in the balancing of the state; temperance, in self-control and social control so that all acted for the public good; and wisdom, in the arrangements for making political choices.

Because self-seeking rather than civic virtue was natural to human beings, there was an ever present danger of corruption. For a society, corruption was a change in its constitution from a good form, in which the good of the whole society was sought, to a corrupt form in which solely the good of the ruling part was the object. For the individual citizen, corruption involved devoting oneself to the pursuit of wealth or pleasure or power at the expense of the social good – private vice rather than civic virtue. Polybius had suggested that constitutions tended to degenerate into their bad forms: kingship becoming tyranny; aristocracy, oligarchy; and law-abiding democracy, ochlocracy or mob-rule. In all these cases constitutional corruption resulted from the ruling element turning away from its pursuit of the social good to seek its own benefit: power corrupts. The constitutions followed each other in a cycle; mob-rule would dissolve into anarchy from which government by a single ruler would once again arise. But escape from the cycle was possible by establishing a mixed government, balancing the three pure forms. Polybius had praised Rome for achieving a balance of kingship (the consuls), aristocracy (the senate) and democracy (the popular assemblies and the tribunes) which had resulted in her rise to dominance of the Mediterranean. In such a mixed and balanced constitution each element (ruler, nobility and people) would promote the good appropriate to it (justice and order, wisdom and aristocratic excellence, and liberty) while maintaining the constitutional balance by resisting encroachments by the other elements.

Similarly, Harrington's 'immortal commonwealth' balanced a deliberative senate (composed of the better off) against the representatives of the people who voted without discussion. The constitution would be secured internally against corruption by a periodic rotation of offices and against degeneration resulting from shifts in the distribution of property by an Agrarian Law. Although the experiment with a republic (in the narrower sense of a constitution without a king) had been abortive, it was usually held that Britain was a commonwealth or republic in the wider sense of having a just and good constitutional regime. In the eighteenth century, the British constitution – combining a legislative power composed of king, lords and commons, the first also charged with executive power, the second with special judicial functions and the third privileged to initiate all taxation – was frequently extolled as balancing the three pure forms (as Polybius and Cicero had extolled the Roman constitution).

A constitution which preserved liberty, freedom from arbitrary rule and so rule according to law was always precarious: vigilance and thus opposition to the aggrandising of power was the price of liberty. The constitution had to provide barriers preventing the self-seeking powerful or wealthy from tyrannising over the ordinary citizens; it had to provide constraints upon the people's upsetting the legal order; and it had to provide institutions training all the members of the society to be good citizens. One favoured way of implanting public spirit and impeding tendencies to self-seeking was military training. Machiavelli had advocated a citizen militia on the Roman model: citizens had received military training which taught them to co-operate with their fellows and even, in war, to risk their lives for each other; the nobility could only achieve their ambitions by military service. Consequently, good arms had combined with good laws to produce Rome's greatness; for the rulers had to rely upon the citizens to defend the state and to achieve their own ambitions for glory, and thus the means of defending the constitution were in the citizens' hands. In eighteenth-century Britain, this pattern of thought justified opposition to standing, professional armies, which could be used by the crown to collect taxes without parliamentary consent and thus unbalance the constitution, and it could be evoked as support for a militia, locally formed and officered and so not directly amenable to direct control from the centre.[5]

Liberty implied civic participation; imbued with public spirit, citizens would engage in collective action for the good of the state. Their virtue might not match that of the classical heroes: few could hope to equal Brutus, who had advocated the trial and execution of his own sons when they attempted to overthrow the republic and restore the Tarquins to the throne, or to rival Cato and his allies who had died opposing Caesar's acquisition of the republic.[6] Nevertheless

---

[5] See J. R. Western, *The English Militia in the Eighteenth Century* (London, Routledge and Kegan Paul, 1965).

[6] Indeed it could be doubted that classical virtue as embodied in Brutus or Cato should be emulated by eighteenth-century Christians: see Ian Donaldson, *The Rapes of Lucretia: A Myth and its Transformations* (Oxford, Clarendon Press, 1982), pp. 145–68, for the problems raised about Cato's suicide and Brutus's apparently heartless indifference to paternal affection.

eighteenth-century Britons could be urged to emulate these (and other) classical heroes, so the histories of Rome, Sparta and other classical states were ransacked for incidents which taught lessons of virtue and corruption.

Marcus Cato of Utica, opponent of Caesar, patriotic defender of liberty, was well-fitted to be a Whig hero. He had been a practising Stoic, as dedicated to the Roman republic as to personal virtue – a model of courage, self-control and public spirit. Joseph Addison's play, *Cato: A Tragedy*, resulted in contention between Whigs and Tories to capture its contemporary lesson.[7] Cato provided a frequently cited embodiment of classical virtue for eighteenth-century Britons. For most writers he had obviously been a Whig:

> Had all the *Roman* Patriots been as much Whigs as *Cato*, *Julius Caesar* and his Tories would never have had an opportunity to subvert their Libertys: but when Men are more intent upon raising their Fortunes, and following their Pleasures than preserving the Constitution, Tyranny is the usual and fatal Consequence.[8]

In the 1720s, John Trenchard and Thomas Gordon signed themselves 'Cato' in their attacks on the degenerate Court Whigs under Walpole and the vices and corruptions of the times. They claimed to be upholding the true Whig position. Some credit for the frequent invocation of Cato in eighteenth-century British political rhetoric (on both sides of the Atlantic) must be theirs: *Cato's Letters* were frequently reprinted.[9]

Thus civic humanism provided an ideological framework for discussing politics in eighteenth-century Britain. Because constitutional forms were philosophically definable, that is, not limited to a specific time, or because Britain, having a mixed constitution, was similar to ancient republics, or perhaps because of the cycle of constitutions, the historical record, especially of Rome and other classical states, provided examples relevant to contemporary political controversies. An education in the classics, the type of education common in Britain since the Renaissance, made historians concerned about liberty like Sallust and Tacitus readily available. Civic humanism was one form of neo-classicism. Since it

---

[7] See John Loftis, *The Politics of Drama in Augustan England* (Oxford, Clarendon Press, 1963), pp. 56–61.

[8] *Observator*, X, no. 8 (27 January 1711).

[9] 'Cato's Letters' originally appeared in the *London Journal* and then the *British Journal* between 1721 and 1723; editions in 1723, 1724, 1733 and after. For their frequent appearance in America, see Bernard Bailyn, *The Ideological Origins of the American Revolution* (Cambridge, Mass., Harvard University Press, 1967); see also Reed Browning, *Political and Constitutional Ideas of the Court Whigs* (Baton Rouge and London, Louisiana State University Press, 1982), pp. 2–10.

supposed the natural depravity of mankind, it could approach an Augustinian or Calvinistic pessimism about the tendencies of men, especially those in office, towards a self-seeking pursuit of wealth, pleasure, luxury, power and glory. It was thus particularly useful to an opposition denouncing a ministry. It focused attention on the constitution and the balance of its component elements. These might be identified as institutions (crown, House of Lords, House of Commons) or as classes (nobility and people). It could thereby be used to identify acts of power which threatened the constitutional balance and thus the liberty that it established. The extension of governmental power, arbitrary action by the executive (e.g., the use of blank warrants), increase in influence of the crown in elections, standing armies, multiplication of administrative or military offices and appointments to them, imposition of new taxes (e.g., Walpole's excise, the Stamp Act in the colonies), all provided occasions when civic humanist rhetoric seemed apposite. But corruption and vice, although likely dangers to be guarded against, were not inevitable; it was possible to maintain a balanced constitution, preserve liberty and promote public spirit. Virtue could prevail – usually if the public would heed the civic humanist prophet and resist the impending evil.[10]

Civic humanist ideas were not the only ones available to political thinkers and propagandists in the eighteenth century. It was always possible to turn to a 'providentialist' account, perceive the hand of God moving in history and base the duty to obey on Romans 13. Edmund Bohun set out a justification of obedience acceptable both to William III and to Tories by contending that the new regime had a right to rule resulting from conquest. Providential, patriarchal and *de facto* theories were embedded in the doctrines and literature of Christianity; they were particularly prominent in the Church of England – in its doctrine of 'passive obedience', in the Book of Common Prayer, in the writings of seventeenth-century divines, in the 30th of January service for 'Charles the Martyr'. Nor did the

[10] Reed Browning has described the characteristics of what he calls 'the Catonic perspective' and summed up the views that united the opposition to the Court Whigs as containing 'four irreducible basic ideas that defined the realm in which political understanding was possible': 'one assumption about human nature', the natural depravity of mankind; 'two laws of politics', that power threatens liberty and that regimes are subject to corruption; and 'one prescription for political order', viz., 'a regime in which men were pitted against men, power against power, principle against principle'; see *Political and Constitutional Ideas of the Court Whigs*, pp. 21–6. See also J. A. W. Gunn, *Beyond Liberty and Property: The Process of Self-Recognition in Eighteenth-Century Political Thought* (Kingston and Montreal, McGill-Queen's University Press, 1983), pp. 7–42.

beliefs that God had conveyed authority to kings and fathers disappear at the Glorious Revolution. The Divine Right of Kings and 'patriarchalism' retained some hold on many British minds for decades after 1690. The repeated assertions of Charles Leslie that he had made an unanswered and unanswerable case for the legitimate succession to the crown were based on the deployment of patriarchalist arguments. These positions were not necessarily crypto-Jacobite. William Sherlock accounted for his own conversion to obedience to William and Mary in providentialist terms. Bishop Blackall, a moderate Tory, was attacked by Charles Leslie as well as Benjamin Hoadly when he ventured to account for the duties of subjects and the rights of magistrates. He recognised that God had allowed a variety of constitutional forms for different peoples, but held that, in each, absolute obedience was owed to a sovereign. However the sovereign was not necessarily a single person, but the legislative authority. So in England, obedience was owed to crown in parliament. By 1710, Sacheverell's counsel were able to argue that their client's obscure fulminations in favour of obedience to the sovereign were to be interpreted as advocating obedience to the supreme legislative power according to the constitution, viz. queen-in-parliament. Thus the British constitution fell within the injunction of Romans 13.[11]

A theory which accorded divine right to the constitution was not far from the doctrine expounded by John Locke. According to him, political society was instituted when individuals devolved their natural rights to judge and execute the law of nature to a society. These powers were entrusted to whomever the majority chose to exercise the supreme, or legislative, authority; and as long as those powers were used justly and for the good of the society, they were

---

[11] For the persistence of 'old Tory' views into the beginning of the eighteenth century, see G. M. Straka, 'The final phase of divine right theory in England', *English Historical Review*, LXXVII (1962), 638–58; their survival through the eighteenth century, including a resuscitation at mid-century and a re-emergence (without implicit Jacobite undertones) to combat radical and revolutionary ideas at the end of the century, has been documented by Gunn, *Beyond Liberty and Property*, pp. 120–93. See also Mark Goldie, 'Edmund Bohum and *ius gentium* in the Revolution debate, 1689–1693', *Historical Journal*, XX (1977), 569–86; William Sherlock, *The Case of the Allegiance due to Sovereign Powers* (London, 1690; reprinted Exeter, The Rota, 1979); Offspring Blackall, *The Subject's Duty* (London, 1705) and *The Divine Institution of Magistracy and the Gracious Design of its Institution* (London, 1709); Henry Sacheverell, *The Perils of False Brethren, both in Church and State* (London, 1709; reprinted Exeter, The Rota, 1974); Geoffrey Holmes, *The Trial of Doctor Sacheverell* (London, Eyre Methuen, 1973); J. P. Kenyon, *Revolution Principles: The Politics of Party, 1689–1720* (Cambridge, Cambridge University Press, 1977), esp. pp. 21–34, 63–4, 109–11, 125, 128–45, 200–8; H. T. Dickinson, *Liberty and Property*, esp. pp. 92–5.

unalterable in the hands that the people had placed them. So, John Somers, defending himself against impeachment, could deploy a constitutional and conservative Lockeanism by arguing that, not the House of Commons, but the whole legislative of king-in-parliament, represented the people in the English parliament.[12] In Locke's theory, the law of nature, which was a law of God, backed the authority of the constitution at one remove. The *Two Treatises* could readily supply a justification for the people's resistance to unjust or arbitrary government; but it could also be read as a defence of entrenched property rights and the existing constitution.

Doctrines of natural law and natural rights were widely available in the eighteenth century. John Locke's *Two Treatises of Government* may not have aroused much careful exegesis, but they were readily available and frequently invoked. Other major works in this tradition, like Samuel Pufendorf's *De jure naturae et gentium* and Hugo Grotius's *De jure belli et pacis*, were translated into English with the learned commentaries of Jean Barbeyrac. Moreover, natural rights and constitutional rights were not incompatible; Britain had a good, mixed and balanced constitution which fulfilled the requirement of civic humanism while being in accord with the laws of nature.[13]

Civic humanism was thus not the only way of discussing politics available in the eighteenth century, but it was the prevailing political ideology. Talk of natural rights or natural law could not focus on what seemed to be the major political issues: the power of the ministry, use of money and influence in public affairs, placemen and standing armies, the position of the opposition and the dangers to a good constitution. Since the British constitution provided rights for Britons, it was not necessary to consider natural rights. Professor

[12] John Somers, *Jura Populi Anglicani*, quoted in Kenyon, *Revolution Principles*, p. 57; cf. John Locke, *Two Treatises of Government*, ed. P. Laslett (Cambridge, Cambridge University Press, 1960), II, x, para. 132, p. 372.

[13] See John Dunn, 'The politics of Locke in England and America in the eighteenth century', in *John Locke: Problems and Perspectives*, ed J. W. Yolton (Cambridge, Cambridge University Press, 1969), pp. 45–80. For other modes by which Locke's influence was communicated, see Richard Ashcraft and M. M. Goldsmith, 'John Locke, revolution principles and the formation of Whig ideology', *Historical Journal*, XXVI (1983), 773–800 and James Moore and Michael Silverstone, 'Gershom Carmichael and the natural jurisprudential tradition in eighteenth-century Scotland', in *Wealth and Virtue: The Shaping of Political Economy in the Scottish Enlightenment*, ed. I. Hont and M. Ignatieff (Cambridge, Cambridge University Press, 1983), pp. 73–87. See also Jean Barbeyrac's translations with commentaries on Grotius (French: Amsterdam, 1724, 1729, 1746; English: London, 1738) and especially Pufendorf (French: Amsterdam, 1706, 1712, 1750; English, 2nd edn, 1716, 1729, 1746). Pufendorf's *The Whole Duty of Man*, also with Barbeyrac's comments, is also important, as is Barbeyrac's *Historical and Critical Account of the Science of Morality* (London, 1729).

Gunn has documented the continuity of traditional providential language; he has even discovered Whig bishops, like Francis Hare, employing it and thereby evoking the reprimands of their contemporaries. Clearly, 'old Tory' sentiments were always attractive to the clergy. But the attractions of this language were more than balanced by its disadvantages. Paradoxically, the more elaborate, emotive and extravagant the invocation of obedience and royalism, the more suspect of disloyalty the invoker. For high-flying language reeked of Jacobitism. Thus, with Charles Leslie, it was safer to ridicule the state of nature and the social contract than to promote Filmerism. Calls for obedience to the sovereign or the supreme power or even the king were acceptable as long as the Pretender was not clearly named; a decent obscurity avoided ministerial wrath. Nevertheless, as long as there was a question about the legitimacy of the Hanoverian dynasty, the language of loyalty hinted at rebellion. After the accession of George III, and the end of the proscription of the Tories, a Jacobite restoration seemed increasingly remote and 'old Tory' language was released from its Babylonian captivity for use against reformers, radicals and revolutionaries.[14]

Commentators have sought to identify an ideology of Court Whiggery. Several useful candidates have been suggested: a moderate Ciceronianism against civic humanist Catonism; the defence of luxury and modernity; the working out of a materialist theory of social development in the Scottish enlightenment; the critique of vulgar Whiggism. It has even been suggested that the events surrounding Robert Walpole's retirement from politics induced a new political scepticism.[15]

Although there is much plausibility and some truth in all these views, civic humanist language remained dominant. Court Whigs might invoke Cicero, a less stern moralist than Cato, a proponent of natural law as well as the Roman constitution, who had argued that justice and utility were compatible. If the anti-minister, Bolingbroke, could be identified with Catiline then a modern Cicero might also be called on to crush a conspiracy against the state.

[14] See Gunn, *Beyond Liberty and Property*, pp. 153–4; the emergence of conservatism is treated on pp. 164–93 and in Dickinson, *Liberty and Property*, pp. 270–318.
[15] See Browning, *Political and Constitutional Ideas of the Court Whigs*, pp. 175–256; Kramnick, *Bolingbroke and his Circle*, pp. 39–55, 111–36, 188–204; Gunn, *Beyond Liberty and Property*, pp. 96–119; Duncan Forbes, *Hume's Philosophical Politics* (Cambridge, Cambridge University Press, 1975); M. M. Goldsmith, 'Faction detected: ideological consequences of Robert Walpole's decline and fall', *History*, LXIV (1979), 1–19 and 'The principles of true liberty: political ideology in eighteenth-century Britain', *Political Studies*, XXVII (1979), 141–6.

Nevertheless, Ciceronianism, in so far as it existed, remained within the boundaries of civic humanism: warnings against fanaticism paralleled the attack on faction and party within civic humanist rhetoric; denunciation of license and of scheming demagogues reiterated the emphasis on the balance of the constitution. The defence of luxury, as we shall see below, did challenge civic humanist ideology, as did the development of theories of social evolution and critical exposure of the simplicities of that doctrine.

Yet none of these types of thought, not even the putative growth of scepticism about the validity of the truths of civic humanism, supplanted it. It was too useful to an opposition to be discarded and too Whig for a Whig ministry to abandon. Moreover, it was an extremely flexible doctrine. That flexibility had been demonstrated by Jonathan Swift as early as 1701 when he had successfully manipulated civic humanist ideas to defend the Whig 'Lords Partitioners' against attacks by a Tory House of Commons. He had argued that Athens and Rome had declined because excessive popular power had unbalanced their constitutions. He even cited Cato as a precedent in defence of bribery.[16] Civic humanism served the purposes of the Opposition of the 1730s both by attacking an undeniably Whig ministry for sins identified by Whig doctrine and by providing a basis on which a heterogeneous collection of dissident Whigs, Tories and covert Jacobites could unite.[18] At the same time it remained the staple of Ministerial propaganda. For the standard line was not to embrace luxury and corruption as positively beneficial, nor even to question the relevance of civic humanist ideals and models – political scepticism involved a retreat from partisan commitment, or at least implicit faith in party doctrine; it did not provide a rhetoric suitable for political journalism. Ministerial writers responded to the Opposition by attacking their pretensions to virtue and by asserting the Ministry's civic humanist credentials.

[16] Jonathan Swift, *A Discourse of the Contest and Dissentions between the Nobles and the People at Athens and Rome*, ed. Frank H. Ellis (Oxford, Clarendon Press, 1967), pp. 126–7. Henry Fielding seems to have followed Swift in suggesting that Cato engaged in bribery in 'A dialogue between a gentleman of London . . . and an honest alderman of the country party', in *The Jacobite's Journal and Related Writings*, ed. W. B. Coley (Oxford, Clarendon Press, 1974), p. 32.

[17] For the argument that civic humanism provided a language especially useful against a Whig ministry, see Quentin Skinner, 'The principles and practice of opposition: the case of Bolingbroke versus Walpole', in *Historical Perspectives: Studies in English Thought and Society in Honour of J. H. Plumb*, ed. N. McKendrick (London, Europa, 1974), pp. 93–128; Linda Colley, *In Defiance of Oligarchy: The Tory Party, 1714–60* (Cambridge, Cambridge University Press, 1983), pp. 85–117, shows that Bolingbroke's line was accepted for purposes of unity, despite some reservations, by Tories.

Thus, Bolingbroke and his colleagues were denounced for lacking the public spirit they pretended to. In fact they were not patriots but traitors, really Jacobites, who were attempting to undermine the government for their own advantage. It was they, not the ministers, who were self-seeking opportunists. All they aspired to was office, even at the price of bringing back a popish monarch. The government, on the contrary, had the support of the people, or at least those who were enfranchised and not deluded; and it certainly had the support of the independent gentlemen of the House of Commons. Since the Revolution, liberty had not been eroded but established; the constitution was not being corrupted but was working properly to protect liberty. So, civic humanism was sufficiently malleable to defend ministries as well as to attack them. And later in the century, it was turned to advantage by radicals who defined the people broadly and demanded less oligarchy and more democracy.

Civic humanism was thus widely purveyed, not confined to a single political party or temperament, but adopted by quite diverse writers. Jonathan Swift, a good Church-of-England man, having failed in his attempt to court the Whig ministers, shifted his political attachment to Robert Harley and the Tories, but did not change his political language. Harley himself had a Whig background. There is no reason to suppose that Swift saw his new position as a betrayal of principle. Moreover, his 'natural' Tory preference for order, hierarchy and stability was quite consistent with civic humanism.[18] By 1701, Charles Davenant had anticipated Bolingbroke, claimed that 'Whig' and 'Tory' no longer meant what they had and denounced the 'new Whigs' for having abandoned their principles and become a court party.[19] Civic humanism was utilised in plays, poems and novels, by Brooke, Fielding, Pope and Thomson – and even built into the design of gardens.[20] It could be stretched to advocate reform and even democracy, but often had an aristocratic bias. Algernon Sidney, whose *Discourses* were a staple of eighteenth-century political education, may have hated kings like a Roman, but he argued no brief for popular power. Liberty should not be allowed to become 'license'. Andrew Fletcher of Saltoun thought that classical virtue required that the lower orders be enslaved. The American 'Founding

---

[18] See F. P. Lock, *Swift's Tory Politics* (London, Duckworth, 1983), p. vii.

[19] Charles Davenant, *The True Picture of a Modern Whig* (London, 1701).

[20] See the poems of Alexander Pope and James Thomson, Henry Brooke's *Gustavus Vasa, the Deliverer of his Country* (London, 1739), Henry Fielding's *Jonathan Wild, Joseph Andrews* and *Tom Jones,* and the gardens at Stowe. See Goldsmith, 'Faction detected'.

Fathers', especially Thomas Jefferson, feared that the emergence of an urban proletariat would undermine the republic. 'Cato' and 'Caleb Danvers' deprecated corruption, deplored the rise of 'moneyed men' and castigated the ministry for its nefarious practices which were undermining the British constitution.

Being broad, flexible and widespread, civic humanism could remain neither exclusive nor pure. Elements of it, like the maxim that power follows property or the prescription of a balanced constitution, crop up in writers whose main line of thought is not civic humanist. It was also easy to combine a Christian concern with sin with a fear of constitutional decline. Selfishness and self-seeking turned a man away from his duty as a good citizen, but it also turned humans away from God. Not looking too closely at the ideal of the virtuous citizen, with its attendant commitment to sacrificing one's private concerns for the state, advancing its power by war and achieving for oneself glory, obscured its incompatibility with such Christian virtues as humility, love and forgiveness. In any case, Christianity was rarely held to preclude service in war, participation in public life or concern for the well-being of one's society. It was thus easy to fuse selfishness, sin and corruption and to oppose them with Christian and civic virtue.

In the early eighteenth century, public corruption was widely feared. To combat the decline of the nation, Societies for the Reformation of Manners were established. Encouraged by the monarchs, William and Mary, Anne and George I, who all issued proclamations, and by much of the church hierarchy, the Societies sought to stem the tide of vice and sin. Clerics like Matthew Heynes preached virtue:

Now secure but the virtue of a Nation and you make it Rich: For Industry, Temperance, and Frugality are most inexhaustible mines, and make the certainest, if not the most ample Returns to the Publick; whilst Luxury, Prodigality and Idleness are continually preying upon it, and dayly tending to enervate by Impoverishing it.[21]

Heynes was especially forthright in promising virtue its reward in gold, but other preachers were no less convinced that the reformation of manners would be beneficial to Britain. Jonathan Swift too, and probably seriously, suggested that the existing corruption in morals and religion was harmful and that authority should act against it – initially by making vice a disqualification for place or

---

[21] Matthew Heynes, *A Sermon for the Reformation of Manners Preach'd in St. Paul's Church in Bedford at the Assizes there held March the 15th 1700* (London, 1701), pp. 7–8.

preferment. Isaac Bickerstaff, Esq., a character invented by Swift, but developed by Richard Steele as the author of the *Tatler* and promoted into the 'Censor of Great Britain', also adhered to the Societies for the Reformation of Manners. Although he was usually engaged in instructing the nation about whether canes were to be worn on buttonholes, castigating the wearers of red heels and examining the foibles of 'platonnes', coxcombs, 'very pretty fellows', 'beaus' and 'perts', he regarded his office as empowered to deal with more serious offences. He declared that 'whoever resides in the World without having any Business in it, and passes away an Age without thinking on the Errand for which he was sent hither, is to me a Dead Man to all intents and purposes'. Thus, all those who selfishly spent their time walking, talking, smoking their pipes and sipping their coffee, activities devoted to their own pleasure, were dead. 'The Living are only those that are in some way or other laudably employed in the Improvement of their own Minds, or for the Advantage of others.' The 'walking dead' he ordered to report to the Company of Upholders for burial.[22]

Bickerstaff's proposal for burying those who did nothing but eat, drink and adorn themselves supposes civic humanist values; those who are engaged in improving themselves or benefiting society are socially useful; the rest are not. Apparently Bickerstaff's pretentious moralism stimulated Bernard Mandeville into objecting. In November 1709, Mandeville had become two members (Lucinda and Artesia) of the 'Society of Ladies' that had taken over writing the *Female Tatler* after no. 51. That paper was one, perhaps the best, of the flurry of imitators precipitated by Steele's success in placing his paper not only in the coffee houses but also on the ladies' tea tables. Imitation is a form of parasitism as well as a form of flattery; the *Female Tatler* was committed to attacking Bickerstaff. Mrs Crackenthorpe (probably Thomas Baker) had done so and so did the Society of Ladies; indeed Mandeville had discussed duelling and honour (frequent subjects in the *Tatler*) in his first paper and ridiculed

[22] Jonathan Swift, *A Project for the Advancement of Religion and the Reformation of Manners* (1709) in *The Prose Writings of Jonathan Swift*, ed. Herbert Davis, 14 vols. (Oxford, Blackwell, 1939–68), II, pp. 43–63; T. C. Curtis and W. A. Speck, 'The Societies for the Reformation of Manners: a case study in the theory and practice of moral reform', *Literature and History*, III (March 1976), 45–64; *Tatler*, nos. 1, 3, 96, 99 (12 April, 16 April, 19 November, 26 November 1709). See also M. M. Goldsmith, 'Public virtue and private vices: Bernard Mandeville and English political ideologies in the early eighteenth century', *Eighteenth-Century Studies*, IX (1976), 477–510 and *Private Vices, Public Benefits: Bernard Mandeville's Social and Political Thought* (Cambridge, Cambridge University Press, 1985), pp. 1–27, 35–8.

Bickerstaff's account of a cure of blindness in his fourth paper.[23] But *Tatler*, no. 99, with its 'Comical remonstrance of the Upholders Company' requesting that Bickerstaff provide for some way of making the walking dead turn themselves in for burial, seems to have provoked a special reaction, for Mandeville wrote a series of three essays in which he denied that public spirit and learning had benefited humanity.

Female Tatler, no. 62 appeared on 28 November, just two days after *Tatler*, no. 99, and the conversation reported by Artesia supposedly took place the very afternoon on which that issue appeared. Lucinda, rejecting Arsinoe's Hobbesian position that 'there is no Animal that is naturally inclined so little to be Sociable as Man' and consequently that laws and government are necessary for peace, agrees with Bickerstaff in asserting that 'none are to be counted Alive, but such as, setting aside all private Interest and Personal Pleasure, are Generous enough to labour and exert themselves for the benefit of others'. To 'those who ever invented anything for the Public Good' we are infinitely indebted for the difference between the conditions in the civilised countries of Europe and the 'groveling State and despicable Condition' in which savages live. But Lucinda's triumph is interrupted by an 'Oxford Gentleman':

Madam, said he, it is unquestionable, that the greatest and most immediate Benefactors to Human Society, are the idle Favourites of blind Fortune, that having more Money left to them than they know what to do with, take no other care than to please themselves, and studying as well to create new Appetites as to gratify those they feel already, are given over to all Sensuality, and value neither Health nor Estate in the purchase of Delight.

Ridiculed for holding that Roman emperors 'Infamous for Luxury and Extravagancy' are praiseworthy, and questioned about how the wise Roman Senate could allow 'the pernitious Tenets of the *Cato's*, the *Seneca's*, and other Moral-Mongers that extolled Content and Frugality, and preach'd against Gluttony, Drunkenness and the rest of the Supporters of the Commonwealth', the Oxford gentleman does not retract. Instead he denies that the selfish hedonists are useless: to be clean, to 'wear Cloaths that are Sumptuously Fashionable', to live in 'Stately Dwellings, adorn'd with Rich and Modish Furniture', to 'Eat and Drink Deliciously, Treat Profusely' and to have what contributes to the 'Joy and Splendor' as well as the 'Ease and Comfort' of life,

[23] *Female Tatler*, nos. 52, 58, (4, 18 November 1709).

is without doubt to be very Useful and Beneficial to the Publick; nay I am so far from allowing these to be Dead, that I think they are the very Springs that turn the Wheels of Trade, and if the Metaphor is ever to be used, it is much more applicable to Men of Letters.

Thus, if anyone is to be counted useless, it is the practitioners of the learned arts and professions, the clergy, the lawyers and even the physicians, who cannot claim to have substantially improved human life. Learning, especially classical learning, is overvalued; compare the achievements of artisans – shipbuilders, millwrights, engineers, clockmakers and the producers of comfortable cane chairs and the furbeloned scarf.[24]

Although in the *Female Tatler* Mandeville stated his rejection of civic humanism at two removes – the views of the 'Oxford Gentle man' being reported by 'Lucinda' – that rejection is foreshadowed in his earlier works and carried forward in his later ones. *The Grumbling Hive* (1705), later embodied in *The Fable of the Bees*, contends that the ideals of civic humanism are 'a vain Eutopia seated in the Brain'. Power and prosperity cannot be achieved without the concomitant vices:

> Fraud, Luxury and Pride must live,
> While we the Benefits receive
> . . .
> So Vice is beneficial found,
> When it's by Justice lopt and bound;
> Nay, where the People would be great,
> As necessary to the State,
> As Hunger is to make 'em eat.
> Bare Virtue can't make Nations live
> In Splendor; they that would revive
> A Golden Age, must be as free,
> For Acorns, as for Honesty.[25]

For a great, flourishing, prosperous commercial society, the ideals of civic humanism are inappropriate.

Mandeville's attacks on civic humanism were devious rather than direct: the *Female Tatler* objected to the pretensions of the learned and put a case for hedonistic self-seekers as society's benefactors, thereby opposing the pre-eminence of the noble, publicly virtuous, founders of states and their imitators. *The Fable of the Bees* did not openly argue that a commercial society was superior to the classical

---

[24] *Female Tatler*, nos. 62, 64, 66 (28 November, 2 December, 7 December 1709).
[25] Bernard Mandeville, *The Fable of the Bees: Or, Private Vices, Publick Benefits*, ed. F. B. Kaye, 2 vols. (Oxford, Clarendon Press, 1924), I, pp. 36–7.

ideal. Instead it insisted that vice was inseparable from a prosperous, commercial society: vice was not desirable, merely unavoidable. Consequently, Mandeville has been identified both as an advocate of capitalism and as a deplorer of luxury.[26]

To arrive at an accurate assessment of Bernard Mandeville's thought and the extent to which it served to justify the social and political order of eighteenth-century Britain, it is necessary to compare his views with those of his contemporaries. On one side we have what Isaac Kramnick has called 'the politics of nostalgia': the exploitation of civic humanist ideas with their emphasis on public virtue as an opposition ideology by Bolingbroke and his allies. But it is difficult to find an unambiguous celebration of commerce and money. Addison and Steele, both Whig publicists, are often cited as proponents of 'middle-class values'. Yet, as I have argued elsewhere, their attitudes to commerce and money-making were hesitant and ambiguous.[27] Although Richard Steele, Joseph Addison and Daniel Defoe have been regarded as favourable to the middle and commercial classes, none of them fully accepted the values of a commercial society or discarded the values of civic humanism completely. True, they did urge that commerce was respectable and that those engaged in it ought to be respected; they argued for according a higher status to the commercial classes. But that is not enough to justify the claim that they were justifying a new social order. For Steele and for Addison, and probably also for Defoe, the aristocratic values of civic humanism remained supreme.

Neither adherents of civic humanism nor Tories necessarily thought all trade and commerce evil. Indeed, Charles Davenant, Josiah Child, Nicolas Barbon and Dudley North were all Tories. Public virtue and a moderate prosperity were often thought compatible and sometimes causally related. Jonathan Swift, in attacking the

---

[26] See Kramnick, pp. 201–4, who identifies Mandeville as the philosopher of Walpole's commercial society and holds that 'The *Fable* not only undermined the Tory position of 1714, but ... it persisted as the most telling critique of the humanist values dear to the Opposition, and accepted the values implicit in the new socioeconomic order' (p. 203); Thomas A. Horne, *The Social Thought of Bernard Mandeville: Virtue and Commerce in Early Eighteenth-Century England* (New York, Columbia University Press and London, Macmillan, 1978); Gunn, *Beyond Liberty and Property*, pp. 96–119, at p. 98: Mandeville 'of course was hostile to the traditional view [of luxury]'; but compare Istvan Hont and Michael Ignatieff, who mention 'Mandeville's strongly Augustinian insistence on the corrupting influence of luxury', 'Needs and justice in the *Wealth of Nations*', in *Wealth and Virtue*, p. 6.

[27] See M. M. Goldsmith, *Private Vices, Public Benefits*, pp. 129–35; see also 'Mandeville and the spirit of capitalism', *Journal of British Studies*, XVII (1977), 63–81.

moneyed interest in the *Examiner*, was not rejecting trade and commerce; for he identified the moneyed interest as 'consisting of Generals or Colonels, or of such whose Fortunes lie in Funds and Stocks', that is, stockjobbers and war profiteers – those who, with Swift's chief target, the Duke of Marlborough, were allegedly prolonging the war for their selfish interest, amassing fortunes out of supplying the army.[28] Money and credit could best be defended by connecting them with trade or with other accepted values. That is what Addison does in *Spectator*, no. 3 (3 March 1711) in the allegorical vision of 'Publick Credit', that beautiful virgin who is 'almost frighted to Distraction' by phantoms representing tyranny, anarchy, atheism, bigotry, republicanism and the Pretender but who recovers in the presence of liberty, monarchy, moderation, religion, 'the Genius of *Great Britain*' and the Electoral Prince of Hanover. While the first set of spirits shrinks the mound of money bags behind her throne, the second transmutes the heaps of paper money into gold. When Mr Spectator visits the Royal Exchange in *Spectator*, no. 69 (19 May 1711) what he discovers in not just a market filled with self-seeking merchants, but a set of men who are 'what Ambassadors are in the Politick World', negotiating treaties, maintaining connections between distant peoples and promoting the public good. In Mr Spectator's club, Sir Andrew Freeport stands for 'the *moneyed* Interest' as Sir Roger de Coverley does for the landed interest. But Freeport is not a petty trader but an eminently respectable merchant. He is wealthy, engaged in foreign trade (which was nearly universally regarded as beneficial to the country) and a knight as well.[29] Daniel Defoe was interested in the petty trader, for whom he wrote *The Complete English Tradesman*, explicitly distinguishing the 'tradesman' or shopkeeper from the merchant and from the craftsman who used tools to make things rather than just selling, but he also wrote a number of virulent pamphlets against stockjobbers. He accused them of manipulating the prices of stocks for their own benefit by spreading false reports of good and bad news; he described them as worse than pirates; he argued that they were constructively, if not legally, guilty of treason, because their actions helped the nation's enemies; he warned against their manipulating parliamentary elections; he denied that they were suitable MPs because they could only think in terms of their selfish material

[28] *Examiner*, no. 5 (2 November 1710).
[29] *Spectator*, no. 126 (2 March 1711); for Freeport's defence of foreign trade, see *ibid.*, no. 174 (19 September 1711).

advantage.[30] For our purposes it does not matter whether Defoe believed in these accusations; it is enough that he thought they could be convincing to his readers.

Thus, even among writers who are frequently taken to be expressing the views appropriate to a commercial society, we find a limited acceptance of some aspects of eighteenth-century British commercial life: credit is chimerical – it needs to be linked to established values, for Addison to the political order or to trade, for Defoe to the good faith of the conscientious small tradesman; funds, stocks, financial manipulations and institutions and those who engage in them are suspect. Mercantile wealth and mercantile activity is acceptable, but it does not displace landed wealth. Sir Roger de Coverley is senior to Sir Andrew Freeport; in his *A Tour through England and Wales*, Defoe is concerned to indicate the extent of production and trade for the London market and to describe the activities and the prosperity of the localities, but although he identifies the establishments of the newly risen merchants, he takes care to place them in the context of the grander houses of the gentry and the aristocracy. Trade may have been 'the whore' Defoe 'doated upon' but it is a trade through established channels aimed at a modest competence for all its participants, not a free market scramble for gain. Because Defoe was profoundly conscious of the sinfulness of luxury as well as fearful of its corrupting effect, he favoured taxes on luxuries, especially imported ones, even as he grudgingly accepted that some luxury seemed essential to trade.[31]

Bernard Mandeville's attitude to trade and commerce is quite different. He was almost as fascinated by the elaboration of manufacturing and trading operations as Defoe. Moreover he accepted the possibility that a commercial way of life may be itself an end for some. Thus Laborio, in *Female Tatler*, no. 105 (15 March 1710), is teased for rising at five and spending his day at his counting house although he is eighty years old and has no children to provide for; why doesn't he retire and take his pleasure? He replies, 'No body takes it more than I; but the question is, *Sir*, what you call Pleasure, I

---

[30] Daniel Defoe, *The Complete English Tradesman* 2 vols. (London, 1725–7); *The Freeholder's Plea against Stock-Jobbing Elections of Parliament Men* (London, 1701); *The Villainy of Stock-Jobbers Detected* (London, 1701); *The Anatomy of Exchange Alley* (London, 1719). For a discussion of Defoe's views, see Maximillian E. Novak, *Economics and the Fiction of Daniel Defoe* (Berkeley and Los Angeles, University of California Press, 1962) and for some excerpts with a commentary, Laura Ann Curtis, *The Versatile Defoe: An Anthology of Uncollected Writings by Daniel Defoe* (London, George Prior, 1979).

[31] See Novak, *Economics and the Fiction of Daniel Defoe*, pp. vii, 134–9.

declare I know none so great as getting of Money.' In fact he denies that his nephew gets more pleasure from spending money on his luxurious and aristocratic tastes (books, pictures and furnishings) that he receives from money-making. Laborio is not presented as a model for all to imitate. Lucinda, one of Mandeville's two personae, objects is no. 107 (20 March 1710), that it exhibits 'a wretched Taste of Pleasure' to fall in love with the toil necessary to achieve greater felicity, and she is supported by a gentleman who believes that Laborio must have 'a very depraved Palate' because he 'only lives to get an Estate'. But Artesia (the other of Mandeville's female masks) replies:

I Remember I was a good big Girl before I could be perswaded, but that they were all Fools that did not love Cheese. Such Wise-acres as I was then are all People that esteem others less for not loving and hating the same Things, and in short for not being of the same Opinion with themselves.[32]

Thus Laborio cannot relish hunting, a noisy, tiring, dangerous rush 'for no other satisfaction than seeing a Glympse' from time to time of a hare or a stag, but he is willing to allow that the hunters must enjoy it.

Both Lucinda's hedonism and Artesia's acceptance of different modes of achieving pleasure reject civic humanist and classical proprieties: not only can endless money-making, an activity Aristotle and others rejected as unnatural, be a satisfying way of living, but also the pursuit of happiness is conceived of as pleasure-seeking rather than the cultivation of virtue. Indeed, Laborio is a far more sympathetic character than Versailles, a hypocrite whose wealth is derived from legal chicanery and cheating those with whom he deals. Versailles has joined a 'Company of Merchants' which excludes tradesmen until 'they first have done Pennance in the appearance of Gentlemen for a considerable time, fix'd by the Company, to Air and Clear 'em from their Mechanick Scent'. Similarly, Urbano, who is rich but spends the time in which he is not further enriching himself in his pleasures – 'lives in Splendor, minds only himself, and lets every body do as they please' – is a more attractive character than the frugal Sylvio, who lives within his income and 'wonders at the slavery which *Urbano* submits to for love of Money'; he 'boasts of being completely Happy, and yet inwardly consumes himself with thinking, that *Urbano*, who makes no brags of it, enjoys more Happiness than himself'. Those who preach rules of happiness to others and

---

[32] *Female Tatler*, no. 109 (24 March 1710). For the variety of trading and manufacturing operations, see *Fable of the Bees*, I, pp. 356–9 (the passage on scarlet cloth).

pretend to be contented 'when they are only too Proud or too Lazy' to change their condition are not to be credited. Horatio, turned out of his place, embraced poverty and wrote a treatise praising his country retirement, but he abandoned that tranquillity quickly enough when recalled at a change of ministry.[33]

Mandeville's moral, expressed by Artesia in *Female Tatler,* no. 109, extends '*De gustibus non est Disputandum*' to ways of life:

For whether a Man loves to get or to spend Money, a great hurry of Business or a quiet Country Life, he that seems always to be pleased, and shews himself easy in his Station, is certainly the Man that is Happy. As to Virtue, one may have as much of it in a Croud as he can in an open Field, and the spending of Money leads a Man into as many Vices, if not more, than the getting of it.

As in *The Fable of the Bees*, Mandeville holds that both avarice and prodigality are needed in society, just as the city and the country cannot do without each other. So, 'every body is Happy that thinks himself so'; a position that leaves no room for a hierarchy of values attached to different ways of life. Philosophers endeavoured to convince everyone that they enjoyed true happiness, being truly contented. But most philosophers were 'morose, ill-natur'd Fellows', 'a parcel of unaccountable Hypocrites, full of Spleen and Superbity, and had not one Grain of Felicity in them'. 'Content' has two meanings:

As for the first, no State or Condition, how full of Uncertainty, Trouble or Anxiety soever it may seem to others, exempts a Man from it; he may be a Stock-Jobber, a Gamester, a Foot Soldier or a Galley Slave, and enjoy it. This is what we call *Suo sorte Contentus esse*, to be Content in one's Station, and signifies in reality nothing else than a Man's endeavouring, let happen what will, to make himself as easy as possible, and always the best of a bad Market. But Content in its large and unlimited Acceptation, to which have all along been and still are so many Pretenders, signifies something so great, that it cannot be an attribute to Mortals; they mean by it, *a Self-Sufficiency within, by which a Man creates himself a Happiness out of a continual delight in his present Condition, from which nothing from without can either bribe or frighten him.*

The ideal proposed by Seneca in *Thyestes*, fearing nothing and desiring nothing, is inconsistent with human nature. We are beings of time and motion: 'Humane Nature delights in a Progress, and being perpetually sensible of advancing toward something it has in view.' Thus, in the sense in which contentment and happiness are possible for humans, one may be happy as a money-getting Laborio or even as

---

[33] *Female Tatler,* nos. 107, 109 (20, 24 March 1710).

a stockjobber; taking care of one's back and belly is also a way of pursuing happiness. Not only is the classical ideal of virtue and self-sufficiency not the only one, but it is a 'pretence to a Chimera, and a Romantick Notion'.

Mandeville's account of the pursuit of happiness subverts the classical order of values. Since neither money-grubbing nor hedonism is unnatural, there can be no identification of the virtue of temperance as an absolute. The same point is made in Mandeville's discussion of luxury in *The Fable of the Bees*:

> If every thing is to be Luxury (as in strictness it ought) that is not immediately necessary to make Man subsist as he is a living Creature, there is nothing else to be found in the World, no not even among the naked Savages; of which it is not probable that there are any but what by this time have made some Improvements upon their former manner of Living; and either in the Preparation of their Eatables, the ordering of their Huts, or otherwise, added something to what once sufficed them. This Definition every body will say is too rigorous; I am of the same Opinion; but if we are to abate one Inch of this Severity, I am afraid we shan't know where to stop.

Wants are boundless; indeed, 'neither the World nor the Skill of Man can produce any thing so curious or extravagant, but some most Gracious Sovereign or other, if it either eases or diverts him, will reckon it among the Necessaries of Life; not meaning every Body's Life, but that of his Sacred Person'.[34]

Instead of retreating to some less absolute definition, Mandeville goes on to deny that luxury is harmful. Firstly he denies that the importing of luxury goods is in itself harmful to national prosperity, e.g., attempting to halve the amount of Turkish luxury goods consumed in England would result in the English being worse off.

> What is laid to the Charge of Luxury besides, is, that it increases Avarice and Rapine: And where they are reigning Vices, Offices of the greatest Trust are bought and sold; the Ministers that should serve the Publick, both great and small, corrupted, and the Countries every Moment in danger of being betray'd to the highest Bidders: And lastly, that it effeminates and enervates the People, by which the Nations become an easy Prey to the first Invaders.

But luxury should not be blamed for bad politics. 'Good Politicians by dextrous Management' can control trade; they will follow a mercantilist policy, preferring trade with countries which can pay in

[34] *Fable of the Bees*, I, pp. 107–8.

specie or goods and not trading with countries that accept only bullion, but above all ensuring a favourable balance of trade. In those circumstances, 'no Nation can ever be impoverish'd by Foreign Luxury'. In addition, property is to be secured and justice administered, foreign affairs wisely directed, the 'Multitude aw'd, no Man's Conscience forc'd' and the clergy kept out of politics.

These are the Arts that lead to worldly Greatness: what Sovereign Power soever makes a good Use of them, that has any considerable nation to govern, whether it be a Monarchy, a Commonwealth, or a Mixture of both, can never fail of making it flourish in spight of all the other Powers upon Earth, and no Luxury or other Vice is ever able to shake their Constitutions.[35]

Moreover, such a nation need only fear God's punishment through the ordinary (secondary) causes: it occurs through bad politics and mismanagement.

Does luxury enervate? A sober and temperate people may be healthier, but, although considering the meaning of 'enervate' was salutary for Mandeville when he was a schoolboy, 'the Consequences of Luxury to a Nation' no longer seem dreadful to him.

As long as men have the same Appetites, the same Vices will remain. In all large Societies, some will love Whoring and others Drinking. The Lustful that can get no handsome clean Women, will content themselves with dirty Drabs; and those that cannot purchase true *Hermitage* or *Pontack*, will be glad of more ordinary *French* Claret. Those that can't reach Wine, take up with worse Liquours, and a Foot Soldier or a Beggar may make himself as drunk with Stale-Beer or Malt-Spirits, as a Lord with *Burgundy*, *Champaign* or *Tockay*. The cheapest and most slovenly way of indulging our Passions, does as much Mischief to a Man's Constitution, as the most elegant and expensive.

The trappings of a wealthy society are not physically harmful; the 'most viciously luxurious' do not indulge themselves so much by excessive eating and drinking as by 'the operose Contrivances, the Profuseness and Nicety they are serv'd with, and the vast Expence they are at in their Tables and Amours'. But even supposing that the wealthy are unfit for military service, the common soldiers will be drawn from the hardy poor. That only leaves the officers to suffer from the dreaded enervation. However, a general does not need physical strength but 'a consummate Knowledge in Martial Affairs, Intrepidity to keep him calm in the midst of Danger, and many other Qualifications that must be the Work of Time and Application, on Men of quick Penetration, a distinguish'd Genius and a World of

[35] *Ibid.*, pp. 108–17.

Honour'. Lesser officers will be hindered from the debauchery that might ruin them by the expense of maintaining themselves in the expected style. In fact they are so controlled by 'a sense of Honour' that 'embroider'd Beaux with fine lac'd Shirts and powder'd Wigs' have shown at least as much of the necessary (artificial) courage as 'it was possible for the most stinking Slovens to have done in their own Hair, tho' it had not been comb'd in a Month'.[36]

So, everything may be called luxury or 'there is no such Thing'; under a wise, mercantilist administration, 'all People may swim in as much Luxury as their product can purchase, without being impoverish'd by it' and enervation is not a real danger.[37]

If some of Mandeville's language seems close to Defoe's view that luxury is evil, but perhaps allowable for the good of trade, the tone is quite different. That he is not actually hostile to luxury is shown again and again. He delights in demonstrating that human vices, especially pride, lead to emulation and so to the poorest labourer's wife starving herself and her husband to purchase a dress and petticoat because she 'scorns to wear a strong wholsom Frize'. Sneering at the possibilities that the well-to-do might be motivated to consume by the intention of providing work for the poor, or that people could humbly consume what is appropriate to their stations, Mandeville points out the near universality with which 'We all look above our selves, and, as fast as we can, strive to imitate those, that in some way or other are superior to us'. Thus, the craftsman dresses like a tradesman, the retailer like the wholesaler, the shopkeeper like a merchant, the merchant's wife takes her fashions from the gentry and nobility which is alarmed into contriving new modes.

The same Emulation is continued through the several degrees of Quality to an incredible Expence, till at last the Prince's great Favourites and those of the first Rank of all, having nothing else left to outstrip some of their Inferiors, are forc'd to lay out vast Estates in pompous Equipages, magnificent Furniture, sumptous Gardens and princely Palaces.

The striving is endless, but 'in trumping up new' fashions and reviving old ones 'there is still a *plus ultra* left to the ingenious; it is this, or at least the consequence of it, that sets the Poor to Work, adds spurs to Industry, and encourages the skilful Artificer to search after further Improvements'.[38]

Thus luxury and pride, endemic to human beings, result in a continuous stimulation of trade, providing work for the poor, delights for the hedonists and prosperity for the society. It is the idle

[36] *Ibid.*, pp. 117–22.　[37] *Ibid.*, p. 123.　[38] *Ibid.*, pp. 129–30.

rich, caring only for their backs and their bellies, 'studying as well to create new Appetites as to gratify those they feel already', who are 'the greatest and most immediate Benefactors to Human Society'. It is therefore not the virtuous, public-spirited statesmen of civic humanism who have provided the institutions which make a good society. What that tradition denigrates as bestiality and vice are now shown to provide those goods which humans actually and unavoidably seek (short of almost miraculous virtue or godliness). 'But be we Savages or Politicians, it is impossible that Man, mere fallen Man, should act with any other View but to please himself while he has the Use of his Organs, and the greatest Extravagancy either of Love or Despair can have no other Centre.'[39] Not heroism but hedonism is the motor of history.

Mandeville's social theory retained the inherent selfishness of humans postulated by civic humanism but rejected its remedy, the imposition of a virtuous order by a statesman in a 'Machiavellian moment'. Instead of the founding of a new social order by a religious or political hero (Moses, Cyrus, Theseus, Lycurgus or Romulus) who persuaded, forced or awed a people into civic discipline, Mandeville postulated a long development from savagery, in which humans were animals with some unusual characteristics, to the civility of a developed commercial society. What had caused this development were human wants and actions aimed at satisfying them.

The restless Industry of Man to supply his Wants, and his constant Endeavours to meliorate his Condition upon Earth, have produced and brought to Perfection many useful Arts and Sciences, of which the Beginnings are of uncertain Æra's, and to which we can assign no other Causes, than human Sagacity in general, and the joynt Labour of many Ages, in which Men have always employ'd themselves in studying and contriving Ways and Means to soothe their various Appetites, and make the best of their Infirmities.[40]

A long process of development lay behind the current state of the arts and sciences: among those that had been the 'joynt Labour of

---

[39] *Ibid.*, p. 348. In Remark O, pp. 147–68, Mandeville argues that 'the real Pleasures of all Men in Nature are worldly and sensual, if we judge from their Practice'. So the theory of virtue is like an ornamental jar, it makes 'a fine shew' but contains only 'Dust and Cobwebs'; the virtues are found in dedications and epitaphs 'and no where else'. By defining virtuous and religious motives as requiring self-abnegation, Mandeville is able to treat all other motives as selfish. These motives thus include not only those derived from self-love, which lead to self-preservation, but also those based on what he later called 'self-liking', a passion which is, or causes, pride and shame. See *Fable of the Bees*, II, pp. 130–1 and for the later explication of self-liking, *An Enquiry into the Origin of Honour, and the Usefulness of Christianity in War* (London, 1732; reprinted London, Frank Cass, 1971), pp. 3–13.   [40] *Fable of the Bees*, II, p. 128.

many Ages' are brewing, baking, shipbuilding, sailing, soap-boiling, agriculture, astronomy, medicine, architecture, painting and metallurgy. Mandeville emphasises that the intricate technological processes involved could not have been invented by individuals in remote ages which lacked the advanced scientific understanding of natural processes, some of which were not understood in his own time. But it is not only the useful arts which have taken a long time to develop; language, manners, reasoning, laws and government have resulted from the same process.[41]

The consequence of this long, slow development has been that 'many things which were once look'd upon as the Invention of Luxury, are now allow'd even to those so miserably poor as to become the Objects of publick Charity, nay even counted so necessary, that we think no Human Creature ought to want them'. Among these advances on savage simplicity, Mandeville mentions white linen and the capacity for washing clothes, bread, beer, soft beds, well-proportioned houses, even Chelsea, Greenwich and Les Invalides for the poor and meat-eating (despite the obvious cruelty involved in slaughtering the higher animals, and a natural repugnance to doing it – overcome by the 'arbitrary Power of Custom, and the violence of Luxury'). But the outcome of the pursuit of happiness has been prosperity.

> Thus Vice nurs'd Ingenuity,
> Which join'd with Time and Industry,
> Had carry'd Life's Conveniencies,
> It's real Pleasures, Comforts, Ease,
> To such a Height, the very Poor
> Liv'd better than the Rich before,
> And nothing could be added more.[42]

On Mandeville's account political heroes were no more necessary than intellectual giants. Just as the progress of the arts and sciences had taken vast tracts of time, so too had the development of social and political institutions. True, Mandeville does refer to 'skilful Politicians' at the beginning of the *Fable*; they, along with 'Moralists and Philosophers of all Ages', 'Lawgivers and other wise Men', are supposed to have flattered humankind into exchanging immediate

---

[41] For various arts and sciences, see *ibid.*, I, pp. 170–1, II, pp. 141–6, 186–8, 267, 287, 319; for social development, pp. 130–9, 286–9, 306–8, 320–3. See also *Female Tatler*, no. 62 (28 November 1709): the arts and sciences 'have all come to the Perfection they are in by very slow Degrees, and the first Rudiments of most of them have been so small, that the Authors are hardly worth naming'.

[42] *Fable of the Bees*, I, pp. 26, 169–75. For a fuller exposition, see Goldsmith, *Private Vices, Public Benefits*, pp. 61–77.

satisfaction of desires for gratification of its passion of self-liking, thus introducing the 'first Rudiments of Morality', this 'Foundation of Politics' being the basis of civilisation. This, along with the statement that 'Good Politicians by dextrous Management' could control trade, has deceived otherwise astute commentators into believing that the publicly virtuous statesmen of civic humanism retain their roles in Mandeville's conception of society. But Mandeville's theory has no real place for such persons. The 'skilful Politicians', apparently charged with a variety of immense tasks, including even extracting harmony from the 'jarring Discord of Contraries' composing society, turn out to be a convenient shorthand way of referring to the mechanism of social development.[43]

Exemplary statesmen are no longer necessary to found states and to discipline citizens into public spirit; the consummate wisdom needed to establish a good constitution is a consequence of 'long Experience in Business, and a Multiplicity of Observations' over a long time. A city's complex government is likened to a knitting frame or a clock; each part has taken skill and effort to develop, but the whole thing can be operated by quite ordinary persons. Even a prime minister needs no special virtues; quite an ordinary man will do, that is, someone of moderate intelligence, a decent memory, fairly healthy, somewhat vain, capable of attending to business without being flustered, but 'bold and resolute, so as not to be easily shock'd or ruffled'. Not virtue, public spirit and intellectual genius, but a thick skin and the abilities to flatter the prince and control a number of subordinates are what are needed for political office. If the employments are divided and each official's powers limited,

the weightiest Affairs, and a vast Multiplicity of them, may be managed with Safety as well as Dispatch, by ordinary Men, whose highest Good is Wealth and Pleasure; and the utmost Regularity may be observed in a great Office, and every part of it; at the same time, that the whole Oeconomy of it seems to be intricate and perplex'd to the last degree, not only to Strangers, but the greatest part of the very Officers that are employ'd in it.

So the political system, far from being the work of a 'Machiavellian moment', becomes a machine like a striking clock, the product of technologies developed over time. 'The wisest Laws of human Invention are generally owing to the Evasions of bad Men, whose Cunning had eluded the Force of former Ordinances, that had been made with less Caution.'[44]

[43] See Goldsmith, *Private Vices, Public Benefits*, pp. 47–64.
[44] *Fable of the Bees*, II, pp. 319–37; see Goldsmith, *Private Vices Public Benefits*, pp. 101–19.

Public and personal virtue are no longer necessary qualifications for office. Civic humanist rhetoric, whether praising or condemning politicians, is irrelevant. Politics has become a matter of keeping the machine going rather than a theatre for displaying virtue and gaining honour. All the rectitude and wisdom that is necessary is provided by the system itself; and it will be improved by gradual adjustments of its faults over time. But if the aristocratic elements of civic humanism are lost, and politicians are reduced to ordinary mortals driven by their passions for wealth and esteem, so too are any implications of the desirability of civic participation. For Mandeville, political commitment is ridiculous:

I could excuse a man, who chuses a side, and stands up for it with obstinacy to oblige his customers, his relations, or a friend, whom he has some expectation from; but it is unpardonable, that a man should be serious and vehement to maintain a cause, which in the first place he is conscious he knows nothing of, in the second he is sure he never can, or so much as proposes to get any thing by, in behalf of others, whom he never was acquainted with, and often never saw or heard spoke of, but with the utmost partiality, and such as despise him, and would not dirty their shoes to save him from hanging, unless they were paid for it.[45]

Some, mainly courtiers, may wish to pursue the pleasures of a political career; for the rest of the population, Mandeville's message is one of scepticism about the virtues of politicians and the virtue of participation. Citizens should cease grumbling. Moreover, in a commercial society they may reject the aristocratic and classical virtues recommended in civic humanist ideology. Thus Mandeville, by showing that luxury was not 'the source of every corruption in government' but that it stimulated the progress of the arts and sciences, contributed to a new conception of morality and politics in which the pursuit of happiness replaced the pursuit of virtue.[46]

[45] Bernard Mandeville, *Free Thoughts on Religion, the Church and National Happiness*, 2nd edn (London, 1729; reprinted Stuttgart–Bad Cannstatt, 1969), pp. 407–8.
[46] See David Hume, *An Enquiry Concerning the Principles of Morals*, in *Enquiries Concerning the Human Understanding and Concerning the Principles of Morals*, ed. L. A. Selby-Bigge, 2nd edn (Oxford, Clarendon Press, 1927), p. 181.

11

The language of sociability and commerce: Samuel Pufendorf and the theoretical foundations of the 'Four-Stages Theory'

ISTVAN HONT

The aim of this essay is to reconstruct Pufendorf's theory of sociability so as to bring out its relation to a theoretical model of commercial society. This theory, it will be argued, was the result of Pufendorf's attempt to reconstruct Grotius's jurisprudence by applying the intellectual method of Thomas Hobbes. By doing this, Pufendorf committed himself to an individualistic premise for his argument and to an anthropology, which systematically compared human with animal nature in order to underline the contrast between civilisation and barbarism. The product of this approach was a new concept of sociability which led some eighteenth-century commentators to describe Pufendorf and his close followers as 'socialists'.[1] This same model of sociability and its concomitant anthropology played a key part in Adam Smith's theory of commercial society and in his conception of the 'Age of Commerce' as the decisive fourth stage in human history.

The intimate continuity between earlier natural-law theories of property and Smith's four stage theory of history does not need elaborate demonstration.[2] But it is commonly believed at present

---

I would like to thank John Dunn and Anthony Pagden for their help with the final version of this essay.

[1] Gottlieb Hufeland, *Lehrsätze des Naturrechts und der damit verbundenen Wissenschaften* (Jena, 1790), p. 16.

[2] See Hans Medick, *Naturzustand und Naturgeschichte der bürgerlichen Gesellschaft: die Ursprünge der bürgerlichen Sozialtheorie als Geschichtsphilosophie und Sozialwissenschaft bei Samuel Pufendorf, John Locke und Adam Smith* (Göttingen, 1973) and Peter Stein, *Legal Evolution: The Story of an Idea* (Cambridge, 1980). On the relevance of the natural jurisprudence connection for the Scottish Enlightenment, see, amongst others, Duncan Forbes, 'Natural law and the Scottish Enlightenment', in R. H. Campbell and A. S. Skinner (eds.), *The Origins and Nature of the Scottish Enlightenment* (Edinburgh, 1982), pp. 186–204; James Moore and M. Silverthorne, 'Gershom Carmichael and the natural jurisprudence tradition in eighteenth-century

that his predecessors and contemporaries in legal theory, while recognising the three earlier stages – hunting–gathering, shepherding and agriculture – had no clear conception of commerce as a further and distinct stage. A closer look at Smith's own position, however, reveals a certain incoherence. His explanation for the emergence of the fourth stage was quite different in kind from those which explained the first three.[3] The principle of progress in the first three stages was simple. Mankind found itself compelled to turn from hunting to shepherding and then to agriculture as the primary ways of material self-preservation under the double pressure of depleting natural resources and growing population. Smith claimed that the age of commerce was just as much a 'natural' development. But it was a development of not quite the same kind. It was not marked with any further step in the natural acquisition of property through occupation or accession. Commerce itself could not possibly be a *primary* mode of acquiring property, since barter presupposed that the objects offered for exchange were already owned. Limited specialisation and limited markets, Smith admitted, were clearly possible before the age of commerce. But once it became clear that commerce, even if 'very much clogged and embarrassed in its operation', had already existed in the rude ages of society, it was also clear that commerce did not succeed the previous stages of subsistence, but rather developed in parallel throughout all four stages. The age of commerce followed on that of agriculture only in a purely quantitative sense. Once a major proportion of a society lost its immediate access to land and 'the division of labour has been once thoroughly established', the majority of society had to live 'by exchanging' or to become 'in some measure a merchant'. When this occurred, Smith claimed, then 'the society itself grows to be what is properly a commercial society'.[4]

The foundation of the division of labour and commerce lay in the human 'propensity to truck, barter, and exchange one thing for

Scotland', in I. Hont and M. Ignatieff (eds.), *Wealth and Virtue: The Shaping of Political Economy in the Scottish Enlightenment* (Cambridge, 1983), pp. 73–88. On Hume's relationship to natural law, not touched upon in this essay for reasons of space, see Forbes's excellent *Hume's Philosophical Politics* (Cambridge, 1975) and Moore, 'Hume's theory of justice and property', *Political Studies*, XXIV (1976), 103–19. A number of complementary themes to the present argument were developed in I. Hont and M. Ignatieff, 'Needs and justice in the *Wealth of Nations*', in *Wealth and Virtue*, pp. 1–44.

[3] Ronald L. Meek, *Social Science and the Ignoble Savage* (Cambridge, 1976), pp. 227–8.
[4] Adam Smith, *An Inquiry into the Nature and Causes of the Wealth of Nations*, ed. R. H. Campbell, A. S. Skinner and W. B. Todd, 2 vols. (Oxford, 1976) [henceforth *WN*], I.iv.1.

another',[5] a consequence of the most paradoxical of contrasts between men and animals. 'Man has received from the bounty of nature reason, ingenuity, art, contrivance, and capacity of improvement, far superior to that which she bestowed on any other animals', observed Smith, 'but is at the same time in a much more helpless and destitute condition with regard to the support and comfort of his life'.[6] Animals were fully equipped for self-preservation, men were not. But once they co-operated they could easily surpass animals. A multiplicity of new needs could be satisfied, completely transforming their way of living. The higher standard of living was a result of the separation of occupations made possible by men bartering selfishly on their own behalf. It was 'not from the benevolence of the butcher, the brewer, or the baker, that we expect our dinner', Smith explained, 'but from their regard to their own interest'.[7] This preoccupation with personal interests did not, however, cause society to collapse into internecine war. When men help each other from benevolence and charity, their society may be a happy place; but when they address themselves exclusively not to the 'humanity' of their fellows, 'but to their self-love', Smith declared,

the society, though less happy and agreeable, will not necessarily be dissolved. Society may subsist among different men, as among different merchants, from a sense of its utility, without any mutual love or affection; and though no man in it should owe any obligation, or be bound in gratitude to any other, it may still be upheld by a mercenary exchange of good offices according to an agreed valuation.[8]

Smith's contemporaries recognised that the famous passage on the benevolence of the butcher, the brewer and the baker was a direct comment on the central issues of natural law. The distinction between benevolence and charity on the one hand and the strict justice of contracts and bargains on the other was a most important premise of post-Grotian jurisprudence. At least one observer, Governor Pownall, in his famous 1776 open letter to Smith, also

---

[5] Smith, *WN*, I.ii.1; compare with *Lectures on Jurisprudence*, ed. R. L. Meek, D. D. Raphael and P. G. Stein (Oxford, 1978), 'Report of 1762–3' [henceforth *LJ(A)*], vi.44; 'Report dated 1766' [henceforth *LJ(B)*], 219; 'Early draft of part of *The Wealth of Nations*' [henceforth *ED*], 2.12.

[6] Smith, *LJ(A)*, vi.8; compare with *WN*, I.ii.2; *ED*, 2.12.

[7] Smith, *WN*, I.ii.2; compare with *LJ(A)*, vi.46; *LJ(B)*, 220; *ED*, 2.13.

[8] Adam Smith, *The Theory of Moral Sentiments*, ed. D. D. Raphael and A. L. Macfie (Oxford, 1976), II.ii.2. The whole section is entitled 'Of the Utility of this constitution of Nature'. What Smith meant by this 'constitution' was that 'man can only subsist in society' where all members 'stand in need of each others' assistance, and are likewise exposed to mutual injuries'.

recognised that by reconstructing the theory of 'that community, which is the basis and origin of civil government' Smith was joining in the debate over the origins of government and of political and social obligations. The issue here was to discover the true 'efficient cause of government as *the true state of nature* to man, not as an artificial succedaneum to an imagined theoretic state of nature'.[9]

This latter viewpoint was of course the infamous theory of Hobbes. The opposite theory, the creation of a principle of society independent of and prior to the foundation of the *civitas*, was known in pre-Smithian natural jurisprudence as the theory of natural sociability. As his use of the language of natural jurisprudence indicated, the theoretical foundations of Smith's fourth stage represented a qualified restatement of the natural jurists' theory of sociability. In his brief introductory lecture on its history with which Smith opened his lectures on jurisprudence, he summarised the opponents of Hobbes as claiming 'that the state of nature was not a state of war but that society might subsist, tho' not in so harmonious a manner, without civil institutions'. 'With this design', he continued, 'Pufendorf wrote his large treatise. The sole intention of the first part of it is to confute Hobbes.'[10]

But Smith insisted that Pufendorf was wrong to believe that there was any point in treating 'of the laws which would take place in a state of nature, or by what means succession to property was carried on' for the simple but devastating reason that there was 'no such state existing'. In order to grasp the nature of Smith's objection, it is necessary to look at Pufendorf's theory of the state of nature in some detail, since it is not entirely clear whether Pufendorf himself believed that a 'state of nature' ever existed.

One of the hallmarks of Pufendorf's natural jurisprudence was precisely its denial that a 'pure' state of nature had ever in fact occurred. All that could be claimed on historical grounds, he argued, was that in the early ages of mankind there was a 'state of natural liberty' amongst the different families roaming the various regions of the world. These men were all counted as equals, were in full moral control of themselves and without any form of subjection or subordination to each other. Their connection with other groups, after they had wandered away from their root family, was no more than the tie of their common humanity. In a wider historical

---

[9]   *A Letter from Governor Pownall to Adam Smith, L.L.D.F.R.S., being an Examination of Several Points of Doctrine, laid down in his 'Inquiry in to the Nature and Causes of the Wealth of Nations'*, reprinted in *The Correspondence of Adam Smith*, ed. E. C. Mossner and I. S. Ross (Oxford, 1977), p. 339.   [10] Smith, *LJ(B)*, 3.

perspective, the state of natural liberty was not simply the 'original' state of mankind, as many jurists had maintained. On the contrary, Pufendorf argued, it was not even the earliest state in which men found themselves. In the first family the children did not confront their parents as bearers of natural liberty, but as subjects of paternal authority. Natural liberty presupposed relationships outside the structure of the family. Hence, the state of nature, 'as it was really', was a product of history; it had developed, Pufendorf argued, as mankind evolved communities, tribes, kingdoms and nations. In this sense it was not merely a matter of the past. The state of nature, the state of natural liberty, he wrote, 'at this Time is the Case of many Kingdoms and Communities, and of the Subjects of the same, with respect to the Subjects of the other; and the same was anciently the State of the Patriarchs, when they liv'd independently'.[11]

The 'state of man' could 'be distinguish'd into either Natural or Adventitious' only for purely theoretical purposes. A theoretical 'state of nature', as opposed to the 'adventitious' or 'acquired', the state of nature 'as it is really and indeed', was a pure fiction. But its 'fictional' status in this context did not vitiate its theoretical contribution. Provided that its fictional character was constantly kept in sight, the utility, indeed the necessity of a method based upon the 'state of nature' within 'natural' jurisprudence was evident. It played a key role in the shaping of Pufendorf's theory of *socialitas*. To grasp this role it is helpful to consider the agenda of natural jurisprudence which Pufendorf put forward in his history of the discourse.[12] To do so will also indicate more clearly the connections

[11] Pufendorf, *De officio hominis et civis juxta legum naturalem libri duo*, translated into English by Andrew Tooke under the title *The Whole Duty of Man According to the Law of Nature; The Fourth Edition with the Notes of Mr Barbeyrac, and many other Additions and Amendments* (London, 1716), 2.1.6. (References to this work will follow the form *OHC* and 'book, chapter, section' numbers.)

[12] The main textual foundation for this account of Pufendorf's views is the essay entitled 'De origine et progressu disciplinae iuris naturalis', first published in the polemical pamphlet *Spicilegium controversiarum* (1680) and then reprinted as the first chapter of Pufendorf's collected answers to his various critics, *Eris Scandica, qua adversus libros de iure naturali et gentium obiecta diluuntur* (1686). The references follow the pagination of the version of *Eris Scandica* added to Hertius's edition of the *De iure naturae et gentium*, 2 vols. (Frankfurt am Main, 1712), II. Pufendorf also included short, but important, sketches of the history of jurisprudence in the introductions to his major works. Another major source is the very important 1663 correspondence between Pufendorf and Baron Boineburg, with Conring's and Johann Heinrich Boeckler's famous critique of the Pufendorf letters, published in Christian Thomasius, *Paulo Plenior historia iuris naturalis* (Halle, 1719), Appendix II. See a modern critical edition of Pufendorf's letters in Fiammetta Palladini, 'Le due letteri di Pufendorf al Barone do Boineburg: quella nota e Quella "perduta" ', *Nouvelles de la République des Lettres*, I (1984), 119–44. All the relevant contemporary controversies around Pufendorf are summarised in her excellent *Discussione seicentesche su Samuel Pufendorf: scritti latini: 1663–1700* (Bologna, 1978).

between the intellectual undertakings of Pufendorf and Smith. The sharp break attributed to Grotius in the history of natural law, such a prominent feature of Smith's account both in the *The Theory of Moral Sentiments* and in the lectures on jurisprudence,[13] can be regarded as essentially an 'invention' of Pufendorf. Smith singled out three great seventeenth-century systems of natural jurisprudence in his introductory lecture. That of Grotius was the first, since he had begun the discourse; Hobbes's was the second, and the third, in sharp reaction to Hobbes, was Pufendorf's own. By pointing out this pattern, Smith was not merely offering a very selective history. For the identification of Grotius and Hobbes as the true makers of natural jurisprudence,[14] when Pufendorf first established the pattern, furnished an 'apology' for the German's own complete break with Scholastic Aristotelianism and his firm support of the moderns.

In philosophy he saw the change coming with Bacon,[15] in jurisprudence with Grotius. 'The vestiges of previous scholarship', he said of Grotius, 'had no influence over his course.'[16] It was Grotius who first clearly understood that natural jurisprudence could be valid only if it was 'of use for the whole human race'. Positive and arbitrary law must be distinguished carefully from the common or 'natural' laws of the whole of mankind. Of these last Grotius's provided the first real and complete system.[17] All previous systems of jurisprudence had been compromised in this respect. Aristotle had 'before his eyes the custom of his own Greek states'.[18] The Roman lawyers were genuinely preoccupied with systematisation and with first principles, but their minds were also focused on considerations which 'originate in the special character of the Roman state'.[19] The same charge was levelled by Pufendorf against any purely Christian natural law. Since Christianity was not the universal religion of the whole of humanity, it could not serve as the basis of universal jurisprudence.[20]

In Pufendorf's eyes even Grotius had in fact to some extent

---

[13] Smith, *TMS*, VII.iv.37; *LJ(B)*, 1.

[14] In his first work, the *Elementorum jurisprudentiae universalis* (1660) Pufendorf cited no authors other than Grotius and Hobbes. For the very revealing pattern of citations in his later work, see the 'Verzeichnis der Zitate in *De iure naturae et gentium*', in Horst Denzer, *Moralphilosophie und Naturrecht bei Samuel Pufendorf: eine geistes- und wissenschaftsgeschichtliche Untersuchung zur Geburt des Naturrechts aus der Praktischen Philosophie* (Munich, 1972), pp. 333–57.

[15] For Pufendorf's views on Bacon and Descartes, see his essay 'De novitatibus philosophicis', in *Eris Scandica*, pp. 170–5.   [16] 'De origine et progressu', p. 167.

[17] 'De origine et progressu', p. 163.   [18] 'De origine et progressu', p. 166.

[19] 'De origine et progressu', p. 166.   [20] 'De origine et progressu', p. 165.

compromised his own enterprise. For by admitting as a means of establishing the law of nature the common custom of the more civilised nations,[21] he had given a place within his own system to the sceptical view of history as cultural diversity. While accepting the relevance of the humanist insistence on *consensus* both in international law and in the theology of tolerance, Pufendorf himself believed that this concession to Aristotelianism was inadmissible. For if one really accepted the force of the sceptical argument there could be little point in referring to the custom and laws of a few selected countries. Scepticism entailed that the criteria of civilisation were also matters for legitimate dispute.[22]

In this instance the weakness of Grotius's system lay in its incompleteness. It lacked an epistemology and a proper study of human nature. It was here that Pufendorf saw the relevance of Hobbes. He did not wish to defend what he called Hobbes's 'Epicureanism' or his perverse theology. But amongst the great errors in Hobbes, he remarked, there were also great lessons to be learnt, particularly from his method. "These very falsehoods which he passes on', he wrote,

provide a foothold by which moral and political science can be led to the highest peak. Thus, much of what helps to complete this study would never have entered anybody's mind if it were not in Hobbes' writings.[23]

Attention to Hobbes was thus the first way forward from Grotius. The second invoked the heritage of the Stoics. As a major relaxation of his aggressive modernism, Pufendorf admitted, that 'among the various schools of the ancient philosophers, the tenets of the Stoics, with a few alterations, could, it seems, be easily incorporated in a consistent system of natural law'.[24] For in Cicero and the Stoics he had found a counterbalance to Hobbes's doctrine of virtue.

[21] Grotius, *De iure belli ac pacis*, 1.1.12.1; compare with 'Prolegomena', 40, 46.
[22] See the point put very sharply in Pufendorf's first letter to Boineburg, 13 January 1663, in Palladini (ed.), 'Le due lettere di Pufendorf', pp. 134–5.
[23] 'De origine et progressu', p. 168. In his defence of Hobbes's character and doctrines Pufendorf referred to Samuel Sorbière. For a characterisation of the important network of Hobbes's followers on the Continent, see Quentin Skinner, 'Thomas Hobbes and his disciples in France and England', *Comparative Studies in Society and History*, III (1965–6), 153–67.
[24] 'De origine et progressu', p. 166. See also Pufendorf's praise of Cumberland's use of Stoic doctrines in countering Hobbes, p. 168. The relevance of Cicero for Pufendorf can also be seen from his possession of several editions of his work. See the sale catalogue of Pufendorf's library, *Catalogus bibliothecae illustris, selectissimis varii generis atque idiomatis libris refertae, cujus auctio consueta lege habebitur Berolini die 20. Septembr. et seqq.* (Berlin, 1697). Pufendorf's point about the relevance of the Stoics was reiterated by Jean Barbeyrac in his influential 'Historical and critical account of the science of morality' which he published as a preface to his French

With a clear view of Pufendorf's master strategy in mind one can understand why he was willing to exploit the ambiguities in the word 'nature', and to use the phrase 'state of nature' to describe both the 'real' historical condition in question and a hypothetical analytical device. Many of the apparent ambiguities of his jurisprudence would disappear, if he had demarcated the relation between these two distinct 'states of nature' more consistently in each of his particular arguments.[25] His failure to do so was itself an index of the enormous difficulty that he experienced in attempting to reconstruct the theory of Grotius with the help of Hobbes's method and without committing himself to Hobbes's own conclusions.

It was a central and conspicuous feature of Pufendorf's mature jurisprudence that it deployed the apparatus of Hobbes's 'state of nature' in an instrumental and two-sided fashion. There was more to this instrumental use of Hobbes's method than a simple endorsement of his strategy for countering scepticism. The analytical concept of the 'state of nature' effectively supplanted the use of Aristotle' concept of the common custom of civilised nations. But the content of this idea, a contrast between civilisation and barbarism, remained eminently present. For what Pufendorf saw clearly was that in important ways Hobbes himself had not destroyed but preserved the view of human nature accepted by the protestant Aristotelians. By dividing the object of analysis into two parts, with cultural diversity entirely on the one side, and 'pure' human nature in the abstract on the other, the humanist message of the late sixteenth-century sceptics could be rescued from their own scepticism. The content which Hobbes gave to the contrast between *civitas* and 'state of nature' preserved the humanist and sceptical valuation of the modern world as something genuinely human in its cultural diversity in opposition to the bestial and primitive uniform-

translation of Pufendorf's *De iure naturae et gentium* in 1706. It was in this spirit that Hume could juxtapose Cicero's *Offices* to Pufendorf's *Whole Duty of Man*, even if he preferred the Roman moralist to his German follower; see his important letter to Francis Hutcheson in *The Letters of David Hume*, ed. J. Y. T. Greig, 2 vols. (Oxford, 1932), I, p. 34.

25 Pufendorf was highly aware of the fact that the 'vocabula *naturae* & *naturalis* ... maxima esse ambigua'. Despite his prominent and lengthy treatment of the 'state of nature' theorem in his major works he also felt the need to answer his critics in a highly combative fashion in two separate essays: 'De statu hominum naturali' in *Eris Scandica*, pp. 176–186 and in 'De statu hominum naturali' (respondens H. Fleming) in *Dissertationes academicae selectiores* (Uppsala, 1677), pp. 458–96. The above quote is in *Eris Scandica*, p. 177. In this piece in particular he attempted to answer his vociferous theological critics.

ity of the early beginnings of mankind.[26] It was in this sense that Pufendorf could claim that Hobbes had been right in *De cive*, both descriptively and evaluatively, in his assessment of the 'inconveniencies' of the 'state of nature' when compared with the *civitas*. This evaluative contrast, which was as essential to the positions of Montaigne and Charron as it was to that of Hobbes, furnished an effective defence of the humanism of modernity. In Pufendorf's words:

There cannot be a more effectual way found out to silence the Complaints and Murmurs of the Common People, when they pretend to find fault with the Miscarriages and the Impositions of the Government than if we would lay before them a true Prospect of the Misery and Confusion which attends a Natural State. (2.2.2)[27]

But this judgement did not make Pufendorf a Hobbist. Adam Smith was quite right to observe that the first books of Pufendorf's *De iure naturae et gentium* constituted a defence of natural jurisprudence against Hobbes, despite their analytical use of the concept of the 'state of nature' methodology and their acceptance of the sceptical humanist anthropology which this carried with it. Both poles of the contrast which underlay this anthropology entailed conclusions which were unacceptable to Pufendorf. At one pole there lay an irrevocably individualist premise – solitary individuals living outside any 'City' – at the other, the political community itself, the *civitas*. The direct juxtaposition of the 'fiction' of discrete individuals and the state implied that society was constituted solely on the basis of each individual's interest in his own self-preservation and on the dynamics of human nature. Pufendorf was well aware of the unsavoury consequences of this position. The sceptical theory of politics had reappeared. Even if the diversity of the laws and customs of mankind was now irrelevant, the contemplation of human nature in itself had shown that only a contractual artefact, the political power of the state, was sufficient to form a structure within which

---

[26] For an example, see P. Charron, *Of Wisdome*, transl. S. Lennard (London, n.d. [before 1612]), ch. 33, 'The second Consideration of Man, by comparing him with all other creatures' and ch. 53, 'A comparison of the civill and sociable life with the solitarie'. Pufendorf cited this work thirty-four times. Montaigne was also a favourite author of Pufendorf.

[27] *De iure naturae et gentium libri octo*, translated by B. Kennet as *Of the Law of Nature and Nations*, 4th edn (London, 1729). (References to this work in the text will be by plain 'book, chapter, section' numbers. Otherwise the abbreviation *ING* will be used.)

individual self-preservation could be guaranteed. The possibility of natural society, it appeared, had been eradicated.

The essence of Pufendorf's 'socialism' lay precisely in his answer to the problem raised by Hobbes. As Pufendorf realised, his task was to re-establish Grotius's fundamental law of nature, the preservation of human society, the *custodia societatis humanae*, on the methodological principles of Hobbes. Grotius started off from two fundamental aspects of human nature: the instinct of self-preservation and the instinctive propensity for society, the *appetitus socialis*. There was no difficulty in the use of individual self-preservation. Indeed, Hobbes had stressed its relevance even more than Grotius, by insisting that it offered the only incontrovertible anthropological foundation for natural law.[28] Pufendorf agreed since, as he explained, to put natural jurisprudence on a secure foundation, it was not enough just to re-emphasise sociability as an observed fact of human existence. Rather, this fact itself had to be re-expressed within the framework of a Hobbesian analysis of the 'state of nature'. To do this Pufendorf transformed Hobbes's unitary model of the state of nature into a triadic model.

Pufendorf's first 'state of nature' did not in fact correspond with the fictive procedure he described. It was rather a restatement in observational terms of the sceptical humanist anthropology of Hobbes. But it did involve the use of the technique of contrast employed in the genuinely fictive presentations of the 'state of nature'. Human life could be best understood by supposing that 'contrary to this State is the Life of Brutes' (*OHC*, 2.1.3). The real difference between man and animal could be captured by the fundamental disparities between needs and the ability to satisfy them. Both man and animals desired self-preservation. The animal's abilities, his faculties, were matched to his needs and in this respect he was superior to man. But this close match also had its limitations. The needs of animals were finite and firmly bounded by natural abilities. If they lived or acted together in society they co-operated solely under the guidance of their appetites and instincts, which were uniform in all members of the species. With the satisfaction of present need their co-operation ceased. Man's position in creation was truly paradoxical, inasmuch as man was at the same time both inferior to and superior to the animals. Although created with the

[28] For an analysis of the intellectual relationship between Grotius and Hobbes, see Richard Tuck, 'Grotius, Carneades and Hobbes', *Grotiana*, n.s., IV (1983), 43–62.

same basic need for self-preservation he lacked the corresponding ability. Man was a 'mute and ignoble Animal, Master of no Powers or Capacities', displaying nothing else but 'exceeding Weakness', a 'wonderful Impotency' and 'natural Indigence'. But this condition of *imbecillitas* and necessitousness, *indigentia*, was not the end of the matter. In contrast to animals the structure of man's needs was radically different. Human needs were neither finite nor uniform across the species. The desires generated by the working of men's minds did not cease when the instinct of self-preservation was minimally satisfied. Even the most elementary needs were transformed by man's nature. Food had not only 'to satisfy his Belly, but tickle his Palate'. Similarly, despite the initial handicap with which he began his life, man was able to turn 'the Infirmity of his Nakedness into an Occasion of Vanity and Pride'. 'Besides,' Pufendorf continued, 'do not Men float in a whole Tide of Affections and Desires, utterly unknown to Beasts?' (2.1.6). The chief of these, Pufendorf went on, was 'an endless Thirst after Things superfluous'. Furthermore, the desires of man were not only often insatiable, but also infinitely varied. 'There is', he said, 'no more Diversity of living, than there is Opinions and ways of living; each of which is cry'd up, with wonderful Perversness, by the several Patrons of them.' Beyond this desire for well-being and for infinite kinds of the 'elegancy of Living' man also harboured desires which moved him far beyond material covetousness. Man was ambitious, was willing to enter competition not only for riches but also for honour; and most importantly, he had a restless desire after power. The consequences of this plasticity and diversity of needs and desires could be read in two ways. On the one hand, Pufendorf argued, man was thus subject to 'prodigious Corruption and Degeneracy'; on the other, however, he was perfectible, 'more capable of fruitful Culture and of useful Improvement' than any other creature.

To analyse the 'state of nature' validly, Pufendorf maintained, it was necessary to 'contemplate the Natural State of Man, by seriously forming in our Minds an Idea of what his Condition would be, if every one were left alone to himself without any Help from other Men' (*OHC*, 2.1.4). In this respect the crucial question for Pufendorf was whether all the relevant features could be captured by a single abstraction. Such non-social men would lack the material comforts of society, but they would also be tied to no system of political and social subordination. They would be indigent but free. If it was true that these were analytically separate properties then Hobbes was wrong in trying to specify both by a single analytical procedure, founded upon the contrast between the natural state and the *civitas*. Accordingly, Pufendorf divided Hobbes's single model into two.

In order to decide in what 'Sense it is, That a Natural State is distinguished from a Civil State', that is, the 'State of Man in a Community (*status civilis*)' (*OHC*, 2.1.5), Pufendorf had to give a definition of the *differentia specifica* of the *civitas*. He decided that its essence was the renunciation of man's natural liberty. Thus, in contrast to the *civitas*, 'those are said to live reciprocally in a State of Nature, who acknowledge no common Superior, and of whom none can pretend Dominion over his fellow' (*OHC*, 2.1.5). In the state of nature the only link obtaining between individuals was the one 'which results from the Likeness of their Natures'. Superficially it might seem as if this model was identical with the state of natural liberty. While the emphasis in both cases was on the autonomy of agents, the thoroughgoing individualist version was a pure fiction. In the real world men could not normally be found outside society. 'It is then taken for manifest', he went on, 'that all Mankind never were universally and at one in the former Natural State' (*OHC*, 2.1.7).

By dividing Hobbes's model of the state of nature into two distinct components, Pufendorf eliminated the possibility of an immediate generic link between the anthropology of the first specification of a 'state of nature' and the construction of political government. His approach also implied that men were able to form society and to acknowledge plain obligations without making a contract, which Pufendorf, like Hobbes, took to be the foundation of the *civitas*. How could the conception of human nature which he presupposed, following Hobbes, produce this startingly un-Hobbesian result? Pufendorf's first point was an insistence that the contrast between animal and human nature made co-operation between men an absolute necessity. A human being on his own could not survive. Even a cursory look at the achievements of the contemporary world would prove, Pufendorf claimed, that human co-operation in society necessarily took the form of a process of cumulative learning. He asked his readers, what would happen 'should we suppose a Number of such helpless Wretches thrown together by Nature on some uninhabited Soil'?[29]

[29] The picture of a group of castaways on an uninhabited island formed an alternative representation of a fictional 'state of nature'. Such a fiction was also used by Smith as a point of departure for his own theoretical history of property, see *Lectures on Jurisprudence, LJ(A)*, i.27; *LJ(B)*, 149.

We cannot but think that they would so long however continue in a brutal Wildness and Disorder, till at last, either by their own Wit and Experience, or by some Hints and Instructions taken from the conduct of Mute Creatures they should by Degrees arrive at some Method and Elegancy of Living, as Virgil says, "Studious Need might beat out Useful Arts". This will easily be acknowledge'd by any one that looks about on the numerous Improvements and Assistances which we make use of in our daily Actions, and at the same time considers how difficult it would be for any Man to invent all these of his own Head, if he were not put in the Way by previous Labour and Guidance of others . . . (2.2.2)

In 'this sense', Pufendorf concluded, 'the Natural State is opposed to a Life cultivated by the Industry of Men' (*OHC*, 2.1.4): in short *cultura*.[30] The opposite of *cultura* was not natural liberty, but the result of man's *imbecillitas*, his initial condition of need, *indigentia*. But *indigentia* did not just cover this initial condition. As an explanatory principle bridging the two poles of the contrast between *natura* and *cultura* it also expressed the intrinsic perfectibility or corruptibility of human nature – the fact that its moving principle was the unsuppressible creation of ever pressing new needs. It was, that is to say, a general principle of human social action. This laid bare, as Pufendorf realised, the Aristotelian foundation of the contrast between civilisation and the condition of need. Originally it had been Plato who had argued in the *Republic* that *chreia* or *indigentia* was the 'sole or the principal Cause' of the rise of the *polis*.[31] Pufendorf himself had no doubt that Plato was wrong to link the concept of need directly to the origins of the state. Aristotle too had been wrong in just the same sense in claiming that man was naturally a political being, a *zoon politikon*. But Aristotle also offered another and more promising approach to social understanding. For in Aristotle's theory *chreia* was the principle not of the state, but of society or community, *koinonia*. Having thus established, or re-established, the concept of society as an organisational form independent of the *civitas*, Pufendorf was now in a position to offer a coherent explanation of the central category of his jurisprudence, *socialitas*, sociability. He had no desire to argue, as against Hobbes, that the consequences of man's paradoxical nature needed no regulation through a system of obligations. But these 'plain' obligations now had their own separate foundation in men's sociability, rather than in state power founded upon contract.

[30] The emergence of this very important concept of Pufendorf's jurisprudence was first analysed in detail in Joseph Niedermann, *Kultur: Werden and Wandlungen des Begriffs und seiner Ersatzbegriffe von Cicero bis Herder* (Florence, 1941).
[31] Plato, *Republic* 369b-c.

ISTVAN HONT

Here the fundamental differences between the inner construction of Pufendorf's and Grotius's concept of sociability become evident.[32] Grotius's *appetitus societatis* was a theory based on the observation that man was 'naturally' fond of society.[33] But Pufendorf was in no position to accept this premise, since he was now committed to a radically individualist explanation of the very possibility of human social association. His fiction of the state of nature had abstracted from social interaction and presupposed juxtaposed and discrete individuals. His account of human nature also began by conceiving a single individual outside society, unable to speak or relate to other human beings. The model of *koinonia* consisted in the mutual satisfaction of needs through commerce. But to construct this model he returned directly to the ideas of *De cive*. Hobbes had explained that 'men do not seek each other's company for its own sake, but for honour or profit'. In this second case, 'if they meet for Traffique, it's plaine every man regards not his Fellow, but his Businesse' and if the reason is 'to discharge some Office', the relationship which obtains is 'a certain Market-friendship'. The reference to 'Market-friendship' in the English version might mislead the modern reader. Hobbes's Latin is more prosaic. What he meant was that 'Law-friendship'[34] which occurred in the *forum*, the market square. It is 'Traffique' which is directly relevant here. For in Hobbes's Latin *commercium* (*si coaeant enim commercii causa*), referred to people who wanted each other's goods (*non socium, sed rem suam colit*). It was this which Pufendorf paraphrased in the following way: 'They who unite in a Body for promoting of Traffick, are led to it purely by Hopes of advancing their Goods more in Conjunction with others, than they could by their private Industry: and whatever disappoints or puts an end to these Hopes, prevails with all, but Fools or Madmen, to put an end likewise to the Society (*societati*)' (7.1.2). *Commercium* thus corresponded to *societas*, not to *civitas*. Pufendorf followed Hobbes's argument with a discussion of Aristotle's notion of man as *zoon politikon*,

---

[32] There is a sharp analysis of the different concepts of sociability in 'The fourth dialogue' of Part II of Mandeville's *The Fable of the Bees*, ed. F. B. Kaye 2 vols. (Oxford, 1924), II, pp. 177–191.

[33] Grotius, *De iure belli ac pacis*, 'Prolegomena', 7. Grotius's difficulty in reconciling the tension between his principle of sociability of community and his individualistic theory of rights is discussed by Richard Tuck in his *Natural Rights Theories: Their Origin and Development* (Cambridge, 1979), pp. 68–74.

[34] The passage in question is *De cive*, 1.2. See Howard Warrender's new edition of both the Latin and English versions, 2 vols, (Oxford, 1983). 'Law-Friendship' is Kennett's translation from Hobbes's own Latin, hence the text is not absolutely identical with that of the *Philosophicall Rudiments Concerning Government and Society*.

as one 'born fit for Society'. The 'Greeks', Hobbes wrote, had built their whole 'Doctrine of Civill Society' (*doctrinam civilem*, there is no *societas* here in Hobbes's Latin) on this principle. Their error becomes apparent if one observes that in this case society had to include everybody, since all were equally humans, and not only those who could reciprocate with each other in matters of 'Honour or Profit'. From this Hobbes turned to a contractual model, arguing that men form 'all manner of Society' only if there is a common aim 'which every one of those, who gather together, propounds to himselfe for good'. Pufendorf refused to accept the 'common will' element of Hobbes's conclusion on the grounds that Hobbes had confused the principles of voluntary associations with the origins of society at large; instead he connected the model of a commercially constituted society with the idea of industry or industriousness which lay at the centre of his model of *cultura*.

With this insight he could now reconstruct Grotius's interpretation of the *custodia societatis humanae* by bridging the gap between the acknowledged primacy of individual self-preservation and the peaceful preservation of society without introducing any such notion as social appetite or social faculty. His own concept of *socialitas* was built firmly on the notion of self-preservation.[35] Here Pufendorf turned to Stoic foundations. If, he claimed, 'in seeking out the true Condition of Men we have assign'd the first Place and Influence to Self-Love', this was not out of approval of a morality founded on selfishness, but rather in recognition of the force of the Stoic argument which pointed to the simple fact that every man naturally was 'sooner sensible of the Love he bears towards himself, than of that which he bears towards others' (3.2.14).[36] He strongly resisted any trivialisation of the concept of sociability as the antithesis of self-regarding behaviour. Sociability was not any trifling prescription of 'kindness and courtesy to Fellow subjects' (7.1.4). In *socialitas* self-regarding and other-regarding motives were not in opposition, rather they formed a distinctive combination. What Pufendorf had in mind at this point was precisely what Kant was later to christen man's 'unsocial sociability'. His initial premise was precisely that human self-preservation itself depended directly on others. But his strategy thereafter was to follow the argument of the Stoics, rather than attempt to represent this mutual need by a

[35] See the recognition of this shift in J. H. Hertius, *Dissertatio de socialitate primo naturalis juris principio occasione 1.3. D. de justitia et jure* (respondens J. C. Bauer) (Giessen, 1694), 1.3–4.
[36] Compare with Smith's account of this essential Stoic point, *TMS*, VI.ii.1.1.

contract. The essence of the Stoic argument had been pointed out by Hobbes himself when he wrote in *De cive*, 'when a Man doubts whether what he is going to do to another be agreeable to the Law of Nature, let him suppose himself in the other's room'. In order to arrive at a correct evaluation of the balance between self-regarding and other-regarding motives, 'Self-love and the other Passions, which weigh'd down one Scale' had to be put in imagination 'into the contrary Scale' (2.3.13).[37]

The technique of role-switching, of mirroring one's own motives in the position of others, if repeated and multiplied, was the model of sociability in action, and as Pufendorf remarked, 'the same Precept was made use of by Ynca Manco Capace, the Founder of the Peruvian Empire; in order to the reducing his Subjects to a Life of Civility' (2.3.13). It was a very basic insight into the operation of human society. Reciprocity in itself, Pufendorf admitted, was not however the fundamental point, because it was, on reflection, 'only a Corollary of that Law which obliges us to hold all Men equal with our selves; and therefore may be demonstrated a priori' (2.3.13). But because of their direct link to self-preservation and the consequent need for co-operation, the dictates of mutuality could be taken as the operational manifestation of the unsocial and yet sociable nature of man. For Pufendorf this was then the fundamental law of nature itself.[38]

Here therefore was a 'law of nature' based on no naturalised concept of sociability at all. Just as the real state of nature, the state of natural liberty, was, in fact an adventitious state, so sociability was a historical product. But this did not imply that it was in any sense inappropriate to describe the fundamental law itself as 'natural'. Sociability was natural even though it was not given directly by nature. To understand the true merits of Hobbes's approach, Pufendorf argued, one had to consider 'diligently the Ambiguity of the Word Nature' (2.3.16). The fact that something is not there in the beginning *by* nature should not be taken to mean that its later development is not natural. To deny the epithet of 'natural' to sociability simply because it was not innate, was like arguing that 'Speech is by Nature actually born with no Man; therefore all Speech which is afterwards learnt is against the Design of Nature.'[39] However paradoxical it might seem, Pufendorf claimed, 'natural' sociability was a 'social' construct.

[37] Pufendorf's reference is to *De cive*, 3.26.
[38] For the full formulation of the law, see *ING*, 2.3.15.
[39] Speech was an important component of Grotius's demonstration of natural sociability, see *De iure belli ac pacis*, 'Prolegomena', 7.

Having restored the Grotian principle of *custodia societatis humanae* to its full vigour by applying strictly Hobbesian principles, Pufendorf had two more essential tasks. He had to clarify the law-like nature of *socialitas*, and he had to set out at least some guidelines concerning its operational content as a law. In view of the insatiability of desires and infinite diversity of human practices, the claim that mutual sociability was capable of sustaining itself was open to obvious doubts. One could not hope that 'Rules would be observ'd out of bare Regard to Interest', even if the 'Usefulness and Expediency of them be clearly apparent'. Sociableness made it possible for men to live together and ensure their self-preservation. Nonetheless, diversity of desires, the 'endless Methods of Living', cried out for natural regulation. Hobbes was wrong in thinking that social diversity and the difficulty of survival required the creation of the *civitas*. But, Pufendorf argued, 'it is not agreeable to the Nature of Man that he should live without Law':

The more Voices there are, the more harsh and unpleasant would be the Sound, unless they join'd in Consort and Harmony; so would human Life be nothing else but Noise and Confusion, were not the jarring Dissonance compos'd and sweet'ned by Law, and turn'd into a Musical Agreement. (2.1.7)[40]

This made it absolutely necessary to introduce a higher agency or principle into the picture, since 'all Law supposes a Superior Power'. Sociability had to be underpinned by a command of God.[41] As its Maker, God had to provide his Creation with the means of survival. Apart from the material resources for survival, he gave man reason. In doing so, and in addition to the fundamental law of sociability and before there was any other law founded on human agreements, he willed man to follow the dictates of reason: 'the Natural Liberty of Man, such as really and truly agrees to him, and not only in the abstracted Sense, must always be understood as guided and restrain'd by the Ties of Reason, and by the Laws of Nature' (2.1.8).

[40] Similar musical metaphors were used by both Hume and Smith to develop their own theory of sociability. For Smith's theory of market sociability, see Nicholas Phillipson, 'Adam Smith as civic moralist', in *Wealth and Virtue*, pp. 179–202.

[41] For a suggestive analysis of this requirement as a criterion of demarcation between the seventeenth-century natural jurists and Smith, see John Dunn, 'From applied theology to social analysis: the break between John Locke and the Scottish Enlightenment', in *Wealth and Virtue*, pp. 119–35. For the character of Pufendorf's theological assumptions, see James Moore and M. Silverthorn, 'Natural sociability and natural rights in the moral philosophy of Gershom Carmichael', in Vincent Hope (ed.), *Philosophers of the Scottish Enlightenment* (Edinburgh, 1984), pp. 1–12 and Pierre Laurent, *Pufendorf et la loi naturelle* (Paris, 1982), pt 3.

The theory of sociability, with its apparatus of dictates of reason imposing duties directly on each and every man, also helped Pufendorf to create a historical account of the rise of property which in no way predetermined or foreshadowed the historical outcome. His famous theory of negative community was a resolution of a many-sided argument. For, besides refuting Hobbes's initial theory of community as everybody's right in everything he, like Locke, had to fight the revived Adamite theory which placed the origin of private property at the very beginning of human history. In the negative community there were no property rights. In this state, Pufendorf claimed, 'rights' had to be understood exclusively, but as 'indefinite Dominion, not formally possess'd, but absolutely allow'd; not Actual, but Potential' (4.4.3). As Barbeyrac remarked, these could be regarded as rights if one allowed the name right to cover 'any sort of right', including a mere 'shadow of Property, or a power of possessing with Property' instead of 'true and actual Property' (4.4.3. n.1). In the negative community first occupation was guided by the dictate of reason, expressed as a proviso of moderation, commanding that no man, or family, should occupy more than what was needed for self-preservation. In the case of land this amounted to the territory that the occupier was able to cultivate.[42] The proviso was meant to operate in the peaceful world of abundance. Apart from miserable, worthless wretches who were always 'in a Humour of invading' others, it was just not the case that 'the All-wise Creator [has] been so unkind or so sparing in his Provisions for the human Race, that two persons must always lay Claim to the same Thing' (2.2.8).

The theory of property in Pufendorf was genuinely historical in the sense that it described a process in time. Mankind moved slowly and gradually, Pufendorf argued, 'according as the Temper or Condition of Men, the Nature of the things themselves, and the difference of place required' (4.4.13). The change in the type of social bond, in the shape of communities, had a curious elliptical trajectory in Pufendorf's theory. From the weak links of sociability obtaining in the state of natural liberty which characterised the early negative community, the direction of movement was towards a

[42] See *ING*, 4.6.3. and 4.5.9. Barbeyrac recognised that Pufendorf's argument of a 'proviso' of good usage was essentially the same as Locke's, see 4.4.4.n.4. The present interpretation runs counter to certain themes in James Tully, *A Discourse on Property: John Locke and His Adversaries* (Cambridge, 1980). Locke was praised by his contemporaries for making the notion of primeval community more consistently 'negative', i.e., non-contractual, than Pufendorf. For a fuller argument, see I. Hont and M. Ignatieff, 'Needs and justice in the *Wealth of Nations*', pp. 26–43.

multiplicity of positive communities, in the agricultural stage reaching such complex agricultural and shepherding groups as those described by Tacitus in his *Germania*. In Pufendorf's theory, just as in Smith's, this process involved a number of contracts, or rather joint decisions. But once the agriculturists agreed to the establishment of full private property, their community reverted to a kind of intra-communal state of natural liberty. Every family was now an island to itself. In their capacity as private-property owners communal relationships between families came to an end; and their isolation, in some ways, reproduced artificially the atomised structure of Hobbes's and Pufendorf's fictional state of nature, although on a much higher level of material culture. If these men wanted to live 'happily and conveniently', Pufendorf argued, then they had to have 'continuall Occasion for the Works and for the Supplies of their Neighbours'. He emphasised two aspects of this mutual dependence. First, they needed their fellows 'as much as their own Time as well as Power would fail them to procure the most useful and the most necessary Things'. But, second, since they could only offer things in exchange 'which they themselves do not want', they also needed their neighbours as consumers and partners in exchange. Without such 'takers' the creation of surplus would have had to come to an end, since it 'would turn to no Use or Account, unless they were thus bestow'd and dispensed' (2.3.14). It was a commonplace of jurisprudence that the rise of private property brought with it the advent of commerce, prices and the introduction of money. But what is most significant here is that the sentences just quoted belong to the core of Pufendorf's definition of sociability. The commerce of private-property owners relied on a reconstitution of society by the mechanisms of sociability.

Since Pufendorf had already established the viability of such a society by his fundamental theory of *socialitas*, he could now ask Smith's question from, as it were, the opposite direction. Why was it that the society of direct co-operation could not survive? Why did the joint owners of communal land agree to its privatisation? Ordinary moral language was heavily loaded in favour of the old community. The notions of abundance and 'Liberty' attached to primeval communities, 'flattering us with being free from all manners of Subjection', were hard to counter. Pufendorf also had to be careful not to re-admit Hobbism through the back door. He could not argue that these communities of property were anarchical. 'Communion considered by itself', he emphasised, 'doth not render Life altogether lawless and unsociable, but only more simple and unpolish'd' (4.4.13). Thus the whole burden of legitimating property had to be carried by the analysis of developing refinement and politeness which underpinned the theory of sociability. The conceptual emphasis had to fall on need and desire rather than on liberty and power. Pufendorf agreed with Hobbes that the *civitas* had to come into being when the destructive and anti-social traits of human nature became incompatible in practice with the peace of a relatively complex *cultura vitae*. But as envy, covetousness, ambition and the desire for domination were permanent features of human nature, they themselves could not have been agents of the change. What changed was the sheer extent of *cultura*.

Primeval communities were societies 'strangers to Delicacies and Excess' and as yet 'ignorant of Wealth', 'finding an easie Supply of Food from Nature's Store'. 'What matter they could have for Bounty', Pufendorf asked, 'When there was no Occasion to scrape up Treasure'? (4.4.8). One strong 'natural' motivation for change came from the heavy pressure of population growth. In the long run, population growth was capable of making the whole Earth too small for mankind. But local scarcities appeared quite early. Most things 'which are applied to the ends of Nourishment and Cloathing, are not by bare inassisted Nature produc'd every where in so great an abundance, as to yield a plentiful supply to all' (4.4.6). Self-preservation increasingly became a matter of the consumption of the 'fruits of industry'. The competition for scarce resources dramatically raised the potentiality for social conflict. The rationale of the communal system of property was to replace the increasingly disregarded proviso of moderation with conscious regulations.

Grotius had earlier suggested that the early communities could persist only as long as men continued to live 'with great plainness and simplicity'. Generalising this insight, he had also suggested that community as a mode of living was possible if 'Men liv'd under the Influence of an Eminent Charity and Friendship towards each other', such as had been the case in the life of the modern 'Ascetick' communities or amongst the old Christians and Essenes. Pufendorf was quick to point out that such societies were modelled on small voluntary communities. Such a system could be maintained amongst no more than a 'few Persons'. Furthermore, it presupposed men of 'singular Modesty and Goodness'. It also ran directly counter to the sceptical conception of what human beings are really like. This radical departure from a realistic assessment of human nature had been the great mistake of More and Campanella in their plans for communitarian utopias, 'it being much more easie to fansie perfect Men than to find them' (4.4.7).

The critique of the society of humanity and beneficence in Pufendorf's theory of property returned quite consciously to Aristotle's critique of Plato's advocacy of community of property in the *Republic*. This in itself was plainly no innovation. It already underlined Hobbes's explanation of the impossibility of living within a system of common rights.[43] But Pufendorf proceeded to apply it directly to the abandonment of the early communitarian stage of mankind. The communitarian arrangement of simplicity and equality was now shown to be not a solution for disorder and strife, but a major cause of it. The placing of the products of a man's labour in a common store for redistribution according to his communally sanctioned needs was a major cause of strife because it cut the natural link between his efforts and his share in consumption. The protection of a man's rights to the products of his own labour, although corrosive of direct community, was now upheld as a precondition for the peace of society. Aristotle's critique of Plato had, furthermore, suggested that the communitarian redistributive system failed even to leave any scope for humanity and beneficence. With the introduction of property the 'Matter and Occasion' was supplied for 'liberality and Beneficence'. 'To gratifie and assist a Friend, a Guest, or a Companion, fills us with Sensible Satisfaction and Delight', argued Pufendorf, 'and this we cannot do, unless we have a separate Share of Good things to ourselves' (4.4.7). Pufendorf's argument entailed that the peace of society would be better preserved if communally organised artificial beneficence gave way to the mutual sociability of selfish agents. For the deconstructed society of private-property owners could still be linked sufficiently through the mutual needs of its members. In order to exchange their goods they had to barter, they had, that is, to form themselves into a commercial society. While self-preservation and population growth could explain mankind's passage from hunting and gathering to agriculture, no account of the transformation of society after the decision to introduce private property in land could be expressed in terms of the origins of property. The fourth stage, which succeeded the overwhelmingly agricultural one, was dominated by the matter of the secondary acquisition of goods. In his discussion of the ensuing system of mutual barter, the rise of money, the rules of commercial

---

[43] See *De cive*, 'The Epistle Dedicatory', 9–10.

sociability embodied in the principles of value and price formation, Pufendorf returned to purely Aristotelian foundations.

According to Aristotle's theory, as cited by Grotius, society, *koinonia*, was held together by need.[44] The cause of bargaining was want, *indigentia*, *chreia*. Once sociability had been expressed as commerce, every further step in social development could be directly derived from an analysis of the mechanisms of human need. At first there was only simple barter, *permutatio*, 'Work was paid in Work, or else in Commodities.' But the craving for refinement and a more commodious life demanded ever further increasing extensions of the system. The matching of needs through direct exchange was, therefore, clearly possible only in small communities. Soon, it would necessarily become 'hard for many to possess such Goods, for which any other would be willing to barter those Commodities he wanted, or which, indeed, could be exactly equivalent of them' (5.1.11). Society based on the mechanisms of sociability depended on the extension of the market. The introduction of money and foreign trade followed logically and inevitably from the stage of *permutatio*.

With the introduction of foreign trade, Pufendorf rounded off his analysis. Sovereign states and their citizens were truly in the state of natural liberty even when they associated through commerce. Hence commercial sociability was perfectly capable of creating 'society' without its agents uniting under 'the same Government and Constitution' (7.1.6). The theory of society and the theory of the state now had to be separated even more sharply. In most historical cases Hobbes's suggestion was entirely correct. Civilised standard of living was associated with the presence of government. But this was not a necessary connection. 'Instances can be given of People living', argued Pufendorf, 'for many Ages, under Civil Establishments, in a condition no way superior, for Plenty and Abundance to that of the Fathers of Families in ancient Time' (7.1.6). By divorcing the origins of government from the satisfaction of human need, Pufendorf could also distance himself from any moral endorsement of the spiral of insatiability and from the endless diversification of the content of need. He could now define the modern *cultura vitae* more sharply, and distinguish it from *vera cultura*, by identifying with great accuracy the institutional outcome of commercial sociability.

The good life was a simple life, fully attainable in the moderate plenty of the early agricultural state. But the trajectory opened up by

---

[44] See *ING*, 5.1.4. Pufendorf cites Aristotle from Grotius, the reference is to *Nicomachean Ethics* 1133a.

men's 'Prospect of living in a better Fashion and greater Plenty, when united together, than they can possibly do in a Condition of Solitude' leads to an urbane society, to *magnes urbes*, not to *civitates*. 'All the mighty Plenty and Luxury, which now reigns in some Parts of the World', he declared, was a product of 'great Cities' (7.1.6). It was in the cities that the negative features of human nature, ambition, vanity, emulation, could easily prosper, trades could establish themselves which had nothing to do with 'the Relief of Men's real Necessities' (7.1.6). *Civitates* 'could very contentedly be without' the luxurious objects manufactured in the towns.[45]

Having constructed his jurisprudence around the concept of commercial sociability, Pufendorf could not end his analysis on quite such a critical note. Once a system of private property in land has made its appearance, once cities have developed, the dynamics of progress becomes irreversible. As Pufendorf observed, luxury progressed in the cities, because 'the meaner People (*vulgus*), having no Income from Cattel or Land, are forced (for Livelihood) upon improving divers Arts and Inventions' (7.1.6). Once private property was established in a society, the extension of the links of market sociability had to be permanent. Despite his misgivings, Pufendorf endorsed the introduction of money as a generalised means of exchange. As he explained, 'in a well-regulated State, where the subjects are divided into various Orders and Ranks, there must be several Sorts of Men which would not be able to subsist, or at least very hardly, did the simple way of Bartering still prevail' (5.1.11). Because of this, the theoretical history of private property could not simply end with the establishment of exclusive private property by men in the age of agriculture. A fourth stage had to be added to clarify the preconditions for the secondary acquisition of the means of self-preservation (as well as the goods that fulfilled the needs of luxury) which allowed everybody, and not only the owners of cattle and land, to survive. Jean Barbeyrac, noting the moral opposition to the corruption caused by the rise of commerce and the great cities, felt the need to underline the force of Pufendorf's conception of sociability. Such denunciation of corruption, he argued, was more a matter for divinity than for civil law. In the human world as this had come to be it was clear that commerce had to be included firmly within the scope of natural jurisprudence. As Barbeyrac wrote:

[45] For Pufendorf's rather traditional casuistry of luxury, see the dissertation he directed and largely wrote as a Professor of Lund, 'De legibus sumptuariis' (respondens Daniel Lossius) in *Dissertationes academicae selectiores*, pp. 404–28.

It is sufficient, that in the State that Things now are, Commerce, as well as Propriety of Goods, is necessary among Men, in the Condition they are; so that we may say, that the Settlements of Commerce in General are very conformable to the most pure Reason, and the Law of Nations, so called in the most agreeable Sense.[46]

It was in this spirit that the 'four stages theory' was conceived in the eighteenth century. It is an attempt, not to create a new definition of commercial society which then could be added to the existing historical theory of the origins of property, but rather to integrate the fragmented aspects of Pufendorfian natural jurisprudence into a single theory of the history of civilisation.[47] The foundations of a theory of commercial society were already fully present in Pufendorf's 'socialism'.

[46] Smith owned Barbeyrac's French translation of Pufendorf, and referred to Barbeyrac's footnotes in *The Theory of Moral Sentiments*, VII.iv.11. See Hiroshi Mizuta, *Adam Smith's Library* (Cambridge, 1967), p. 49. The passage above is in Barbeyrac's first footnote to *ING*, 5.1.1. The immediate target of the criticism was Thomasius, who had been the first to break away from the 'socialists', replacing sociability with happiness at the centre of his jurisprudence.

[47] On the relevance of 'commercial humanism' and its place on the discursive map of European intellectual history, see J. G. A. Pocock, 'Virtues, rights and manners: a model for historians of political thought', in *Virtue, Commerce and History: Essays on Political Thought and History, Chiefly in the Eighteenth Century* (Cambridge, 1985), pp. 37–50.

12

◁ ═══ ▷

'Da metafisico a mercatante' – Antonio Genovesi and the development of a new language of commerce in eighteenth-century Naples

RICHARD BELLAMY

Genovesi's appointment in 1754 to the specially created chair *di commercio e di meccanica* at Naples university marked, as Franco Venturi has noted, the full flowering of the complex of political and cultural developments which made up the Neapolitan enlightenment.[1] Yet this event is perhaps too easily seized upon as representing the birth of a secular science of politics, a transition, as Genovesi jokingly said of his new position, from *metafisico* to *mercatante*.[2] In this essay I wish to show how these two elements were fused as Genovesi sought to give them coherent expression in a new language of politics adapted to the needs of modern commercial society.

Born in 1713 at Castiglione near Salerno, Genovesi was the first

Professors Raffaele Ajello and Guiseppe Ricuperati very kindly encouraged my early Neapolitan studies, whilst Dott. Eluggero Pii has generously shared his intimate knowledge of Genovesi with me. I am grateful for his comments on an earlier version, and for those of Anthony Pagden, the participants at the Florence conference and John Robertson and Judith Shklar. Research for this paper was made possible by a Leverhulme study abroad studentship and a grant in aid of research from the British School at Rome.

[1] Franco Venturi, *Illuministi italiani*, T.V., Riformatori napoletani, (Milan–Naples, 1958), pp. ix–xiii, 3–43, 'Il movimento riformatore degli illuministi meridionale', *Rivista Storica Italiana*, LXXIV (1966), 5–26, *Settecento riformatore*, I (Turin, 1969), ch. 8, pp. 523–644 and 'Antonio Genovesi', *Terzo Programma*, n.s., II (1970), 15–24.

[2] Letter of 23 February 1754 to Romualdo Sterlich in 'Lettere familiari' in *Autobiografia e lettere*, ed. G. Savarese (Milan, 1962), p. 78. This view, held by Venturi, e.g., *Settecento riformatore*, I, pp. 552–3, 'Antonio Genovesi', pp. 18–20, and with a different emphasis by R. Villari, 'Antonio Genovesi e la ricerca delle forze motrici dello sviluppo sociale', *Studi Storica*, XI (1970), 26–52, has been criticised by Paola Zambelli, *La formazione filosofica di Antonio Genovesi* (Naples, 1972), pp. 421–37, who has demonstrated the continuity of Genovesi's theological interests, though without reference to his economic doctrine (esp. pp. 709–94). The most recent analysis of the reason for Genovesi's change of chair, based on the various versions of his autobiography, is provided by Eluggero Pii, *Antonio Genovesi – dalla politica economica alla 'politica civile'* (Florence, 1984), pp. 9–24.

son of a family of small landowners fallen on hard times. He was educated for the priesthood, being ordained in 1737, when the death of his uncle gave him enough money to continue his studies in Naples.[3] Neapolitan intellectual life was at this time undergoing a profound change. The Cartesian and Platonist philosophies which had dominated the last fifty years still prevailed, but their three main representatives, Pietro Giannone, Giambattista Vico and Paolo Mattia Doria, were all to die in the 1740s and an important new current of thought, fervently anti-metaphysical in character and stressing the experimental method of Newton, was growing up in opposition to them.[4] As Vincenzo Ferrone's recent study has shown, these two intellectual traditions were grouped into two opposing camps centred on the Accademia degli Oziosi, founded in 1733 and supported by Vico and especially Doria, and the Accademia delle Scienze, formed by Celestino Galiani and Bartolomeo Intieri the year before.[5] Whilst the *veteres* attacked the 'material and carnal science' of the *Principia* and the *Opticks*,[6] the *novatores* regarded them as models for the study not just of the natural world but of man and society as well, reading Mandeville, Bayle and above all Locke to this purpose.[7] As a result, Vico and Doria's dispute with the *novatores* was more than a simple defence of humanist learning. Their complaint was that the rigorous application of the empirical method of the natural sciences to the study of society was incompatible with Catholic morality and indeed was likely to have a deleterious effect on social mores *tout court*. This was a central issue in contemporary Naples. The formation of an independent Neapolitan state, free from Austrian or Spanish domination, under Carlo Borbone in 1734, had produced hopes for a comprehensive reform of the adminis- tration and legal system to revive a society hitherto crippled by feudal privileges and systematically plundered by foreign rulers.[8]

---

[3] *Vita di Antonio Genovesi* in *Autobiografia*, pp. 7–14.

[4] In addition to the books and articles by Franco Venturi cited in n.1, see Raffaelo Ajello, 'Cartesianismo e cultura oltramontana al tempo dell' *Istoria Civile'*, in *Pietro Giannone e il suo tempo*, ed. R, Ajello, 2 vols. (Naples, 1980), pp. 3–181, esp. 88–105 and Vincenzo Ferrone, *Scienza, natura, religione – mondo Newtoniano e cultura italiana nel primo '70* (Naples, 1982), esp. chs. 5 and 6.

[5] Ferrone, *Scienza, natura, religione*, pp. 501–15, 525–45. On Intieri and Galiani see, in addition to Ferrone, Franco Venturi, 'Alle origini dell'illuminismo napoletano: dal carteggio di Bartolomeo Intieri', *Rivista storica italiana* (RSI), LXXI (1959), 416–56 and Fausto Nicolini, *Un grande educatore italiano, Celestino Galiani* (Naples, 1951).

[6] P. M. Doria, quoted in Ferrone, *Scienza, natura, religione*, p. 539.

[7] Their manifesto declared that 'We expressly ban the discussion of metaphysics or general systems', quoted in *ibid.*, p. 502.

[8] Franco Venturi, *Settecento riformatore*, I, pp. 29ff.; R. Ajello, 'La vita politica napoletana sotto Carlo di Barbone: "La fondazione ed il tempo eroico" della dinastia', in *Storia di Napoli* VII, (Naples, 1972), pp. 461–984.

The Accademia delle Scienze had been formed with the express aim of providing suitable intellectual tools for this purpose. Its chosen models were Holland and especially England, whose commercial success was attributed less to the intervention of the sovereign than to the existence of a culture and laws favourable to economic achievement, a conclusion drawn from Melon's influential *Essai politique sur le commerce* (1734).[9] The debate between *veteres* and *novatores* was therefore motivated by two divergent views of the nature and merits of economic development. The former stressed the social character of commerce. This aimed not at individual enrichment but at 'mutual aid', a practice which required 'a most virtuous education and good training'.[10] The latter sought to legitimise commercial practice by elaborating a lay, utilitarian model of society, based on immutable economic laws reflecting those of the Newtonian cosmos, the principle of which was human self-interest. The contrast between the two was thus that whereas Doria's concern with Christian morality led him to place economic development within a general scheme of social justice, Intieri and Galiani's view of morality and justice was entirely economic in orientation.[11] This led to a revised theory of human nature, involving the reduction of human psychology to certain basic passional drives which can be, in A.O. Hirschman's suggestive term, 'harnessed' to the needs of society.[12] The essential elements of this vision are clearly deployed in Ferdinando Galiani's *Della moneta* (1750) – a work which, as Ferrone has shown, completed the programme for a new social ethic begun by his uncle Celestino in the 1730s. Ferdinando argues against 'the disdain and loathing of those few, who arrogate the venerable name of "savants" ' for human acquisitiveness. Rather, 'the desire for gain; or to live happily' is the equivalent in the moral sciences to gravity in the physical. Since 'man is a complex of passions, which move him with unequal force' these can be studied and used to procure for humanity the maximum utility or happiness.[13]

According to his autobiography, Genovesi began by maintaining

[9] Ferrone, *Scienza, natura, religione*, pp. 554–67.
[10] P. M. Doria, *Del commercio del regno di Napoli* (1740), in E. Vidal, *Il pensiero civile di P. M. Doria negli scritti inediti: con il testo del manoscritto 'del commercio del regno di Napoli'* (Milan, 1953), p. 162, quoted in Ferrone, *Scienza, natura, religione*, p. 597.
[11] See R. Ajello, 'La critica del regime in Doria, Intieri e Broggia', in *Arcana iuris: diritto e politica nel settecento italiano* (Naples, 1976), pp. 389–427.
[12] A. O. Hirschman, *The Passions and the Interests – Political Arguments for Capitalism before its Triumph* (Princeton, 1977), pp. 16–20.
[13] Ferdinando Galiani, *Della moneta* (1750), ed. Alberto Merola (Milan, 1963), pp. 36, 39, 55–6.

his independence from these two camps, filling the gaps in his provincial education with elements gleaned from both. In many respects his distinctive contribution resides in the manner in which this continued to be the case, so that his work reflects the conflicts felt by contemporaries in adopting the new theory of society as elaborated by Galiani. His greater affinity with the *novatores* is nevertheless clear in his admiration for Newton.[14] Newton did not, however, move him in the direction of scepticism or atheism but rather provided him with a key for resolving traditional religious concerns by the new commercial ethic. An attempt at such a solution can be found in his early works on metaphysics, but this route was eventually closed to him when ecclesiastical opposition prevented his gaining the chair of theology in 1748. His subsequent involvement with Intieri and Galiani is explained in the *Vita* entirely in terms of these external circumstances and leads almost immediately to the setting up of the new chair *di commercia e di meccanica* by Intieri, with him in mind.[15] This suggests that the shift from *metafisico* to *mercatante* was less a change of purpose than of the path by which he chose to pursue it. The first part of this essay will therefore show how he fused the new and the old in a theory of human nature inspired by Newtonian cosmology. The second part will then illustrate how he used this 'moral anthropology' to reconcile the claims of morality and commerce.

I

The group gathered around Celestino Galiani had already gone some way towards developing on Newtonian science of society. The following example of his thinking will serve as a useful point of comparison with Genovesi's rather different use of these ideas:

Just as in Newtonian physics one traces the forces and the laws with which these function, and having found out what they are we use these as principles to reason about other phenomena, so in the study of man, one who

---

[14] E. Pii, *Antonio Genovesi*, pp. 11–12.
[15] See Franco Venturi, 'Alle origini dell'illuminismo napoletano: dal carteggio di Bartolomeo Intieri'. Intieri quickly realised the potential of Genovesi as an educator, e.g., letters to A. Cocchi in *ibid.*, no. viii, 12 December 1752 (pp. 440–1), no. x, 16 January 1953 (p. 443), no. xi, 20 February 1753 (p. 444), no. xiv, 12 February 1754 (p. 448), and regarded Genovesi's appointment to the new chair as the culmination of his life's work (no. xv, 18 June 1754, p. 449). Genovesi records his debt to Intieri in his autobiography (*Autobiografia*, pp. 29–34) and the 'Discorso sopra il vero fine delle lettere e delle scienze', dedicated to Intieri (reproduced in *ibid.*, pp. 275–6).

knows how to reason and observe well, can deduce from certain of his constant traits the forces, which are usually one or more passions combined together and having traced what these are, understand his [man's] character (. . .) to the extent of being able to act as a fortune teller or prophet by predicting without danger of erring what he will do in the various positions, or combination of circumstances in which he might find himself.[16]

Although Genovesi's willingness to read and comment on authors such as Hobbes and Mandeville got him into difficulties with the religious authorities, there can be little doubt about the orthodoxy of his views.[17] He could not therefore accept Galiani's theory without considerable modification. He certainly appreciated the potential of both Newtonian method and cosmology to provide an unassailable basis for the new political and moral sciences:

The *Mathematical Principles* of cavalier Newton, the *Physico-Theology* of Derham, the work of Niewentit, and others of a similar kind, are worth a hundred thousand volumes of the idle tales and equivocations of these Avincennists, Averroists etc . . . Here is the real metaphysics.[18]

His use of Newtonianism was not, however, free from a continuing concern with certain axioms of traditional Christian theology. He was particularly worried that certain Newtonian ideas, such as the concept of the ether and of empty space as God's sensorium, could lead to the Spinozist heresy of identifying God and Nature.[19]

---

[16] Letter to Bottari, 12 August 1730, quoted in V. Ferrone, *Scienza, natura, religione*, p. 569. Particularly useful for an understanding of Galiani's ideas is the unpublished manuscript 'Della scienza morale', discussed by Ferrone in *ibid.*, pp. 420–42.

[17] See G. Galasso, 'Il pensiero religioso di Antonio Genovesi', *RSI, LXXXII* (1979), 800–23 and, more generally, P. Zambelli, *La formazione filosofica di Antonio Genovesi.*

[18] *La logica per gli giovanetti* (1766), 7th edn (Naples, 1836), Bk V, ch. 5, para. xiv (*II V*, p. 268 – where possible I shall quote from Venturi's selection of Genovesi's writings in *Illuministi italiani*, T.V., pp. 47–330, hereafter *II V*). Genovesi followed Newton in making this transition from natural to moral philosophy; particularly the 31st question of the *Optics.*

[19] *Delle scienze metafisiche per gli giovanetti* (1763) (Venice, 3rd edn 1803), 1, ch. 6, para. xv and 2, ch. 3, para. ii. Ferrone, following N. Badaloni, *Antonio Conti: un abate libero pensatore tra Newton e Voltaire* (Milan, 1968), pp. 203–8 and 'La cultura', *Storia d'Italia*, III (Turin, 1973), pp. 825–8 and E. Garin, 'Antonio Genovesi storico della scienza', in *Dal rinascimento all'illuminismo* (Pisa, 1970), pp. 223–40, argues that in the earlier *Disputatio physico-historica de rerum corporearum origine et constitutione* (1745) Genovesi had read Newton in a Neo-Stoic key, seeing the universe as a self-sufficient system, a theatre of active processes ordered by an immanent *anima mundi* (*Scienza, natura, religione*, p. 612). Yet here too Genovesi seems to be saying that although Newton *could* be read in this manner, citing Clarke and Whiston as examples, it would be against both Newtonian method ('non fingo . . .') and religion to do so – regardless of the motives of those like Clarke who aimed to defend religion in this way (*Disputatio* in *Disciplinorum metaphysicarum elementa*, T.V., new edn (Venice, 1779) pp. 99–100). Thus, whilst Genovesi fully appreciated the cultural significance of

Genovesi objected to such ideas on the grounds that they denied the doctrine of creation. For Genovesi the universe was to be considered as the product of God's will, its laws being in conformity with its nature and hence not binding God, Who existed outside and separated from His creation.[20] He therefore accepted the argument from design but firmly attacked concessions to any kind of hylarchic principle, because, in his view, this led to atheism,[21] and to the rejection of the freedom of God's will, and of man's. He preserved both by seeing each component of the universe as endowed with its own principle of action proper to its nature, and governed by the mechanical laws whose working was directly dependent on the will of God.[22]

Genovesi had essentially discovered a *via media* between a passive conception of matter, acted upon by an omnipresent and omnipotent God, and a view of matter as active and dynamic and self-ordering. There are, therefore, two tiers in Genovesi's view of the world system – a rational order created by God and a secondary system of self-regulating natural processes. The first is constituted by an underlying created order in which man in common with everything else has his place, the second by the mechanisms which preserve this order and develop it. The two taken together constitute the basis of Genovesi's moral science: 'Therefore the first foundation of the moral sciences is human nature: the second the relations between things, which surround us: the third the laws of these relations'.[23]

In an analogous manner, Genovesi also divided human nature into two parts – animal and rational. By virtue of our animal nature we are subjected to all the 'animal laws' (*leggi della animalità*) and all those of the spirit and of reason with respect to the mind.[24] Humans qua animals are sensate beings with an infinite number of appetites and natural desires which they seek to satisfy.[25] Genovesi examines the consequences for humanity of this state both internally and externally,

---

Newton, he was very careful, right from the start, to disassociate himself from both 'conservative' and 'radical' wings of Newtonianism. See too the Proemio to the *Elementa physicae experimentalis*, 2 vols. (Naples, 1791) (published posthumously), I, p. vii and II, Bk IV., ch. 13, paras. ix, x.
[20] *Metafisica*, pt 1, ch. 1, and ch. 6, para. xiii.
[21] *Ibid.*, pt 1, ch. 2, para. v and the passage of the *Elementa physicae* cited in n. 19, where he praises the natural theology of Ray, Derham and Nieventit.
[22] *Ibid.*, pt 1, ch. 6, para. xii.
[23] *Logica*, Bk V, ch. 5, para. xxxi (*II* V, p. 270). See too the Proemio to the *Della Diceosina o sia della filosofia del giusto e dell'onesto* (1766), ed. F. Arata (Milan, 1973), pp. 25–7.
[24] *Diceosina*, Bk I, ch. 1, para. i, p. 32.   [25] *Ibid.*, Bk I, ch. 1, para. ii, p. 32.

each time invoking the laws of mechanics to do so. There are two forces which govern the world system – 'the *centripetal* and the *centrifugal*' (*la centripeta e la centrifuga*).[26] Man, as a finite limited being, is subject to the same laws which regulate all other bodies in the universe, the laws of attraction and collision.[27] The dialectic of these two forces preserves the natural order. It is therefore the source of all good but also, because of the imperfect nature of finite beings, of all evil. Political evil derives from man's living in society and the inevitable clash of individuals seeking to satisfy their private interests (force of collision). On the other hand, the force of attraction is a source of gain for man, society providing him with the security and company necessary to his existence. Happiness and the good for man are to be found in the equilibrium of these two forces.[28] Genovesi therefore rejects the idea that the public good can develop out of the pursuit of selfish ends. He takes this argument further with reference to the internal structure of man. The conflict of desires, the pressures of the external world, cause pain and arouse passions within him. To describe this phenomenon Genovesi again has recourse to the two universal forces of attraction and repulsion derived from Newtonian cosmology. These two forces, called at different times *concentriva* and *diffusiva* or *espansiva* and *coattiva* and *direttiva*, are also defined in the more usual terminology as 'self-love' (*l'amor proprio*) and 'love of the species' (*l'amor della spezia*).[29] Genovesi uses this schema in order to criticise those theorists who sought a metamorphosis of destructive passions stemming from self-love into virtuous social action. His principle targets were Hobbes and Mandeville. The verisimilitude granted to Mandeville's theory derives, he argues, from its superficiality – he is *un filosofo di corteccia*. Self-love is basic to human survival but, here following Shaftesbury, so is sympathy with the rest of mankind and the latter can in no sense be seen as derivative from the former.[30] Both, claimed Genovesi, explicitly breaking with the associationist psychology of Locke

---

[26] *Metafisica*, pt 1, ch. 2, para. i.
[27] *Ibid.*, pt 1, ch. 8, para. i, *Diceosina*, Bk I, ch. 1, para. x, p. 37.
[28] *Metafisica*, pt 1, ch. 8, 'Dei mali'.
[29] *Logica*, Bk V, ch. 5, para. xxxiv (*II* V, p. 271), *Diceosina*, Bk I, ch. 1, para. xvii, p. 42, where they are also called 'due interni principi motori, simpatici ed energetici, che sono essenziali all nostra natura'.
[30] *Metafisica*, pt 3, ch. 7, paras. x–xv. P. Zambelli has demonstrated the influence of Vico's criticism of Hobbes on Genovesi (*La formazione filosofica di A. G.*, pp. 557–61). This has suggestive consequences for his later economic theory (see *Elementorum metaphysicae*, T. IV (Naples, 1754), Bk I, ch. 4, paras. xxxii–iii and A. O. Hirschmann, *The Passions and the Interests*, pp. 17–19 for a revealing discussion of Vico's *Scienza nuova*, paras. cxxx–xxxv).

which had been adopted by Galiani and others, are innate, fixed principles within man.[31] On the same grounds he attacks what he calls the Hobbesian view that society can be seen as the product of enlightened self-interest:

the error of both of them is to have made the *concentriva* alone the primary force, and the other the effect and result of that. Shaftesbury has shown the error of this: and if there is something in nature which the philosophers have demonstrated, it is this truth in the learned work of this Englishman.[32]

Human happiness is thus to be found in the harmony of these two forces which regulate both the world and human nature. Genovesi consequently rejects any suggestion that different political systems could affect human behaviour as artificial. For example, he criticises Montesquieu's tripartite division of the forms of government, each with its own principle, as a 'Fable (*Romanzo*): neither well founded in nature, nor in the principles of nature'.[33] Different forms of government simply reflect the balance of the two forces within man. As Enrico De Mas has observed, such a view is strange given that he had earlier accused Montesquieu of subverting religion and morals by attempting to see them as the outcome of natural processes.[34] Genovesi resolves this possible contradiction by appealing to the laws of the created natural order.

Genovesi raises the problem that his theory might appear to lead to some form of determinism itself. Taking on the role of the devil's advocate, he argues that if man is to be seen as being moved solely by 'physical causes' rather than moral imperatives, then there would

[31] Genovesi's rejection of this aspect of Locke is clearly shown in his epistolary exchange with Antonio Conti on the origin of ideas (*Lettere familiari*, 2nd edn (Venice, 1787), pp. 2–30, esp. letter 2, pp. 3–28). Genovesi defines innate ideas as 'naturali inclinazioni dell'animo, . . . naturali leggi, per cui siam portati al nostro ultimo fine, simili in ciò alle leggi naturali della materia; ovvero quei giudizi, che naturalmente vengono in capo a tutti, e che son dette prime e naturali verità' (pp. 23–4).
This debate forms the core of G. Gentile's chapter on Genovesi in *Storia della filosofia italiana: dal Genovesi al Galluppi*, 2nd edn, 2 vols. (Florence, 1937) I, ch. 1, which is to my mind more accurate in its conclusions that N. Badaloni, *Antonio Conti*, pp. 204–10 and 'La cultura', pp. 823–8.

[32] *Logica*, Bk V, ch. 5, para. xxxvi (*II* V, pp. 272–3).

[33] *Spirito delle leggi del Signore di Montesquieu con le note dell'Abate Antonio Genovesi*, 4 vols. (Naples, 1777), I, Bk III, ch. 4, n.2, p. 56.
Genovesi's annotations to Montesquieu's *Esprit des lois* (written 1766–9) were published posthumously. They have been discussed in detail in Enrico De Mas, *Montesquieu, Genovesi e la edizione italiane dello 'Spirito delle Leggi'* (Florence, 1971), esp. pp. 59–169. De Mas's study provides in many respects the best philosophical treatment of Genovesi's social thought. He omits to mention, however, Genovesi's concept of 'collisione' and this to my mind flaws his discussion of the linking of passion, reason and interest.

be no point in engaging in moral philosophy at all.[35] To counter this he takes a qualitative, if not strictly logical, leap in his argument. Human nature is unchangeable, but not unmodifiable – man is 'elastic' (*la forza della natura umana è elastica*).[36] Man is led by nature, but an understanding of this is communicated to him by the passions. Passions derive from the law of collision. But since Genovesi maintains the mind–body distinction,[37] an aspect of how the external world affects us is our rational perception of it:

A false and harmful point of view will arouse a harmful passion and man will be led by that passion (that is by nature whipped up by the passion) to his misery. A truer view of the same thing, and more connected to our interests, will arouse a useful passion; and we will be led by it to our happiness. Our happiness or our misery therefore depends upon what aspect things present to us, and make us love or hate them. So do, or should do, the true and good theories of morality. The theory of relations is therefore essential to good morals.[38]

This passage (and there are many like it) demonstrates the crucial bridge Genovesi created between the naturalistic and rationalistic models of human action which he had adopted. Hirschman has shown how the concept of 'interest' became a new paradigm in eighteenth-century moral theory, mediating between selfish and socially orientated passions.[39] Genovesi puts it to much the same use, though in his own way. He identifies utility, happiness and interest as the rational perception of the natural order which enables man to avoid the pain consequent on the force of collision.

Reason is simply defined as 'the calculating faculty' (*la facoltà calcolatrice*).[40] Reason cannot of itself, therefore, provide moral guidelines. These derive from the law of nature, which man knows by a religious and moral sense or instinct and which reason seeks to interpret.[41] Thus, although man is susceptible to an infinite variety of habits and customs, his essential nature remains the same, ruled by the law of nature 'which links all the parts of this world, fixing in each its nature, its relations and the particular laws'.[42] This law necessarily forms the basis by which man must order himself if he wants to achieve the 'minimum of ills' (*minimo de' mali*) – viz. the best

[34] E. De Mas, *Montesquieu, Genovesi*, pp. 108–9.
[35] *Logica*, Bk V, ch. 5, para xxxviii (*II* V, p. 273).
[36] *Diceosina*, Bk I, ch. 1, para. xvi, p. 41, 'Discorso sopra il vero fine delle lettere e delle scienza', *II* V, p. 119. [37] *Metafisica*, pt 3, ch. 2, para. xv.
[38] *Logica*, Bk V, ch. 5, para. xl (*II* V, pp. 273–4).
[39] *The Passions and the Interests*, pp. 42–8. [40] *Diceosina*, Bk I, ch. 2, para. i, p. 44.
[41] *Ibid.*, para. iii, p. 45. [42] *Ibid.*, *Logica*, Bk V, ch. 5, paras. XLV–VII.

possible happiness which limited and imperfect beings can enjoy.[43]
To adopt other criteria is to court disaster:

If the nature of things; if man; if the relations which man has; if the civil
body, and its relations, if the interest of man and of the Republic, etc . . . are
not the foundation of the laws, the laws clash with physical nature, and do
not endure, or are undermined in an infinite number of ways. The true rule
therefore, the first, the immutable, is to turn to nature herself.[44]

This is achieved by rationally using the springs of human action, the
passions, to encourage man to pursue his interest – what Genovesi
calls the maxim of *etica fisica* – namely that:

IT IS NOT REASON WHICH RESTRAINS THE PASSIONS, BUT ALWAYS THE GREATER
[passion] RESTRAINS THE LESSER: and if reason acts as a restraint, it does so by
exciting a greater [passion].[45]

The art of government thus consists in leading men from false and
harmful passions and seeks to imprint in their hearts 'a stronger
passion, but truer, that is more in accord with personal and common
interests'.[46] Genovesi had therefore discovered a use for theory in
the moral world, since knowledge of the law of nature is necessary to
promote human happiness. Moreover, such action is not to be
regarded as morally indifferent, or a mysterious manipulation of vice
to good ends, but is the outcome of virtue. Virtue is precisely this
perception of the moral order without which man would be led not
just to evil but equally to pain and unhappiness.[47] If man's reason
were not involved, as Genovesi thinks Mandeville for example
argues, he could be no more capable of virtue than an animal or a
plant.[48] Instead Genovesi follows Shaftesbury in believing that man
has a natural propensity for virtuous action which develops with his
intellect – that is his rational perception of the moral order.[49] Virtue
and interest necessarily coincide; to separate them is only
hypothetically possible, as in the false theories of Hobbes and
Mandeville. Occasional ambiguities in Genovesi's opinion here
merely reflect the uncertainties in the political language of the
time.[50] Genovesi firmly rejects the notion that a society could be
built on interest alone, or indeed that a people exists without virtue,
since morals and religion are innate sentiments within man.[51] Like

[43] *Diceosina*, Bk I, ch. 2, para. ii, p. 45.   [44] *Logica*, Bk. V, ch. 5, para. xliv.
[45] *Ibid.*, para. 1 x (*II* V, p. 279).   [46] *Metafisica*, pt 3, ch. 6, para. xxi.
[47] *Diceosina*, Bk I, ch. 1, para. viii, p. 35, ch. 2, para. v, p. 46.
[48] *Ibid.*, ch. 1, paras. iv, v, pp. 33–4.   [49] *Metafisica*, pt 3, ch. 7, para. xiv.
[50] A. O. Hirschman, *The Passions and the Interests*, pp. 46–7.
[51] *Metafisica*, pt 2, ch. 4, para. iv. See Enrico De Mas, *Montesquieu, Genovesi*, pp. 112–21
for an important discussion of Genovesi's notes to *Esprit des lois*, Bk III, ch. 7.
Diceosina, Bk I, ch 10, para. viii, p. 164.

Shaftesbury he argues that man's self-interest can only be truly found in reference to his end as implanted in his nature. Each creature, plant etc., is part of a universal system of things, in which the end of each is resolved with that of the whole. Virtue and interest are identified since to do evil to oneself and to subvert the order of things are one and the same thing.[52] Genovesi has simply refined upon this theory of morals with his physical description of the workings of human passion inspired by Newtonian cosmology. Reason cannot change man's end, which is fixed by his natural constitution, but is merely the means by which he fulfils it.[53]

It would be wrong to see Genovesi's moral order as immutably fixed, his concept of virtue based on the traditional Christian qualities of restraint and abnegation – ideas developed by Muratori and Doria earlier on in the century.[54] It was noted above how Genovesi's conception of Newtonianism achieved a middle way between the set laws which govern the component parts of the world and active properties inherent in these parts themselves. Genovesi transfers this to the moral sphere when he argues that the ethical code governing human actions can be reduced to the axiom 'preserve the equilibrium by preserving rights' (*serba l'equilibrio con serbare i diritti*).[55] Genovesi in this respect provides an early prototype for the minimalist liberalism of today. A baseline of rights is there to provide a safety net against the abuse of freedom, but not a set of goals for human action. This is simply, again in liberal fashion, the pursuit of happiness. Man's rights are simply those properties of mind and body with which he is endowed as a created being. These in turn are preserved by the law of nature which orders the whole chain of being.[56] The dynamic element is provided by man's reason, which develops with experience and eases man's passage through this vale of tears.

[52] Shaftesbury, *Inquiry Concerning Virtue and Merit* (1699):

> We have found, that to deserve the name of *good* or *virtuous*, a creature must have all his inclinations and affections, his dispositions of mind and temper, suitable, and agreeing with the good of his *kind*, or of that *system* in which he is included, and of which he constitutes a PART. To stand thus well affected and to have one's affections *right* and *entire*, not only in respect of oneself, but of society and the public: this is *rectitude, integrity*, or VIRTUE. And to be wanting in any of these, or to have their contraries, is *depravity, corruption* and VICE.

Bk II, pt 1, sect. i in *British Moralists 1650–1800*, ed. D. D. Raphael, 2 vols. (Oxford, 1969), I, para. ccv, p. 175. Compare *Diceosina*, Bk I, ch. 3, para. xviii, p. 60.

[53] *Metafisica*, pt 3, ch. 6, para. xxxii.
[54] On Doria, see R. Ajello, 'La critica del regime in Doria, Intieri e Broggia', and compare Muratori's chapter on luxury in *Della pubblica felicità* (1748), ch. 19, with its attack on Melon, to the view of Genovesi in *Lezioni di commercio*, pt 1, ch. x (*II* V, pp. 177–208), discussed below.
[55] *Diceosina*, Bk I, ch. 1, para. xx, p. 44, ch. 3, and 4.
[56] *Diceosina*, Bk I, ch. 3, para. xiv, p. 58, *Lezione di commercio*, pt 1, ch. 1, paras. x–xv.

It is here, in his adoption of a programme for progress through the practical use of reason, that Genovesi's second debt to contemporary scientific culture becomes evident. Reason, he argued in his inaugural *Discourse on the True End of the Arts and Sciences* (1753), is what separates man from the brutes, bringing him closer to God. It is what directs his other faculties. Through its use he is able to satisfy his wants in increasingly better ways. Tracing the hypothetical development of a nation from barbarity to civilisation he notes how:

Reason, on the basis of the relations of the things which surround us in our life, makes the arts and perfects them with regard to their relations to our end... Experience, which is the point arrived at by reason in different times and subjects, discovers in brief new relations and new uses, and therefore improvements and perfections, and will do so to the extent that such a nation, which in its origin was closer to dumb beasts than reasoning beings, finds itself as superior to the former as it had been similar to them at its birth.[57]

There can thus be a science of politics which can be put to practical use to educate the populace and promote good habits in them.[58] The progress of society is not inevitable, but goes hand in hand with the development of reason and the consequent regulation of the passions in man.[59] Hirschman has suggested that the attractiveness of interest as a new paradigm for explaining human motivation was its predictability – the constancy with which it was held to operate within man. For Genovesi interest still had unpleasant notions of egoism which he diffused by linking it with reason and virtue. Only then would man's interest emerge, for only by the practical application of reason to discover and observe nature's laws could man lessen the burden of his earthly existence, cease to be an animal and become truly human again.[60] That the arts and sciences should be put to the useful task of furthering human (as opposed to individual) happiness was thus a moral obligation which it was the duty of the intellectual class to spread amongst the people.[61]

The *Discorso* clearly aligns Genovesi with the *novatores* and against

---

[57] 'Discorso sopra il vero fine delle lettere e delle scienze', *II* V, p. 89.
[58] *Ibid.*, p. 100.
[59] 'Ragionamento sul commercio in universale', *II*, V, pp. 136–7.
[60] Hirschman, *The Passions and the Interests*, pp. 48–56.
Genovesi's 'Letter accademiche su la questione se siano più felice gli'ignoranti che gli schienziati' (1764) in *Autobiografia*, pp. 359–66, deals with this theme, e.g., letter 2, p. 375.
[61] 'Discorso sopra il vero fine delle lettere e delle scienze', *II* V. pp. 118–25. My interpretation of the *Discorso* follows E. Pii, *Antonio Genovesi*, pp. 23–44.

the *veteres*. The culture of contemplation, of *ozio*, runs the risk of corrupting the community and precipitating a return to the bestial state.[62] It is, in the modern sense of the word, otiose; and he significantly justifies this view via a criticism of Greek philosophy, which, he claims, produced the dark ages of scholastic thought.[63] The decisive break came with the Renaissance and the works of Galileo and Bacon, which liberated Europe from the 'barbarism' into which it had fallen.[64] Progress requires the enlightenment of the populace. Reason must therefore cease to be the preserve of an intellectual elite:

One cannot say that reason has reached maturity in a nation, when it still resides more in the abstract intellect than in men's hearts and hands . . . It is like the jewels which sparkle but do not nourish us. Reason is not useful until it has become a practical reality, nor does it become such until it is so diffused in the customs and arts, that we adopt it as our sovereign rule, almost without realising it.[65]

The *Discorso*, dedicated to Intieri, ends with a survey of the state of the kingdom of Naples and looks to the spreading of enlightenment (*lume*) amongst the country's artisans and peasants[66] and the consequent 'multiplication, improvement and the perfectioning of foodstuffs, commerce and the arts'.[67]

The *Discorso* has been called 'the manifesto of the Neapolitan Enlightenment',[68] assigning a definite role to the intellectuals in promoting economic progress via a programme of cultural reform and education of the populace. The emphasis on education is important for a correct understanding of the precise nature of Genovesi's endorsement of commercial practice. He specifically avoids the essentially naturalistic theory of the development of human morality of Hobbes and Mandeville which Celestino Galiani adopted. The framework of Genovesi's thinking remains essentially theocentric and hence anti-sociological.[69] It is not the development of society as such which produces the improvement of human customs and manners, but the influence of the latter which leads to the former. This view was no doubt reinforced by the bitter experience of Neapolitan history, where intellectual repression went hand in hand with a backward and archaic social system. The duty and rationale for human improvement therefore required a foundation outside the contingencies of social progress in the God-given laws of attributes of human nature and reason.[70] Our

[62] *Discorso*, p. 89.   [63] *Ibid.*, pp. 92–6.   [64] *Ibid.*, pp. 96–7.
[65] *Ibid.*, p. 100.   [66] *Ibid.*, p. 110.   [67] *Ibid.*, p. 123.
[68] E. Pii, *Antonio Genovesi*, p. 26.   [69] *Discorso*, p. 88.   [70] *Ibid.*, pp. 89–90, 124–31.

obligations to others and to ourselves are therefore fixed in a manner which avoids the moral parody of *The Fable of the Bees*. The elements of a commercial ethic are nevertheless clearly present. Our goals are no longer prescribed by our place in the hierarchy of being. The cosmic order is not fixed for all time but is a complex of interrelated and dynamic atoms. The result of the application of the atomistic model to the microcosm of society is that the individual, ruled by his own thoughts and desires, becomes the basic unit for explaining and legitimating social relations. Our purposes are closely related to our moral duty to use our God-given cognitive and physical capacities. In practice, this entails us finding our goals within our own nature and devising the means to satisfy and fulfil our desires, a duty enshrined in certain basic and inalienable rights. Genovesi was able to provide thereby a theological motive for the capitalist way of life. The life of endless accumulation, which in Doria's neo-Platonist perspective was one of vice and slavery to the passions – a turning away from what is intrinsically good – is endorsed by Genovesi as the exercise and fulfilment of our spiritual capacity. Reason ceases to be concerned with contemplation of the eternal forms, but is instrumental to the pursuit of our worldly goals. Genovesi therefore provided a model of capitalist man, who works to satisfy his desires as a God-given vocation, which would be almost archetypally Weberian were it not for the fact that it arose in a Catholic rather than a Protestant milieu. Finally, it is to be noted that although Genovesi's theory is in many respects paradigmatically liberal and individualist in character, he is careful to avoid the dangers of egoism. The individual's pursuit of his own good is related at a basic level with the rights of others to act similarly. In this manner he reconciled the new language of commerce with the concern with morality and social justice of Doria and Broggia.

II

Having outlined the main features of Genovesi's *antropologia morale*, I wish briefly to sketch how he adapted it to the needs of commercial society. The impetus to translate his social theory directly into a study and defence of commerce came less from his new teaching duties than from the terrible famine of 1764.[71] It was generally agreed that this had arisen from the series of bad harvests which had

---

[71] E. Pii, *Antonio Genovesi*, pp. 165–70.

occurred since 1758. It thereby brought to an end a period of general European prosperity which had encouraged an optimism in the inherently progressive nature of social processes amongst Neapolitan reformers.[2] The spectacle of this national disaster had a profound effect on Genovesi, convincing him of the need to put forward a programme for the reform of the practices – most particularly those stemming from numerous local and feudal privileges – which had so weakened agricultural production. Genovesi's observations were informed by an attempt to provide empirical documentation of the kingdom's ills. However, what was strikingly new and original was the organisation of these ideas within a general theory of economic development derived from his revised account of human nature. The principle aspect of Genovesi's proposals was the need to erode the feudal landlords' hold on the land and to free the peasants from their virtual serfdom so that they were in a position to profit from their own labour.[73] The rationale for the theory was provided by his justification of the acquisitive ethic examined in the previous section.

The two volumes of his *Lezioni di commercio o sia di economia civile* appeared in 1765 and 1767 respectively. He begins by making the step from *metafisico* to *mercatante* outlined above.[74] Man is born, he argues, with certain innate properties:

But although these things are inseparable from us; they can nevertheless be modified in an infinite number of ways. Our happiness depends on a wise modification of them, and from the reasoned use, that we make of them: misery from their abuse.[75]

This is increasingly the case as societies grow and become more complex. Needs increase and their satisfaction becomes more complicated so that friction and hence pain is potentially greater. Yet in reality it is the opposite which occurs, since the increased number of ties bind society tighter together and enable more people to be sustained above subsistence level than in primitive society.[76] These are the two objects of trade and industry (both products of

---

[72] P. Villani, *Mezzogiorno tra riforme e rivoluzione*, 2nd edn (Bari, 1973), p. 26.
[73] A. Genovesi, Preface to Cosimo Trina, *L'agricoltore sperimentato* (1764), in *Autobiografia*, pp. 342–55.
[74] On the genesis of Genovesi's economic theory see, in addition to the articles and books already cited in n. 1, Franco Venturi, 'Le *Lezione di commercio* di Antonio Genovesi – Manoscritti, edizioni e traduzioni', in *RSI*, LXXII (1960), 511–38 and E. Pii, 'Le origini dell'economia "civile" in Antonio Genovesi', *Il Pensiero Politico*, XII (1979), 334–43, and *Antonio Genovesi*, ch. 5.
[75] *Delle lezioni di commercio o sia d'economica civile*, 2 vols., 2nd edn (Naples, 1768–70), pt 1, ch. 1, para. xxi, p. 36.   [76] *Ibid.*, Proemio, p. 12.

human reason) – to increase the wealth of the nation and hence the population.[77] What holds society together is the law of nature, duty to which is encouraged by education and religion.[78] Man is educated via his passions – above all the desire to eschew pain, which Genovesi calls his interest. But it is not simply a selfish desire. There are the two forces, the self-regarding and the social, which operate in man. The latter, 'the sympathetic principle' (*il principio simpatico*), which he distinguishes from 'rational self-love' (*un amor proprio riflesso*), being 'the source of three quarters of human actions'.[79] Again he rebuts the suggestion that any sort of felicific calculus could be applied by a benevolent legislator to encourage good customs in people without appealing to reason and virtue.[80] In debate with Rousseau, he argues that the arts and science, in so far as they are used to promote social and economic progress, can only spread virtue rather than vice.[81] The traumatic effect of the plague and famine of 1763–4 made his attack on the supposed happy condition of primitive man all the more poignant.[82] Man in his primitive state is little better off than an animal, moved by physical springs alone and incapable of virtue. It is only when he can consciously take control of his own destiny that man can be capable of moral action. Commerce is thus rehabilitated by Genovesi as the free application of the arts and science to the pursuit of the *summum bonum*, human happiness.[83]

Nothing better illustrates the transformation of morals achieved by Genovesi than his treatment of luxury.[84] Vico and Doria had both regarded luxury as pernicious to society. Vico's 'ideal eternal history' is often regarded as an early prototype of the stadial theory of social progress, but it clearly emerged from an intellectual framework which its proponents (notably the Scots) consciously sought to supersede. For Vico the founding of society is an act of God for man's preservation and greater ease. Man's attempts to better his condition determine the phases of history, but this process has a limit in the final stage of luxury. Thus:

Men first feel necessity, then look for utility, next attend to comfort, still later amuse themselves with pleasure, then grow dissolute in luxury, and finally go mad and waste their substance.[85]

[77] *Ibid.*, introduction to pt 1, pp. 17–18, ch. 16, para. i, p. 342.
[78] *Ibid.*, ch. 1, para. xxxii.   [79] *Ibid.*, ch. 2, para. vi.
[80] *Ibid.*, ch. 1. para, xxxii, and note a.   [81] *Ibid.*, ch. 10. para. ii.
[82] This is essentially the message of the 'Lettere accademiche' (e.g., letter 1, p. 373). See F. Venturi, *Settecento riformatore*, I, pp. 605–10.
[83] *Lezioni di commercio*, pt 1, ch. 22, paras. ix, xxxiii, *II* V, pp. 224–5, 243–4.
[84] *Ibid.*, pt 1, ch. 10, in *II* V, pp. 177–208.
[85] G. B. Vico, *La scienza nuova* (1744), ed. Fausto Nicolini, 2 vols. (Bari, 1974), 'degnita' LXVI, para. ccxli, see also LXVII, para ccxlii.

Significantly applying his theory to the history of Rome, Vico argued that the objective of statecraft should be the direct furtherance of the public good. Only when this became the chief priority of all members of the community was a state likely to escape entering the cycle of decadence and decline. The decline of Rome and the *ricorso* to a second barbarism is attributed to the importing of 'Asiatic' luxury. Vico's condemnation of luxury was thus very much that of the civic moralist and was endorsed by Doria, who regarded it as something 'which by its very nature is a vice and poison in the republic'.[86] It was crucial to Genovesi's defence of commerce that he amend this view, for it set an unacceptable limit to human progress and was at odds with the individualist premises of his theory of economic growth. The originality of this step is underlined by the fact that even Ferdinando Galiani, in *Della moneta*, had argued that despite its good effect '[i]t is nevertheless always true that luxury is the infallible sign and warning of the imminent decadence of a state.'[87]

Hume played a crucial role in providing Genovesi with arguments to counter these objections. Hume's *Essays* and his *History of England* provided a model of economic development which Genovesi in many respects made his own. There are various reasons for the affinities between their thought, mainly deriving from a common concern with the relative economic development of rich and poor countries and the key role played by agriculture in providing a surplus to be spent on manufacture. For both, their commitment to the undoubted benefits accruing from commercial wealth necessitated a concomitant reappraisal of the moral consequences of luxury.[88] Hume, in the essay 'Of refinement in the arts', had defended luxury from the views of both moralists and libertines:

---

[86] P. M. Doria, *Del commercio*, p. 209, quoted in Ferrone, *Scienza, natura, religione*, p. 599.   [87] *Della moneta*, p. 242.

[88] 'Of commerce', *Essays Moral, Political and Literary* (Oxford, 1963), pp. 259–74. Hume's *Essays* and *History* were appreciated early on in Italy. As the Florentine *Novelle letterarie* noted:

Il signor Hume si è proposto in questi suoi Discorsi Politici il grande oggetto d'essere utile anche agli homini che nasceranno; e di più non li ha scritti per la sola nazione. Il commercio è una delle parti più esseziale della sua opera. (Tomo XVI, n. 3, 17 January 1755, p. 42)

The *History of England* was regarded as 'un modello per tutti quei che vogliono accingersi a scrivere una qualche storia' (Tomo XIX, n. 48, 1 December 1758, p. 67). On the Italian reception of the Scottish Enlightenment, see F. Venturi, 'Scottish echoes in eighteenth-century Italy', in *Wealth and Virtue*, ed. I. Hont and M. Ignatieff (Cambridge, 1983), pp. 345–62. I am indebted to John Robertson's chapter, 'The Scottish Enlightenment at the limits of the civic tradition', in *ibid.*, pp. 137–78, for my understanding of Hume's economic theory.

by proving, *first*, that the ages of refinement are both the happiest and most virtuous; *secondly*, that wherever luxury ceases to be innocent, it also ceases to be beneficial; and when carried a degree too far, is a quality pernicious, though perhaps not the most pernicious, to political society.[89]

Genovesi essentially repeats Hume's arguments, using them to steer a careful path between Mandeville and Rousseau. Both Mandeville, who regards it as the product of vice, and Rousseau, who sees it as productive of vice, are wrong. There is rather, Genovesi believes, a level of luxury which is essential to both the civilisation and virtue of a nation, without which a people is subject simply to the gifts of fortune. Genovesi agrees that amongst the springs of human action is greed. But although one cannot change vice into virtue, it is possible to take advantage of it for the public good – 'Human art cannot make nature, but it can regulate it (*reggerle*).'[90] Genovesi followed Hume in maintaining that whilst excessive luxury was destructive of society in arousing the desire for gain and hedonistic pleasure above all else, a certain degree was required if a nation was to leave the savage state:

this moderate luxury should rather be called propriety, decency, and gentility of a civilised people, than luxury: and far from being a vice is a virtue, being a mean between rough and sordid parsimony, and foolish and vain prodigality.[91]

Genovesi's reappraisal of luxury went hand in hand with a revised view of how wealth was created in a community. Vico and Doria had argued that wealth must be sought as a public rather than a personal good if its corrupting effects were to be forestalled. Genovesi, however, drew upon Hume to argue that economic growth was the end product of the individual pursuit of personal and family interest; since 'the nature and main force and activity of political bodies derives from the nature and force of families and the nature and force of persons'.[92] Luxury and wealth are a product of the human desire to 'distinguish ourselves' (*di distinguersi*).[93] This desire exists in even the most primitive peoples, who adorn themselves with bangles or brightly coloured clothes – a point illustrated by a quote from the description of 'the character of the Anglo-Saxons marvellously painted by Sig. Davide Hum'.[94] It becomes much more complicated in commercial society, where the marks of distinction

---

[89] *Essays*, p. 267.
[90] *Lezione*, pt 1, ch. 10, para. ii, pp. 178–9. *Ibid.*, para. vii, p. 181.
[91] *Ibid.*, para. xli, p. 206.   [92] *Lezione*, pt 1, ch. 1, para. ii, p. 19.
[93] *Ibid.*, ch. 10, paras. xv–vi, in *II* V, pp. 187–8.   [94] *Ibid.*, n. 1, pp. 188–9.

are 'no longer natural, but representative' (*rappresentatrici*)'.[95] Once money and manufactured goods have been introduced, the incentive to work is potentially inexhaustible. For these provide an infinite source of different forms of wealth by which individuals can distinguish themselves from each other.[96] Genovesi had no wish, as previous moralists had done, to attack this natural human propensity, merely to regulate it.[97] This is again done with reference to both the laws of nature and the laws of mechanics.[98] The former merely confer the obligation to respect the rights of others in their individual pursuit of happiness, the latter provide the means of educating the passions in conformity with the social interest.[99]

Genovesi shared the view of the Scottish economists that luxury distributes wealth and destroys privilege, in particular that stemming from feudalism.[100] Again following Hume, he gave a classically Scottish account of the decline of feudalism which was to become a standard feature of the works of Neapolitan reformers.[101] 'In a polite nation (*una nazione polita*)', he says, 'one cannot do without a thousand things which luxury begins to make necessary.'[102] As a result, the landowners begin to dissipate their wealth and hence their economic power in conspicuous consumption. The consequent substitution of cash for service relationships frees the peasants from oppressive feudal dues and ultimately enables them to become a class of independent small proprietors. Genovesi believed that this would inevitably be a slow process. He significantly regarded the role of the state to consist not in the outright abolition of feudalism, but in the protection of the individual's right to his labour, 'the capital

---

[95] *Ibid.*, para. xvii, pp. 189–90.   [96] *Ibid.*, paras. xviii–xxv, pp. 190–4.
[97] *Ibid.*, para vii, p. 181.   [98] *Ibid.*, para. viii, p. 181.
[99] *Diceosina*, Bk I, ch. 3, para. v, pp. 52–3.
[100] *Lezioni de commercio*, pt 1, ch. 22, para. xxiv, in *II*, pp. 193–4. I have discussed the interpretation by the Scottish economists of the Idea of Progress in 'From feudalism to capitalism: history and politics in the Scottish Enlightenment', in *The Promise of History*, ed. A. Moulakis (Berlin–New York, 1985), pp. 35–50.
[101] *Lezione*, pt 1, ch. 22, *II* V, pp. 218ff. and is discussed in G. Giarizzo, 'La storiografia meridionale del settecento', *Vico– la politica e la storia* (Naples, 1981), pp. 175–239, esp. 198–201. Genovesi's own version of the stadial theory is in *Lezione*, pt 1, ch. 17, paras. i–vii, pp. 140–9 and is analysed by E. Pii, *Antonio Genovesi*, pp. 230–3. Genovesi's follower, G. M. Galanti, had the relevant passages of Hume's *History* (Appendix III) and William Robertson's *A View of the Progress of Society in Europe* translated, and applied their insights in his own study *Della descrizione geografica e politica della Sicilia* (Naples, 1782). This use of the stadial theory for the analysis of the transition from feudalism to capitalism in Naples culminated in David Winspeare's *Storia degli abusi feudali* (Naples, 1811). See G. Giarrizzo, 'La storiografia meridionale', for the fullest account of this movement.
[102] *Lezione*, pt 2, ch. 9, para. xi, pp. 215–16.

of the poor'. This would eventually have the desired effect of increasing the wealth of the nation and, more importantly, would result in its being distributed in an equitable fashion.[103] It does not lead to a classless society, since individuals will still be distinguished by natural talents, skills, occupations etc., but to a meritocracy suited to the desert ethic of a market society.[104] Finally, he did not believe that the bonds between states created by commerce would replace war, as Melon and Montesquieu had argued.[105] The Seven Years War had provided ample evidence that this was not necessarily the case, and he maintained a strong neo-Mercantalist attitude with regard to the dealings between states. This largely derives from the realistic strain in Genovesi and does not contradict the principle of a fundamental equilibrium which is at the heart of his social theory. It is simply a recognition that relations between states are likely to be harder to regulate than those within them, so that the desire for gain is likely to get the upper hand. Nations must simply be prepared for this eventuality.[106]

The commercial growth of England in particular represented for Genovesi a model of economic development for the new kingdom of Naples. This had nothing to do with the English constitutional arrangements, but with the principles which had been applied to arouse the commercial instinct in man.[107] Genovesi, unlike many later Neapolitan thinkers such as Filangeri, was not particularly interested in the institutional arrangements of individual governments but grounded his theory, as we have seen, on eternal laws of nature identifiable by reason. What was important was the constancy of human nature at all times and places and of the natural order which regulated it.[108] This was realised not by constitutional reform, but via a system of legally recognised rights.

Although Hume's defence of English commercial practice is at the heart of Genovesi's view of the modern economy, he takes issue with

[103] Ibid., ch. 221, paras. xxii, xxxv–vii, pp. 461, 483–7.
[104] Ibid., pt 1, chs. 3 and 4.
[105] Hirschman, The Passions and the Interests, p. 80, E. De Mas, Montesquieu, Genovesi, pp. 157–61, Spirito delle leggi, Bk XXI, ch. 14, n. 2, I, p. 346.
[106] Spirito delle leggi, Bk XX, ch. 2, n. 1, I, p. 266, Lezione di commercio, pt 1, ch. 19, para. vii, p. 406.
[107] As De Mas notes, Genovesi barely comments on Montesquieu's famous chapter on the English constitution except to mention that it is about England (Montesquieu, Genovesi, p. 157, n. 46, Spirito delle leggi, Bk XIX, ch. 27, II, n. 1, p. 250). He makes the reasons clear in his introduction to J. Carey's An Essay on the State of England, where he emphasises not the political structure of England, but the principles which have been used to arouse the commercial drive within man (II V, pp. 144–56). [108] Diceosina, Bk I, ch. 3, para. xvi, p. 59.

him on two key points which reflect both the special circumstance of Naples and salient differences in their social theory which reveal the nature and limits of Genovesi's endorsement of commerce. First, he notes a certain inconsistency between Hume's analysis of money and luxury and his criticisms of banks and paper credit. In a chapter of the *Lezioni* devoted to the topic, he argues that an influx of money stimulates labour and industry by increasing demand and that Hume ignored these beneifts, outlined in the essay 'Of money', when he came to attack Law's schemes in 'Of public credit'. After all:

Signor Hum himself calls money 'the oil of the commercial wagon'.[109] Therefore when he claims not to have ever understood the force of this word 'circulation', wishing to declaim against the abuses of paper money, he pretends to be ignorant of its true utility, in order to be able to become more severely heated [in his criticisms].[110]

Genovesi was free from his British contemporaries' concern with the undermining of values in an economy based on money and credit.[111] In part this reflects the perspective of a poor country, which did not run the dangers of pricing itself out of the market,[112] but his faith in the continued industriousness of the workforce also derived from his different view of the springs of human action. Hume regarded morality and justice as a product of the progress of society. His reservations therefore sprang from the fact that he had never completely overcome his scepticism about the long-term prospects for virtue under capitalism. Genovesi, on the other hand, grounded moral identity in man's God-given rational capacities to follow and develop his nature according to certain eternal and immutable laws. For Genovesi, reason is not the mere slave of the passions, constrained by the conventions and requirements of society. Religious qualms apart, he was all too aware that social arrangements, such as those of his own country, often arise in a quite arbitrary fashion and can be thoroughly bad, and was therefore unwilling to accept such a theory. Rather, human reason mirrors divine reason in making society as well ordered as the natural world. For it to be otherwise could be to put in question the meaning and value of human existence.

---

[109] Hume's actual words are: 'it is the oil which renders the motion of the wheels more smooth and easy', *Essays*, p. 289.
[110] *Lezione*, pt 2, ch. 7, para. xv, pp. 96–7.
[111] On this debate, see J. G. A. Pocock, *The Machiavellian Moment* (Princeton, 1975), chs. 13 and 14.
[112] See Istvan Hont, 'The "rich country – poor country" debate in Scottish classical political economy', in *Wealth and Virtue*, pp. 271–315.

Commercial activity is thus an extension of Genovesi's view of human activity in general. Seen in terms of Genovesi's social theory it becomes the expression of human virtue rather than in conflict with it. It derives from the free, rational exercise of man's innate faculties towards his end – the least possible pain.[113] This does not lead to a rapacious war of conflicting individual appetites but a higher development of the equilibrium of passion which exists at all times, reflecting the forces which regulate the motions of celestial bodies. The preservation of the laws of nature hence represents man's true duty and interest.[114] Although commercial, civilised societies are not free from evil and pain, and luxury has a tendency to increase human greed, on balance man is immeasurably better off. He is freed from the bare struggle for existence and tied to his fellows by stronger mutual bonds.[115] Utility and interest are in this way redefined to coincide with virtue and justice:

From all of the above one easily understands that in nature these words, just, honest, virtue, useful, interest, can only be foolishly separated. If keeping intact our God given rights, our own and those of others, is justice, it is also honesty and true moral virtue. And if this is the law of equilibrium between the *concentriva* and *espansiva* forces; and this equilibrium alone can provide our present happiness; it alone is truly useful and our real interest. If injustice is but to offend the rights either of the ruler of the world or others; this same would be vice. And if this tends to divide our basic forces, to put them in conflict with each other and bring us pain and misery; vice cannot be the true utility . . . Who is wise or stupid enough that he would know or dare to arrest the course of the universe? We are subject to it, fools or wise men, whether we like it or not, inspite of our scorn.[116]

Genovesi was too religiously orthodox to accept the secular theory of utility based on a hedonistic individualism propounded by Celestino Galiani. Indeed Galiani's *Della scienza morale* was too out of tune with the dominant mores of the age for it even to be published. Genovesi sought to devise a theory of utility which was both more social in orientation and in tune with traditional religious ethics. The *metafisico* was thus never absent in his writings on commerce. His

---

[113] *Lezione di commercio*, pt 1, ch. 1, para. xv, pp. 30–1. Genovesi's moral reservations and maintenance of a theocentric framework in his justification of modernity invites comparison with the similar project of Locke – see John Dunn, 'From applied theology to social analysis: and break between John Locke and the Scottish Enlightenment', in *Wealth and Virtue*, pp. 119–36.

[114] *Ibid.*, para. xxxix, p. 51.

[115] *Ibid.*, ch. 16, para. ii, n.a., pp. 343–4, ch. 19, para. v, n.b., pp. 404–5 and whole chapter generally.

[116] *Diceosina*, Bk I, ch. 3, para. xviii, p. 60.

moral philosophy presupposed a total philosophy of the created order of nature, hingeing on a metaphysics and natural theology of design, the Chain of Being, teleology, order, hierarchy, and mind–body dualism. His achievement was to exploit the language of the theologian to express the new values of the merchant.

PART IV

13

◁ ═══ ▷

The criticism of rhetorical historiography and the ideal of scientific method: history, nature and science in the political language of Thomas Hobbes

GIGLIOLA ROSSINI

I

Hobbes's first published work, which appeared in 1629, was a translation of Thucydides's *Eight Books of the Peloponnesian War*,[1] and it was a work which was to have a deep and lasting, if also sometimes ambiguous, influence on the subsequent development of his political ideas and on the language in which he couched them. In his introduction to the work he had this to say of Thucydides's political ideas:

> For his opinion touching the government of the state, it is manifest that he least of all liked the democracy. And upon divers occasions he noteth the emulation and contention of the demagogues for reputation and glory of wit; with their crossing of each other's counsels, to the damage of the public; the inconsistency of resolutions, caused by the diversity of ends and power of rhetoric in the orators; and the desperate actions undertaken upon the flattering advice of such as desired to attain, or to hold what they had attained, of authority and sway among the common people.[2]

In addition to his rejection of rhetoric and demagogy, Thucydides had also condemned superstitious beliefs as causes of controversy

---

I wish to thank Professor Quentin Skinner and Dr Anthony Pagden for their helpful suggestions on an earlier version of this essay.

[1] *Eight Books of the Peloponnesian War written by Thucydides . . . interpreted . . . by Thomas Hobbes* (in *The English Works of Thomas Hobbes of Malmesbury*; now first collected and edited by William Molesworth, London 1839–45, vols. VIII–IX. Henceforth this work will be indicated as *E. W.*). The *Eight Books* was published in London in 1629, but Hobbes himself wrote, in the epistle 'To the Readers', that he had finished the translation some time before (see *E. W.*, VIII, p. ix; also *T. Hobbes Malmesburiensis vita, authore seipso*, in *Opera latina*, ed. Molesworth, I, pp. xiii–xiv).

[2] Hobbes, 'Of the life and history of Thucydides', in *Eight Books*, pp. xvi–xvii. For Hobbes's aversion towards 'rhetorical' knowledge, see also *De corpore politico*, P. II, c. IX, 8 (*E. W.*, IV, p. 219); *Leviathan*, P. IV, c. XLVI, (*E. W.*, III, pp. 676–7); *Behemoth* (*E. W.*, VI, p. 215).

and dissent. For this, for his belief in 'natural reason' and his denunciation of the 'ridiculous religion' of the common people, he had been unjustly accused of atheism.³ Hobbes was similarly hostile to superstitious beliefs and in *Leviathan* he described the Catholic church as a 'Kingdome of Darkenesse' because it used liturgy to reinforce its political power. There are, too, in the definitions of the 'state of war' and of the 'war amongst nations' to be found in Hobbes's later works, analogies with Thucydides's descriptions of the security risks implicit in democratic government. In *Leviathan*, for instance, Hobbes analysed the way in which, in both a democratic and an aristocratic system, some individuals will always seek to take advantage of civil war and treachery, whereas a sovereign will always pursue the benefit and security of his own subjects, since his own reputation depends on them.⁴

Civil war is, for Hobbes, the historical image of man's war against another in the manner described by the notion of the 'state of nature'.⁵ Outside the commonwealth the state of war is always present.⁶ Neighbouring nations, as they are not subjected to a common international authority, fight each other because each is jealous of the other's power.⁷

Hobbes's interest in Thucydides was also inspired by his admiration for the man. Although he had the qualities required to become a powerful demagogue, Thucydides took the decision not to have any part in the government of his own state at the moment when it would have been impossible to provide the community with 'good and profitable counsel'. For this, he claimed, was a time when citizens had achieved such an opinion of their own power that they were prepared to listen only to such men as swayed the assemblies and 'put them upon the most dangerous and desperate enterprises'. Believing that it was impossible for him to play any useful part in politics, Thucydides had preferred to lead a private life and took to the writing of history.⁸ In 1640 Hobbes too, after he had completed *Human Nature* and *De corpore politico or the Elements of Law Moral and Politic,*⁹ the first works in which the principal concerns of his later

³ 'Of the life and history of Thucydides', p. xv.
⁴ *Leviathan*, P. II, c. XIX (*E.W.*, III, p. 174).
⁵ *Ibid.*, P. I, c. XIII, pp. 114–15. ⁶ *Ibid.*, p. 113.
⁷ See *Behemoth*, p. 203. ⁸ 'Of the life and history of Thucydides', p. xvi.
⁹ I quoted Hobbes' *Human Nature* and *De corpore politico* (both first published in 1650) as in Molesworth edition, IV. F. Tönnies published a critical edition of the two treatises from unprinted Mss (*The Elements of Law Natural and Politic*, London, 1889).

thought are apparent, chose voluntary exile in France soon after the summoning of the Short Parliament.

When he began his translation of Thucydides, Hobbes had not yet developed any systematic interest in mathematics and natural science. Although the bibliographical list that he wrote down between 1627 and 1628 and between 1631 and 1632 (Chatsworth Ms E 2), after the interruption of his second trip to the Continent in 1629–30, could be interpreted as a programme of reading by which he may have intended to deepen his scientific and linguistic knowledge,[10] there is no evidence to suggest that Hobbes's interest in Thucydides constituted, as such, a premise for the construction of a scientific model for the explanation of reality. It is possible, however, to read Hobbes's appreciation of Thucydides as a reflection of his recognition of the need to build historical knowledge upon a set of rigorous methodological criteria and, consequently, to prise it away from relativism and from the ideological use of rhetoric. Thucydides, besides representing the model of a way of life, provided Hobbes with an example of a notion of historiography whose methodological aspects and speculative aims he shared.[11]

The political situation in England had made Hobbes acutely aware of the ways in which ideological conflict could lead to political insecurity. This experience deepened his pessimism, compelled him to broaden the scope of his observations and to articulate them as a rational scheme. Particular historical events seemed to reveal that men's life is the 'life of bodies'; passions and the search for individual usefulness are the only expressions of human nature. Hobbes's theoretical interests were strongly inspired by political aims and remained so even when mathematics provided a method applicable to philosophical explanations. When describing the aim of history, he cited the work of Thucydides as the highest level reached by historiography because it was organised around a rationalistic ideal of history.

What I want to do in this essay is to show that Hobbes's need for a scientific method began with his repudiation of 'rhetorical'

---

[10] A. Pacchi has published the only available edition of the Chatsworth Ms E2 in his article 'Una "biblioteca ideal" di Thomas Hobbes', *Acme, Annali della Facolta di Lettere e Filosofia dell'Università di Milano*, XXI (1968), 1.

[11] As a further proof of Hobbes's interest in Thucydides, see *T. Hobbes Malmesburiensis vita, carmine espressa* (*O.L.*, I, p. xxxvi). On Thucydides's presence in the English culture of the sixteenth and seventeenth centuries and for the reason why Bacon and Hobbes were concerned with the Thucydideian historiographical model, see R. Schlatter, 'Thomas Hobbes and Thucydides', *Journal of the History of Ideas*, VI, 3, (1945) 350–62.

historiography and that his acceptance of a scientific ideal of knowledge was already present in the Introduction to the translation of Thucydides.

Hobbes wrote about Thucydides's conception of the aim of history that:

the principal and proper work of history being to instruct and enable men, by the knowledge of actions past, to bear themselves prudently in the present and providently towards the future: there is not extant any other (merely human) that doth more naturally perform it, than this of my author.[12]

Hobbes, however, did not conceive of history in terms of the Ciceronian notion of *magistra vitae*. The *object* of history should, he claimed, consist only of the careful and objective reconstruction of facts.

The pedagogical value of history derived, for Hobbes, precisely from that methodological rigour which led Thucydides to avoid any attempt 'to read a lecture, moral or political' into his material.[13] Hobbes's 'discovery' of Thucydides as a model for historiography meant, together with the condemnation of ideology and extrinsic ethical principles, the acknowledgement that questions concerning the 'truth' of historical facts were fundamental. There are indeed, Hobbes says, many excellent and profitable histories written by historians who have nevertheless limited themselves to providing observations independently of the narrative. Such observations, he claims, 'commend the knowledge of the writer, but not the history itself: the nature whereof is merely narrative'.[14] Other historians have introduced subtle conjectures about the secret aims and inward cogitations of historical agents. Since, however, the narrative itself would not have been sufficient to suggest these conjectures to the reader, they are nothing but stylistic exercises, the devices of a rhetorical historiography whose aim is to move human passions instead of representing facts objectively. Hobbes stressed that, precisely because he rejected a rhetorical use of narrative,

Thucydides is one, who, though he never digress to read a lecture, moral or political, upon his own text, nor enter into men's hearts further than the acts themselves evidently guide him: is yet accounted the most politic historiographer that ever writ . . . He filleth his narration with the choice of matter, and ordereth them with that judgment, and with such perspicuity

[12] *Eight Books*, 'To the Readers', p. viii.   [13] *Ibid.*, p. viii.   [14] *Ibid.*

and efficacy expresseth himself, that, as Plutarch saith, he maketh his auditor a spectator.[15]

Hobbes was as aware as Thucydides of the risks, for the historian, of partiality and the temptation to manipulate his narrative. When defining the object and the method of historiography, Hobbes sets: (1) truth as the central object of history; (2) the search for truth as the methodological problem concerning the author's impartiality and the critical shifting of the witnesses; (3) the use of correct methodologies of inquiry in order to understand the dynamics of history.

According to Hobbes there are two main qualities to be considered in historical writing: *truth* and *elocution*;

for in *truth* consisteth the *soul*, and in *elocution* the *body* of history. The latter without the former, is but a picture of history; and the former without the latter, unapt to instruct.[16]

The aim of history, for Thucydides, should not consist in flattering the audience but in the pedagogical function 'to instruct the age to come'.[17] In his Introduction to the translation of the *Eight Books of the Peloponnesian War*, Hobbes opposed Dionysius of Halicarnassus to Thucydides as a negative model of an historian who used a rhetorical style to express moral contents. Dionysius could never have made the economical and political degradation of his own country the object of a history since he was concerned only with the depiction of splendid and glorious actions.

Dionysius aimeth still at the delight of the *present* hearer; though Thucydides himself profess that his scope is not that, but to leave his work for a *perpetual possession for the posterity*.[18]

From Thucydides Hobbes learnt that a rigorous and objective reconstruction of the past, rather than a set of aprioristic, ethical principles, is the necessary premise for a better understanding of the political present.

Hobbes's interest in Thucydides derived also from his concern with the priority given to philology by a number of humanist historians, particularly Lorenzo Valla; and it is worth pointing out, in this context that, when Valla himself picked Thucydides as a model, he formulated a new relationship between rhetoric and history founded precisely upon a connection between history and

[15] *Ibid.*   [16] 'Of the life and history of Thucydides', pp. xx–xxi.
[17] *Ibid.*, p. xxi.   [18] *Ibid.*, p. xxvii.

science. According to Valla the function of rhetoric had to be sub-ordinated to the 'historical truth', and in the proper relationship between rhetoric and science the former provided only functional instruments able to present factual objectivity.[19]

Hobbes employed a similar notion of the 'functional' or instrumental role of rhetoric. When defending Thucydides from the accusation of Dionysius of Halicarnassus that he wrote in an 'obscure' style, Hobbes praised Thucydides's non-ideological use of rhetoric and said that his so-called 'obscurity' was limited to the description of multiform and complex aspects of reality. Having a perfect mastery of the rules of rhetoric, Thucydides made a very skil-ful use of antitheses in dialogues in order to outline with verisimilitude the psychology of characters and the historical disparity between intentions and praxis. The capacity of history to teach is dependent upon the possibility, for historical subjects, to operate in the present. Hobbes expressed such a 'pragmatical' notion of history-writing by saying that Thucydides's language of history *secretly* instructs:

Digression for instruction's cause, or other such open conveyances of precepts (which is the philosopher's part), he never useth; as having so clearly set before men's eyes the ways and events of good and evil counsels, that the narration itself doth *secretly* instruct the reader, and more effectually than can possibly be done by precept.[20]

We have seen that what Hobbes praised in Thucydides was his research into the objective conditions under which human actions take place and his attempt to apply a kind of 'medical' rationalism to history which meant the reconstruction of historical man as 'natural object'. When discussing Thucydides's conception of history, Hobbes also stressed his research into the rules which regulate human nature:

He was far from the necessity of servile writers, either to fear or flatter. And whereas he may peradventure be thought to have been malevolent towards his country, because they deserved to have him so; yet hath he not written

---

[19] Lorenzo Valla, *Historiarum Ferdinandi regis Aragonae, libri tres*, proemio:
    Oportet in historico esse, praeter ipsam mirabilem quandam et multis sane dotibus exaggeratam scribendi scientiam, alia multa, sine quibus non possit suum munus implere, primum in cognoscenda re solertiam, acumen, iudicium ... Nonne igitur ad huiusmodi veritatem eruendam historico opus est non minori accuratione ac sagacitate, quam aut indici in deprehendendo vero ac justo, aut medico in previdendo morbo atque curando? (ed. O. Besomi, Padua, 1973, pp. 3–8).
[20] 'Of the life and history of Thucydides', p. xxii.

any thing that discovereth such passion. *Nor is there any thing written of them that tendeth to their dishonour as Athenians, but only as people.*[21]

Thucydides tried to operate, within the context of history, a subtle and complex connection between the objectivity of historical conditions and the dynamism of particular historical processes, and this meant that man had to be understood not only with respect to his biological–anthropological nature but also in terms of his specific actions as historical subject.

At the time Hobbes began his translation of Thucydides, events in England revealed to him that the conflicts of passions, the will for supremacy and the search for individual usefulness constituted man's 'naturality'. In the development of his philosophical thought after 1629, Hobbes clearly stated that man is primarily nature. As man is himself enclosed within nature, he cannot be the artifex of the natural world. Passions originate as 'adversions' and 'desires'. Egotism and competition are therefore 'natural' as well as the state of anarchy and civil war, whereas civil society is 'artificial'.[22] But if organised society is a product of 'man's art', it is nevertheless always true that man *is* nature and that his history is indissolubly bound to his naturalness. For Hobbes, history and nature belong on the same level. And beside the common ground where they meet, there is also a level where history and political praxis are connected. Therefore the historical narrative, guided by the acknowledgement of human nature in general, is able to establish precise connections between political 'science' and 'art'.

It has already been pointed out that Hobbes defined the search for historical truth, expressed through a 'coherent, perspicuous and persuasive' narrative, as the main quality of Thucydides's work. Given that in truth consists the soul and in elocution the body of history, Hobbes was able to distinguish a double aspect of elocution:

---

[21] *Ibid.*, p. xxi.
[22] The difference between 'natural' and 'artificial' is clearly set out in Hobbes's 'Introduction' to *Leviathan*:

> NATURE, the art whereby God hath made and governes the world, is by the *art* of man, as in many other things, so in this also imitated, that it can make an artificial animal. For seeing life is but a motion of limbs, the beginning whereof is in some principal part within; why may we not say, that all *automata* (engines that move themselves by springs and wheels as doth a watch) have an artificial life? ... *Art* goes yet further, imitating that rational and most excellent worke of nature, *man*. For by art is created the great LEVIATHAN called a COMMON-WEALTH, or STATE, (in latin CIVITAS) which is but an artificial man; though of greater stature and strength than the natural, for whose protection and defence it was intended. (*E.W.*, III, pp. ix–x)

disposition or method and *style*.[23] Before describing the war between Athens and Sparta, Thucydides had briefly discussed the processes which characterised the development of Greece from its origins to the present; and he had carefully analysed the customs, institutions and sentiments of those people who had taken part in the war. He also made a distinction between the 'avowed' causes of the war (e.g., the quarrels about Corcyra and Potidea), and the 'true' cause, namely Sparta's fear and envy of the greatness of Athens.[24]

The methodological value of Thucydides's work was, for Hobbes, pre-eminent:

> the grounds and motives of every action he settleth down before the action itself, either narratively or else contriveth them into the form of *deliberative orations* in the persons of such as from time to time bare sway the common-wealth. After the actions, when there is just occasion, he giveth his judgment of them; shewing by what means the success came either to be furthered or hindered.[25]

Once causal links have become pre-eminent within the narrative, the sequence of facts, the *dispositio* according to the rhetoric of classical terminology, acquires a fundamental importance. The order of the exposition becomes the fulcrum of the historical narrative. Thucydides expressed this order in a careful chronological sequence. He avoided making any personal judgements before actions themselves had been described and he made every attempt to discover the deep causes of the historical phenomena with which he dealt. Also for Thucydides the 'order' of rhetoric was functional to the 'order' of history. He confirmed Hobbes's distrust of the stylistic–esornative role of *elocution* which had occupied a pre-eminent position in some of the most famous handbooks of the Quattrocento such as Pontano's *Actius* and the *Rhetoricorum libri quinque* by Trapezunzio.

II

As we have seen, in translating Thucydides, Hobbes had already displayed a concern with an ideal of scientific knowledge. The full acceptance of a scientific ideal of knowledge was only to become explicit, however, in his 'conversion' to Euclid. The demonstrative ideal of a Euclidean science appears in the *Short Tract on First Principles*,

---

[23] 'Of the life and history of Thucydides', p. xxi.
[24] *Ibid.*, pp. xxi and xxvii.   [25] *Ibid.*

written around 1631,[26] and then in the two treatises *Human Nature* and *De corpore politico*.

The critical literature has usually made a distinction, within Hobbes's philosophical and political thought, between an early period when the influence of a 'humanistic' culture was particularly strong and a 'scientific' period when Hobbes's interests were mainly concerned with first principles as a means of explaining natural phenomena.[27] In the so-called scientific period, motion and substance are said to be the methodological presupposition for any explanation of reality. Upon these two first principles Hobbes created a rigorous, universal and deductive science which proceeded, according to the Aristotelian model, from a limited number of proper definitions, postulates and axioms. His pre eminent political interest was thus capable of being integrated within the 'scientific' methodological order.

One of the most influential of Hobbes's commentators, Leo Strauss, in his work *The Political Philosophy of Hobbes. Its Basis and its Genesis*, first published in 1936, intended to demonstrate, however, that the real basis of Hobbes's political philosophy was not modern science. Strauss characterises Hobbes's pre-scientific thought as an adhesion to a moral Aristotelianism in which definitions of the aims of human actions are fundamental. According to Strauss, Hobbes distanced himself from Aristotle's physics and metaphysics and became more interested in his morals and politics: this meant 'the

---

[26] F. Tönnies attributed to Hobbes the *Short Tract on First Principles*, and published it as Appendix I of *The Elements*. The *Short Tract* is divided into sections, each one proceeding from 'principles' to 'conclusions'. Important philosophical themes are introduced: abstract concepts of body, motion, agent, patient, explanation of such phenomena as sensation, light, colours. There is also an outline of ethics which follows a deductive—materialistic presentation where the most relevant statement is the identification of 'what is good' with 'what is desirable'. This identification implies a relativism of the concept of good (pp. 203ff.).

[27] G. C. Robertson in his *Hobbes* (London and Edinburgh, 1886) propounded the thesis that Hobbes fixed the main lines of his political thought when he was still an 'observer of men and manners', not yet a 'mechanical philosopher'. Leo Strauss reinforced Robertson's thesis in his *The Political Philosophy of Hobbes: Its Basis and its Genesis* (Oxford, 1936, reprinted Chicago, 1952). J. W. N. Watkins challenged the Robertson–Strauss thesis and demonstrated that Hobbes's political ideas can only be understood as part of a systematic philosophy encompassing both natural and political science. Hobbes's psychology, ethics, and civil philosophy can be interpreted, according to Watkins, as an application of Galileo's 'resolutive–compositive' method to politics. See Watkins, 'Philosophy and Politics in Hobbes', *Philosophical Quarterly*, V (April 1955), reprinted in *Hobbes's Studies*, ed. K. C. Brown (Cambridge, Mass., 1965); also *Hobbes's System of Ideas* (London, 1965).

replacement of theory by the primacy of practice'.[28] Since, according to Strauss, Hobbes conceived the aim of history to be to act as a guide for human behaviour, he believed that the virtue of 'honour' should be the directive for all human action. It was, in Strauss's view, the 'humanist' Hobbes, still sensitive to the Renaissance theme of the *cortegiano*, who recommended to the young William Cavendish, third Earl of Devonshire, the writings of Thucydides as 'having in them profitable instructions for noblemen, and such as may come to have the managing of great and weighty actions'.[29] Hobbes therefore ascribed to 'history and civil knowledge' an exceptional importance for the aristocracy.

It is certain that when, in the Epistle Dedicatory of his translation of Thucydides, Hobbes praises 'honour' as the aristocratic virtue which can guide all human behaviour, he is expressing a typically humanistic sentiment. But it is also necessary to emphasise the deeper significance of the model of 'virtue' which Hobbes claimed to have discovered in Sir William Cavendish, second Earl of Devonshire. Because of his solid, rigorous political and historical culture, Sir William represented the antithesis of the demagogue, and of that erudite culture whose aims were ostentation and the influence of human passions.[30]

It seems to me, therefore, that in the ideal of a 'scientific' historiography Hobbes had already expressed that criticism of rhetorical knowledge which, in his later works, he was to identify with the use of language as an instrument of falsehood, bad faith and deceit.

In *De homine* (published in 1658), Hobbes wrote:

it sometimes happens to those that listen to philosophers and Schoolmen that listening becomes a habit, and the words that they hear they accept rashly, even though no sense can be had from them (for such are the kind of words invented by teachers to hide their own ignorance), and they use them, believing that they say nothing. Finally, on account of the ease of speech, the man who truly doth not think, speaks; and what he says, he believes to be true, and he can deceive himself; a beast cannot deceive itself. Therefore by speech man is not made better, but only given greater possibilities.[31]

To a rhetorical knowledge Hobbes opposed 'authentic' know-

[28] L. Strauss, *Political Philosophy of Hobbes*, p. 34.
[29] *Eight Books*, 'Epistle Dedicatory', p. v.
[30] See C. A. Viano, 'Analisi della vita emotiva e tecnica politica nella filosofia di Hobbes', *Rivista critica di Storia della Filosofia*, XVII (1962), 355ff.
[31] *De homine*, Eng. trans. by Charles T. Wood, T. S. Scott-Craig, and Bernard Gert, in *Man and Citizen*, edited with an Introduction by B. Gert (Garden City, New York, 1972), c. X, 3, pp. 40–1.

ledge which was built upon a proper use of language provided by definitions of the meanings of words and of their order within speech.[32]

The aim of this 'authentic' knowledge was to improve intersubjective relationships through the establishment of the supremacy of reason over the passions. Bacon had already defined rhetoric as an apparent or false mode of knowledge, capable only of inspiring conflict and disagreement and of feeding the passions and political struggle. And although he recognised his greatness, Bacon had also seen Aristotle as essentially a proponent of just such knowledge. Bacon had attempted to eliminate what he saw as the negative aspects of classical ethics and which he identified as the primacy of the contemplative over the active life, a lack of any doctrine of social obligation and of a scientific theory of the emotions directed towards the control of human passions.[33]

For the Hobbes of *The Elements of Law Natural and Politic*, Aristotle is also the advocate of a rhetorical, passional, factious kind of knowledge, and he wrote of the University teachings inspired by Aristotelianism that they·

have delivered nothing concerning morality and policy demonstratively: but being passionately addicted to popular government, have insinuated their opinions by eloquent sophistry.[34]

It appears that, when translating Thucydides, Hobbes stressed the role of history as an alternative to rhetoric, rather than as the expression of a concern with morals founded upon a humanistic conception of history. To a non-rhetorical historiography Hobbes assigned the duty of presenting facts and the relationship between them. Politics should then make use of such teaching in order to better organise human society through a reciprocal conformity of ends and means.[35]

I doubt, however, that Hobbes drew the inspiration for his original political thought from his early humanistic–rhetorical culture, as Strauss claims, for this would have been to give to politics

[32] Hobbes exalted language as the 'human specific' in *Leviathan*, P. I, c. IV. Similar reasonings are to be found in *Human Nature*, c. V, and in *De corpore*, P. I, c. II, 1.

[33] On Bacon's views on rhetoric, see Lisa A. Jardine, *Francis Bacon, Discovery and the Art of Discourse* (London, 1974). For Bacon's consideration of Aristotle's philosophy and of classical and Renaissance culture in general, see P. Rossi, *Francesco Bacone: dalla magia alla scienza* (Bari, 1957), pp. 132ff., 400ff. In *The Works of Francis Bacon*, collected and edited by J. Speeding, R. L. Ellis, and D. D. Health (London, 1879), see especially *De dignitate et augmentis scientiarum*, I.

[34] *De corpore politico*, P. II, c. IX, 8 (*E. W.*, IV, p. 219).

[35] C. A. Viano (see n. 30), p. 360.

a moral foundation;[36] and it is only in his anti-rhetorical instance, which he also praises in Thucydides, that we find the revolutionary element of Hobbes's political thought and language. The criticism of rhetoric in itself implies the development of a scientific method.

As an alternative to Aristotelian ethics which speculated upon the 'highest good', Hobbes concentrated upon the construction of a political science able to guarantee stability to human society. The genuine originality of Hobbes's political thought consisted in its evolution as a self-conscious scientific mode of explanation and in its acceptance of the explanatory models of physics and geometry. Once such models had been accepted, it was no longer possible to consider political theory strictly as the product of a political philosophy, as a doctrine in itself or as an emanation of moral theory. Hobbes's main concern for politics, as it is expressed within the 'constructive rigour' of the system, cannot be reduced to the merely *political* parts of that system. The criticism of rhetoric, which Hobbes directed against Aristotelianism and traditional historiography, should be considered as a prelude to the discovery of a scientific method to which history itself had to be subordinated.

III

In *The Elements of Law Natural and Politic*, which Hobbes completed in the form of two treatises in 1640, his anti-rhetorical position appears fully integrated with the new scientific method. In the Epistle Dedicatory he wrote:

From the principal parts of Nature, Reason and Passion, have proceeded two kinds of learning, *mathematical* and *dogmatical*: the former is free from controversy and dispute, because it consisteth in comparing figure and motion only; in which things, *truth*, and the *interest of men*, oppose not each other: but in the other there is nothing undisputable, because it compareth men, and meddleth with their right and profit; in which, as oft as reason is against man, so oft will a man be against reason.[37]

The opposition of science and rhetoric is now particularly clear.

[36] Criticising Strauss's attribution to Hobbes of a bourgeois concept of virtue as the expression of his turning from philosophy to history in search of a normative guidance for politics, Raymond Polin writes that 'la politique de Hobbes ne comporte pas de fondement moral. Ou plutôt, le fondement moral de sa politique, c'est qu'il n'existe pas de fondement moral pour une philosophie politique' (*Politique et philosophie chez Thomas Hobbes*, Paris, 1953, p. 151).
[37] See *Human Nature* (*E.W.*, IV), 'Epistle Dedicatory'.

So-called 'learned' men should be divided into two groups: the *dogmatici*, for whom knowledge derives from persuasion and uncritical acceptance of opinions, and the *mathematici* who found knowledge upon demonstration.[38] Only mathematical knowledge can be taught; dogmatical knowledge, whose sign is controversy, serves only to persuade.[39]

The contrast between these two forms of knowledge becomes even more explicit when Hobbes establishes a new link between politics and geometry. In order to preserve politics from vain eloquence, ideology and abuse, it is necessary to submit it to control. The procedure is twofold: on one side, we must be aware of the historical, and therefore relativistic, origin of our opinions concerning what is just and unjust. This will expose the mystification implied in the presupposed universality of such opinions, and it will then become possible to denounce the state of perpetual war caused by those individuals whose culture is dogmatical or who are instigated by such a culture. On the other side, Hobbes wished to regenerate and to ascribe to politics a new value: once politics has been submitted to the same cognitive model as mathematics and geometry, it would become, he believed, a science of the just and the unjust, a deductive and conventional knowledge proceeding from definitions.

In the Epistle Dedicatory to *The Elements*, Hobbes underlined the many contradictions which are present in writings about justice and politics:

> they who have written of justice and policy in general, do all invade each other and themselves with contradictions. To reduce this doctrine to the rules and infallibility of reason, there is no way, but, first put such principles down for a foundation, as passion not mistrusting, may not seek to displace; and afterwards to build thereon the truth of cases in the law of nature (which hitherto have been built in the air) by degrees, till the whole have been inexpugnable.[40]

In *The Elements* Hobbes accomplished his first coherent attempt to apply the methodologies of the mathematical and physical sciences to the ethical–political world. In particular he established a correspondence between the demonstrative order of geometry and the constructive models of ethics, politics and right.

In the mature period of his philosophical thought, Hobbes imputed the difference between 'modern time' and 'ancient barbarousness' to geometry. In the Epistle Dedicatory to the English

---

[38]   *Ibid.*, XIII, 4, pp. 73–4.   [39]   *Ibid.*, p. 73.   [40]   *Ibid.*, 'Epistle Dedicatory'.

De cive, entitled *Philosophical Rudiments concerning Government and Society*, he claimed that:

If the moral philosophers had as happily discharged their duty, I know not what could have been added by human industry to the completion of that happiness, which is consistent with human life. For were the nature of human actions as distinctly known as the nature of *quality* in geometrical figures, the strength of *avarice* and *ambition*, which is sustained by the erroneous opinions of the vulgar as touching the nature of *right* and *wrong*, would presently faint and languish; and mankind should enjoy such an immortal peace, that unless it were for habitation, on supposition that the earth should grow too narrow for her inhabitants, there would hardly be left any pretence for war.[41]

Hobbes believed that moral philosophy did not determine any progress in the science of natural rights and laws. On the contrary, moral philosophy represented a regressive kind of knowledge which, in many circumstances, had determined the relapse into the *bellum omnium contra omnes*. For Hobbes, the science of rights, as well as any other science, should start from proper principles. An analysis of 'natural justice' could show that *rights* are sanctioned by men's covenants and not by nature. In fact, from two postulates of human nature, which are man's *natural desire* to enjoy for himself communal goods and the dictate of *natural reason* to avoid anything dangerous to his self-preservation, it becomes necessary for covenants to be respected and for moral virtue, as the fulfilment of social duties, to be instituted.[42]

Hobbes described language as the most important of human inventions. The definitory power of language is an indispensable instrument for science and represents the means by which men can stipulate the social contract and hence accomplish peace; but even in the state of nature, language is an instrument and an 'art', and it is precisely the 'art of words' which enables humans to deceive their fellow creatures.

The possibility of falsehood was born together with language itself and it is such as:

some men can represent to others, that which is good, in the likeness of evil; and evil, in the likeness of good; and augment, or diminish the apparent greatness of good and evil; discontenting men and troubling their peace and their pleasure.[43]

---

[41] *Philosophical Rudiments concerning Government and Society*, 'Epistle Dedicatory' (*E. W.*, II, pp. iv–v); my italics. Hobbes expressed similar considerations in *Human Nature*, c. XIII, 3.

[42] *De cive* (Eng. edn), 'Epistle Dedicatory' (*E. W.*, II, pp. v–vi).

[43] *Leviathan*, P. II, c. XVII (*E. W.*, III, p. 157).

The capacity for lying, or the moral indifference of language itself, which every man utilises in order to assert his own superiority over individuals, is one of the reasons why men have to live in societies subjected to a coercive power.

Language and society are, in Hobbes's doctrine, closely connected: the danger implied in vain eloquence, in rhetoric, in words as mere chatter and falsehood, is the risk of a regression to the state of nature, a state not understood, in the Rousseauian sense, as a lost island of happiness behind history, but as an empty space filled with violence, cunning and self-interest. Hobbesian man creates and improves language by working against nature with the aim of controlling nature. The creation of linguistic definitions is a condition of the growth of human reason in the form of scientific knowledge. The opposition of dogmatical and mathematical knowledge, of passions and reason, of logic and rhetoric, may also be set out as the contrast between two different conceptions and contrary uses of *eloquence*.

Now eloquence is twofold. The one is an elegant and clear expression of the conceptions of the mind; and riseth partly from the contemplation of the things themselves, partly from an understanding of words taken in their own proper and definite signification. The other is a commotion of the passions of the mind, such as are *hope, fear, anger, pity*; and derives from a metaphorical use of the words fitted to the passions.[44]

The rejection of scientific anarchy, present in all human sciences that lack the rigour of mathematics and geometry, coincides, in Hobbes's moral consciousness, with a resolute disapproval of ethical–political anarchy, while the need for a universality of knowledge corresponds to the need to create a political community. Hobbes is the philosopher of the commonwealth. This can explain his tendency to sacrifice the possibility of any individualistic–democratic action in favour of the overriding need to defend that community. Rational and mathematical knowledge, which Hobbes in *The Elements* opposes to the emotional and dogmatical one, is thus a universal and communal kind of knowledge. Conventional and artificial language, which is the instrument of science built up *ex definitionibus*, also founds man's moral existence not upon natural law alone, but necessarily upon the enunciation of conventions and positive laws.

The ethical need, present in Hobbes's political and philosophical thought, first of all expresses itself as the ideal of an authentic

[44] *De cive* (Eng. edn), c. XII, 12 (*E. W.*, II, pp. 161–2).

philosophical science as far as this can be really deductive. Only ethical–political science can defeat the war of man against man and it is language which makes possible the construction of such a science, because of its quality as 'anti-nature' and because it represents the first social institution. The significance which Hobbes ascribes to language in its cognitive and ethical–political function has the moral meaning of entrusting man himself with the complete responsibility for his own destiny. Hobbes's realistic observation on human selfishness, in cases where individualism is not corrected by the pedagogical action of institutions, is undoubtedly one of the most modern and lasting aspects of his philosophy.

IV

In *The Elements*, Hobbes described history as a part, not of science, but of prudence. This distinction between 'prudence' and 'science' dates back to one of Hobbes's first drafts of *De corpore*, known as *De principiis*, which was probably composed around 1637.[45] In *De principiis* Hobbes distinguished two kinds of knowledge: 'original' knowledge, which is prudence or 'experience of fact', and 'derivative' knowledge or 'evidence of truth', which is the only true *scientific* knowledge.

'Prudence', which consists of a train of particular effects, impressions and images produced by bodies 'working upon' our senses, is such that we can affirm: 'there is nothing that truly exists in the world but single individuall Bodies producing single and individuall acts'.[46]

Prudence or original knowledge provides science with perceptual data as images or 'phantasmata', stored in the memory. These data are elaborated by means of the linguistic and calcolistic models which belong to 'derivative knowledge'. Hobbes also made the same distinction between two kinds of knowledge in *The Elements*:

there are *two kinds* of knowledge, whereof *one* is nothing but *sense*, or knowledge *original* . . . and *remembrance* of the same; the *other* is called *science* or knowledge of the *truth of propositions*, and how things are called, and is derived from understanding.[47]

---

[45] The Ms 5297 of the National Library of Wales (*De principiis*) was first published by M. M. Rossi, 'L'evoluzione del pensiero di Hobbes alla luce di un nuovo manoscritto', in *Civiltà Moderna*, XIII (1941), 125–50; 217–46; 366–402. A second edition with critical notes is in M. M. Rossi, *Alle fonti del deismo e del materialismo moderno* (Florence, 1942) and I refer to this edition; pp. 103–7.

[46] *De principiis*, fol. Ir, rr. 21–3.   [47] *Human Nature*, c. VI, 1 (*E.W.*, IV, p. 27).

Clearly we can only ascribe the term 'science' to the second kind of knowledge whose truth emerges as evidence from the linguistic order in which experience is organised. Truth was, for Hobbes, a property of speech and not of things themselves.

For the truth of a proposition is never evident, until we conceive the meaning of the words or terms whereof it consisteth, which are always conceptions of the mind.[48]

Both, science and original knowledge, derive from experience; but whereas science originates from the experience of the correct use of words, original knowledge, which is reducible to sense-data, is the experience of those effects which things have on us.

Different sciences are 'registers' of linguistic conventions which establish a concomitance of concepts and the words that signify them.[49] Therefore, if the sciences proceed from the 'remembrance' of the logical–linguistic organisation imposed upon experiential materials, history consists of 'registers' of 'experience of fact'.[50]

In *The Elements*, history is described as nothing but the remembrance of past experience. Remembrance is the way in which experiences have been connected according to a sequence of antecedents and consequents; but to expect things to occur in any particular manner, on the basis of past experience, is merely a presumption of the future.[51] In the same way, to believe that the links which have been observed between past events will repeat themselves in the present is 'conjecture of the past, or presumption of the fact'.[52] The fact that the same antecedents are followed by the same consequents means only that the antecedent and the consequent are '*signs* one of another, as clouds are signs of rain to come and rain of clouds past'.[53] Prudence is therefore the highest level that original knowledge or the experience of facts is able to attain. As Hobbes wrote in *Human Nature*:

Prudence is nothing but conjecture from experience, or taking of signs from experience warily, that is, that the experiments from which he (man) taketh such signs be all remembered; for else the cases are not alike that seem so.[54]

In conclusion, prudence is coterminous with remembrance, and it can be usefully exploited only if its limitation as an exclusively conjectural kind of knowledge, without certainty and evidence, is

---

[48] *Ibid.*, 4, p. 28.
[49] The term 'registers' is used by Hobbes in *Human Nature* (*E.W.*, IV, p. 27).
[50] *Ibid.*   [51] *Ibid.*, c. IV, 7 (*E.W.*, IV, p. 17).   [52] *Ibid.*, 8 (*E.W.*, IV, p. 17).
[53] *Ibid.*, 9 (*E.W.*, IV, p. 17).   [54] *Ibid.*, 10 (*E.W.*, IV, p. 18); my italics.

recognised. As history itself is the remembrance of the past, historical knowledge is nothing but prudence and must therefore be excluded from the ambit of philosophy.

This theoretical position is made clear in the final version of *De corpore*, published in 1655:

we must consider, first, that although Sense and Memory of things, which are common to man and all living creatures, be knowledge, yet because they are given us immediately by nature, and not gotten by ratiocination, they are not philosophy.

Secondly, seeing Experience is nothing but memory; and Prudence, or prospect into the future time, nothing but expectation of such things as we have already had experience of, Prudence also is not to be esteemed philosophy.

By *ratiocination*, I mean *computation* . . . all ratiocination is comprehended in these two operations of the mind, addition and substraction.[55]

The fact that, between translating Thucydides and writing *The Elements*, Hobbes diminished the value ascribed to history and clearly excluded prudence from the ambit of philosophy, is indicative of an evolution of his epistemological model towards a scientific ideal of knowledge. Such a scientific ideal was both the confutation of a Pyrronian scepticism which Gassendi had defended on the grounds of the subjectivity of all sensible phenomena, and a rejection of the theories of substantial forms and of the metaphysical constructions which derived from Aristotle and Descartes.

Hobbes criticised the metaphysical and spiritualistic aspects of Descartes's philosophy but shared with Descartes the project of building up a unitary scientific system founded upon a demonstrative methodology capable of explaining all sensible phenomena. If Hobbes rejected the ontology of substantial forms, he nevertheless, together with Galileo and Descartes, tried to place scientific explanations on an ontological basis. Hobbes intended that scientific knowledge should have in itself the 'evidence of truth' which derives from the logic of scientific discourse.

In his *Objectiones* to Descartes's *Meditationes de prima philosophia*, Hobbes rejected the Cartesian notion of evidence, founded upon the clarity and distinctiveness of the 'idea' or mental content.[56] The only Cartesian principle Hobbes accepted was the validity of rational deduction, which he used to confirm the empirical origin of mental

[55] *Of Body*, P. I, c. I, 2 (*E.W.*, I, p. 3).
[56] Hobbes, *Objectiones ad Cartesii Meditationes* (*O.L.*, V); especially Objectio II, III and IV.

ideas and the causal links between phenomenal appearances and their supposed external reality.[57]

The same ideal distance which had separated Descartes's epistemological model from Gassendi's and Mersenne's, also separated them from Hobbes's interpretation of scientific knowledge. For Mersenne's mechanism provided a scheme for the representation of natural phenomena but did not arrive at any demonstrative dimension, while in Gassendi's model of scientific explanation, experimental practice had no connection with the constructive dimension of science nor with the mathematical order of scientific theories.[58]

A comparison between Hobbes's and Descartes's views of history might be enlightening at this point. Descartes denied any value to history as true knowledge since he had based his principal methodological presupposition on the rejection of all probable and conjectural knowledge. In the second of his *Regulae ad directionem ingenii*, Descartes wrote that we should be interested only in those objects whose 'certain' knowledge derives from the 'evidence' of our mental ideas:

Science in its entirety is true and evident cognition . . . Hence it were better not to study at all than to occupy one's self with objects of such difficulty, that, owing to our inability to distinguish true from false, we are forced to regard the doubtful as certain; for in those matters any hope of augmenting our knowledge is exceeded by the risk of diminishing it.[59]

In the same *Regula II*, he went on to make a distinction between two sources of knowledge, of which the former, experience, is often fallacious, whereas the latter, deduction:

cannot be erroneous when performed by an understanding that is in the least degree rational . . . none of the mistakes which men can make (men, I say, not beasts) are due to faulty inference; they are caused merely by the

[57] See also *Leviathan*, P. I, c. I: 'All which qualities, called *sensible*, are in the object, that causeth them, but so many several motions of the matter, by which it presseth our organs diversely. Neither in us that are pressed, are they any thing else, but divers motions; for motion produceth nothing but motion' (*E.W.*, III, p. 2).

[58] See Pierre Gassendi, *Excercitationes paradoxicae adversus Aristoteleos* (1624), in *Opera omnia*, 6 vols. (Lyon, 1658, reprinted Stuttgart–Bad Cannstatt, 1964); Marin Mersenne, *Harmonie universelle, traitez de la nature des sons, et de movemens de toutes sortes de corps* (Paris, 1636; facsimile edn Paris, 1963). On Gassendi's empiricism, see T. Gregory, *Scetticismo ed empirismo: studio su Gassendi* (Bari, 1961). On Gassendi's and Mersenne's 'constructive' scepticism, see R. H. Popkin, *The History of Scepticism from Erasmus to Descartes* (Assen, 1960); on limitations of Gassendi's empiricism, see O. R. Bloch, *La Philosophie de Gassendi* (The Hague, 1971).

[59] *Rules for the Direction of Mind*, by René Descartes, Eng. transl. by Elizabeth S. Haldane and G. R. T. Ross (Cambridge, 1972), I, p. 3.

fact that we found upon a basis of poorly comprehended experiences, or that propositions are posited which are hasty and groundless.

This furnishes us with an evident explanation of the great superiority in certitude of Arithmetics and Geometry to other sciences. The former alone deal with an object so pure and uncomplicated, that they need make no assumptions at all which experience renders uncertain, but wholly consists in the rational deduction of consequences.[60]

This means, as Descartes states in the *Discours de la méthode*, that we should regard all that is only probable as nearly completely false.[61] The impossibility of building a science upon probable opinions means, for Descartes, that all disputes should be condemned. Discussions and debates are, indeed, signs of the absence of that evidence on which knowledge ought to be built. In the *Regula X*, Descartes excluded the possibility that dialectics might be useful in any search for truth, and relegated them to the status of rhetoric. According to Descartes, history is a 'prejudice' because it is fallacious knowledge depending on experience and usually only on indirect experience. History cannot be identified with the ideal of truth and any historical interest should be connected with an awareness that:

in our search for the direct road towards truth we should busy ourselves with no object about which we cannot attain certitude equal to that of the demonstrations of Arithmetic and Geometry.[62]

For Descartes, then, history is a mere object of erudition which can at best provide only models of moral behaviour or information about the habits of different people. As an object of erudition pragmatically oriented and as a mere rhetorical exercise, history does not seem to provide any knowledge of the past which might allow us to interpret the present. In the *Discours*, Descartes claimed that to spend time reading histories and the 'fables', contained in ancient books, carried the same danger as 'travelling' and 'becoming foreigners in our own country'. Indeed, he claimed, if a man is too attracted by past events, he usually remains ignorant of present facts.[63]

Both Hobbes and Descartes excluded any form of merely conjectural knowledge from the ambit of philosophy. But, when translating Thucydides, Hobbes showed an interest in history which

---

[60] *Ibid.*, pp. 4–5.
[61] See *Discours de la méthode*, in *Oeuvres de Descartes*, ed. Charles Adam and Paul Tannery (reprinted Paris, 1973–4), VI, p. 8, and p. 31.
[62] *Rules for the Direction of Mind*, p. 5.
[63] See *Discours de la méthode*, ed. Adam and Tannery, VI, pp. 6–7.

clearly constituted a rejection of the Cartesian identification of erudition and history. Indeed, Hobbes understood history to be not 'erudition' at all but the 'knowledge of facts'. It is, however, inevitable that Hobbes, like Descartes, should come to the later conclusion that no historical science could ever become a truly 'demonstrative' science.

If, at least in his translation of Thucydides, Hobbes was willing to ascribe to facts a 'specific certainty', he was nevertheless unable to relate such certainty, based as it was only upon a careful judgement of the witnesses to specific human events, to any logical – rational or intuitive evidence. As far as historical facts are concerned, the only legitimate interpretation must be based solely on the internal and external circumstances of those facts themselves. There is, here, not a contradiction, but a real continuity in Hobbes's evaluation of the cognitive status of rhetorical knowledge, from his translation of Thucydides to *The Elements*. For if, in *The Elements*, 'history' is compared to 'prudence', this must be understood to mean that historical knowledge has two important functions. The first of these is to unmask the metaphysical foundations and the supposed universality of the theories of rights and civil society. It is necessary, Hobbes insisted, to emphasise the historical, and therefore neither necessary nor universal, origin of the values of justice:

As in conjecture concerning things past and future, it is prudence to conclude from experience, what is like to come to pass, or to have passed already; so it is an error to conclude from it, that *it is* so or so *called*; that is to say, we cannot from experience conclude, that any thing is to be called *just* or *unjust*, *true* or *false*, or any proposition *universal* whatsoever, except it be from remembrance of the use of names imposed arbitrarily by men: for example, to have heard a sentence given in the like case, the like sentence a thousand of times is not enough to conclude by: but it is *necessary*, for the drawing of such conclusion, to *trace* and *find out*, by many experiences, what men do mean by calling things just and unjust.[64]

Theories concerning politics and rights are, he claimed, imputable to particular social and historical contexts:

Though words be the *signs* we have of another's *opinions* and intentions, because the *equivocation* of them is so *frequent according* to the *diversity of contexture*, and of the company wherewith they go, which, the presence of him that speaketh, our *sight* of his *actions*, and *conjecture* of his *intentions*, must help to discharge us of; it must therefore be *extremely hard* to find the *opinions* and meaning of those *men* that are *gone from us long ago*, and have left us no other signification thereof than their books, which cannot possibly be understood

[64] *Human Nature*, c. IV, 11 (*E.W.*, IV, pp. 18–19).

without *history*, to discover those aforementioned circumstances, and also without great prudence to *observe* them.[65]

For the Hobbes of *The Elements*, then, history could not belong to the domain of science because it had revealed the 'relativism' of all human behaviour. But the second function which history was to perform was precisely that of disclosing the negative consequences of relativism together with the necessity of defining what is *just* and *unjust* within 'authentic' knowledge. The conclusion was, of course, that science should take the place of history and that we should construct our ethics, jurisprudence and politics as a process which is essentially synthetic. As Hobbes wrote in *De homine*:

So, just as the proverb hath it, 'So many men, so many opinions', one can also say, 'Many men, many different rules for vice and virtue'. Nevertheless, what is to be understood about men insofar as they are men, is not applicable insofar as they are citizens; for those who are outside of a state are not obliged to follow another's opinion, while those in a state are obliged by covenants. Whence it is to be understood that they, who consider men by themselves and as though they existed outside of civil society, can have no moral science because they lack any certain standard against which virtue and vice can be judged and defined. For all sciences begin with definitions, or otherwise they must not be called sciences, but mere verbiage.[66]

The role played by history is therefore fundamental to our understanding of the development of Hobbes's philosophical thought, because history allowed all men to achieve a better understanding of the practical world as well as the recognition that the adherence to true political *science* was the means to fulfil those social duties which are required by every member of civil society.

[65] *Ibid.*, c. XIII, 8 (*E.W.*, IV, p. 75).
[66] *De homine*, Eng. transl. c. XIII, 8, pp. 68–9.

14

Saint-Simon and the passage from
political to social science

ROBERT WOKLER

I

In perhaps the most profound of several remarkable contributions
to social theory, Michel Foucault has claimed that man as a subject of
science was invented around the end of the eighteenth century. It
was then, he contends in *Les Mots et les choses*, that our conceptions of
labour, life and language were transformed from taxonomies of the
mind, body and action into etiologies of forces, causes, and origins
which the human sciences have ever since sought to uncover.[1] In this
metamorphosis of Western thought, the period from 1775 to 1795
is portrayed as decisive. During that interval, Adam Smith's perception of labour as the measure of value is judged to have been superseded by Ricardo's view of labour as productive activity which lay at
the source of value – a principle held to be fundamental to the
modern science of economics. Around the same time, Jussieu's
classification of the structures and functions of bodily organs came
to be replaced by Cuvier's account of an organic structural plan of
living beings around which the science of biology has since been
shaped. So too was Wilkins's theory of universal grammar,
conceived as a system of verbal signs, supplanted by Bopp's analysis
of language in terms of historical roots and origins, which have
thereafter come to be traced by the modern science of philology.

Of course these representative thinkers are only illustrative of the
striking changes in the new map of scientific knowledge which
Foucault plots, and it may be unimportant for his purposes that their
writings span a period of more than one hundred years before, and

[1] See Michel Foucault, *Les Mots et les choses* (Paris, 1966), chs. 8 and 10. For a more
general assessment of Foucault's contribution to the history of the human sciences,
see especially Pamela Major-Poetzl, *Michel Foucault's Archeology of Western Culture*
(Brighton 1982).

nearly half a century after, the year 1795 which he suggests is pivotal. More disconcerting is Foucault's extremely dense language, which obscures many of his specific points and indeed renders great tracts of his argument unintelligible. And yet, writ large in his manner, the overall case he presents is grandly impressive. With regard to the development of the human sciences, it confirms the importance attached to the period around the end of the eighteenth century by more mundane practising historians of ideas, most notably Sergio Moravia, who locates the *idéologues* at the nexus of a new *science de l'homme*, and Georges Gusdorf, whose immense history of the human sciences draws to its close then, with the fulfilment and fruition of already established disciplines.[2]

On the evidence which no doubt underpins Foucault's account, it does appear to be the case that at least the period from around 1780 to 1810 marks, in linguistics, the demise of universal grammar and the birth of philology, as well as the passage from eighteenth-century natural history to nineteenth-century biology. More problematic, no doubt, is his claim that modern economics draws its impetus from the displacement of Smith's analysis of the wealth of nations by Ricardo's political economy, but, on the other hand, the same epoch also brings to their end the speculative or conjectural histories of the Enlightenment, and gives rise to craniology, phrenology, and the sciences of the brain as alternatives to earlier philosophies of the mind. Even the fundamental terminology of the modern human sciences – for instance, anthropology, psychology, and biology – was either invented or took on new meanings then, and in 1796 there appears for the first time the word *idéologie*, in its original sense as the science of ideas, to be followed not very long afterwards by the doctrines of 'liberalism' and 'socialism' – ideologies which, with their associated institutions, shaped much of nineteenth-century political and intellectual life.

Whether or not our modern human sciences first arose around the end of the eighteenth century, they certainly acquired new forms then that were unlike any of the studies of human nature before. The history of these developments, some of whose deeper structures have now been excavated by Foucault, still remains to be written. My aim here is to sketch a very preliminary contribution to that history with reference to the idea of a social science, which also dates from this period. It is regrettable that Foucault should have ignored the unfolding of *la science sociale* in his account of the metamorphosis

[2] See Sergio Moravia, *Il pensiero degli idéologues: scienza e filosofia in Francia (1780–1815)* (Florence, 1974), and Georges Gusdorf, *Les Sciences humaines et la pensée occidentale*, 8 vols. (Paris, 1966–78).

of *les sciences humaines*, since in its proper place it would have lent more substantial weight to his argument as a whole. But I shall equally try to show that its early history points to other defects of Foucault's account, which similarly stand in need of revision or correction, and this in four main ways.

First, it shows that in order to understand the genesis of the so-called human sciences around the end of the eighteenth century, historians will need to take note not only of new concepts and their vocabularies but also of the newly born scientific institutions and societies which in the 1790s promoted and sponsored the study of *la science de l'homme*. Second, it shows that at least with regard to the political and social sciences it is impossible to ignore the significance which their early exponents attached to the greatest political and social upheaval they believed the world had ever known, and through which they lived – that is, the French Revolution. Third, it accords pride of place in the early development of the social sciences, and particularly their disengagement from a previous association with political science, to the contribution of Saint-Simon in particular. Fourth, it suggests, paradoxically, that in the first efflorescence of the human sciences along the lines Foucault conceived, man was not so much invented as discarded, with the new study of the underlying forces that shape our will substituted for the idea of human agency that lay at the heart of the now superseded political sciences.

II

The early history of the term 'social science' has been researched before,[3] and its first recorded usage thus far uncovered can be found in the initial issue of the abbé Sieyes's *Qu'est-ce que le tiers-état?*, published in January 1789. 'Si nous voulons actuellement considérer le même sujet d'après les principes qui sont fait pour l'éclairer,' Sieyes remarked,

c'est-à-dire, d'après ceux qui forment la science sociale, indépendamment de tout intérêt particulier, nous verrons prendre à cette question une face nouvelle.[4]

[3] Chiefly by Moravia (see pp. 743–53); Gusdorf (see VIII, pp. 392–406); Keith M. Baker (see 'The early history of the term "social science"', *Annals of Science*, XX (1964), 211–26, and *Condorcet: From Natural Philosophy to Social Mathematics* (Chicago, 1975), pp. 391–5); and Brian W. Head (see 'The origins of "La science sociale" in France, 1770–1800', *Australian Journal of French Studies*, XIX (1982), 115–32).

[4] Sieyes, *Qu'est-ce que le tiers-état?*, ed. Roberto Zapperi (Geneva, 1970), p. 151. The term *la science sociale* only figured in the first edition of this text, however, giving way in all subsequent editions to the expression *la science de l'ordre social*. Its use in *Qu'est ce que le tiers-état?* has been noted by Head.

In the light of the meanings subsequently ascribed to it, and in view
of the fact that in the same year Sieyes went to some lengths to
dissociate the problems of morals and politics from the methods of
the natural sciences, his use of the term in the most important and
influential of all French Revolutionary political tracts is particularly
striking. For Sieyes, the truths of the natural world and those of the
moral order were distinct, the one dealing with quantities, the other
with qualities, the one pertaining to what is, the other concerned
with the utility of man.[5]

Most of the pioneering uses of the term, however, were less
discriminating. Condorcet cited it apparently for the first time in
January 1792 in his 'Projet de décret sur l'organisation sociale',
where he joined it to the study of morals and seems to have conflated
its meaning with what he had earlier termed *l'art social*, whose aim
was to implement the political principles implied by the science.
In his later writings, according to Keith Baker, Condorcet
distinguished at least two further senses of *la science sociale*, one meaning the principles of social organisation derived from the analysis of
sensations and ideas, the other a statistical science of man in society.[6]
But this last conception, the most peculiar to Condorcet, was to
have no significant bearing upon later thinkers, while the first and
second, as we shall see, were to be developed by Saint-Simon in a new
idiom that launched the social sciences in a direction wholly
different from that which Condorcet had envisaged.

Even before Condorcet's first reference to *la science sociale*, the term
had been employed by Dominique-Joseph Garat in December 1791,
in a pamphlet addressed to Condorcet, in which he had commented
on the political principles of the *Encyclopédistes*, and above all on
Rousseau's notion of popular sovereignty and Montesquieu's
doctrine of the distinction of powers, noting, nevertheless, that such
ideas did not fully embrace *la science sociale* until men of good will
put them into practice in the constitutions of enlightened states.[7]
Pierre-Louis Lacretelle, moreover, in his *De l'établissement des
connoissances humaines*, also dating from 1791, used the term, which he
called *la science par excellence*, to embrace man's general duties,
passions, and faculties and all the principles of our social
relations.[8]

[5] See Sieyes, *Vues sur les moyens d'exécution dont les représentants de la France pourront disposer en 1789*, 2nd edn (1789), pp. 29–33, and Archives Nationales Paris, Fonds Sieyes, 284.AP.2, dossier 3.
[6] See Baker, *Condorcet*, pp. 371–3.
[7] See Garat's letter to Condorcet (Paris, 1791), p. 82, cited in Baker, 'The early history of the term "social science"', p. 219.
[8] See Lacretelle, *De l'établissement des connoissances humaines* (Paris, 1791), p. 54. The

It appears from these early, almost casual, invocations of *la science sociale*, therefore, that the term was at first ill-defined, confusing ideas of both science and art, and of principle and its application. More important, however, is the fact that each author assimilated his conception of a social science with other human sciences, including, as Lacretelle put it, *la morale* and *la politique*, whose integration it was the task of *la science sociale* to achieve. Garat supposed that such political principles as Rousseau and Montesquieu had devised were themselves actually constitutive elements of *la science sociale*, while Condorcet frequently defined the human sciences in general as *les sciences morales* or even *les sciences morales et politiques*, now at long last, he believed, set to advance on the model of the physical sciences. In each of these rudimentary formulations *la science sociale*, then, was to be politically realised in a new social order already launched by the French Revolution, which in its advent had for the first time in human history made possible the political fulfilment of a true science of society.

This first association of *la science sociale* with politics and the Revolution is scarcely surprising, since every one of its authors was in 1790 a member of the Société de 1789,[9] a club formed to commemorate the Revolution and ensure the success of its reconstruction of French society. The task the Société de 1789 set for itself was no less than that of promoting political stability through constitutional reforms based upon the prevailing *sciences morales et politiques*, encapsulated in Condorcet's declared aim in the Société's prospectus, to investigate the principles and means of perfecting *l'art social*. Just as the Académie des sciences, of which Condorcet was the permanent secretary, had as its object the improvement of the sciences of nature, so the Société de 1789 sought to discover, promulgate and implement the truths of society, 'elaborating a rational constitution on the basis of the principles of social science'.[10] The term *la science sociale* may well have entered into public discussion at meetings of the Société de 1789, and it is no doubt in the light of its association with the Société's programme of promoting a new social order that

same discussion, incorporating a reference to *la science sociale*, appears in Lacretelle's article 'Science' for the section on logic, metaphysics and morals of the *Encyclopédie méthodique* which he edited. Because the first volume of this section was published in 1786, Gusdorf dates Lacretelle's use of the term from that year, but the fourth volume, including the article 'Science', actually appeared in 1791, around the same time as *De l'établissement des connoissances humaines*.

9 For a history of the Société de 1789, see especially Augustin Challamel, *Les Clubs contre-révolutionnaires* (Paris, 1895), pp. 391–443, and Baker, 'Politics and social science in eighteenth-century France: the "Société de 1789" ', in *French Government and Society 1500–1850*, ed. J. F. Bosher (London, 1973), pp. 208–30.

10 Baker, 'The "Société de 1789" ', p. 213.

the political character of its first formulations took shape. Here, finally, was heralded the triumph of the philosophy of *les lumières*. The new politics and social science, as Destutt de Tracy observed later about Montesquieu, were the same.[11]

III

Of course, as with so much else in the Revolution, dusk settled quickly over this political dawn of the Enlightenment, and the promise of the Société remained unfulfilled, as the French nation was over-taken by new crises. By 1791, with the defection of many of its members to the ranks of the Jacobins, Feuillants, or Club mon-archique, the Société de 1789 was dissolved. Yet the idea of a general social science which had been kindled in the political imagination of its adherents was soon to be pursued further when several among them, most notably Sieyes, Garat and Cabanis, were elected to the Classe des sciences morales et politiques which formed part of the Institut national des sciences et arts established by the Convention in 1795. One of the six sections of the Classe des sciences morales et politiques was in fact named 'Science sociale, et législation', perhaps thus confirming the connection between political reform and the requisite programme of social science already envisaged by members of the Société de 1789. By 1798, the idea of a social science had indeed become sufficiently familiar for a member of that section, Jean-Jacques-Régis de Cambacérès, to treat the subject in general in a 'Discours sur la science sociale', probably the first work ever published to contain the term 'social science' in its title.[12] In his essay Cambacérès contended that the social sciences embraced the arts, laws and morals, though he focused more attention upon the importance of property for the maintenance of social order, and on the role of government to safeguard that institution. *La science sociale*, he claimed, is in need not only of perfection but indeed of creation, and he called upon artists, scientists, and perhaps above all legislators and jurists to promote it, thereby appealing to that very class of men whose influence Saint-Simon was later to decry in his campaign to promote social sciences of another sort.

Neither the 'Discours sur la science sociale' nor its author were to exercise much influence upon French thought in this period

[11] See Destutt de Tracy, *Commentaire sur l'Esprit des lois de Montesquieu* (Paris, 1819), p. vii.
[12] See the *Mémoires de l'Institut national: sciences morales et politiques*, III (Paris, an IX, 1801), pp. 1–14.

(although Cambacérès later became Napoleon's Second Consul), but other members of the Classe des sciences morales et politiques were to make a considerable impression. It was in his 'Mémoire sur la faculté de penser', presented to the Classe in 1796, that de Tracy, an associate member, introduced the term *idéologie* and his conception of the science of ideas around which many interpretations of the human sciences were soon to be formed. It was to the same Classe des sciences morales et politiques that Cabanis delivered the text which was to become his *Rapports du physique et du moral de l'homme*, in which he expounded his doctrine of *la science de l'homme*, and even *l'Anthropologie*, to denote a synthesis of physiology, morals, and the analysis of ideas. Until its dissolution by Napoleon in 1803 the Classe des sciences morales et politiques bore witness to the ascendancy of the *idéologues* over France's intellectual life and newly established educational system in general, while its members' formulations of *la science de l'homme* were to exercise a preponderant influence, in particular, upon the development of Saint-Simon's own conception of the nature of the social sciences. Some of his contemporaries, especially such liberal thinkers as Constant and Mme de Stael, propounded theories of society and of the evolution of civilisation which had a markedly Scottish flavour, inspired most immediately by the writings of Smith, Ferguson, or Stewart. The principal sources upon which Saint-Simon drew, however, were closer to home, and they were much more fundamentally rooted in a science of man incorporating both *le physique* and *le moral* on the lines set forth by Cabanis and the *idéologues* of the Classe des sciences morales et politiques.

IV

If it was the Enlightenment which had sparked the Revolution with its social doctrines, it was men such as Saint-Simon who fuelled the initial flame. Recollecting the enthusiasms of his youth in a prospectus for an *Encyclopédie* of his own, he maintained that the ideas of Rousseau, Voltaire, Diderot and other *philosophes* had formed the essence of his education, which had accomplished its aim: 'Elle nous a rendus révolutionnaires.'[13] As a French officer in the campaign supporting the War of Independence in America, moreover, he found himself drawn to political science rather than military strategy

---

[13] Saint-Simon, *Projet d'Encyclopédie*, second prospectus (1809), in his *Oeuvres*, 6 vols. (Paris, 1966), VI, p. 281.

and soon resolved to pursue a new career – to study the advance of
the human mind in order to promote the improvement of civilisation.[14] By the late 1790s, as a devotee of courses at the Ecole
Polytechnique and Ecole de Médecine, in letters addressed to the
Société du Lycée Républicain, and in the salon of intellectuals he
established at the Hôtel Chabanis, he had come to concentrate all his
energies upon the advancement of science and of scientific education as the principal generators of humanity's progress.

His first major work, the *Lettres d'un habitant de Genève* of 1802, set
forth the proposition that such progress had always been due to the
efforts of great scientists, artists and men of towering intellect like
Newton, who had seized the sceptre of public opinion, thus
vanquishing the force of inertia and pointing the way to the happiness of mankind. By 1804, in an 'Extrait sur l'organisation sociale',
he had come to the view that this happiness could only be attained
through a positive *science de l'organisation sociale*, which in the
nineteenth century must follow in the train of the progress already
made by the exact sciences in the previous century.[15] That thesis was
subsequently elaborated at length in his *Introduction aux travaux
scientifiques du XIXe siècle* of 1807–8 and was taken up again in his
Mémoire sur la science de l'homme of 1813, where he claimed that it was
vital to deal comprehensively with all the sciences of man, so as to
promote the reconstruction of our systems of morality, religion and
politics, and thereby the reorganisation of Europe society itself.

In all these and several other works of the same period and later,
Saint-Simon faithfully adopted his precursors' schemes of establishing an exact social science on the model of the natural sciences and
furthermore of implementing it in public policy. His writings very
frequently exhibit and pay tribute to the influence of earlier
thinkers, for instance d'Alembert and especially Condorcet, who is
credited with the central idea developed in his 'Extrait sur l'organisation sociale'. At the same time, however, his acknowledgement and
perception of his intellectual debts shed important light upon differences between his own conception of the social sciences and the
accounts earlier foreshadowed by the *philosophes* of the Enlightenment or envisaged by the members of the Société de 1789. In his
Mémoire sur la science de l'homme, Saint-Simon claimed that his doctrine
was based upon the work of four major thinkers, to whose writings

---

[14] See Saint-Simon, 'Lettres à un americain', in *L'Industrie* (1816–18), *Oeuvres*, I, pt 2,
pp. 148–9.
[15] See Saint-Simon, 'Extrait sur l'organisation sociale', appended to Alfred Pereire's
edition of his *Lettres d'un habitant de Genève* (Paris, 1925), p. 93.

his attention had been drawn by one individual who gave him personal encouragement, and that it only assembled, combined, organised and completed the ideas expressed in these sources, drawing out the consequences from their principles. The four thinkers he cites are Vicq-d'Azyr, Bichat, Condorcet and Cabanis, and his acknowledged patron is Jean Burdin.[16] From Saint-Simon's perspective of the consequences stemming from these figures' works there emerges an idea of the social sciences strikingly distinct from any earlier doctrine – and one which with regard to this subject, and perhaps for the first time, fulfils the conditions stipulated by Foucault as characteristic of the general rise of the human sciences at the end of the eighteenth century.

Burdin, himself the author of a substantial *Cours d'études médicales ou exposition de la structure de l'homme* published in 1803, appears to have inspired Saint-Simon's interest in the construction of a positive science to supplant scientific conjecture, and it was he, claims Saint-Simon, who conceived such a science as formed from the anatomy of Vicq-d'Azyr, the physiology of Bichat, the psychology of Cabanis, and the philosophical history of Condorcet. This positive science was to be physiology, a subject which, throughout his life, Saint-Simon took to be pre-eminent among the human sciences in general. 'C'est en considérant comme phénomènes physiologiques nos relations sociales que j'ai conçu le projet que je vous présente', he had already remarked in his *Lettres d'un habitant de Genève* (*Oeuvres*, I, pt 1, p. 40). And when in 1825, in his last year, his disciple Etienne-Marin Bailly drafted a work entitled *De la physiologie sociale* as a compendium of his views on such a science, Saint-Simon added a postscript reminding his readers yet again of the importance of physiological observations for the study of society, noting, in the language of Cabanis, how moral and physical properties react upon one another, for instance when the moral ferment of eighteenth-century *philosophes* had provoked the physical forces of the Revolution. Through Burdin as well, moreover, Saint-Simon first became familiar with a central tenet of the physiology of his own day – in effect that the level of intelligence of organisms is proportionate to the degree of perfection of their structures. That idea lent itself readily to Saint-Simon's dual conception of 'organisation' as both a complex internal arrangement and equally an organic body as a whole, and it encouraged him to look upon the constitution and

[16] See Saint-Simon, *Mémoire sur la science de l'homme*, *Oeuvres*, V, pt 2, pp. 21 and 175.

morphology of social bodies in an idiom which had not been explored before.

Saint-Simon, as has been noted, never himself used the word *sociologie*, which was coined by his most famous protégé, Comte, nor, so far as I have been able to ascertain, did he ever mention the term *la science sociale* already current in his day. His closest approximation to that language may well be in the passage from the 'Extrait sur l'organisation sociale' I have already cited, in which he speaks of 'la science de l'organisation sociale'. This is, however, a significant expression in Saint-Simon's vocabulary, for the positive science of society he envisaged was indeed the science of social organisation, conceived on the model of a physiology of organised bodies ('les corps organisés'), which included man ('le plus organisé de tous').[17] Durkheim, in whose intellectual formation such a doctrine figured prominently, was mistaken when he later attributed the *Physiologie sociale*, and its comments on *le corps social* animated by the organisation of its parts, to the pen of Saint-Simon himself. But the perspective on the nature of the social sciences embodied in that work, and in its title, were indeed drawn directly from Saint-Simon, and it set apart his own views from earlier conceptions of the social sciences in a number of striking ways.

V

One of these ways is the sense in which it inspired the idea, frequently expounded in his theory of history, that the critical and revolutionary philosophy of the eighteenth century must be superseded in the nineteenth century by a philosophy of organisation. In the light, above all, of physiological knowledge, men of science and letters must now seek to reconstitute the body politic which had come to be disorganised in pursuit of the doctrines of the previous age.[18] Without organisation there could only be anarchy, Saint-Simon believed, a thesis he propounded in his *Mémoire sur la science de l'homme* even in criticism of Vicq-d'Azyr ('ce père de la science positive'), who had wrongly supposed that the formation of vital matter was not subject to the fundamental natural law of attraction.[19] It thus

---

[17] *Ibid.*, pp. 173–4. On the subject of Saint-Simon's debt to Burdin and interest in physiology, see especially Henri Gouhier, *La Jeunesse d'Auguste Comte*, 3 vols. (Paris, 1933–41), II, pp. 180–200.

[18] See the *Mémoire sur la science de l'homme*, *Oeuvres*, V, pt 2, pp. 194–5, and *De la réorganisation de la société européenne* (1814), *Oeuvres*, I, pt 1, p. 158.

[19] See the *Mémoire sur la science de l'homme*, *Oeuvres*, V, pt 2, pp. 202–4.

appears that Saint-Simon's paramount commitment to an idea of social cohesion based on physiological organisation almost undermined his professed enthusiasm for Enlightenment ideals, a factor which may help to explain why this precursor of socialism sometimes found himself in agreement with conservative critics of both the Enlightenment and the Revolution, such as Bonald, who held to a rather less scientifically informed conception of the nature of order in society.

The same physiological perspective may also have had some bearing on Saint-Simon's view of religion, so radically different from what he termed the *anti-théologie* of the *Encyclopédistes*.[20] Again in his *Mémoire sur la science de l'homme*, he took issue with Condorcet's supposition, common to most other *philosophes* of the Enlightenment as well, that the Middle Ages had marked a retrograde step in the development of the human mind. Quite the contrary, for Saint-Simon, they had witnessed both the progress of scientific knowledge under the Saracens and an advance of social organisation – indeed the foundation of European society itself – through the bond of religious association Charlemagne had formed with Rome. Much of Saint-Simon's social philosophy was actually designed to bring science and religion together, either through the passage of spiritual power from theologians to physicists and physiologists, or, as he maintained in his last work, *Le Nouveau Christianisme*, in the re-establishment of Christian worship. If physiology embodied the foremost study of *le physique* of mankind, religion encapsulated the highest pursuit of *le moral*, a point of view which perhaps prompted his conviction that religion was necessary for the maintenance of the social order.[21] When in 1858 Enfantin reissued Saint-Simon's *Mémoire* and *Travail sur la gravitation universelle* together with his own *Lettre sur la physiologie*, all three works were given the collective title *Science de l'homme: physiologie religieuse*.

Third, and most important, Saint-Simon's conception of the organisation of society in terms of physiology appears to have been linked to his general distrust of political solutions to social problems of disorder and derangement. We attach too much importance, he wrote in *L'Industrie*, to forms of government, supposing that the right organisation stems from the mere distribution of power. Rather like Burke and other opponents of the French Revolution before him, Saint-Simon deplored the immense influence exercised

---

[20] See *L'Industrie*, *Oeuvres*, I, pt 2, p. 218.
[21] See the *Introduction aux travaux scientifiques du XIXe siècle*, *Oeuvres*, VI, p. 170.

over the government of France by lawyers and jurists, which had been calamitous both under Robespierre and the Committee of Public Safety and again when the despotism of Napoleon had overnight converted republican lawyers into proselytes of his supreme authority.[22] The *industriels* had not played an active part in the Revolution, he complained; indeed, they had been among its principal victims,[23] and the social organisation of France had suffered as a consequence. Social hygiene, therefore, rather than political power was required to ensure the proper regulation of the interests of all groups in society. 'Si les physiologistes et les philosophes veulent aujourd'hui réunir franchement leurs efforts,' he observed in the *Mémoire sur la science de l'homme*, 'ils parviendront à ramener toutes les questions politiques à des considérations d'hygiène.'[24] Only then could the activities of government be superseded by the functions of administration.[25]

VI

Of course Saint-Simon's scheme of administration as contrasted with government did not dispose of political institutions altogether. On the contrary, he believed that the absence of political organisation meant anarchy rather than administration, and anarchy was the greatest of all scourges, from which even the most ignorant members of society recoil in their need for order.[26] What was required, as he put it in *L'Industrie*, was a *new* system of political organisation,[27] in which the *industriels* themselves – that is, men of the highest intellectual and scientific capacity – would assume responsibility for public administration, and he devoted many of his later writings, as well as his short-lived journal, *Le Politique*, to elaborating the complex details of this system. In his social philosophy there is no lack of emphasis upon the need for individual enterprise, nor did his conception of the organisation of society without government imply any withering away of the state.

[22] See *L'Industrie, Oeuvres*, II, pt 1, pp. 81, 123–7 and 162–8. Cf. Bailly's observation in *De la physiologie sociale, Oeuvres*, V, pt 1, p. 185: 'Quel obstacle s'est jusqu'à présent opposé à l'établissement d'une constitution physiologique des sociétés? La lutte qui a toujours existé entre les organes du corps social, entre les chefs et les administrés.'

[23] See *L'Industrie, Oeuvres*, II, pt 1, p. 166.

[24] Saint-Simon, *Mémoire sur la science de l'homme, Oeuvres*, V, pt 2, p. 212. Cf. *De la physiologie sociale, ibid.*, pt 1, pp. 180–2.

[25] See especially Saint-Simon's *De l'organisation sociale* (1825), *Oeuvres*, V, pt 1, pp. 130–1 and 138–9, and *L'Organisateur* (1819–20), *Oeuvres*, II, pt 2, pp. 186–8.

[26] See Saint-Simon, *Lettres d'un habitant de Genève, Oeuvres*, I, pt 1, p. 33.

[27] See Saint-Simon, *L'Industrie, Oeuvres*, I, pt 2, p. 182.

But his concern with the administrative control of social affairs instead of the exercise of political power marked an important development in the history of the human sciences. For one thing, all formal institutions of government and sovereignty were in his doctrine rendered insignificant against the background of society's infrastructure and organisation. No longer could *la science sociale* envisaged by Condorcet and the other members of the Société de 1789 be deemed the same as *l'art social*, to be implemented and enacted in a programme of legislative and constitutional reform. Neither the Rousseauist general will nor the Napoleonic will of the general could have any real bearing upon his conception of order in society – best preserved, he supposed, by the maintenance of social hygiene, instead of the imposition of political control. With Saint-Simon's doctrine, quite unlike any earlier schemes of social science, we find the fulfilment of the prognosis of Pope's couplet from *An Essay on Man*,

> For Forms of Government let fools contest;
> Whate'er is best administer'd is best.

His idea of social organisation as patterned on the model of a physiological system also turned sharply away from most characteristic Enlightenment perspectives on the nature of man and society in a second and still more important sense, and this along just those lines which Foucault has suggested mark the inception of the human sciences in general. Saint-Simon's perspective, that is, was focused upon the study of mechanisms within the human body, scrutinised at a deeper level of more fundamental causes than could be uncovered from the general principles of the nature of man, which had been the object of scientific reflection before. When Hume had considered whether politics could be reduced to a science and had come to the conclusion that 'good laws may beget order', he had been in no doubt of the fact that this science must refer directly to the human will and to human action. That point of view similarly informed Mirabeau's *La Science ou les droits et les devoirs de l'homme*, for instance, and it was common as well to Ferguson's *Principles of Moral and Political Science* and to Filangieri's *La scienza della legislazione*. Each of these and many other Enlightenment contributions to the human sciences incorporated claims about what it is that persons have a mind to do, and how they ought to behave, in the light of such truths as could be established about man's nature. In the language of Cabanis, one might almost say that they aimed to understand the human passage from *le physique* to *le moral*. Saint-Simon, however, by concentrating upon the internal functions and structures of the social body – upon forces operating independently of the human will,[28] as Marx would later maintain in another idiom – developed a theory which passed from *le moral* to *le physique*. In addressing himself to the physiological foundations of the organisation of society he did not help to invent, but rather cast aside, the sciences of man that had already been formed in the Enlightenment.

[28] See Saint-Simon, *L'Organisateur, Oeuvres*, II, pt 2, p. 199: 'Ces questions ... sont éminemment positives ... les décisions ne peuvent être que le résultat de démonstrations scientifiques, absolument indépendantes de toute volonté humaine.'

15

◁ ════════════════════════════════════ ▷

Alexander Hamilton and the language of political science

JUDITH N. SHKLAR

'These calculations cannot absolutely be relied on because the data are necessarily uncertain; but they are the result of the best information I can obtain.'[1] So wrote Alexander Hamilton to his friend Robert Morris in 1782 about New York's balance of trade with the other states. At the very least we would recognise this as the letter of a very fact-minded man with a strong sense of the difference between social knowledge and good guessing. Given their contemporary resonance, we might even claim that Hamilton's words are still our own. And, indeed, if by vocabulary we mean just words or general expressions, then the continuity of the language of social science would be established by sentences such as this one. However, even if we mean to think of vocabularies that endure more comprehensively, as reminders of the extraordinary capacity of intellectual and moral dispositions to survive intact under the assaults of social change, we would find a significant example of such longevity here.[2] One ought not to claim too much or too little, in this case. Hamilton was in many ways an oddity among the Americans of his time. Some of this ideas were a 'gigantic irrelevancy' for many of them.[3] He was isolated in many ways, especially in his preference for a strong central government. It would therefore be absurd to treat his voice as representative of an age. What can, however, be said is that though his vocabulary does not tell us what words and sentiments were then

[1] *The Papers of Alexander Hamilton*, ed. C. Syrrett and J. E. Cook (New York, Columbia University Press, 1962), III, p. 135.
[2] For a discussion of these issues generally, see Georges Duby, 'The history of systems of values', in *The Chivalrous Society*, translated by Cynthia Postan (Berkeley, University of California Press, 1980), p. 216.
[3] Robert Dahl, *A Preface to Democratic Theory* (Chicago, University of Chicago Press, 1963), p. 11. For his lack of political success in New York, see David H. Fischer, *The Revolution of the Conservatives* (New York, Harper and Row, 1965), p. 20.

in or out of fashion, they do tell us something interesting about what was being discussed and why it was being talked about in still very recognisable and relevant ways. Specifically, Hamilton spoke for and of American political science.

Alexander Hamilton's best-known contributions to social theory are the two reports on economic policy, one on manufactures, the other on public credit, that he submitted as Washington's Secretary of the Treasury. They reveal a man well-read in the literature of political economy of his time, as well as his own avowed admiration for Colbert.[4] They are also extensions of the views expressed earlier as one of the authors of the *Federalist Papers*, written to urge the ratification of the proposed Federal Constitution of 1787. Whatever the contribution of European thinkers to Hamilton's education in economics was, it could not extend to politics. Even Montesquieu, to whom the *Federalist* owes much, could only instruct Hamilton and his collaborator Madison philosophically. The actual practices of representative democracy were wholly unknown in Europe, and Americans had to devise their own vocabulary for dealing with their novel institutions of government. Among the latter were elections, which were frequent and, by European standards, enormously democratic. Although he did not approve of democratic values, Hamilton never doubted the absolute necessity of a broadly based suffrage in a republic.[5] And there is, in principle at least, no contradiction between that view and the active central state which he all but alone proposed. For as he enhanced the social significance of government in general, the importance of those who chose it also grew. That may well be why Hamilton's one essay on elections in the *Federalist* is so peculiarly familiar in tone. The thirty-fifth *Federalist*, which displays all his powers of political analysis at that moment in his public career, is prophetic rather than seminal, since it was not the first in a series of similar writings by him. But it does introduce one of the typical vocabularies of representative democracy; the analysis of voting behaviour. Too bold and too calculating in his public discourse, Hamilton was far too much of a loner to influence

[4]   R. J. Parks, *European Origins of the Economic Ideas of Alexander Hamilton* (New York, Arno Press, 1977) names Montesquieu, Hume, Postlewayt and Richard Price, among others. Clinton Rossiter, *Alexander Hamilton and the Constitution* (New York, Harcourt, Brace and World, 1964), pp. 113–52.
[5]   'Remarks in Favor of a Motion Increasing the Number of the House of Representatives'. Constitutional Convention, 8 September 1787, *Papers*, IV, p. 244. *The Federalist*, ed. Clinton Rossiter (New York, New American Library), no. 22, p. 152. Broadus Mitchell, *Alexander Hamilton* (New York, MacMillan, 1957), I, pp. 441–65.

anyone around him. So the study of elections was left to lesser journalists for well-informed, but not scientific, reporting. It was only in the first decades of the present century, with the availability of precise census figures, that the scientific study of voting behaviour began.[6] It came, one might note also, at a time when central government became preponderant in every way, and when the suffrage had at last become universal.[7] Survey research is relatively new, but the importance of voting was recognised as a central moment in representative democracy from the first. What gives Hamilton's essays in the *Federalist* their present immediacy now is the joining of a concern for the voter with a scientific turn of mind.

If voting is the central ritual of representative democracy, then it is not at all surprising that it should generate its own language. Elections were a common part of American political life long before the Revolution, and with the ratification of the Constitution they acquired their present rhythm. For two hundred years now Americans have voted for a president every four years, and every two for Congressmen in federal elections, not to mention the numerous state and local elections which were far more important for its political life until relatively recently. Elections have always mattered to all those who participated in them in some way. For citizens 'the simple act of voting' is a ritual that is profoundly reinforced by the deepest democratic myth – that even the federal government acts with the 'consent of the governed.' Elections are what I should like to call 'consequential rituals'; that is, they have very real political results, not only in the ultimate choice of office holders, but also in their attitudes and conduct. They have also had an enormous impact upon the most typical forms of social theory, which is now political science, and which has all along been a part of representative democracy. Democracy as a 'consequential myth', and the rituals associated with it, influence actual practices in a self-validating way. The electoral process is decisively important in American government, but not because it registers the preferences of the majority. Nevertheless, even with free-riders and similar well-known considerations, voters do believe that voting delivers the consent of the governed. And

6   Peter Rossi, 'Four landmarks in voting research', in Eugene Burdick and Arthur J. Broadbeck (eds), *American Voting Behavior* (Glencoe, Illinois, The Free Press, 1959), pp. 5–54.
7   Charles E. Merriam saw at once how much the extension of the suffrage to women stimulated research into voting, and that better census figures invited more rigorous research, see his *American Political Ideas 1865–1917* (New York, Macmillan, 1920), pp. 82–106, 375–76.

oddly, it does, by keeping the elected leaders responsive to the non-leaders, that is to all the rest of us. The capacity to constrain the elected depends on their awareness that they must soon stand for election again, but also on the beliefs they share with most other voters: that their mandate to act at all depends on the voters' choice.[8] The word 'grass roots' is not a trivial one psychologically, rhetorically or practically. Hamilton's associate in the *Federalist*, Madison, certainly knew all this. He had learned it in Virginia as Hamilton had received his political education in New York.

That elections may be recognised as rituals which, among other functions, serve to reinforce democratic beliefs does not alter their practical significance for the process of government. They legitimise and constrain officials and policies. They are as such consequential on several levels and this too has been part of the self-understanding that brought the constitutional project into being. The scientific study of politics has, moreover, similar roots. The actualities of electoral rituals and myth are not masks, nor are they remote from the overt purposes of democracy, and they even achieve some of its ideal aims, even if that be in indirect, complex and partial ways. Those who study voters with a view to an accurate understanding of these phenomena need not separate or distance themselves from the political practices and beliefs of which their science is also a part. For their quest, though different, is not alien to the political world which they study.

From the first, democracy has required a considerable amount of accurate information. Along with regular elections, Americans have also, as mandated by the Constitution, a national census that is published every ten years without fail (Act I, sect. 2). And beyond that there is the need, recognised inevitably by any group of freely elected representatives, to know as much as possible about their constituencies. The demand for information about almost the entire white male population, for the suffrage was very broad, even before most property and tax qualifications for voting disappeared in the 1840s, imposes a radical democratisation on political inquiry. How to assess the behaviour and attitudes of the anonymous many who compose the electorate was a wholly novel intellectual task. So new a democratisation of inquiry and values demanded considerable theoretical effort in 1787, and again when it was taken up with new vigour in the early 1930s. Among the earliest political thinkers, it has always seemed to me, Alexander Hamilton's was one of the most

[8]   Robert Dahl, *Democratic Theory*, p. 131.

significant voices in setting the terms of what is now called political science. In fact, he had already known those words and their uses. Among them was their application to the study of voting. For then, as now, it is the tortuous and long road from the individual voter to the public policies of the federal government that has excited the greatest interest. It obsessed him and it is central to a very substantial part of contemporary survey research. The active, planning, central state of which Hamilton merely dreamed is, to be sure, the political actuality of this science in its present phase. The sources of authority and its ultimate exercise are, however, in either case the focus of calculation. It is of course true that the mathematical refinement and therefore the accuracy of the framed hypotheses and of their disposition is far greater now than it was in the eighteenth century, nor is the population being counted and viewed the same. However, the real puzzle is that given that the culture, geography, economy and technology of America have been transformed, the structure of political discourse has changed so little and that the most characteristic institutions of its representative democracy seem so immune to change. The claim that political science is a new enterprise and that it must first imitate and then catch up with the natural sciences is more an expression of a multiplicity of frustrations than a reflection of either the age or the inner structure of America's typical political science. In fact, the practices of political science are responses to the oldest and most enduring political values and as such prove, if anything, the resilience of at least one of America's earliest vocabularies.

No vocabulary of representative democracy was, however, available to Americans of Hamilton's generation. They had to create it, and did so with considerable floundering and difficulty. Even the phrase 'the people' had by 1787 a different meaning than it had in British English. It meant everyone, as in 'we the people', not a part of the population only.[9] Hamilton's political education, like that of his fellow farmers, was therefore local and indigenous. As the British parliament became increasingly oligarchic, American representative institutions began their steady movement towards political democracy and towards the practices that made the individual voter the ultimate unit of representation.[10] All these changes in all their novelty were the substance of Hamilton's political science. And

[9] Gordon S. Wood, *The Creation of the American Republic* (Chapel Hill, University of North Carolina Press, 1969), pp. 593–612.
[10] J. R. Pole, *Political Representation in England and the American Revolution* (New York, St Martin's Press, 1966), pp. 385–405, 513–16, 526–39.

indeed New York's political history and recent experiences must have provided him with a quite remarkable education. Even in colonial times New York politics aroused much interest because of the intensity of its factional struggles. When the conflict with Great Britain became the paramount issue, these local battles were no longer mere family feuds, but real struggles between interests. By the time New York became a state it was ready for considerable changes. To be sure, the new constitution did retain property qualifications for voting, especially for governor and the senate, but they were not high for the assembly, which was elected annually.[11] Most of New York's free males could vote frequently and by secret ballot. By 1790, 65% to 70% of the male population voted for assembly and it was at a higher rate for local elections. They did so at voting places now deliberately accessible to the common voter. The only major restriction allowed only 30% to vote for senators and the governor.[12] Most striking of all was the suffrage for the convention which met at Poughkeepsie in 1787 to ratify the Federal Constitution. All free male citizens of twenty-one years or over could vote for delegates. The results of that election showed that class was not a decisive issue. Both factions included both wealthy and poor voters whose interests appeared to coincide for some economic or geographic reason. The Federalists, for example, did well in New York City, both among mechanics and merchants.[13]

The states differed considerably from each other politically, but all were by 1787 very remote from any European pattern of government. If New York taught Hamilton about the new politics, Virginia had formed Madison. Madison's was, however, in the *Federalist* another, though equally significant, aspect of political science. He was less concerned with voters. His great claim to fame is that he began that part of political sociology that flourishes in a pluralistic society and which concerns itself with the formation and interactions of interest groups. The model of these was the multiplicity of protestant sects which Madison knew in his native state and from which he extrapolated the likely behaviour of those other groups that regional diversity, social inequality and a free and growing

---

[11] Patricia Bonomi, *A Factious People: Politics and Society in Colonial New York* (New York, Columbia University Press, 1971), pp. 5–16, 279–86. David H. Ellis *et al.*, *A History of New York State* (Ithaca, Cornell University Press, 1967), pp. 113–14, 119–33.

[12] Chilton Williamson, *American Suffrage: From Property to Democracy: 1760–1860* (Princeton, Princeton University Press, 1960), pp. 13, 16–17, 27–8, 107–8, 111–12, 121–2, 124.

[13] Forrest McDonald, *We The People* (Chicago, University of Chicago Press, 1958), pp. 283–310.

economy nurtured. This is also a field now cultivated by survey research and it has obvious bearings on every aspect of politics. However, as general public opinion is not identical with specifically electoral opinion, so the relationship between the two sciences is itself a subject of scholarly dispute. Hamilton is significant for that major part of political science in which electoral acts and their implications count most heavily, not for the sociology of public attitudes generally. Indeed, as an aside, even radical American social scientists use 'critical' elections as their focus of investigations of major social changes in American history.[14] It is not surprising, because it is impossible to think of American politics apart from the processes of representative democracy with its peculiar terms: majority and minority rather than class; local and central, partly because elections are geographically determined, and also because of federalism; voters and candidates, choice and its limits, indifference and activity, habits and issues, and factions and parties. And these terms impose themselves whatever the ideological preferences of the observer–speaker may be. Hamilton, as it happened, was not an enthusiastic supporter of the system he helped others to understand, while most of today's political scientists, on the contrary, tend to be ardently loyal to the constitutional order. It makes no difference; when you enter a ritual, you are going to speak its language. And that language tells us of a huge premium put upon prediction: for everyone cares about the outcome of elections and that itself stimulates science.

The intellectual structure of electoral survey research is not particularly complicated. It works to establish valid generalisations about voters by correlating increasingly detailed and accurate versions of expressed opinions. Mathematically sophisticated and now computerised, it remains basically within the realm of common sense. You test probable abstract statements by correlating the responses of individuals, the only directly observable indivisible units: the voters. This is solid Baconian science and it is just what Hamilton wished to develop as well. A known reader of Hume's essays, and of Montesquieu, he was sure that 'history' taught political psychology. According to his friend Chancellor Kent, he contemplated 'a full investigation of the history and science of civil government . . . and to have the subject treated in reference to past experience upon Lord Bacon's inductive philosophy'.[15] The questions

---

[14] See, e.g., Walter D. Burnham, *Critical Elections and the Mainsprings of American Politics* (New York, Norton, 1970).

[15] William Kent, *Memoirs and Letters of James Kent* (Boston, Little, Brown & Co., 1898), pp. 327–8.

that such a science would ask were not remote from those of voting studies. They were about the responsiveness of governments to the governed, the ability of systems to reconcile groups of people in conflict, and the governability specifically of the American people.[16] It is indeed not surprising that at fifty years of age survey research recognises itself as a legitimate part of political historiography, intellectually, and as a contributor to the public good, ethically.

Unlike Hume, whom history taught that whatever lasted must be good, Hamilton, no less than his successors, was open to novelty and to the constructive efforts of the political will. 'The science of politics ... like most other sciences, has received great improvement. The efficacy of various principles is now well understood, which were either not known at all, or only imperfectly known to the ancients.'[17] Among the things that the science of politics had discovered was the efficacy of representative democracy. Moreover, there was something that the very act of establishing a completely new form of government could prove: 'whether societies of men are really capable or not of establishing good government from reflection and choice, or whether they are forever destined to depend for their political constitution on accident and force'. If Americans chose to make the wrong decisions it would be not only a mistake for them but a 'general misfortune of mankind'.[18] Electoral politics obviously imply a fair degree of voluntarism, voters make their destiny, especially when they vote for a constitution in the first place. That also introduces an element of unpredictability into politics. Discussing the future of military policies Hamilton, for instance, admitted 'how the national legislature may reason ... is a thing which neither [his adversaries] nor I can foresee'.[19] And this again is an invitation to calculation and inferences from past to present. Voters change, representatives have wills. Politics as voting is, in short, a subject for constant investigation, because it is uncertain and yet needs to be grasped.

The kind of information that was really needed was psychological. It is taken for granted that both social groups and individual political agents are moved by 'ambition, avarice and vindictiveness'. Of these the first two are the most important, which makes political behaviour relatively predictable, at least when the most active political people are involved. Hamilton was not disposed to 'view human nature'

[16] Norman H. Nie, Sidney Verba and Jolen R. Petrocik, *The Changing American Voter* (Cambridge, Harvard University Press, 1979), pp. 2–13.
[17] *Federalist*, no. 9, p. 72.   [18] *Ibid.*, no. 1, p. 33.   [19] *Ibid.*, no. 29, p. 185.

other than 'as it is, without either flattering its virtues or exaggerating its vices'.[20] That made him neither anxious, nor excessively optimistic. Indeed, 'utopian' was a word of scorn in his vocabulary.[21] What really impressed him politically, however, was 'the alarming indifference discoverable in the exercise of so valuable a privilege' as voting.[22] All these observations referred back to known behaviour in the several states. Moreover, this mix of ambition, avarice and voter indifference was not random in his view. Like everything else it occurs in a setting that is also subject to reasonably accurate descriptions. The relevant circumstances are the natural wealth and 'the genius of the citizens', the degree of information they possess, the state of commerce, of acts of industry, and 'many more too complex, remote or adventitious to admit of particular specification'. This constitutes 'the wealth of nations' and it is measurable.[23] Apart from voting, politics is in fact highly depersonalised and, indeed, this is necessary for a predictive science of politics. It is also inherent in representative democracy, and for Hamilton that was a sign of the durability of the 'great' republic. Majorities are aggregates, solid wholes. That, in any case, was given: there could be no alteration of majority rule. The 'fundamental maxim of republican government ... requires that the sense of the majority should prevail' and that 'the deliberate sense of the community should govern the conduct of those to whom they intrust the management of their affairs'.[24] Majority government as such was simply 'there', and it was subject to objective investigation.

Like most political scientists, Hamilton thought little of the intelligence or knowledge of the voters.[25] Nevertheless he did not blame them for defects in their conduct. It was always the fault of the candidates and of those who misled or failed to present issues properly to the voters. Among distinguished political scientists it was particularly V. O. Key who came to emphasise that the quality of voters' choices depended on the choices put before them, and articulated for them by candidates. The political science profession's long-standing *cri de coeur* for a 'responsible' two-party system in America carries the same message. It was Hamilton's as well, especially when he argued, for example, for a single executive, whom voters could easily size up and hold fully responsible for his

[20] *Ibid.*, no. 76, p. 458.   [21] *Ibid.*, no. 6, p. 54.   [22] *Ibid.*, no. 61, p. 373.
[23] *Ibid.*, no. 21, pp. 142–3.   [24] *Ibid.*, no. 22, p. 146; no. 71, p. 432.
[25] John C. Miller, *Alexander Hamilton and the Growth of the New Nation* (New York, Harper & Row, 1959), pp. 185–86.

performance in office.[26] It must be said that recently voters have certainly exercised that real if rather negative power.

With all these considerations in mind, Hamilton turned to the composition of the majority, given its primacy in the whole political scheme. How do electors behave? Like present-day researchers Hamilton was no formalist; he looked to 'social alignments'. Today these are perceived as depending on ethnicity, religion and status. Since it was a white and overwhelmingly protestant electorate, Hamilton looked at status and region, the South and North, as also at the more agricultural and the more commercial areas, respectively. Status was, however, the chief object of interest. What he saw in New York, his own state, was as follows: 'Mechanics and manufacturers will always be inclined, with a few exceptions, to give their votes to merchants in preference to persons of their own professions or trades.' They regard a merchant who trades in their products as their 'patron and friend' and they think their interests safer in his hands than in their own. What you have here is an account of deferential voting, but without the usual sneer that often accompanies such observations. The confidence that small landowners have in great planters, Hamilton went on to observe, is equally strong and again rooted in well-understood self-interest. For the psychology is here not one of class deference, but of calculated self-interest, brought out by capable candidates. 'If we take fact as our guide', in short, we will know that rural voters elect moderate proprietors as a rule. Even more than these statistical constants, what matters is the confidence that an individual candidate, rich or poor, can arouse in voters.[27] That is indeed the argument of today of those interested in accurate short-term predictions of voting behaviour, which makes sense, given the very low ideological temperature of American voters and their declining tendency to identify with one of the two parties.[28] There will, therefore, be candidates who succeed without being members of any of the obvious economic groups: the 'learned professions . . . who truly form no distinct interest in society' but who, 'according to their situation and talents', will be 'objects of the confidence and choice' of their communities. By 'learned professions' Hamilton meant lawyers. Voters certainly want candidates who understand 'their

---

[26] V. O. Key, *The Responsible Electorate* (Cambridge, Harvard University Press, 1966); *Federalist*, no. 70, pp. 427–31.

[27] *Federalist*, no. 35, pp. 214–17.

[28] E.g., Stanley Kelley Jr, *Interpreting Elections* (Princeton, Princeton University Press, 1983).

feelings and interests', but to bring diverse groups together to frame policies the latter need to do more. They must amalgamate in the legislatures and make governable their very heterogeneous electors. Mediation and brokerage in Hamilton's view was the chief task of the 'neutral' representatives, those who belonged to the learned professions.

What of the candidates? Information is their greatest need if they are to function at all. 'Extensive inquiry' will inform a potential or actual representative of 'the dispositions and inclinations' of the voters. He must, therefore, whether he be learned or not, be a primary consumer of local political and general psychological knowledge, the kind that only scientifically sampled survey research can and does, in fact, yield.[29]

Hamilton, of course, had special reasons for emphasising the possibility of representatives being equipped with 'sufficient knowledge of local circumstances' and also of their ability to forge solid majorities out of disparate interests. For these were the necessary basis for policy planning, especially for centralised economic and fiscal policy grounded in political economy. Because members of the same class, such as different kinds of artisans, often have more conflicts with each other than with people who may be better off than themselves, but engaged in their own line of production, they vote in keeping, not with their social status, but with their vertical economic interest group. This is fortunate as it is likely to result in a representative assembly whose members can be reconciled for purposes of fiscal policy, not to mention the sort of economic planning Hamilton hoped for, and which the contemporary federal government pursues. Voters, in short, choose not necessarily their own mirror image as individuals or members of groups, but as their more diffuse sense of confidence in an individual dictates. That is, of course, not a quality that can be divorced from issue voting. Especially when the issues are as confounding as welfare, defence, race relations and, as ever, taxation.

There are few papers in the *Federalist* that can match the two on which I have just drawn. There is in them, as in many others, a larger purpose that must and does inspire the scientific temper in all its manifestations. That is the necessity to combat non-scientific or pre-scientific modes of thought. Americans are notoriously, though not, I believe, uniquely, addicted to one form of pre-scientific thinking: conspiratorial explanations of political events. In a brilliant essay,

[29] *Federalist*, no. 35, pp. 214–17; no. 36, pp. 217–20.

Gordon Wood has argued that conspiratorial thinking in this period of American history was a response to a new intellectual climate created by science and naturalistic philosophy generally. There now had to be a causal, natural explanation for all events, social as well as physical. Given rather frightening and complex events, the appeal to common sense and suspicion that conspiracy offers – not to mention its psychological gratifications, its certainties and simplicities – was and is the most obvious answer for those who are remote from scientific modes of thought.[30] Among the anti-Federalists there were indeed many such men, who, fearful of the new constitution and terrified by the men who had drawn it up, saw deep plots behind the proposals. Monarchies, standing armies and generally the connivance of 'the wealthy and well-born' were seen as dooming republican freedom. 'Where in the name of common sense', Hamilton exclaimed, 'are our fears to end if we cannot trust our brothers, our neighbors, our fellow citizens?',[31] but he also argued from the analogy of the natural sciences to try to induce his readers to think through complexities, rather than to look for sinister agents.[32] Above all, he wanted to persuade them to try 'rational calculation of probabilities', to think carefully of the 'permanent causes, moral as well as physical' rather than to abandon science in favour of wild speculation.[33] The other source of irrationality in politics was obviously passion and self-interest. There were in Hamilton's view 'utopians, who disdain the admonitions of experimental instruction', who thought that one could have government without coercion.[34] But clearly there are many far from 'utopian' dreamers who also resist the instructions of scientific thought. Pre-scientific, unscientific, anti-scientific thinking about politics generally, and elections specifically, flourishes, right and left, north and south. The newspapers and television, both of which often conduct unscientific surveys, treat them as solid public opinion though they are often vaguely defined, and regard as definitive, guesswork, moralism and ideology. The whole use of polls to promote candidates and policies, and of course every form of conspiracy thinking, are still rampant forms of semi-science in the U.S.A. It is impossible to understand the passion for accuracy apart from these essentially non-scientific mind-sets which play at being scientific, even though they are in truth anti-scientific. The refinements

[30] Gordon S. Wood, 'Conspiracy and the paranoid style: causality and deceit in the eighteenth century', *The William and Mary Quarterly*, ed. Sevieries, XXXIX (1982), 401–41.   [31] *Federalist*, no. 29, p. 186.
[32] *Ibid.*, no. 31, pp. 193–4.   [33] *Ibid.*, no. 60, p. 367.   [34] *Ibid.*, no. 28, p. 178.

of survey research have other sources and intellectual justifications, to be sure, but the spectacle of science abused and misapprehended must always figure as an important one. Exposing fallacies was one of Hamilton's self-set tasks and it remains one for political science.

The scientific study of voters, specifically their psychology, responses to events and the outcome of elections, has finally a bearing on what survey researchers frankly call the 'democratic myth': that the voter decides. The voter does not care, is ignorant and generally feels that what he does on election day does not matter. For him it is a civic ritual. Nevertheless, it is psychologically extremely important that representatives and officials think of themselves as dependent upon 'grass roots'. They want and need the security of this base which guarantees their place in the structure of representative democracy as a whole. To this quandary science has no answer.[35] It may not need to worry, because its findings are not new politically and indeed have always reflected these realities. Political science need not look back with regret to the formalism of the nineteenth century, which was always subject to challenges, even in its strongest period. There is, in fact, every reason to suppose, especially when one considers Hamilton's writings even *before* legal and political institutions had become established, that an informal, demystifying, scientific and individualising political science is built into the rituals of electoral politics and is in fact a part of their structure. Those who seek votes will want to know all they can about the voters, and they will always have reason to fear their constituents. There is therefore a built-in impetus to scientific surveying and one that in the end sustains rather than unsettles the whole ritual because, far from diminishing, it enhances the sense of its ultimate importance. For, looked at historically, scientific historiography, which is what survey research knows itself to be by now, is itself an integral part of the complex dialectic of democratic politics.

There are of course some very serious objections to be made to my whole argument. Did not political science exist in the eighteenth century in countries whose governments were wholly unlike that of the United States? Am I not making too much of the ties between representative democracy and the scientific ethos in matters of politics? Moreover, were there not alternative, quite different sorts of social science even in the new republic? To begin with this latter

---

[35] These are the implications of both Angus Campbell, Philip E. Converse, Warren E. Miller and Donald Stokes, *The American Voter* (New York, Wiley, 1960), and Norman H. Nie *et al.*, *The Changing American Voter*.

consideration: Jefferson did indeed differ from Hamilton intellectually as in every other respect. They disagreed about Montesquieu
whose relativism Hamilton admired and whom Jefferson came to
distrust as too fatalistic. In this Jefferson was decisively influenced
by his French friends, Helvetius and Destutt de Tracy.[36] More
significantly, in his *Notes on the State of Virginia*, he offered a
thoroughly well-informed survey of the government as well as of the
natural conditions of his native state. The latter were, however, his
main concern. In fact his account of the native Indian population
forms part of the chapter on the flora and fauna of Virginia. Here
one can indeed recognise the origin and character of American
anthropology, so much of it concerned with the Amero-Indians. It is
a science that owes nothing to the experiences of republican government, and everything to the permanent and inescapable contact of
Europeans with the local Amero-Indian population and imported
black slaves. Though such encounters were to be widespread
everywhere, they were more enduring and integral to American
society than to any other group of Europeans. Hence the habit of
'looking at' and describing these alien peoples, along with the
natural resources and topography of the continent, became a settled
intellectual style. The great difference between this 'science of man'
and a political science such as Hamilton's is that the latter does not
have to pretend that it is concerned with persons unlike the observer
in any significant way. It therefore makes fewer demands on the
imagination, and greater ones on the sense of a scientific obligation
to accuracy. Indeed, the comparison between Jeffersonian anthropology and the political science of the *Federalist* only highlights the
dependence of the latter on representative democracy. It is, to be
sure, only one of the sciences of man to emerge during the
eighteenth century in America, but its identity as a quite specific
endeavour is also clear.

Hamilton was hardly Montesquieu's only heir. Conjectural
history, closely patterned on *L'Esprit des lois*, had flourished for some
time in Scotland especially.[37] Hamilton, as we saw, shared the
psychological assumptions on which these studies of historical
change were based. A uniform human nature displayed under altering circumstances a limited and knowable number of responses.

---

[36] Gilbert Chinard, *Pensées choisies de Montesquieu tirées du 'Commonplace Book' de Thomas
Jefferson* (Paris, Les Belles Lettres, 1925), pp. 7–29.
[37] Nicholas Phillipson, 'The Scottish Enlightenment', in *The Enlightenment in National
Context*, ed. Roy Porter and Mikulas Teich (Cambridge, Cambridge University
Press, 1981), pp. 19–40.

Historical examples therefore could yield general truths, highly useful to any potential legislator who might choose to promote a stable
and just order of laws. This sort of political science, which Hume
proposed, amounts to little but maxims of good sense.[38] It calls for
no great efforts of observation and assumes that nothing novel will
occur. That is what Hamilton knew to be wrong. America had in fact
no part in the prudential calculus of European authors before the
Revolution. The vaunted Baconianism of the Scots was, moreover,
more of an ideological advertisement than a method of research. It
took providence out of historical theory, but it did not necessarily
indicate an interest in minute, irreducible facts and inadequate data.
Baconian professions did not even mean an absence of speculation,
as long as it was marked by common sense and shared information.
Often vast numbers of phenomena were organised under a few principles in these speculative histories. Since they purported to be
factual, they remained, in their authors' view at least, Baconian. It
also meant that neither heroes nor miracles were used as explanations of events. Impersonality was very much a mark of this
history. Hamilton's Baconianism may not have been deeper than
that of the Scottish authors he admired, but there is reason to
suppose that it was more than mere window-dressing. For he did
take his political science down to the last irreducible atom of social
life, the voter, and built from there up. Moreover, 'the legislator' was
no abstraction in his vocabulary. Gone were those ancient
demigods, to be replaced by elected representatives of the voters.
Conjectural history and its broad theory of change may not have
been able to survive the actual hurly-burly of New York politics. The
phenomena of local contests for votes do not lend themselves to the
broader forms of social speculation. They do, however, invite a
Baconianism that is data-based in a way that a commonsense
empiricism resting on examples drawn from world history is not.
The two are, of course, in no sense incompatible, and Hamilton
practised both. Nevertheless, there is a vast difference between
a science of history designed for 'the legislator', and the science
of politics that surveys the actual conduct of voters and their

---

[38] Gladys Bryson, *Man and Society: The Scottish Inquiry of the Eighteenth Century*
(Princeton, Princeton University Press, 1945), pp. 17, 109, 148–72. Duncan
Forbes, 'Sceptical Whiggism, commerce and liberty', in Andrew Skinner and
Thomas Wilson (eds.), *Essays on Adam Smith* (Oxford, The Clarendon Press, 1975),
pp. 179–201. Andrew Skinner, 'Science and the role of the imagination', in *A System
of Social Sciences: Papers Relating to Adam Smith* (Oxford, Clarendon Press, 1979), pp.
14–41. For Hume's brand of Baconian social science one need look not only to
'That politics may be reduced to a science', but to the Essays generally.

representatives. The first does not presuppose representative democracy while the latter is virtually an off-shoot of that political system. The self-selected elite at Philadelphia may not have thought of themselves as legislators, but they knew well enough that very soon they would have to face the voters, and to behave like citizens in a way no one in Europe did in 1787.

There is finally a political science in the eighteenth century that is close to Hamilton's. That is the rational decision theory of Condorcet.[39] Quite unlike Hamilton, Condorcet was a radical intellectual and a professional mathematician, fully in command of the calculus of probabilities. First at the request of Turgot and then as a deputy to both a legislative assembly and a constitutional convention, he applied probability theory to voting in legislatures. Turgot had hoped to decentralise government by establishing municipal assemblies, and both he and Condorcet were concerned to make sure that the decisions of these elected bodies would be rational and in the public interest. That continued to be Condorcet's great interest even when he was considering, and indeed a member of, a democratically elected national legislature. The outcome of deliberations remained his chief preoccupation. The bureaucratic origins marked his political science even when he had become a convinced democrat. The aggregation of the individual interests of the deputies must, moreover, have been a mathematical challenge for him. The result was a political science more sophisticated and far less Baconian than Hamilton's, though the two were pefectly compatible with each other, expressing as both did the contingencies of republican government. It is only monarchy, where hereditary status delineates the political authority of political agents, which limits the possibilities of an individualising political science such as that of either Hamilton or Condorcet. For both, the analysis of the voting behaviour of citizens and the theory of decision-making in assemblies presuppose electoral authorisation. Condorcet knew as well as Hamilton that Solon and Lycurgus had been replaced by assemblies, but his experience of administration had left its mark on him, as it eventually would on Hamilton: it moved Condorcet towards the science of rational decision-making, while Hamilton would turn to economic planning.

There is, however, nothing surprising in a movement back and forth between a bureaucratic and parliamentary social science.

---

[39] The followng remarks rely entirely on Keith M. Baker, *Condorcet* (Chicago, University of Chicago Press, 1975), pp. 197–263, 320–5, 330–42.

Bureaucratically devised policies are a part of the picture. That is why Hamilton, the first and most significant early American partisan of such policies, is so prophetic and why his language re-emerges in the age of Progressivism and especially with the New Deal and after. The uniqueness of his political science as contrasted with the purely policy-oriented studies of bureaucratic governments is that the behaviour of the electorate is primary. The science of understanding the voters is not subservient to policy, as it is in Condorcet. The voters count and active public policy only make them more problematic. Within the context of representative democracy the science of politics remains, in fact, subordinate to the imperatives inspired by the belief in 'the consent of the governed', though it becomes vital only when it is confronted by national politics framed and executed *far* from the arena in which 'the simple act of voting' occurs. For political science to be a science, as it now is, it must make the understanding of the individual, elementary phenomena its primary goal, and that occurs only within the political context of representative democracy. American political science may well be stimulated by the political demands of an active central state, but it looks first to its ultimate basis in the rituals and habits of two centuries of uninterrupted (even by a Civil War!) electoral activity.

INDEX

358   INDEX